To Xa

Contents

PART III
Towards a Culture-Led Olympic Games?

Figures

Tables

Acronyms

ABC: Australian Broadcasting Commission
AC: Australia Council
CoS: City of Sydney
IOC: International Olympic Committee
NSW: New South Wales
OAF: Olympic Arts Festivals
OAF'2000:   abbreviation for the Olympic Arts Festival taking place in
            year 2000
OCA: Olympic Coordination Authority
OCOG: Organising Committee for the Olympic Games
ORTA: Olympic Roads and Transport Authority
SMC: Sydney Media Centre
SMH: Sydney Morning Herald
SOCOG: Sydney Organising Committee for the Olympic Games
TOK: Transfer of Knowledge
VIK: Value in Kind

Preface

When Pierre de Coubertin developed his vision for the modern Olympic Games, the union of sport and art was a central part of his philosophy of Olympism. Yet, the cultural and artistic dimensions of the Games are typically regarded as being of secondary importance to the supposedly more media friendly and more lucrative Olympic sports programme, which is underpinned by the powerful global sports industries. This book challenges this trend and argues that the cultural dimensions of the Games should be considered as pivotal to the Olympic programme for both the host city and the international Games stakeholders—the Olympic Movement. These cultural dimensions, and the Games cultural programme as their implementation vehicle, are the main mechanism through which the Olympic Movement can fulfil its ideological aspirations and the host city can achieve a lasting and meaningful Games legacy.

This is not to say that delivering a successful Olympic cultural programme is easy. Indeed, achieving the right balance between representing the cultural identity of the local host and embracing the cultural aspirations of communities worldwide is one of the most ambitious and less understood dimensions of the Olympic Games staging process. As well, developing audiences for new cultural activities is a challenge, not to mention trying to convince audiences—and producers—that arts and cultural activities can be in any way connected to an event that has sport at heart. These and other related challenges inform the research underpinning this book, which offers the most comprehensive and detailed ethnographic study of an Olympic Games cultural programme, and provides a thorough account of how current Olympic organisational structures limit the ability of culture and the arts to fulfil their potential within the Games and the Movement.

While delivering a cultural programme during Games time is a formal requirement from the International Olympic Committee (IOC), the research within this book shows how there are only limited guidelines and evaluation structures to inform this process. In contrast, almost all other dimensions of the Games involve extensive and detailed guidelines and knowledge transfer to inform (and monitor) the host city's decisions. These circumstances have led to the marginalisation of cultural programming at the Games since very early in their modern life. Nevertheless, on the few occasions where these circumstances have not prevented a host city from giving prominence to culture, it is apparent how much of an advantage these Games have had in making their mark on Olympic history and, indeed, on the importance given to their Games by their host population.

It is also apparent that, while the delivery of an Olympic cultural programme can often be left wanting, it can play a central part in distinguishing an Olympic bid and setting a candidate proposal apart from the rest. For example, Barcelona 1992 introduced the idea of a four-year Cultural Olympiad to ensure maximum inclusiveness and diversity in the Olympic programme, and to overcome the heavy restrictions of a 16-day city-focused elite-sport competition. Atlanta 1996 promised to use its cultural programme to celebrate the American South and its black-communities. Sydney 2000 gained advantage over its main bid rival at the time, Beijing, thanks to its promise to use the cultural programme to advance societal issues over Aboriginal reconciliation and multicultural understanding and thus addressing international concerns over Australia's human rights record. Athens 2004 aspired to use its cultural programme to reinvigorate the ancient symbols and values of Olympism and to promote Greece as the cradle of the Games. Beijing 2008 promised to use its cultural programme to explore contemporary notions of Chinese culture and its worldwide connections, which resonated with a period whereby China was becoming a global economic superpower. Finally, London 2012 became a last minute, unexpected favourite over its rival candidate, Paris, partly thanks to its emphasis on its cultural and educational ambitions, reflecting the higher ideals of Olympism as a Movement dedicated to the promotion of peace, intercultural understanding and the fulfilment of youth's potentials. The challenge, therefore, is to address the gap between the bid promises and the eventual delivery of the programme to ensure that culture remains a central part of the Games hosting process, well connected with other Games programmes and integral to the priorities and values of the organisations involved with their delivery.

To develop an understanding of the existing opportunities and challenges, this book provides an in-depth analysis of the cultural policy implications of hosting the Olympic Games, extracting lessons from the experience of one of the key referents in recent Olympic Games history: the Sydney 2000 Olympic Summer Games. The central ambition of the book is to provide a critical examination of the principles behind the official Olympic cultural discourse and to highlight how these reflect ongoing tensions between the Games global communication aspirations and its local community dependencies and responsibilities. A detailed study of the Games official cultural programme or Cultural Olympiad is pertinent, as it provides much needed clarity on how the event's simultaneous local and global imperatives may come to clash to their mutual detriment or flourish to their mutual advantage.

The Sydney 2000 Olympic Games has been celebrated for placing the city at the heart of the Games experience and providing a very strong festival atmosphere to rival that of Barcelona in 1992. In particular, Sydney 2000 introduced new hosting techniques that have been adopted by subsequent Games editions, such as the provision of coordinated crowd entertainment outside official sports venues (the so-called '*Live/Sites*'). Sydney also remains distinct in how it developed a strong cultural narrative around the value of hosting the Games, placing a celebration of Australia's multiculturalism and the aspiration to advance reconciliation with its Aboriginal communities at the heart of its original Games bid. From a strict cultural policy point of view, Sydney is also relevant as Australia has led the way in terms of policy discourses for culture, pioneering many of the techniques and research tools that today we take for granted in this field. Many of these were being tested at the time of the Sydney Games. These experiences have been influential for subsequent Games hosts, including London 2012. In this context, a detailed review and critique of Sydney 2000 provides an insight into an influential Games edition as well as an opportunity to reflect on issues that retain their full currency today in terms of how cultural activity is defined, managed and promoted during an Olympic Games hosting process.

Each chapter within this book provides a detailed examination of a specific dimension of the Olympic cultural programme. This work is based on original research conducted over the last eleven years through fieldwork in every Summer and Winter Games edition from Sydney 2000 onwards. Much of the evidence presented here emerged from a two-year residency in Sydney, from early 1999 to the end of 2000. During this time, I conducted over 90 interviews with key Olympic cultural programme stakeholders, undertook direct observations within the Sydney Organising Committee for the Games and gained access to a wide range of unpublished materials that provide an unparalleled insight into the changing design priorities, management needs and relationships development that explain how an Olympic cultural programme is delivered and promoted.

Since my residency in Sydney, I have been funded by the British Academy to investigate each subsequent Olympic Games with fieldwork residencies lasting between two and six weeks at a time. This has involved direct observations, documentary analysis and over 35 interviews with organising committee representatives, cultural partners, media, artists, sponsors and public authorities in Salt Lake City (2002), Athens (2004), Torino (2006), Beijing (2006, 2008), Vancouver (2010) and London (bid stage in 2004 onwards). I have also benefited from the funding and support of the IOC to research the organisation's historical archives in the area of culture. Further, my work is informed by repeated interviews with key decision makers within the IOC and ongoing conversations with international scholars dedicated to the study of the Olympic Games and the Olympic Movement.

The book is structured in three parts and ten chapters. Part I presents the book's conceptual framework, explaining the background to the Olympic Games cultural programme and providing an overview of Olympic cultural policies. Chapter 1 provides a definition of cultural policy and explains why mega-events are an important referent into the uses and implications of cultural programming. In particular, it explains how globalisation has affected cultural policy discourses, how cultural policies have become intimately related to, and dependent on, communication policies, and how cities have become the primary site for such policy experimentation, with major events becoming a key city aspiration to progress local and international cultural policy agendas. Chapter 2 locates these issues within the Olympic Games cultural programme specifically, providing a detailed assessment of the programme. The chapter provides an analysis of relevant terminology as defined by the IOC and discussion about how the programme has evolved since its inception at the turn of the 20th century. Chapter 3 explains and assesses official IOC cultural provisions to establish how the organisation has articulated its cultural policy over the years. This involves an analysis of the positioning of cultural activities within the structure of the Olympic Movement, the IOC in particular, and an analysis of how cultural references and commitments are reflected within the institution's working agenda.

Part II focuses on the four annual Olympic Arts Festivals (1997–2000) of the Sydney 2000 Olympic Games, in order to highlight key issues in the design, management and promotion of any given Olympic cultural programme. Chapter 4 analyses the historical, political and cultural context for the Olympic bid and the ensuing vision for the Games cultural programme. Chapter 5 focuses on the Games structures of management, in particular, the way the cultural programme is embedded within the Organising Committee for the Games (OCOG). This overview extends to Chapter 6, which discusses how the programme fits within the OCOG's external operations and stakeholder relationships. In this case, the emphasis is on key cultural stakeholders including the public sector, the local arts community, the corporate sector and the media. Chapter 7 moves on to the Games communications and marketing framework, providing an overview of the IOC communications policy, which has resulted in one of the most widely recognised and lucrative global brands. The chapter then assesses how this policy is implemented within a specific Games context and how this in turn impacts on the Olympic cultural programme. Chapter 8 moves away from OCOG structures of management to explore the expectations and policy choices of cultural programme stakeholders. In particular, it discusses the cultural priorities of public authorities, arts groups, corporations and media partners when engaging with the Games hosting process. Finally, Chapter 9 shows how the issues noted within previous chapters are reflected in media coverage of Sydney's four-year Olympic cultural programme.

To conclude, Part III considers the future of cultural policy at the Olympic Games. Chapter 10 draws together the different strands of assessment that have been presented throughout the monograph, identifying key ongoing tensions and providing some commentary about ways to overcome current limitations. The main emphasis is on the need to reconcile global communication imperatives with the Games (and Movement) self-proclaimed social mission, which is expected to involve locally sensitive as well as historically informed cultural responsibilities.

Acknowledgments

This book has been possible thanks to the support of many individuals and institutions over the years. Many thanks to Miquel de Moragas i Spà and the team at the Olympic Studies Centre at Universitat Autònoma de Barcelona (UAB), who provided invaluable assistance to coordinate fieldtrips and key contacts at the Sydney Olympic Games and the International Olympic Committee back in 1999, 2000 and 2001. In particular, thanks to Ana Belén Moreno, Berta Cerezuela, Miquel Gómez and Marta Civil. Thanks also to Manuel Parés i Maicas for providing the original contact point with the Centre.

My fieldwork in Sydney was possible thanks to the continued support of academic colleagues at the University of Technology, Sydney (UTS), and the Centre for Olympic Studies at the University of New South Wales (UWS). My thanks go to Christine Burton, Janet Cahill, Tania Tambiah, Richard Cashman and Anthony Hugues.

I was based at the Sydney Organising Committee for the Olympic Games for over six months to develop a detailed ethnography of the Olympic Arts Festivals (OAF) hosting process. Special thanks to Alex Hesse and Kristine Toohey, with whom I was lucky to collaborate at the Publications team, to Angie Rizakos for providing access to the Documentation Centre, and to the OAF team at a very busy and demanding time: Craig Hassall, Karilyn Brown, Stephanie Sulway and Sue Couttie. My work also relied on close conversations with Sydney's diverse artistic community. Particular thanks go to Justo Díaz for his insights into Australia's cultural production networks. I am also indebted to Jonathan Nolan from CostaDesign for his assistance with tracing back relevant images a decade on.

The historical review of archives and documentation about the Olympic Movement's evolving cultural policies was supported by an IOC postgraduate grant and undertaken at the Olympic Study Centre in Lausanne, Switzerland. My very special thanks go to the team that assisted me back in 2001: Nuria Puig, Ruth Beck-Perrenoud, Yoo-Mi Steffen, Patricia Eckert and Marie Villemin. I have also benefited from attending the International Olympic Academy (IOA) Postgraduate Seminar and accessing the Academy's specialist collections. Thank you to Kostas Georgiadis and Themis Artalis.

Between 2001 and 2010, I have been fortunate to continue receiving grant support to develop my work at every subsequent summer and winter Olympic Games edition. My thanks go to the funders, the British Academy and the Universities' China Committee in London, and to the many people that have given me their time to access key documents and share their insights at respective Organising Committees for the Olympic Games and selected cultural key stakeholders. Thanks as well to Jude Kelly for supporting my role as observer of the London 2012 Culture, Ceremonies and Education bid preparations.

I also want to highlight my appreciation of the support received by the network of international scholars dedicated to the study of the Olympic Movement that provided encouragement for this work in the early days, and have remained an invaluable point of contact for the exchange of ideas and access to key informants and documentation at every Olympic Games. Very special thanks to Norbert Müller, Manfred Messing, Holger Preuss, Bruce Kidd, John MacAloon, Laurence Chalip and Jean-Loup Chappelet.

Finally, thanks to my family and especially my husband, Andy Miah, who is my best critic.

Part I

Cultural Policy and the Olympic Movement

1 Introduction
The Cultural Policy of Global Events

This chapter explores the relevance of cultural policy frameworks to interrogate global event hosting processes, the Olympic Games in particular. It starts by reviewing the impact of globalisation on the definition and application of cultural policy principles, arguing that this has led to a convergence between cultural and communication frameworks. The chapter then touches on the implications of such trend for cities and regions and moves on to reflect on the role of mega-events as catalysts for locally-based cultural policies with a global outreach. The last section of the chapter introduces the Olympic Games as a paradigm of all these processes combined. Throughout the chapter, I focus particularly on revisiting the state of cultural policy debates in the late 1990s, as this is the period leading to the Sydney 2000 Olympic Games and the distinct cultural policy choices that framed its four year cultural programme, which will be the main case study explored throughout the monograph.

CULTURAL POLICY AND GLOBALISATION

From the mid 1990s, the United Nations Education, Science, and Culture Organisation (UNESCO) has assessed the impact of globalisation on cultural activity. Numerous studies have been published since then, notably after the publication of the report 'Our Creative Diversity' in 1995, which led to the 'World Culture Report' (UNESCO 1996, 1998a). Both documents included a passage that analysed the effect of globalisation in the shaping of cultural matters and cultural policy making. An important effect was the realisation that culture has an important economic dimension and, thus, that it is possible to talk of *cultural goods*. These works revealed that, in a global era, cultural goods are likely to grow their prominence within contemporary production and industrial systems. Subsequently, in 1998, UNESCO began a series of meetings to study the potential of the trilogy 'culture, the market and globalisation' (UNESCO 1998b). In 2000, this research process resulted in the publication of various working documents on 'Cultural Diversity and Globalisation' (UNESCO 2000a, 2000b,

2000c). These papers emphasised that, as a result of globalisation, there is an increasing influence of new technologies on shaping trends and aspirations within the cultural sector. In particular, they noted that there is a need to consider the role of communication media as a vehicle to transmit these aspirations.

In order to understand the influence of these conclusions on the development and shaping of cultural policy making, it is relevant to start by framing the variety of meanings and uses of the term *cultural policy* in the last quarter of the 20th century. The term cultural policy has only become widely used since the mid to late 1960s. Moreover, it is a term that has never been understood in a homogeneous way throughout the globe. Nevertheless, the origin of cultural policies can be traced to other kinds of concepts, which would appear to address similar concerns for culture. Such roots deserve recognition as they extend earlier than the UNESCO documentation and have significantly influenced today's international cultural policy discourse.

Defining Cultural Policy

To explain the various ambiguities surrounding the term 'cultural policy' Fernández Prado (1991) refers to the wide diversity of uses and associations depending on the language used and country of application. For instance, in English speaking countries it is more frequent to see the term 'arts policy', while in many parts of Africa and Asia the term 'cultural policy' is used interchangeably with 'education policy' (p. 17). According to Fernández Prado,

> differences in the definition of what encompasses the cultural sector . . . derive from important differences in historical processes that have led different states to intervene massively in the most emblematic aspects of cultural life (p. 17, Spanish in the original)

Prado offers some examples of these historical references by pointing out the vast intervention of the state on the management of national communication media in communist countries, while in Western Europe it is common to see a strong presence of the state in the protection of traditional artistic production. These different emphases have influenced the current understandings of cultural policy that are held in respective countries. Prado considers that cultural policy encompasses artistic creation, scientific research and the diffusion of new ideas that lack immediate application and/or are the result of leisure activities, pleasure and the search for personal development (p. 18). However, he acknowledges that these areas are blurring into other spheres. This is due to the growing synergies between cultural and communication policies, and the increasing interaction between cultural, industrial and economic policies that encompass, 'not only the communication media, cinema and audiovisual productions, but also some aspects associated with cultural tourism' (p. 26).

Historically, one can identify a series of key periods that offer a distinctive perspective on the meanings and uses of the term cultural policy. I will focus on Europe and the western world, which are the key referent areas for this monograph. An initial period is found in the 18th century, with the appearance of various forms of state and aristocratic patronage of the arts and the support to academies that would establish aesthetic and scientific criteria. This changed radically in the 19th century, a time dominated by the expansion of social class conflicts and the emergence of grassroots movements that would oppose the power of the state and the domination of the Academy in defining criteria for culture and the arts. During this period, the notion of the *welfare state* emerged. This resulted in the creation of policies for the support of cultural endeavours that transferred the emphasis from the traditional arts to the protection and expansion of educational programmes.

The beginning of the 20th century saw the options and evolution of cultural policy uses marked by World Wars I and II. Prior to and during wartime, most European states emphasised the role of national identity through the regulation and control of national educational institutions and the growing presence of the mass media. In the 1940s, during the post-war era, the dominance of national state organisations was substituted by the cultural leadership of major international institutions, such as the United Nations and the Council of Europe. These institutions supported the moral and cultural reconstruction of nations during the 1950s. During this decade, national and international organisations emphasised *cultural democratisation* as the most important aspiration of cultural leaders and administrators. This meant that the policies of governments and cultural institutions ensured that the kind of arts and culture they were in charge of protecting was appreciated and understood by the general population. The focus was to facilitate access to the arts and cultural experiences that had traditionally excluded the participation of the masses. Typical cultural policy actions at this time were the reduction of prices to attend arts events and the organisation of workshops to explain their value and meaning.

However, it was not until the mid 1960s that cultural policy started to embed itself into the discourse of opinion leaders and was referred to, explicitly, as a tool for protecting and ensuring the fair development of the cultural sector. It was a time when UNESCO focused on guaranteeing the existence of public institutions dedicated to cultural matters in all country members of the United Nations system. Consequently, from the mid 1960s, a series of meetings were arranged to place cultural policy onto the international agenda. This culminated in 1970 in Venice with the first World Conference on Culture, which, according to Ander-Egg (1991), was the first conference to clearly address the question of what cultural policy is and what it can do. A series of conferences followed and culminated in

Mexico in 1982 with the 'World Conference on Cultural Policies'. These conferences focused on debating *cultural democracy* as a substitute to the principle of *cultural democratisation*, which was so popular in the 1950s. Influenced by the expansion of social movements, such as the youth movements of the late 1960s, this process promoted the acceptance of wider notions of culture. However, on this occasion culture was not defined by the elite to keep their supremacy, or to educate the masses. Rather, it was captured at grassroots levels. As summarised by Kelly,

> Cultural democracy (as opposed to the democratisation of culture) is an idea which revolves around the notion of plurality, and around equality of access to the means of cultural production and distribution. (1984: 101)

In this context, the concept of popular culture would be revisited and the traditional distinctions between high and low culture would begin to blur (see Gans 1974).

The last two decades of the 20th century can be seen as another remarkable turning point in the definition and use of cultural policy. The process started in the 1980s, when it became evident that cultural matters were of interest for the private sector and would, increasingly, be funded and promoted by corporations independently from public administrations (see Kong 2000). This process has been termed *privatisation of culture* and motivated dedicated research programmes in institutions such as New York University, under the guidance of Toby Miller and George Yúdice (see Goldstein 1998) leading to defining publications such as Lewis and Miller (2003) and Miller and Yúdice (2002). The work of García Canclini is central to these studies as it argues that this process of privatisation is a direct effect of the movement towards globalisation:

> Néstor García Canclini approached the debate on the privatisation of culture as symptomatic of the broader processes of contemporary global restructuring, linking these processes to the attendant reconfiguration of the concept of modernity. He identified four principal tendencies of the modern project, each of which are eroded in the confrontation between multinational corporations and national societies that attempted to maintain their cultural differences: 'emancipation' (the secularisation of the cultural field); 'expansion' (the conquest of nature, scientific advance, mass education, industrial development, and the diffusion of material and symbolic commodities); 'renewal' (innovation and the endemic obsolescence suggested by [Octavio] Paz's 'tradition of rupture'); and 'democratisation' (dissemination of specialized knowledges through education and mass participation in rational and moral evolution). (Goldstein 1998: Contexts and Conditions of the Support of Culture, paragraph 3)

However, this brief history is not the only antecedent of the modern uses of cultural policy. The evolution of these terms within the process of privatisation is complemented by the re-emergence of the concept *cultural industries*. This concept was first used in the 1940s by Horkheimer and Adorno in reference to 'all existing processes of mercantilisation of culture that have led it to lose its autonomy' (Adorno & Horkheimer 1979). For them, *industrialisation of culture* involved culture becoming a means for achieving non-cultural ends, such as economic benefits and political control (Adorno 1991). In contrast, by the end of the century, the term cultural industries has lost its critical taint, more innocuously referring to the wide range of media vehicles that produce and reproduce culture, information, entertainment and promotional activities (see Hesmondhalgh 2007). Since the turn of the new millennium, the term *creative industries* has become an even more dominant term, particularly within Anglo-Saxon countries (see DCMS 1998, 2001). Its rise has led to major debates on the appropriateness and implications of using the terms creativity or culture in the context of policy-making (eg. Galloway 2007, Garnham 2007, Hearn et al 2007, Hesmondhalgh & Pratt 2005).

Cultural policies in Europe and around the world were revisited throughout the 1990s in order to face these new trends. Since the end of the 1980s, cultural policy initiatives have grown exponentially—this time without the leadership of UNESCO. Many academic professional institutions have emerged with a clear vocation to explore and promote cultural policy. These have ranged from *cultural observatories*, frequently found in Europe and many South American countries (International Network on Cultural Policy 2002, IFACCA 2008)[1], to specialised university research centres—mostly in the UK, Australia, New Zealand and Canada—and a wide array of foundations and other private groups—in particular, in the United States. These various trends and histories suggested the need to re-define what is meant by cultural policy today and how it affects governance and the debate over critical issues such as social inclusion, international understanding, multiculturalism, representation and identity among many others. The establishment of *The International Journal of Cultural Policy*, regularly dedicated international conferences and symposiums, innumerable online networks and platforms, as well as the publication of a growing number of special monographs and dedicated journal editions centred on the cultural policy debate has offered increasingly visible and influential platforms to address these concerns.

The contested concept of cultural policy and its area of influence reflects how the debate has expanded beyond the remit of organisations such as UNESCO and the Council of Europe. Cultural policy has been incorporated into key debates about economic and social questions (eg. DCMS 2004). Consequently, the definition and application of cultural policy principles has become an instrument of analysis and regulation for all kinds of cultural actors, not only traditional governmental organisations and quangos, but also the academic community, private corporations and the associative sector. The effects of such trends, particularly in the 1990s, are considered in the following section.

Cultural Policies in the Global Context: Culture and Communications

As already mentioned, in the 1960s, UNESCO became the leading institution for promoting a debate about cultural policy and ensuring its development and application within most nation states. However, in the context of globalisation, cultural policies require a framework that is different from the one used in the 1960s and 1970s. With that in mind, in the 1990s, UNESCO organised a series of projects aimed at exploring the links between cultural activities and development, notably in the context of the world economy and the global communication media. One such initiative was the World Decade for Cultural Development, which started in 1987 and culminated in 1998. The experiences of the decade were discussed in the 'UNESCO Intergovernmental Conference on Cultural Policies for Development' (UNESCO 1998b) and in the 'Symposium of Experts on Culture, the Market and Globalisation' (UNESCO 1999). A feature of both conferences was the influence of the newly defined cultural and creative industries—in particular, global media networks—and the effects of privatisation on culture. Additionally, a growing link began to emerge between these global processes and the increasing prominence of local actors such as regions and cities, as opposed to the nation state. This new emphasis on locality brought prominence to institutions other than UNESCO to lead on the cultural policy discourse. Whereas UNESCO had traditionally debated cultural matters from the perspective of nation-states and networked with state ministries and parallel bodies as a priority, other institutions such as the Council of Europe, the European Commission and a wide range of cultural observatories and specialised research centres around the world focused their interest on regional and municipal actors.

During the 1990s, the Council of Europe engaged in major collaborative research to analyse current cultural trends across Europe. This resulted in the publication of 'In from the Margins' (Council of Europe 1997) a report that anticipated the findings by UNESCO (1998a, 1998b, 1999) with regard to the influence of the cultural industries, privatisation and the emergence of local movements in cultural development. Within this document, it is argued that cultural policy matters are closely linked to the nature and conditions of a new communication society. This presented a further dimension which had been overlooked until that point.

> 11.2.19 *The role of culture in the new communications society.* Traditionally communication has been the main link between culture and

development. Cultural impulses into society have always been more or less formally 'communicated', and the faster and more widely this is done the greater their impact. The need to communicate culture (especially audiovisual culture) has been one of the motive forces behind technological innovation and the arrival of the 'information society'. (Council of Europe 1997: 245)

Pessimistically, the Council of Europe adds that,

11.2.25 These structural changes in the world of communications, culture and the media cause similar problems in respect of identity and participation. Active participation, in the traditional sense of consciously chosen creative activity, lost much of its meaning after the advent of radio and television. (*op. cit*: 247)

However, established and emerging communication media have also allowed the development of new cultural forms, which mean that the transmission of values and identities can be either empowered or diminished depending on how the links between communication and culture are used. This conveys the importance of considering parallels between cultural and communication media policies when seeking to understand the meaning, utility and function of cultural policy. From the late 1980s, academic as well as policy circles are in agreement of the need for cultural policies to incorporate communication policies within their design (eg. Martin-Barbero 1989). Since the turn of the millennium, this has also meant a progressive convergence between both areas (eg. Crane et al. 2002, Cuilenburg & McQuail 2003, Napoli 2006).

Overall, processes of cultural production and consumption have been developing in parallel with new communication technologies. They have become increasingly accessible and have gained wider visibility depending on their ability to meet the needs of the media required to diffuse them. Indeed, the power of the media to affect the prominence of cultural issues in the global arena has been an object of study and reflection among cultural policy makers (Crane et al. 2002, Council of Europe 1997, Foote 1998, Machet & Robillard 1998, Murray 1998). Nevertheless, the effect of this is ambiguous and confrontations and disagreements have arisen, as there are still many cultural planners that reject the idea of culture as a product to be exchanged or promoted in similar ways to commercial goods. In any case, the now classic argument about the economic value of the arts (Myerscough 1988) and the widely accepted role of culture as a catalyst for regeneration in post-industrial economies (eg. Garcia 2004a) has led to greater incorporation of cultural practices within the market place, and their adaptation to some of the most common rules of the market (see DiMaggio 1983, Gibson & Klocker 2005, Shubik 1999). The importance of these circumstances is analysed further in the following section.

CULTURAL POLICY AND THE PROMOTION OF THE LOCAL

As culture has found its place within the market, new associations have been created between cultural policy and promotional strategies. Yet, the use of cultural policies as promotional tools has occurred mostly at a local level. The promotional uses of cultural policy have been applied as a guide for revitalising the local in a global context, with regions and cities being the preferred points of reference.[2] This situation can be explained on the grounds that the process towards globalisation has brought into question the sustainability of the nation-state as a model for projecting cultural identities (Anderson 2000, Roche 2000). This has accelerated the re-emergence of regions and cities as key actors in defining and promoting notions of cultural policy. The Council of Europe (1997) corroborates this in its study of the state of debates about culture and development in Europe,

> 5.3.1. As the world becomes more homogeneous, it is natural to try to distinguish the experiences we own from the experiences of others. This might be one of the reasons inspiring the development of regionalist movements throughout the 1970s and 1980s . . . 5.3.6. The process of decentralisation has encouraged a great potential for the concordance between culture and the arts and the needs of local and/ or regional governments . . . 5.3.10. The city has been one of the beneficiaries of the weakening of the nation state as a unit for social and political integration. The roots of urban autonomy set up in the Middle Ages and the city-state as a basis for the 'republic' have been re-born and have inspired modern urban strategies. The search for a municipal identity has become very urgent in the light of new factors that signal a trend towards segmentation and alienation, including social mobility and migration, [. . .], the arrival of global culture, the de-regulation of habitation and real state and the cuts in social provision. (Council of Europe 1997: pp.88–90)

These processes have grown throughout Europe and, as noted by UNESCO (1998a), can also be detected in other parts of the world. UNESCO's 'Culture in the neighbourhood' project (UNESCO-Swiss National Commission 1990) is an example of the initiatives supported by international institutions to stimulate the process of decentralisation. Indeed, this situation has increased the influence and global significance of cities. Equally, it has accentuated the challenges cities must face to minimise social inequalities and balance the conflicting needs and priorities of differing urban communities of interest. Definitions of cultural policy have also been framed by these trends, with the term 'urban cultural policy' becoming a common and dominant reference (see García 2004a). In this context, there have been continuous calls to strengthen the role of cultural policy, not only as a tool to promote the outcomes of local development, but also as a guide to decide how this development is to be undertaken (Bianchini 1999, Borja & Subirós 1989, Landry 1999). Moreover, since the late 1990s, the city has been presented as the key unit in cultural and creative development (see Landry 2000)—and culture has, in turn, been presented as one of the key catalysts in urban regeneration, particularly in the process to transform local industrial economies into post-industrial economies, as discussed below.

One factor that has become a visible focus in the process to project cities and regions globally is the importance of culture to contribute to their sustainable development. Notably, the continuous growth of cities has required the strengthening of cultural policies to support the long-term benefits of decentralisation and urbanisation processes (UNESCO 1998a, Borja & Subirós 1989)

> 11.3.11. Culturally sensitive urban planning enriched the economic and social motives which guided regeneration policies during the late 1970s and 1980s. The planners' first priority was to revive city centres, their aims being to abolish slums, reduce poverty and criminality—and also to create more secure environments for business, leisure and tourism. (Council of Europe 1997: 251)

Consequently, the definition of what constitutes the remit and function of a cultural policy is no longer the purview of public institutions exclusively. Private corporations and not-for-profit associations, the media as well as a wide range of community groups, have taken a larger responsibility to survey and promote the application of cultural policy guidelines. Thus, all of these agents have the ability to influence the way culture is administered, regulated and sustained.

However, despite these interests to define and develop cultural policies, there remains a remarkable lack of funding for cultural activities. The decentralisation of responsibilities in the cultural sector accentuated this situation in the 1990s. As argued in a Canadian conference on cultural development,

> It is paradoxical that in the context of financial disengagement by federal and provincial governments, municipalities have become the most effective level for the delivery of cultural policy, yet they face considerable financial constraints. (Fréchete, Roy & Durantaye 1998: 53)

In response, in the approach to and since the turn of the millennium, there has been a trend towards widening fundraising sources for cultural activities and increasing the variety of techniques and mechanisms used to attract and secure these sources. The influence of private corporations became remarkable in the now established use of marketing strategies to promote cities and regions, a trend that had not been fully documented until well into the 1990s (see Ashworth & Voogd 1995, Gold & Ward 1994,

Smyth 1994). In this context, tourism in particular became an important economic tool within which to invest and culture became a key selling point for tourism (Urry 1994). As such, cultural policy discourses have often taken the form of local image strategies and have been transformed into tools for the marketing of cities and regions.

Given the above trends, it has become common to refer to *cultural tourism* as a separate form of leisure activity (see Berg et al. 1995, Dodd & Hemel 1999, Richards 1996, 2001, Towner 1997). These links are not entirely new, since leisure and tourism have long been regarded as major areas for the development of cultural activities (see Council of Europe 1997, par. 11.3.1). Nevertheless, the frequency of the associations and the explicit use of the term cultural tourism as a distinguished form of leisure since the late 1990s, have introduced a new debate that affects the making and definition of cultural policies. Consequently, it has become common to design cultural policies that encourage the promotion of local cultures through tourism and leisure (Bianchini & Parkinson 1993, Bianchini 1999).

A parallel if later trend in urban cultural policy has been the popularisation of the notion of the 'creative city' (Landry 2000) and, subsequently, the 'creative class' (Florida 2002). These two notions highlight the need to explore and facilitate opportunities for cultural production as opposed to (or complementing) the emphasis on cultural consumption that is implicit in leisure and tourism-led cultural policy strategies (see also Mommaas 2004).

Be it consumption-driven or production-driven, the dedication towards city-based culture-led promotions triggered an interest in using special events as a vehicle for developing local cultural policies, particularly from the late 1980s onwards. Getz (1989) argues that events are viewed as an integral part of tourism development and marketing plans for cities, regions and countries alike, and suggests that they can play a number of important roles as image-makers of the local host and as catalysts for other urban development and renewal strategies. On this basis, understanding how culture and policy are affected by globalisation requires investigating the event hosting process, great and hallmark events in particular.

CULTURAL POLICY AND MAJOR EVENTS

Major or 'hallmark' events such as the Olympic Games, Universal Exhibitions and World Cup Finals have become key cultural actors at a global level due to their ability to attract the attention of international communications media, the financial contributions of multinational corporations they involve, and the extensive use they make of global marketing and promotional campaigns (see Getz 1991, Gold & Gold 2005, Hall 1992a, Heller 1999, Roche 2000). Equally, major events are also shaped by the place where they occur, host-city stakeholders in particular. From a cultural policy perspective, one might ask critical questions about how the reliance on media, corporations and marketing campaigns on a global scale affect the image projection of the cities and nations hosting the event. A significant question is whether the global communication opportunities brought by these events are, or can be, leveraged at a local level by the host cultural institutions, policy makers and wider communities.

As I will argue throughout this monograph, the potential to secure an appropriate representation of the event's cultural dimension is dependent on the ability to balance the cultural aspirations of the local host policy-makers with the aspirations and sense of purpose of the event's long-term global partners. Major events can be a useful tool to develop and implement distinctive cultural policies for a local community. However, it is necessary to analyse whether such aspirations can be sustainable in the medium to long term, given the wider social and economic pressures that exist within any global event hosting process.

Cultural Policy as Image Strategy

Using events as a cultural policy strategy for the promotion of cities and regions has been a growing trend since the early 1980s. Bianchini (1993) comments on the use of such flagship schemes to project cities as a distinctive form of cultural policy in something he defines an application of 'cultural policy as an image strategy' (p. 15). Bianchini offers some examples of European cities that used cultural policies to improve internal and external images in the early 1980s,

> Prestigious cultural projects acted as *symbols of rebirth*, renewed confidence and dynamism in declining cities like Glasgow, Sheffield and Bilbao. . . . Cultural policies were used *as symbols of modernity and innovation* in cities like Montpellier, Nimes, Grenoble, Rennes, Hamburg, Cologne, Barcelona and Bologna, that wished to *develop sectors of the economy* such as fashion, crafts and design based manufacturing and high-tech industry. . . . [As such] cultural flagships like the Burrell collection in Glasgow . . . [and] the 160 new public squares created in Barcelona in the build up to the 1992 Olympics all became powerful physical *symbols of urban renaissance*. (1993: 15–16, emphasis added)

Here, Bianchini suggests four different uses of prestigious cultural projects, which can be interpreted as a response to four different objectives in cultural policy. First, these projects can act as 'symbols of rebirth', thus assisting in processes of city regeneration and development. Second, they can act as 'symbols of modernity and innovation', for instance, being at the forefront of city marketing strategies to attract new visitors and corporate business to the city. Third, they can be used as a catalyst to 'develop sectors of the economy' of the city, thus stimulating the cultural sector to be more productive and engaged in market trends. Finally, they can be used as a 'symbol of urban renaissance', which can be interpreted as a stimulus for the growth of the city, originated and informed by the cultural sector. These four uses of events can overlap, but they indicate variations according to the main interests of policy-makers and the characteristics of respective cities or locations. Nevertheless, the four uses embrace a common pursuit for revitalising the image and activity of a location through culture.

Lacarrieu (2001) considers that major events are one of the favourite formats for cities and regions to improve their image, far beyond other sorts of great projects or flagship schemes. Major events are sought after by cultural policy makers because they offer a 'space that condenses a defined notion [an image] of the local . . . and intends to be the sum of the diverse "micro-cultures' or "local cultures" or "local identities" that constitute a city, a region or a nation' (p. 11, Spanish in the original). García (2004b) corroborates the principle that major events are a useful tool for policy-making and for leveraging the image of the cities hosting them. Further, Borja and Subirós (1989) challenge the argument that they are superficial or ephemeral in comparison with other flagship projects such as large architectural developments as, they note, special events can be a catalyst to attract the investments necessary for creating infrastructures and other long-term cultural endeavours (p. 6).

Roche (2000) adds that events have an advantage over other flagship projects in that they are extremely appealing for the media and, thus, more visible. The author cites Verdaguer to support this point,

> Cities are becoming more and more a stage, if not a final destination, as a cultural resource, alongside other new destinations [. . .] Mega-events could be considered [. . .] one of the most visible elements of the current local strategies for [urban] survival. (Verdaguer 1995: 203, cited in Roche 2000: 147)

It is commonplace to find arguments that claim that greater visibility of events is a direct result of their media appeal (see Dayan & Katz 1994, García 2005, Getz 1991, Reason & García 2007, Roche 2000). As noted by Roche (2000), '[m]ega-events are global [and thus particularly visible] events because of the development of media systems' (p. 10). This has led authors such as Moragas (1992, 2001) to assert that the greatest events are also the most appealing media events. Indeed, this also implies that the success of a major event depends strongly on their ability to meet the requirements of the media. As such, the challenge for event organisers and cultural policy makers is to succeed in balancing the interest for promoting an image that represents local cultural values, with the need to adapt them to formats that are easy to communicate and distribute through the global media (Moragas 1988, 1992; Klausen 1999b).

In this context, it is critical to consider the responsibilities of the organisers and supporters of the event. The tension lies between a focus on *representing the local community*, providing a sense of ownership and being coherent with other local cultural policy initiatives; and a focus on *creating a global impact*, projecting an image that is spectacular and appealing for foreign audiences, beneficial for tourism and business purposes, and responding to the needs of the media. In the early 1990s, this dilemma led to re-considering the notion of cultural policy and the uses that had been commonly agreed as more appropriate for its implementation (García 2004a). The question was, and remains today, whether cultural policy should be dedicated exclusively to promote culture as an end in itself, or whether it can be used as a means for other—economic, social, political—purposes. The Council of Europe presents this dilemma in these words,

> 11.3.11 . . . the new focus of cultural planning and cultural protection strategies was to test this utilitarian strategy [the ambition to use cultural policy as a tool for local promotion with an emphasis on flagship projects]. Two schools of thinking appeared, each of them capturing the 'uses' that, ideally, had to be given to culture in the urban environment. Despite possible overlaps [. . .] we can talk, schematically, of a 'political-symbolic' beautification [which is the case of special events and flagship schemes] and culture as a 'resource' of the community. (Council of Europe 1997: 260)

According to the Council of Europe, the first approach is focused on creating extrinsic images for the city, while the second encourages action and auto-determination and thus allows the creation of intrinsic images. In the first case, culture is seen as a finished outcome; in the second, culture is seen as an instrument for the community to define and produce the outcomes that are most relevant to them *(ibid)*.

Thus, the production of major events as a vehicle for cultural policy encounters a series of important challenges. It needs to reconcile the needs and interests of the city and region hosting the event with the needs and mechanisms of the global media. Moreover, the production needs to be appreciated by foreign audiences but also owned by the local communities. Finally, it needs to be visible and spectacular, at the same time as representative and meaningful for its hosts. These challenges will have more or less poignancy depending on the size and scope of the event. Indeed, the greater the event, the greater the impact and chances for cultural policy makers to project the image of a particular place. However, for smaller events, other kinds of considerations should be prioritised. At this point, it is useful to review the meaning of *great* or *mega* event by comparing it with other sort of events of small or medium scale.

Defining Major Events and Mega-Events

In his study of community involvement in a mega-event hosting process, Haxton (1999) includes a review of event typologies. The author starts by offering a list of characteristics that define 'special events or festivals' according to a group of industry experts and academics working for the National Task Force on Data in Canada (Statistics Canada cited in Haxton 1999: 13). This group considered that the most essential characteristics of a special event are,

> it is open to the public; its main purpose is the celebration or display or a specific theme; it takes place once a year, or less frequently; it has predetermined opening and closing dates; it does not own a permanent structure; its program may consist of separate activities; all activities take place in the same local area or region.

According to Haxton, these criteria, although comprehensive, exclude some important event types, such as travelling shows and events that occur more regularly than once a year (*ibid*). Haxton then cites the 'event tourism typology' formulated by Getz in 1991, where events are classified according to number and origin of participants, number and origin of spectators, and media coverage. Haxton explains that these attributes are central to helping to determine the 'scale' or 'size' of an event. As such, depending on the number of participants, media attention and so on, events can be considered 'local events, regional events, national/continental events and mega-events' (*ibid*). In this typology, mega-events have the following characteristics,

> *Participants [number and] catchment area*: usually under 10,000 however, may be as many as approximately 100,000. [They are] *usually* more international than local
>
> *Spectators [number and] catchment area*: from approximately 100,000 to one million or plus. [They are] mainly domestic but a large international contingent move to the place because of the event as *primary purpose* (extremely high international demand for available tickets)
>
> *Media coverage and live demand*: very high levels of international coverage and exposure. Very *high demand* [of live coverage]. Rights for extended media coverage typically require bidding to an international governing body (if not, one or more national networks may provide live coverage) (Haxton 1999: 15, emphasis in the original)

In an attempt to capture the characteristics of each event category and also specific examples or events within categories, Haxton adds that further attributes that help distinguishing event types are,

> [the] *catalysts to event production* (ie. the major reasons behind an event taking place) [. . .] the *event mobile/temporal nature* [fixed, touring or transient], [and the] *activity type* (sporting, cultural, industrial, religious, or community etc.). (*op. cit*:. 20, italics in the original)

For our purposes, the type of event that is most relevant is an event characterised by its great size (mega-event), motivated by an interest to project the cultural image of a location, having a transient nature and involving cultural activities. The reasons for this are as follows. First, a *mega-event* is a clear by-product of globalisation processes. As already suggested, the success and scope of major events is directly associated with their appeal for the communication media, a fact that, according to Getz (1991) makes them 'the largest and most visible events' (p. 340). They are thus, one of the phenomena with a greater ability to have a global impact. Second, a mega events is *transient*, characterised by its mobility and the tightly time-bound pressure it places on respective hosts to choose the messages or 'images' they want to transmit in the context of that event specifically. This pressure will occur every time the event takes place, thus offering continuous opportunities to new hosts to re-evaluate processes, images and the cultural policy strategy that best suits each occasion. Finally, the sort of event that is of interest here is motivated by the political ambition to project *images informed by a cultural narrative*, thus incorporating cultural activities and cultural programmes. On the basis of this conceptual framework, the Olympic Games stand out as the paradigmatic example, offering multiple opportunities for the exploration of each of these processes and their practical implications for cultural policy-makers.

OLYMPIC GAMES, GLOBALISATION AND CULTURAL POLICY

The Olympic Games exhibit rich tensions between the global and the local. It is the event that incorporates the greatest number of simultaneous participant countries and spectators in a common space. It also gathers the largest media audience in a common time and across the largest number of nations. As such, the Games represent an outstanding opportunity for host nations and cities to present themselves to the world. Further, the Games are embedded within a centenary Movement under the auspices of the IOC. This means that the event incorporates an extensive cultural and symbolic background which is integral to its celebration and provides a broader historic context to the contemporary media narrative of any given local host. Thus the production of cultural value at the Olympic Games involves continuous negotiations with cultural actors and policy-makers locally and internationally, and is framed by policy guidelines emerging over one hundred years of symbolic narrative production. The policy implications of this multilayered approach are discussed below.

The Production of Cultural Value in the Olympic Games

By the beginning of the 21st century, the quadrennial celebration of the Olympic Games is considered to be the greatest peacetime event on earth.

Moragas (1992) argues that the global scope the Games have achieved cannot be understood without considering their close relation and dependence on their media stakeholders and their ability to accelerate the production and communication of cultural value. Thus, 'the promotion and selection of values developed through a complex communication production process— signs, rituals, images, *mise en scène*, advertising, information—is the principal cultural—and politic—responsibility of the Olympic Games staging process' (1992: 17, Catalan in the original). This impression is reinforced by Klausen (1999a) in his research on the Lillehammer 1994 Winter Games. Klausen explains how the large-scale media coverage of the event made the Norwegian government realise the cultural potential of the Games beyond the sporting competitions:

> the main scope of the Games was now formulated metaphorically as 'a showcase of modern Norwegian society'. The cultural dimension became very important, both in the sense of culture as artistic activities and in the sense of culture as identity and way of life. (p. 3)

The statements by Moragas and Klausen corroborate the claim that a major event can be a good promotional tool for the local host and a vehicle for the implementation of cultural policy strategies (Garcia 2004a, 2004b). Berkaak (1999) goes on to note the significance of the enduring tension between local and global processes and its impact on cultural value production. The production of values and symbols representing a host culture to the world must consider first, the local and national impact and appreciation of the image that is selected by the event organisers; second, it must understand its international and global interpretation. Berkaak quotes a paragraph from the official newsletter of the Lillehammer 1994 Games, to exemplify this dialectic:

> An Olympic event is an opportunity to be focused on—with an assured benefit. . . . We have a lot to show the world and a lot we can point to and proudly say is typically Norwegian. This we can do standing upright and erect, without losing ourselves in our own reflection in the window-pane. The glass is transparent. It allows us to see from the inside and the outside. It provides us with an opportunity to see ourselves with the eyes of strangers. We can discover our blind spots, our way of life and culture. . . . The sooner we start on this introspective task the sooner we will be able to choose which aspects we want to emulate, which we want to change, and which we want to retain as they are. (*Offisiell Leverandor* published by the Lillehammer Olympic Organising Committee, cited in Berkaak 1999: 68)

Moragas (1992) notes that the local acceptance of a particular set of cultural values requires a complex interaction process among influential host-city institutions. Normally, this involves the organisation in charge of producing the Games or 'Organising Committee for the Olympic Games' (OCOG), public administration bodies, private corporations and political and civic groups. As a departing point, the main objective is typically to summarise the political and cultural personality of the host country in a way that is both representative in the eyes of the local community and easy to understand by foreigners. Nevertheless, once a local agreement is reached, the aspiration to transform this exercise into a global statement will require the involvement of the international media. Indeed, from the moment when the media take on the role to interpret and transmit this constructed image to the world, the host-city loses control of the communication process. Consequently, the global character of the Games, with its ability to put the host-city on the international communication agenda, offers as many possibilities for the promotion of its local and national image, as it does increase the risk of local, national and international misunderstandings, criticism and rejection.

In an effort to avoid such misunderstandings and to manage the media interpretation and transmission of the city's socio-cultural briefing, the host cultural policy-makers tend to define their local culture on the basis of media production mechanisms. As such, their focus is often on those identity signs more suitable for audio-visual expression. Moragas (1992) states that the features and attractions of the local culture can only be successfully displayed if they are presented in an organised and schematic manner within the complex communication network of the Olympic Games:

> the question is to synthesise a complex reality in an image consisting of the adequate attributes. . . . All cultures own some 'brand images' resulting from history, prior tourist promotional strategies or the universal success of some of its more representative features. However the celebration of the Olympic Games also represents an historic opportunity to reconstruct and renovate certain pertinent characteristics [which may be out-dated] or have resulted from situations of politico-cultural domination. (p. 32, Catalan in the original)

Typically, the issues deemed to be more representative or appropriate to showcase the host culture will be selected and those considered to be negative or misleading will be rejected. The selection process will also be conditioned by what can better suit the media production process. Moragas (1992: 30–33) lists the elements included in the strategy for the construction of the Barcelona 1992 Olympic Games image as follows:

- selection of cultural values which already have an international projection
- use of samples from different arts manifestations (painting, sculpture, architecture, music, cinema, video)

- selection of buildings and monuments representing sporting and Olympic architecture complemented by both civil and religious emblematic city examples
- selection of popular culture and folklore together with economic and technology features, and some personal city representation

Moragas adds that these examples are indicative of the way a 'semantic field' is constructed in order to promote a city internationally, according to the selection and simplification criteria of any advertising strategy (1992: 33). These advertising strategies will become national and international campaigns with different emphases depending on their specific target audience and timing. National campaigns will tend to focus on ensuring the approval, pride and sense of belonging of the population in regard to the Olympic project, while international campaigns will share similar characteristics to the promotion of 'films, songs or tourist offers' (p. 34). As such, Moragas concludes that, 'the Olympic Games are a laboratory of incalculable value to understand the logic behind the commercialisation of nowadays culture' (*ibid*). In the same sense, we could add, the Games are also a platform to understand the framing of urban cultural policies attempting to combine local representation with international projection (see also Garcia 2004b).

Olympic Values, Transmission of Culture and Commercialisation

The attempt to commercialise cultural values brings to the fore a series of challenges. An excess of commercialisation may result in an impoverished local cultural discourse, based exclusively on elements that are easily adapted to and appealing for the media but not representative of the host community. For example, the focus on cultural components that are easy to represent through the media, in particular, television broadcasts, may prevent the inclusion of less visual cultural values such as literary, oral and other community traditions not easily adaptable for the screen. This challenge became evident in the Atlanta 1996 Olympic Games in the wake of the widely reported success of the Barcelona 1992 Olympics in promoting the city and its cultural values according to city marketing strategies.

In Atlanta, the replication of Barcelona's Olympic city image strategy became a difficult exercise because the city did not have the same visual icons or 'architectural sophistication' to build on (Turner 1995: 4). The immediate media appeal and subsequent tourist success brought by Barcelona's Games time value production strategy raised the expectations of international Olympic stakeholders but made Atlanta cultural leaders and population sceptical about their ability to position their city's urban landscape of shopping malls, interstates and skyscrapers in a genuinely appealing and representative way. In response to this, Dana White, an Atlanta history expert at Emory University criticised that 'it's kind of cheapening

of a culture to try to capture a complex culture in a few words' (cited in
Turner 1995: 4). In contrast, from a policy point of view, Maria Luisa
Albacar, head of the foreign relations for Turisme de Barcelona, advised
Atlanta on how to use the Games to position the city as a tourist destina-
tion, insisting that the most important task was 'to create a product' noting
that, in its absence 'you can invent one' (Roughton 1996: 9).

The anthropological and cultural theory approach of Martin Klausen
and his team in Norway has become a relevant source for contrasting the
opportunities and dangers that cultural policy makers must face in the context of the Olympic Games (see Klausen 1999a). Berkaak (1999) discusses
the way that the Olympic ideology and its symbolic repertoire fits within
the logic of the market and warns against the reductionist effects that can
result from intertwining symbolic interpretative frames with pragmatic
ones. The author refers to the change of orientation of the Olympic Games
and the Olympic Movement, from the humanistic ideals of its founder,
Baron Pierre de Coubertin (see Carl Diem Institute 1966), to the economic
and pragmatic motivations of the IOC president at the time, Juan Antonio
Samaranch. In Berkaak's words, this has resulted in an Olympic discourse
characterised by the coexistence of two seemingly opposite orientations:

> the hedonism of the festival and the pragmatics of the political arena
> and the market place. . . . The symbolic and artistic elements, the 'signi-
> fying materials of a culture' have clearly become instrumental in a way
> that is . . . typical of all promotional culture. (p. 63)

Consequently, during the 1994 Lillehammer Games,

> it became quite legitimate to evaluate cultural forms and performances
> in terms of their potential to attract customers and secure contract
> partners [. . .] and not to see them simply as expressions of inherent
> identity. [. . .] The athletic achievements and the festive aspects of the
> Olympic events were meant to catch and hold the attention of the world
> and direct the 'eye of the world' to Norway, not just as a nation, but
> as a tourist destination and a production site, or, more generally, as a
> commodity. (p. 65)

Again, this suggests that the Games, even more so than other large-scale
international events, offer as many opportunities as challenges to implement and promote a coherent cultural policy for the host-city. At the same
time as addressing the expectations and demands of international stakeholders, the ambitions of local cultural leaders must be balanced with
those of event sponsors, tourism boards, trade organisations and so on,
even though these represent competing and often conflicting agendas. This
involves a delicate exercise of prioritisation and agreed commitment to the
main policy narrative across city. At this point, it is relevant to explore

which are appropriate referents for the implementation of cultural policy choices within the Olympic Games.

Referents for Cultural Policy-making within the Olympic Games

Moragas (2001) has argued that the cultural policy options of the Olympic host organisers should be focused on constructing the values and symbols of the event to ensure the coherence of its cultural dimension:

> The Olympic Games, in contrast with what is common in other mega-events, demand the host organisers to develop a programme where most of its components are fully defined. The sporting competitions, the organisation and management structures, but also the Games rituals, are all objects that have been pre-planned and are subject to guidelines increasingly controlled and detailed by the International Olympic Committee. . . . Nevertheless, the host-city has a wide autonomy in the creation of one of the key aspects of the event preparations: the cultural programme and the event symbolic production. . . . Thus, in order to 'win the Games' it is necessary to start by appropriately interpreting its cultural dimension. This interpretation requires the development of [five] fundamental axis: (1) know how to define and interpret the event- the Olympic Games—understanding it as a cultural phenomenon; (2) find the appropriate position for the local and global audience of the event; (3) develop a cultural programme that defines the host-city identity—ceremonies, Cultural Olympiad, street celebrations; (4) establish a communication policy, in particular in regards to television; (5) new challenges in the Internet era. (N.p., Spanish in the original)

Building on this, a number of possibilities arise for how Games hosts might derive sources of media-friendly and locally representative cultural value production within the Games staging process. First, as discussed in the previous section, cities can develop and harness *the promotional strategy for respective Games editions and 'brand image' of the host-city*. This includes the construction of city marketing strategies, including the synthesis of attractive local iconic features for promotion, among others. Second, there are the *'symbols' of the Games and the Olympic Movement*. This includes the logo and emblem of each Games, the mascots, all merchandising materials and commercial applications of those symbols, the Olympic posters, the corporate design or 'Look of the Games' (including pictograms, Olympic buildings design, staff uniforms, stationery design, publications design and so on) and other symbols such as the traditional Olympic numismatics (stamps and coins), Olympic slogans and Olympic songs. Third, a host city can optimise the contribution of *Olympic Ceremonies and rituals*. This includes both the Opening and Closing Ceremonies which are considered the peak event of the Games in terms of public awareness and interest and has become the most viewed event in the world due to global television coverage. Additionally, it encompasses the Torch Relay, which is one of the greater Olympic experiences in terms of public participation and community interest. As well, the medal ceremonies which involve the podium, the raising of national flags of winners, and national hymns provide rich, symbolic episodes through which to convey additional meaning. Finally, there is *the official cultural programme* or *Cultural Olympiad*. This refers to the organisation of special cultural and arts events prior to and during the Olympic period. This is the least regulated of all the areas described here and, as discussed below, it is becoming the strongest area of opportunity for the implementation of distinct cultural policies.

These elements constitute a holistic model for image production within a host-city culture framed by its task to deliver Games celebrations. They are also a source for the transmission of values and identity signs that can assist in promoting the host city's cultural policy choices among the international media. For example, the choice of mascot design, Olympic emblem and the Look of the Games in Barcelona 1992 was aimed at reflecting the contemporary, stylised and design-loving character of the city. Yet, many of these elements can flatten the host's values and images. This is the case for logos, slogans and merchandising materials that are designed as marketing and advertising tools with a strong commercial focus but without a clear cultural and symbolic dimension (see Garcia & Miah 2006).

Olympic Opening and Closing Ceremonies also offer great opportunities for the showcasing and representation of a host-city's culture and tend to be perceived as the main source of Olympic cultural value production and, indeed, as the main expression of Games time cultural activity and programming. However, they have become such a restricted media-bound exercise (see Tomlinson 1996) that they often fail to fulfill their symbolic potential. When one considers, for instance, the controversies surrounding the Beijing 2008 Opening Ceremony on its use of digitally created fireworks portrayed as if they were actually taking place across the city (Luo 2010), it is easy to see how claims about lack of integrity can arise from what otherwise might be innocuous programming decisions. During an Olympic Opening Ceremony, every small detail can be exploited by the media for criticism. Indeed, their large scale, strict time concentration, and ever growing dependence on television demands tends to transform such ceremonies into gigantic spectacles where the surprise factor and the scale of components seem far more relevant than the meaning and consistency of the cultural discourse being presented (see Miah and Garcia 2000, Tomlinson 1996). As noted by MacAloon (1996), what is presented in an Olympic Ceremony needs to reach a universal audience simultaneously and needs to be easily transmitted and interpreted through the media. As such, the event must be 'internationally sensitive to very different cultures' and 'avoid offending highly diverse and highly politicised social and cultural groups' (1996: 39–40). This is why, also in Beijing, when the Mayor of London

Boris Johnson receives the Olympic flag with his hands in his pockets or without his suit jacket buttoned, it becomes a national point of discussion for China. These sensitivities create a tendency to produce 'historically deracinated, abstract and culturally neutered representations . . . of Olympic rituals' (*ibid*) and often result in over-simplistic interpretations and articulation by the media.

In contrast, among this ensemble of value production sources, the official Games cultural programme is a component that can be a source for more complex, sophisticated and representative messages about the host cultural identity and policy choices. From Barcelona 1992 onwards, the cultural programme has been implemented as a four-year event or Cultural Olympiad, which has offered host cities greater chances to develop consistent cultural policy initiatives and build up long term strategies to promote and expand awareness of the host-city and nation idiosyncrasies. There are arguments that question the relevance of organising a separate or additional cultural programme to present the host-city cultural identity, noting that the Games are indeed a cultural event in themselves. The next section outlines such arguments but concludes that, from a cultural policy perspective, a distinct cultural programme still plays an essential role at the Olympic Games.

The Olympic Games as a Cultural Event

Traditionally, the existence of a cultural programme within the Olympic Games has been understood as a complement to the sporting components. This is the result of a conception of two separate entities, 'sports plus culture', which comes from the founder of the modern Games, Pierre de Coubertin (see Monreal 1997). This conception is reflected in the Olympic Charter, the main policy document of the IOC, where it is stated that the Olympic Movement is composed of three differentiated strings, 'sport, culture and education' (IOC 2007: 11). Authors such as Good (1998) have also supported the idea of a contrast between sport, education and culture by identifying them with the traditional Greek concept of the balance between the body (sport), mind (education) and soul (culture). The tendency towards understanding these three concepts as separate entities—even if the expressed aspiration of the IOC is to 'blend' them during Games time—explains the low levels of interaction taking place between the programmes created to operationalise them during the Olympic Games celebration. The problem is one of conception as well as implementation.

Rather than separate identities that must be 'blended', sport, culture and education should be seen as dimensions of the very same principle. The sports and recreation science literature understands sport as a cultural manifestation and an activity through which education takes place. Thus, it is not possible to understand the concept of sport or Olympic sport, without reference to the concepts of culture and education (Blake 1996; Horne et al.

1999). For this reason, the concept of a cultural programme separated from the sporting and educative programmes seems to be redundant. One would expect all of them to be integrated and perceived accordingly by everybody involved within the Olympic experience, from athletes to coaches, organisers and spectators. However, the lack of an integrated sporting cultural discourse perceived as such by average Olympic audiences and promoted as such by Olympic organisers, supporters and media, reveals that the idea of a perfect and evident integration of these concepts within people's minds is far from being a reality.

Moragas (1992) corroborates the argument that culture and sport are intrinsic and inseparable components of the Games. In his view, there are two aspects in the cultural dimension of the Olympic Games that must be observed. In the first place, the Olympic Games are a cultural phenomenon and not only the opportunity to implement cultural or other activities alongside the sports competitions. Second, the target audience of the Olympic Games as a cultural event are all Games communication audiences, both local and international, direct and mediate (p. 11). This is why Moragas considers that it is critical to distinguish between the content and scope of the Olympic cultural programme or Cultural Olympiad from what could be defined as the Games cultural project in general.

> If the Cultural Olympiad consists of a programme to promote cultural activities for the Olympiad period, and it is fundamentally destined to host citizens and surroundings, or those who travel expressly to the host-city during Games time, then we should say that we are only considering a part, and very limited, of the Games cultural project. The cultural project must be understood in a wider sense, as all expressions of value production updated through the mass media not only dedicated to the public opinion in the host-city but also to the international public opinion. (Moragas 1992: 12, Catalan in the original)

Moragas advocates that a consideration of the Games as a cultural event should lead to the creation of consistent cultural policies throughout the Games preparations and that this would help to avoid the dangers of excessive commercialism and reductionism in the transmission of meanings and values. He argues that, by accepting the idea of an Olympic cultural project beyond the limits of the Cultural Olympiad programme, the basic levels of organisation and production of the Games should be influenced, 'especially in what regards the production of symbols and the informative coverage of the event' (1992: 12). As a whole, with his cultural analysis, Moragas argues that,

> the idea of the Games being seen as an advertising opportunity to sell local product must be rejected. We cannot forget that, through its organisational decisions, the host-city is converted into a world

meeting point, a point for the dialogue between its own culture and other world cultures. (*ibid*, Catalan in the original)

This argument highlights some of the limitations of the current processes to stage the Olympic Games, where the emphasis on marketing and global business management strategies overshadows the idea of a humanistic movement with the ideal of peace and universal understanding as its reason of being.[3] However, the cultural programme of the Games, now defined as Cultural Olympiad, has a specific and significant role to play as a distinguished element of the Games. This role could be understood as the balanced representation of the host-city and culture not only to local audiences, but to an international public opinion. Partly thanks to the lack of strict Olympic regulations and the freedoms that local hosts enjoy to shape this aspect of the Games, the official Olympic cultural programme offers a context through which it should be possible to balance the commercial aspects of the Games with their cultural policy ambitions, thus reinforcing the notion of the Games as a cultural event. This potential is explored in the following chapter, which dissect the foundations, definitions and current purpose of the official Olympic Cultural programme.

SUMMARY

This chapter has explored how notions and applications of cultural policy have been affected by processes of globalisation and how this, in turn, has led to the positioning of major events as key platforms for the advancement of cultural policy, understood as a communication tool and image strategy, for cities and regions around the world. Such assessment is based in the premises outlined below.

First, in the context of globalisation, the notion and uses of cultural policy are converging with practices in media communication. This implies that, increasingly, cultural policy is being used as a tool for the promotion of the values and practices of differing areas in the cultural sector, which has led to speak of uses of cultural policy as an image strategy.

Second, there is a perception that the use of cultural policy as a guide for creating and sustaining images is applied mainly at a local level, within cities and regions, but that this exercise often has a global vocation. This tendency has led cultural policy makers to seek communication vehicles that work well at the level of cities and regions and that can capture local idiosyncrasies at the same time as having the ability to reach global audiences.

Third, great or mega events have become one of the most sough-after vehicle to advance city cultural policies and the Olympic Games represent the ultimate paradigm, particularly due to the existence of a historically established cultural programme as part of the hosting process.

There is a wide range of research dedicated to study the economic impacts of major events. However, little is known about the mechanisms in place so that major events respond to the cultural policy choices of their hosts as well as the choices of the global networks in charge of sustaining the event in the long term. The interrogation of how such processes are played out within the largest mega-event of all and how purpose-built cultural programmes can assist overcome the shortcomings of existing global media event structures will be the focus of the remainder of the monograph.

2 The Olympic Games Cultural Programme

The introductory chapter explains that the scope and influence of the Olympic Games is a result of its relationship with the global media and multinational corporations, while it also functions as a mechanism for the production of local symbols and the reinforcement of cultural values. This chapter provides a framework for understanding the functions and position of the Olympic cultural programme within this framework. The chapter begins by reviewing the notion of the Olympic cultural programme, understood as a distinct component of the Games celebration, with an emphasis on the period leading up to Sydney 2000. It then describes the historical evolution of the programme since its original inception by Baron Pierre de Coubertin and its first implementation in 1912, up to the latest editions of the Olympic Summer and Winter Games in Beijing 2008, Vancouver 2010 and the lead to London 2012.

DELIMITING THE NOTION OF THE OLYMPIC CULTURAL PROGRAMME

To understand the current definition and practical applications of the Olympic cultural programme, it is necessary to make some initial distinctions over the identification of the programme's key components. This exercise is not straightforward as, to this day, there are no official nor detailed guidelines about the role and main functions that an Olympic Games cultural programme is supposed to fulfill. Instead, Games organisers must rely on a dynamic range of references that underline the importance of 'culture' within the Olympic Movement. Some of these references are specific, but they also extremely brief and, often, contradictory. They include the IOC official regulations in the Olympic Charter and Olympic Candidature guidelines, (which are limited to indicating the compulsory presence of a cultural programme during the Olympic Games), and reports of prior Olympic cities, which vary widely in quality and detail about the conceptualisation and implementation of respective cultural festivals and exhibitions.

A consequence of this situation is that there is no prescribed indication over what might be included within or excluded from the cultural programme. Should it, for instance, comprise part or all elements of other non-sporting Olympic programmes such as Olympic protocol and the Olympic education programme or, as suggested by Moragas (2001) include the host city street celebrations and other local promotional strategies? This section provides a reasoned approach to delimit the scope of the Olympic cultural programme and make explicit what is meant by it throughout this monograph.

Cultural Programme versus Cultural Event

As indicated in Chapter 1, the focus in this book is the analysis of the Olympic cultural programme or Cultural Olympiad understood as a component that represents only a section of the overall Olympic activities taking place prior to and during the staging of the Olympic Games. While a range of other cultural expressions emerge during an Olympic Games hosting process, such as locally organised celebrations within communities, these rich and important aspects of the Olympic experience are not dealt with here, since they tend to operate outside of the organisational structure of the Olympic delivery organisations. A critical document in delimiting what the official Olympic cultural programme consists of is the founding document of the Olympic Movement, the Olympic Charter. Examining references to cultural programming within this document makes it possible to determine how the official cultural programme may be distinguished from the wider notion of the Games *as a cultural event* per se.

Up until 1999, the IOC official reference to the programme read as shown in Table 2.1. This was the formal statement that guided the design of the Sydney 2000 Olympic cultural programme, which is analysed in detail in following chapters. These details do not offer any specific indication about what the Olympic cultural programme should include. Instead, it indicates the main principles that the programme of 'cultural events' is supposed to promote. These principles are identified as: 'harmonious relations', 'mutual understanding', 'friendship', 'universality' and 'diversity' but they are not supported by any specific performance indicator. Consequently, throughout the years, respective Organising Committees for the Olympic Games (OCOGs) have been free to propose an interpretation of these principles and to decide on the most appropriate way to implement them.

Complementing the Olympic Charter, another key document that offers and indication of key regulations and priorities for the delivery of an Olympic Games is the official IOC Candidature Procedure and Questionnaire that leads to the Candidature File or, informally named 'Bid Books', presented by any city aiming to host the Games. The Candidature Procedure and Questionnaire documents vary considerably from one Games to the next but, invariably, the section or chapter dedicated

Table 2.1   Cultural Programme as Presented in the Olympic Charter

Rule 44: Cultural Programme

The OCOG [Organising Committee for the Olympic Games] must organise a programme of cultural events which shall be submitted to the IOC Executive Board for its prior approval.
This programme must serve to promote harmonious relations, mutual understanding and friendship among the participants and others attending the Olympic Games.
By-Law to Rule 44:
    The Cultural Programme must include

- Cultural events organised in the Olympic Village and symbolising the universality and the diversity of human culture
- Other events with the same purpose held mainly in the host-city, with a certain number of seats being reserved free of charge for participants accredited by the IOC

The cultural programme must cover at least the entire period during which the Olympic Village is open.

Source: Olympic Charter (1999a) Chapter 5: The Olympic Games, rule 44 (p.68–69)

to outline the candidate's cultural programming requirements is the one most open to interpretation. Traditionally, the cultural programme has been presented as the final chapter.[1] This chapter tends to introduce the notion of 'Olympism' or 'Olympic Values', where candidate cities are encouraged to outline their interpretation of such concepts. It is also a chapter that often requests outline proposals for the Olympic Ceremonies and Olympic Education programmes, though it is not always the case. In such cases, the Olympic Ceremonies section is the only area supported by a Technical Manual with fixed specifications for protocol, while there is no such manual for the cultural or education programme. Furthermore, the chapter including references to the cultural programme is traditionally the only section within the Candidature Questionnaire that does not require accompanying guarantees, that is, it does not lead to legally binding commitments. This means that the cultural proposals and budgets suggested within the Bid documents may be changed after award of the Games and this is crucial to understanding why it can also be the more vulnerable component of the Games, when difficult budget decisions are being taken. Coming to terms with this trajectory is crucial for cultural programme organisers. The implications of such circumstances for Sydney in 2000 are discussed in detail in Chapter 4.

This absence of fixed requirements is accentuated when one considers that the 2004 and 2007 versions of the Olympic Charter have abbreviated the Rule—also stripping from it the bylaws—to the following:

> The OCOG shall organise a programme of cultural events which must cover at least the entire period during which the Olympic Village is open. Such programme shall be submitted to the IOC Executive Board for its prior approval (IOC 2004a, 2007: Rule 40).

The recent abbreviation to the Rule suggests that, from an official regulation point of view, rather than expanding its area of influence and integration within the Olympic hosting process, the cultural programme may become more marginal. As we will see in following sections, this contradicts the growing aspirations and rhetoric of Olympic host cities, which see the cultural programme as a central platform through which to maximise local distinctiveness, representation and ownership. However, without the support of the IOC and appropriate international regulations sustained from one edition into the next, particularly in terms of monitoring and evaluation, it is unlikely that the cultural programme can grow and reach its full potential. This is because, without a stable framework and explicit requirements for the support of the Games' global partners (sponsors and media in particular), the cultural programme becomes a local affair, disconnected from the Games global projection and poorly documented for the reference of future hosts, which must instead reinvent the concept and delivery mechanisms in every Games edition.

Interestingly, in 2008, the Olympic candidature questionnaire that acted as a reference for 2016 Olympic Games candidates , eliminated 'Culture' as a separate section, instead incorporating it within a more generic reference to the IOC's aspiration for 'The Olympic Games Experience' (IOC 2008a: 10). Rather than diminish its influence, this move may provide an opportunity for better integration of the cultural programme within other Games components. Such potential is discussed in more detail in Part IV, where an indication of future directions for Olympic cultural programming is outlined.

Characteristics of an Olympic Cultural Programme

Of course, opportunities also arise from the brevity and ambiguity of the IOC official definitions and guidelines. For instance, one might argue that a richer cultural programme ensues from this and that it would be philosophically highly problematic for the IOC to impose more stipulative guidelines on the content of a programme that is supposed to reflect the unique cultural values and identity of the Games local host. In the lead up to Sydney 2000, representatives of the then named IOC Cultural Commission argued that it is not convenient to offer too tight a framework for the implementation of Olympic cultural activities,[2] as it would constrain the richness and diversity of expressions that respective Games hosts can provide (IOC 2000d). Indeed, the lack of a concrete definition has allowed a great freedom of action and interpretation and has contributed to incite ambitious cultural bid proposals. Nevertheless, this has also been the source of remarkable discontinuities in respective OCOG's commitment to develop the programme, especially with regards to budgeting and resource allocation. All the same, for this reason, understanding the Olympic cultural programme in a historical or sociological sense requires an assessment of the main characteristics and components of prior Olympic editions—ie. the agendas and actions of differing OCOGs—and the accounts of researchers presenting data on each Games' cultural activities. As such, this chapter infers from previous Games what we might treat as the main components and characteristics of the cultural programme.

A fundamental characteristic that stands out in Olympic documents and related research is the identification of the Olympic cultural programme with an 'arts' programme rather than a broader cultural programme incorporating interpretations of culture as a way of life in its more anthropological sense (for wider notions of culture look at UNESCO 1998a and Williams 1981). In this context, the terms culture and arts, and occasionally, fine arts, have been used interchangeably.[3] Gold and Revill (2007) are perhaps one of the few notable exceptions, as they note how, in recent editions of the Games, particularly from Barcelona 1992 onwards, the ambitions of the Olympic cultural programme have been merging more and more closely with the wider economic and social agendas of host cities and governments, thus combining their artistic aspirations with other dimensions such as identity building, attracting tourism and contributing to urban regeneration. This has not been a continuum though, as is discussed in the following section of this chapter.

As such, with a few exceptions, the Olympic cultural programme has been operationalised, mainly, as an arts programme or arts festival. This interpretation is justified, firstly, because it was the notion of a fine arts showcase that prompted the founder of the modern Olympic Games, Baron Pierre de Coubertin, to advocate for the inclusion of a cultural programme to bring an 'aesthetic setting' to the sporting competitions (IOC 1997a) or, as noted by Gold and Revill, '[to] take up the ethos of the *panegyris* from the [Greek] classical festival—a festive assembly in which the entire people came together to participate in religious rites, sporting competitions and artistic performance'. (2007: 59) Secondly, it is appropriate to make this claim because the principle of artistic expression has inspired most cultural programmes since the first time they were implemented in 1912 (Stanton 2000).

The interpretation of Pierre de Coubertin's conception of Olympic cultural activity as a collection of fine arts expressions, and the review of the recent history of Olympic cultural/arts festivals suggests that, up to the Sydney 2000 Games edition, the notion of Olympic cultural programme referred mainly to the organisation as an arts programme composed by cultural activities or events belonging to the following categories:[4]

- literature (poetry, plays, novels, philosophical theses, historical reviews)
- music (orchestral music, operas, folklore, pop, rock or other sorts of traditional and contemporary musical expression)
- theatre (from classical theatre to contemporary physical theatre and a wide range of stage performances)
- dance (from classical ballet, to folkloric and contemporary dance)
- visual arts (painting, sculpture, decorative arts, photography and public art expressions)
- architecture and city decorations
- cinema and other contemporary audiovisual expressions

This view of cultural programming as a compartmentalised range of traditionally established art-forms is brought under question in an era of creative and cultural industries, as has become manifest in the lead up to the London 2012 Olympic Games. Nevertheless, a focus on arts programming has been the dominant approach and delivery model for most Olympic Games cultural programmers throughout the 20th century, as I describe in detail in the next section.

At this point, it is appropriate to identify which programmes within the Olympic Games staging process are closer to the Olympic cultural programme in their definition, function and/or public perception. These activities are a useful reference point for comparisons about the degree of managerial and promotional coherence, perceived relevance by key Games stakeholders, levels of public awareness and, more generally, degree of interaction between the cultural programme and the overall Olympic project. Traditionally, the cultural programme has been strongly associated with the most historically informed and symbolically rich elements of the Games, which convey 'Olympic values' or the idea of Olympism, the philosophical principles that characterise the 19th-century humanitarian movement that was Coubertin's vision for his revived Olympics. These include the torch relay, the opening and closing ceremonies, Olympic village ceremonies, the education programme, and the youth camp programme. In recent years, particularly since the 1990s, and in line with the increasing alliance between cultural and communication policies, there have also been growing associations with those Games programmes most oriented towards communications, marketing and promotions. These include the Games Special Events programme (mainly involving VIP functions) and the Image and 'Look of the Games' programme. There are three fundamental points of overlap between these different versions of Olympic cultural programming: (1) none of these programmes and activities consists, in essence, of sporting activities; (2) these programmes are not dedicated to reflect or reinforce the notion of sport exclusively but rather to locate sport within a wider context; and (3) all of these programmes offer similar opportunities to showcase the character of the host-city, region and/or country.

The operational relationship between the cultural programme and any of the other programmes listed above has changed considerably from Games edition to Games edition, to the point that it is not possible to outline a consistent pattern of interaction. For a period in the late part of the 20th century, IOC guidelines for bidding cities included the culture, ceremonies, education and youth camp programmes as part of the same 'chapter', however, the articulation of actual operational links has remained vague and, as noted elsewhere, the only programmes to come supported by clear guidelines and background documentation are the Ceremonies and Torch Relay programmes which, consequently, are also the programmes securing greatest sponsorship support and attracting the largest media attention. By the start of the 21st century, and partly as a result of Sydney's experience, a new rhetoric is emerging that places a stronger link between the cultural programme and the Look of the Games programme, but this is not formally supported by IOC guidelines to this date. In the meantime, formal links to the educational and youth camp programmes seem to have weakened over the last few decades.

All in all, these are indications of the ambiguous positioning of the cultural programme and the ever changing nature of its positioning within Games delivery structures. Such situation reinforces the claim that this is one of the few Games programmes that remain open to the interpretation of Games host cities and OCOGs and is not strictly regulated by the IOC. The absence of guidelines and clear definitions of purpose has resulted in unstable levels of financial and promotional support for the programme, which has affected its consistency and ability to raise an international profile comparable to the ceremonies programme and sporting events. The following section provides specific examples of the above by reviewing the cultural achievements and policy limitations of over one century of Olympic cultural programmes.

A HISTORY OF THE OLYMPIC CULTURAL PROGRAMME

The nature and scope of the Olympic cultural programme has changed dramatically over time. While there has been a continuous insistence on its fundamental importance to ensure a holistic Olympic experience, its purpose and formats have been questioned since the beginning of the modern Olympic Games. Today, the programme remains one of the least regulated (and most misinterpreted) dimensions of the Games celebration.

Origins: The Ideal Role of Cultural Programming in the Olympic Games

The principle of holding an arts festival in parallel with the celebration of sporting competitions is embedded in the foundations of the Olympic Movement. The Movement was founded in 1894 by Baron Pierre de Coubertin, a French pedagogue who sought to revive the ancient Greek tradition of quadrennial celebrations of athletics and the arts that had been held in Olympia from 776 BC to 395 AC. Hanna (1999) describes that in the Ancient Games, 'athletes, philosophers, scholars, poets, musicians, sculptors and high-profile leaders displayed their talents, in what Coubertin called the spirit of Olympism' (p. 106). Olympism was often defined by Coubertin as the simultaneous training of the human body and the cultivation of the intellect and spirit, together viewed as manifestations of the harmoniously educated man. On this basis, Coubertin's ambition was to create an environment in modern society where artists and athletes could, again, be mutually inspired. From this, it can be concluded that Coubertin brought the Olympic Games back to life hoping to develop an internationally recognised relationship between art and sport. In support of this ambition, the Olympic Charter establishes that 'blending sport with culture and education' is a fundamental principle of Olympism (IOC 2007: 11).

Coubertin's ability to coordinate and attract the attention of critical decision makers around the world led to the re-birth of the Games in 1896—Athens—and to their continuation in 1900—Paris—and 1904—St Louis.[5] Nevertheless, none of these Games incorporated arts activities alongside the sporting events. To change these circumstances, Coubertin convened a 'Consultative conference on Art, Letters and Sport' at the *Comedie Française* in Paris, 1906. He invited artists, writers and sports experts to discuss how the arts could be integrated into the Modern Olympic Games. The invitation stated that the purpose of the meeting was to study 'to what extent and in what form the arts and letters could take part in the celebration of the modern Olympic Games and become associated, in general, with the practice of sports, in order to profit from them and ennoble them' (Carl Diem Institute 1966: 16). As a result of the conference and in order to ensure a clear association of the arts with sports, Coubertin established an arts competition, which became part of every Olympic Games celebration (Coubertin, cited in IOC 1997a: 92). This competition was called the 'Pentathlon of Muses' and would involve the awarding of medals in the categories of sculpture, painting, music, literature and architecture.

The organisation of the first 'Pentathlon of Muses' was designated to a special commission set up by the Olympic Organising Committee of the host-city staging the first Games after the Conference, London 1908. Nevertheless, time constraints and disagreement over the programme contents led to its cancellation at the last minute (Burnosky 1994: 21–22, Petersen 1989). Consequently, the idea of an Olympic arts competition was not implemented until the Stockholm Games in 1912.

From Competitions to Exhibitions in the Summer Games

Stockholm 1912 to London 1948: Olympic Arts Competitions

From 1912 in Stockholm until 1948 in London, arts competitions were organised in parallel to the sporting competitions, and artists, like athletes, competed and won gold, silver and bronze medals (Good 1999, Stanton 2000). However, regulations and contest parameters changed considerably due to difficulties in defining the different competition sections and disagreement in defining the most appropriate subject for the works presented. Over the years, the competition's sections changed from the five areas composing the 'Pentathlon of Muses' to a long list of sub-categories. Moreover, the appropriate theme for Olympic artworks was also controversial, as it was discussed whether or not to restrict the entries to works inspired in or portraying sports activities. Initially, it was compulsory to present a sporting theme, but this proved difficult and limiting in areas other than architecture or design for sports buildings (Burnosky 1994: 23). Also problematic was the non-universal or localised nature of the arts competitions, as most judges and competitors were European and it was very rare that non-western artists were awarded a medal (Burnosky 1994, Hanna 1999, Good 1999). Other problems were related to transport difficulties, inconsistent support from respective OCOGs and many limitations resulting from the regulation of amateurism in the Olympic Movement.[6] The latter implied that, as in the case of athletes at the time, the participation of professional artists could not be accepted. In an arts context this was particularly problematic because all artists were considered professional in their devotion to their vocation (Hanna 1999: 108, referring to an IOC document from the 44th IOC Session in Rome, 1949).

Hanna adds that perhaps most disappointing was the poor audience participation attracted by the arts competitions, 'Cultural celebrations based on sport were increasingly irrelevant; people watch[ed] sport in real competitions, but their interest did not extend to sport in art.' (*ibid*: 108). This was a remarkable set-back to the promotion of Coubertin's ideals, as a major reason for holding cultural events alongside the sports competitions was to inspire discussion and the promotion of ideas among all Olympic participants and spectators.

In this context, it is interesting to see that, in contrast with other host cities where Olympic arts manifestations had played a minor role, the so-called 'Nazi Games' of Berlin 1936 included a cultural festival of unprecedented dimensions for which, as indicated in the Berlin Games official report, an ambitious publicity campaign was created to ensure maximum recognition and participation.

> Because of the slight interest which the general public had hitherto evidenced in the Olympic Art Competition and Exhibition, it was necessary to emphasise their cultural significance to the Olympic Games through numerous articles in the professional and daily publications as well as radio lectures. (Berlin Organising Committee 1937, vol.2)

The Berlin Games in 1936 offer one of the most ambitious examples of an Olympic art programme in this first period, which have been seen by many as evidence of culture and the arts being used for propaganda purposes—indeed, the Berlin Arts Committee programme was chaired by a representative of the

Reich Ministry of Propaganda (Berlin Organising Committee 1937). The Games had been identified by the local host as an opportunity to promote the ideals of Nazi Germany and cultural activity was seen as a good vehicle to represent the supremacy of the Arian race and Western civilisation. Cultural innovations brough in at the Berlin Games included the first Olympic torch relay, travelling from Ancient Olympia in Greece to the Berlin stadium, and the first artist-led Olympic film, Leni Riefenstahl's 'Olympia'. These cultural manifestations became as central to the Olympic experience as the sport competitions, both during Games time and in their symbolic reconstruction for decades to come. From a cultural programming point of view, the most interesting aspect of this particular experience is the evidence that the Games were used as a mechanism to make Germany's national cultural policy discourse more visible internationally, and the use of artistic expression as a platform to contextualise the Games and use them for propaganda purposes, far beyond simple sport representation.

The 1940 and 1944 Olympic Games and related arts competitions were not held because of World War II. When the Games were re-established in London 1948, the organising committee succeeded in paralleling the sports with arts competitions. Remarkably, after the cultural programme ended, the British Fine Arts Committee that had been set up on occasion of the Games compiled a report of suggestions for future arts contests. This was intended for use as a guide to organising future arts competitions. Good (1998) explains that 'the recommendations included reducing the number of arts categories' and concluded that the 'interest in the exhibitions would be greater if they were more closely linked up with the Games themselves and if a more intensive press campaign had been organised' (p. 20). By 1950, however, the problems and difficulties of hosting Olympic art competitions were perceived to be far greater than the benefits and achievements. To review the situation, an extended discussion process took place within the IOC from 1949 in Rome to 1952 in Helsinki. As a result of this controversial process, which involved a detailed assessment of the 'amateur' nature of Olympic contributions, it was decided that from 1952 on, the presence of the arts in the Olympics would take the form of cultural exhibitions and festivals instead of competitions.

Melbourne 1956 to Seoul 1988: Olympic Arts Exhibitions and Festivals

The first official Olympic arts festival was held at the Melbourne 1956 Games. The festival was coordinated first by a Fine-Arts Subcommittee, elected in 1953 and then by a Festival Sub-Committee created in 1955. The festival had two major components: one of visual arts and literature, and another one of music and drama. Hanna (1999: 76) describes that 'exhibitions and festivals were staged simultaneously in the weeks leading up to and during the Games and featured local, national and international artists and performers'. A special book on Australian arts was published after the Games, entitled 'The Arts Festival: a Guide to the Exhibition with Introductory Commentaries on the Arts in Australia'. The Official Report of the Melbourne Games concluded that 'the change from a competition to a Festival was widely welcomed, since the Festival provided a significant commentary on Australia's contribution to the Arts' (cited in Good 1998: 29).

This new stage in the Olympic cultural programme tradition brought opportunities as well as challenges for the development of local, national and international cultural policy. On the one hand, Games organisers had greater freedoms to define the purpose of such programmes and determine who should be presenting what type of work. On the other, eliminating its competitive nature led to divorcing the programme from strong national delegation following (and related patriotic sentiments), and this situation often led to lesser Olympic participants and audience engagement and lesser international focus. The programme was now mainly a platform for local cultural representation directed according to the specific interests of the host authorities, with much less of a direct involvement and regulations from the top Olympic structures.

Some Olympic host countries saw the programme as an important opportunity to make a statement about a point in their history, and as an opportunity to profile the host nation, far and beyond what was possible within the sporting arenas and the highly regulated Olympic ceremonies and protocol. Host cities became increasingly ambitious in their treatment of the arts festivals, progressively aligning them with the 'growing arts agenda' that developed after the Second World War including an aspiration to address 'audience development, access, and inclusion' (Gold and Revill 2007: 73). In 1968, Mexico presented one of the most ambitious festivals, spanning throughout one year and acting as a showcase, not only of the best international art at the time, but also the best of Mexican contemporary art as well as folklore and heritage. For many, the ambition and quality of the programme proved that Mexico may have been considered a country that was part of the 'developing world' from an economic point of view, but was certainly at the avantgarde of the 'first world' in terms of art and culture (MacAloon 2008, pers. comm., 23 Jun). Interestingly, Mexico viewed the cultural programme in a more holistic fashion than other Games hosts and, beyond the arts, incorporated discussions about education, science as well as advertising, design and communications. Montreal in 1976 also presented an innovative cultural programme, making a clear emphasis in the connections between art and sport and exploring the presentation of arts activitiy within sporting venues, in particular the main Olympic Park avenue and the areas surrounding the stadium.

Throughout the 1960s and 1970s, other areas where artists and related creative practitioners made major contributions were the design of banners and logos—what is now termed 'the look of the Games'. The imagery for Mexico 1968, Tokyo 1964 and Munich 1972 are all exemplars of avantgarde visual design rather than simple marketing and branding exercises, which can be viewed as a foremost example of powerful cultural policy innovation emerging out of the Games. These elements of the Games were however, often not treated as part of the official cultural programme (Mexico 1968 was a notable exception), and subsequent editions of the Games (excepting Barcelona 1992 and Torino 2006) have failed to use these environments as an expression of advanced place-sensitive creative practice.

Barcelona 1992 to London 2012: Cultural Olympiads

Another stage in Olympic cultural programming was initiated with the Barcelona 1992 Olympic Bid, which proposed that the implementation of a Cultural Olympiad (a term already used in Mexico 1968 amongst others) should in fact take place during the four years of the Olympiad—from the end of one Games edition to the start of the next. Barcelona's Cultural Olympiad thus started in 1988, at the end of the Seoul Games, and evolved up to 1992 with a different thematic emphasis for each year. Guevara (1992) explains this ambitious decision by referring to the organisers' strategic intention to use the Games to improve the city's urban landscape and assist in its international projection far beyond the Games staging period. Indeed, Barcelona 1992 has come to be remembered and portrayed by the international media as the Games that placed the city at the heart of the Olympic experience. The festive use of public space was at central to its success, while it is less clear whether the official cultural programme, restricted as it was to traditional arts venues rather than establishing direct synergies with other Games activities, played a role within the Olympic city's narrative (see Moragas 2001).

Regardless of the actual effectiveness of specific activities within the Cultural Olympiad, the four-year format has been maintained in subsequent summer Games editions. This has been on the initiative of respective host cities rather than an IOC directive, as there is no formal requirement to create a four year cultural programme. As noted later, the Winter Games have also grown their ambitions for the Cultural Olympiad and have presented the first full four-year Olympiad programme in the lead to Vancouver 2010. This last stage in Olympic cultural programme development has been characterised by two main phenomena. On the one hand, there has been a clearer alignment of the programme with local and national cultural policy ambitions than ever before, and set objectives have been in line with standard cultural event objectives (such as using the Games period not only to expand sport audiences but also cultural and arts audiences, and using the event to advance local creative development aspirations); social agendas (using the event to improve community inclusion, expand access to marginal or deprived communities, strengthen local or national identity); and economic agendas (advancing urban regeneration, repositioning cities, growing cultural tourism) (Garcia 2004a, 2004b). The kinds of 'political agendas' that were common in previous periods have

also been maintainted, particularly for countries aspiring to overcome negative stereotypes related to their military past or human right issues, or for
countries aspiring to present a more complex picture of their local identity,
beyond fixed monocultural nation-state perceptions. On the other hand,
the branding tension in relation to the main Olympic programme of sporting activity has become increasingly apparent, and there have been varied
attempts at establishing separate Cultural Olympiad or Olympic Arts Festival
brands, with various degrees of success (Garcia 2001).

The Cultural Olympiad of Athens 2004 provides an example of the
extremes organisers have been ready to go to in order to establish a strong
Olympic cultural programme identity and brand. The programme was given
a prime position within the event hosting process, as the city celebrated the
contribution of Greece and Greek heritage as the cradle of European civilisation and the birthplace of the Olympic Games. The Cultural Olympiad
was thus utilised as a platform to convey ancient Olympic values and claim
ownership of the Games in ways not accessible to other Olympic hosts. This
involved the promotion of the Olympic Truce as a particularly important
component of the Olympiad[7] and the establishment of a Cultural Olympiad
Foundation in 1998 with backing from UNESCO, with the aim of becoming a permanent institution to coordinate Olympic cultural programming
in the same way that the IOC coordinates the sporting programme.[8] At the
time of writing, more than a decade on from the establishment of this institution, the role of this foundation remains unclear, providing yet another
indication of the persistent challenges embedded within the Olympic cultural programme tradition.

The Olympic programmes for Beijing 2008 and London 2012 also incorporate a Cultural Olympiad. In Beijing, this took the form of 'Olympic Cultural Festivals' taking place over a month each year from 2003 to 2008—so,
over a six-year period.[9] In London, the Cultural Olympiad started at the
end of September 2008 and involves a nation-wide programme of activities
up to 2012, coordinated by thirteen specially appointed regional creative
programmers, plus an additional London 2012 Festival to take place over
two and a half months in the Olympic year.

Cultural Programming at the Winter Games and Paralympic Games

While this monograph focuses predominantly on the Olympic Summer
Games hosting process, it is important to note that there are crucial differences in cultural programming that arise within the Olympic Winter
Games and the Paralympic Games. While I do not intend to focus on either
of these in depth, it is valuable to provide a brief indication of what has
been achieved as this also provides a rich counterpoint for the Summer
Games cultural policy discourse, on occasion, representing a more successful variation that could be taken as a point of reference for better Olympic
cultural policy implementation.

The artistic programme of the Winter Games was not formally established until Cortina d'Ampezzo in 1956 and was a minor affair. However, more ambitious cultural programmes comparable to the Summer Games began with Grenoble 1968, the same year that Mexico hosted the Summer Games and presented the most extensive cultural programme to date. In the three most recent Winter Games—Salt Lake City 2002, Torino 2006 and Vancouver 2010—it is evident that the ambition of host cities to attract attention building on a cultural discourse has grown year upon year (see also Müller, Messing and Preuss 2006).

Given the smaller scale of operations at the Winter Games, there are interesting nuances that allow for different kinds of programming and growing differentiation from Summer Games protocols. This differentiation has evolved since Nagano 1998. A particularly relevant phenomenon from a cultural point of view is the emergence of the '*medals plaza*' as a distinct mixed-venue within the host city centre. This is a space where medals are awarded to athletes, thus extending and changing the ceremony that would normally take place within sport venues exclusively. The justification for this extension has been that winter sports take place mainly within mountain resorts away from any urban conurbation and thus have limited people critical mass and festival atmosphere. The staging of a medals plaza as an additional Olympic venue allows organisers to re-constitute the city space each evening around a hallmark event. Integral to this ceremony each night is the programming of a range of other cultural activities. For instance, in Torino and Salt Lake City, it was typical for medals ceremonies to be followed by feature performances by international singers and musicians. This is one clear example in which the Winter Games has affected the Olympic protocol in a way that is conducive to more effective festival programming. Also in Torino 2006, there were connections made between the OCOG and the host city promotional programmes, particularly through the Look of the Games programme, which, for the first time, was accompanied by a Look of the City programme featuring cultural rather than sporting icons (see Garcia and Miah 2006).

Innovation continues to occur at the Winter Games. For instance, the Cultural Olympiad of Vancouver 2010 lasted four years, a first for any Olympic Winter Games, and it became a visible element within the city's dressing strategy, with dedicated flagpoles in the years leading to the Games and during the Games fortnight in 2010. Further, the launch of a Cultural Olympiad Digital Edition (CODE) ensured engagement with new technologies that resulted in new creative art-form interventions as well as innovative ways to engage disperse communities throughout Canada, which were invited to reflect on their sense of identity via social media environments and share them within a dedicated online platform, Canada CODE (Young 2010). This expansion of the cultural dimensions of Olympic programming reinforces the view that it is becoming more and more central to local host ambitions and their projections to ensure a Games legacy.

With regard to the Paralympic Games, its cultural programme has evolved slowly over the years and has received even less attention than the Olympic cultural programme. However, this trend has changed since Sydney 2000, which was the first Games to provide the same team to manage the official Olympic and Paralympic cultural programme. Further, in the wake of Sydney 2000, a series of agreements between the IOC and the International Paralympic Committee (IPC) have resulted in ever closer synergies between the two Games, including the decision to establish a single organising committee for both Games (Brittain 2010: 29–30) which effectively means that all key programmes are organised under the same operational framework. In the context of London 2012, the team responsible for the cultural programme have committed to expanding such organisational synergies into an all-encompassing Games cultural policy narrative, where there is no distinction between Olympic and Paralympic cultural activity. Indeed, the London 2012 Cultural Olympiad incorporates a celebration of long established UK disability arts organisations as part of its four year national programme and a range of regional cultural programmes have placed an emphasis on presenting activity that questions the notion of 'normality' as a way of bridging the gap between perceptions of abled bodies or disabled bodies and the work they can engage with, be it in the realm of sports or arts.[10] Further, the Games-time cultural programme, named London 2012 Festival, spans over both Olympic and Paralympic fortnights without interruption, thus acting as one of the key symbolic bridges between both events. The sharing of a common team and a single programme of activity is critical since most other Games programmes, from the sport competitions to symbolic events such as the torch relay or the ceremonies, follow a very different planning and delivery cycle. Indeed, this places the official cultural programme in a very central and significant position to create additional synergies between the two Games, an aspiration that is becoming increasingly important to the Olympic Movement.[11]

ONGOING OPERATIONAL ISSUES FOR THE OLYMPIC CULTURAL PROGRAMME

The dynamic nature of the Olympic cultural programme is clearly manifest in the diversity of formats, objectives and management structures put in place to implement it. While the sports competitions and virtually every other Olympic programme have become heavily rationalised and standardised, the cultural programme remains an area open to free interpretation by respective hosts. Guevara (1992) documented the diversity of interpretations through a comparative analysis of Olympic Games cultural programmes from Mexico 1968 to Barcelona 1992. This section builds on and complements Guevara's study with an analysis of Games editions beyond 1992 and points out at significant new areas of disparity in terms of brand recognition and stakeholder support, all of which reinforces the impression that there is no appropriate cultural policy framework to support the programme.

Programme Design: Objectives, Themes and Delivery Format

One of the main differences between programme editions is its actual duration. While the only formal request by the IOC is that 'cultural activities take place during the time the Olympic Village is open', since Mexico's year long cultural celebration in 1968, the length of the cultural programme has varied from three weeks in Moscow 1980, to ten weeks in los Angeles 1984 and four years in the summer editions of Barcelona 1992 onwards. Despite the growing popularity of the four year format, the duration of a Cultural Olympiad is not completely set either. Indeed, while one might expect that a host city cannot promote its Cultural Olympiad until the previous city has concluded its Games, there are no rules that indicate this. As such, Beijing 2008 began its Olympiad during 2003, before the Athens 2004 Games had even begun. While Barcelona 1992, Atlanta 1996, Sydney 2000 and Athens 2004 presented activities distributed throughout each of the four years leading to the Games, in Beijing, the Olympiad involved a period of between one week to a month of activity every year between 2003 and 2008, mainly to commemorate the day of the Games award.

In terms of core objectives, one can identify five major and non-exclusive categories which have varying degrees of economic, political, social or cultural undertones: (1) acknowledgement of the city's artistic and cultural capacities, (2) improvement of the city cultural services or infrastructure, (3) showcase of the country's folklore and cultural diversity, (4) international projection, and (5) change of image (Guevara 1992; Garcia 2000). The first objective was paramount to Munich 1972 and Los Angeles 1984. Both cities were already linked to important cultural circuits and counted on the appropriate budget to present a festival of international significance. Using the Games as an opportunity to *improve the city's cultural services* was a major drive for the Barcelona 1992 Cultural Olympiad, which expanded the programme over four years and established its leading team with close ties to the City Council in order to ensure that key programming aspirations were retained beyond Games time and had an impact on the city's cultural infrastructure.

The showcase of the country's *folklore and cultural diversity* was a fundamental factor in the design of the Mexico 1968, Montreal 1976 and Moscow 1980 cultural programmes. This was also the case for Beijing 2008 and is linked to a deeper political agenda of reinforcing national pride on the country's heritage.[12] The aim to achieve an *international projection* was dominant in Seoul 1988, Barcelona 1992, Sydney 2000 and Athens 2004. In the case of Seoul and Barcelona, the Games brought both cities the opportunity to be known world-wide. As such, the Games cultural policy combined an emphasis on local inclusion and representation with ambitious international communication strategies for culture. Finally, the objective to achieve a *change of image* was key in the cultural agenda of cities such as Munich, Seoul and Beijing, all of them cities within countries with a prominent and controversial militaristic character in the past, aspiring to overcome dated international stereotypes.

In the approach to London 2012, additional aims that are emerging as core Cultural Olympiad aspirations are the growth of cultural as well as sporting *audiences and participation* and, in line with late developments in cultural policy definitions, the use of the cultural programmes to advance wider *urban regeneration* objectives that link to social as well as economic agendas (see Garcia 2004a, 2004b).

The thematic focus of Olympic cultural programmes has traditionally responded to these five to six types of set objectives. As such, they have varied from strongly rooted national festivals to international festivals, and from a focus on community events to a focus on high arts manifestations. For example, Mexico 1968 presented a year-long national and international festival while Montreal 1976 presented a small scale but highly popular festival with a marked national character. In contrast, Los Angeles 1984 was a large-scale, well promoted festival focused on elite national and international events with few open-air popular manifestations. Seoul 1988 also presented some international elite artists but combined them with local popular events. Remarkably, Munich 1972 was paradigmatic in the configuration and production of the arts festivals because the festival was completely integrated within the Olympic sporting events. Munich understood the Games as a cultural event in itself and presented the arts manifestations in a way more open to spontaneous community appropriation. This was particularly evident in its so-called *Avenue of Entertainment* which was composed of street theatre shows, mimes, clowns and acrobats (Burnosky 1994: 47) and incorporated performances focused on the interpretation of sports through art.

Additionally, since the creation of the Cultural Olympiad model, a common feature has been the design of thematic festivals, one for each year of the event. In Barcelona, the themes evolved from a *Cultural Gateway* in 1988, to the *Year of Culture and Sport* in 1989, the *Year of the Arts* in 1990, the *Year of the Future* in 1991 and the *Olympic Art Festival* in 1992. Atlanta also covered a wide range of subjects during the four years of festivals, arranged into two main themes: *Southern Connections* at a national level, and *International Connections*. Sydney offered a taste of the many and diverse Australian cultural communities through presenting an indigenous festival in 1997, a festival dedicated to multicultural groups and the waves of immigration in 1998, and international festivals in 1999 and year 2000. Finally, Athens reflected on major philosophical and humanistic principles by exploring the notions of 'Man and Space', 'Man and the Earth', 'Man and the Spirit' and 'Man and Man'.

Another operational dimension not considered by Guevara in her 1992 study is the geographical spread of cultural activity. While most Olympic Games editions have concentrated their cultural programmes in the host city (mainly within central areas or, in some cases, within the Olympic park and related Olympic venues), since the establishment of the Cultural Olympiad, the ambition has been to involve communities beyond the host city to ensure that the Games are owned at a national level—and, sometimes, internationally. This has brought an additional challenge, as the more disperse the activity, the more difficult it has been to ensure that the programme is widely visible and it can have an impact at a large scale— particularly from the perspective of media coverage (García 2000, 2001). The first nation-wide cultural programme took place in Mexico 1968, with various attempts at following this trend taking place in the lead to Sydney 2000, Athens 2004 and, currently, London 2012. The latter has established an Olympic first by supporting the creation of thirteen regional 'Creative Programmers' posts that are to coordinate and encourage Olympic cultural activity without depending directly on the OCOG.[13] Sydney 2000 and Athens 2004 have also aspired to incorporate an international dimension, with artworks being presented across the five continents.

Management and Promotional Structures

Despite the ongoing revisions to the cultural programme design framework, objectives and thematic priorities, the underlying challenges in terms of visibility and linkage to other Games activity have remained. Good (1998) argues that the shift from art competitions to exhibitions did not solve these problems because it did not study or analyse the 'management issues' that had been repeatedly raised in official Games reports up to the 1950s (p. 31). These problems might have been accentuated by the absence of an international cultural organisation comparable to the international sports federations in its ability to coordinate and support Olympic arts initiatives (Masterton 1973). Indeed, recent attempts to address this gap (such as the notion of a permanent Cultural Olympiad foundation in Greece) have failed to fully materialise. In the meantime, management styles have varied considerably from one Games to the next. Building on Guevara's (1992) analysis, it is possible to identify five main types of management structure in the context of the Games: central management model to shared management, state management, private management and mixed management.

Central management occurs when the cultural programme is the sole responsibility of the OCOG. This was the case in Mexico 1968, Munich 1972, Seoul 1988 and Sydney 2000, the latter of which is analysed in detail in Chapter 5. *Decentralised management* or *shared management* has occurred when the Olympic cultural responsibilities have been the obligation of the OCOG in partnership with other organisations either private or public. A representative case was Montreal 1976, where Canadian provinces were in charge of designing the arts programmes, while the OCOG's cultural department was in charge of the logistics. A similar situation applies to London 2012, which counts on a culture team within the OCOG but also benefits from the appointment of 13 regional creative programmers to manage its four-year cultural Olympiad, building on separate funding and organisational support via the Arts Council and other non-profit organisations. *State management* has occurred when the control of the cultural programme has been directly in hands of one or various public bodies. This was the model for the management, planning and production of the Moscow 1980 Games arts component as well as the Cultural Olympiad in Athens 2004, which was entirely managed via a special branch of the Hellenic Ministry of Culture. In contrast, the clearest example of *private management* has been Los Angeles 1984. On that occasion, the OCOG was established as a private company and its cultural department hired co-producer agencies to organise the arts events. This was also the case in Atlanta 1996. Finally, there have been some cases of *mixed management* such as in Barcelona 1992, where a special organisation for the cultural programme was created with name *Olimpiada Cultural SA* (OCSA). OCSA was at the same time separated and dependent upon the Olympic Organising Committee: on the one hand, it had an administrative committee composed of public administration representatives independent of the OCOG; on the other, the Major of Barcelona presided over the OCSA Board of Directors and was also President of the OCOG, which effectively implied a common set of priorities and a dependence on the Games organising committee key delivery agendas.

From a promotional point of view, little is known about the approach to communicating and attracting interest on the festivals before the advent of global branding techniques and the creation of complex Olympic marketing guidelines. As discussed in Chapter 7, however, such techniques have had little application for the cultural programme. Barcelona 1992 created a separate brand to promote its Cultural Olympiad, an approach also used by Athens 2004. In both cases, authors have argued that there were important communication gaps and a lack of promotional synergy with mainstream Olympic activity (Moragas 2001, Panagiotopoulou 2008).

In the lead to London 2012, further branding discussions have emerged, this time trying to establish a Cultural Olympiad brand that does not conflict with Olympic sponsor interests (such as protecting their exclusive access to the use of the rings), but allow cultural contributors to search alternative sources of funding or acknowledge their own long term sponsors. This has involved the establishment of an 'Inspired by 2012' mark, which is clearly associated with London 2012, but does not include the Olympic rings, which is a protected IOC trademark only accessible to its global corporate partners and media right holders. Such distinction offers a clear example of the different dimensions of cultural value associated to the Games: on the one hand, the local or national festival dimension

(Inspire mark), mainly oriented towards those who will experience activites as live specatators in the lead to the Games; on the other, the global media event dimension (Olympic rings), which is mainly oriented towards broadcast audiences worldwide. As will be discussed in more detail throughout the monograph, in such a division, it becomes apparent that the Cultural Olympiad is clearly rooted within the local and national festival sphere, while only the Ceremonies and 16 days of sport programme are central to the Games as a global media spectacle.

Challenges and Potential Contributions by the International Olympic Committee

Traditionally, there has been a large gap between the eagerness of potential host cities to propose activities for the cultural Olympic programme at the bid stage and the readiness of the chosen Olympic organising committee to implement them. This gap might be a direct result of the ambiguous description of the cultural programme in the Olympic Charter guidelines. As discussed earlier, this situation has allowed a great freedom of action and interpretation and has contributed to incite very ambitious cultural bid proposals. Nevertheless, this is also the source of remarkable discontinuities in the OCOG's commitment to realise them, especially when the question of budget and resource allocation is debated.

Further, as noted in Chapter 5 and six, Olympic cultural programmes, whether they have been organised by an independent institution or by a department within the OCOG, have had difficulties to sustain their association with other Olympic activities and to benefit from the Games' extensive promotional opportunities (García 2001). This is indicative of a potential conflict that prevents the integration of the cultural programme within the overall Olympic Games preparations. Ultimately, this suggests that, although the Olympic Movement aims to be a humanistic project encompassing sport, culture and education, the commercial imperatives of the Olympic Games staging process have led to the absolute predominance of the competitive elite sport programme over cultural and educational activities. The prior statement is reflected in the operational structure of the OCOG, within which the team in charge of the cultural programme tends to be operate almost independently to the rest of the organisation. This does not only provoke an understandable separation of the cultural programme from the departments in charge of sporting competitions but also from the departments in charge of Olympic ceremonies, marketing, communications, media and institutional relations. This lack of cohesion of programmes and activities has led to an unnecessary duplicity of resources and to a lack of visibility for the Cultural Olympiad.

Finally, it is relevant to note the continuous difficulties to guarantee appropriate fundraising for respective cultural programmes, a topic we return to in Chapter 7. This may be a direct result of the way the current

Olympic marketing strategies have been designed. None of the fundamental sources of Olympic revenue–the successful worldwide Olympic sponsorship programme (TOP) and the national sponsorship programs or the sales of television rights- include concrete references which favour investment in or coverage of Olympic cultural activities. In this context, considering the low status of the cultural programme when compared to such activities as the sporting competitions, the ceremonies and the torch relay, it is to be expected that Olympic sponsors will almost unanimously tend to invest in the latter areas rather than in a cultural programme. Further, the exclusivity principle lying behind all Olympic marketing arrangements has traditionally limited the possibility of attracting funders for cultural activity other than public entities (see García 2001).

All these considerations make a case for a better regulation of the cultural programme management and production system. More specifically, it calls for the creation of a more clearly defined IOC cultural policy that can protect and enhance such an important but misunderstood dimension of the Olympic Games. The following chapter assesses the intrinsic limitations of the programme as a result of an ambiguous cultural policy at the heart of the International Olympic Committee.

SUMMARY

The notion of Olympic cultural programme has a long tradition within the Olympic Movement, though it is not accompanied by a clear definition of its role. As such, respective Olympic Games organisers have had freedom to interpret this notion and implement it in the form most appropriate to their interests and the particularities of their countries. This has (sometimes) encouraged creativity, but it has also led to inconsistencies and variable levels of political and financial assurances. The consequence of such instability has been a tendency for the programme to be pushed to the margins of an OCOGs delivery structure, which is evident from the absence of connections to various other parts of the Olympic infrastructure. In turn, this has led to a relatively low profile.

The Olympic cultural programme has traditionally been understood as an artistic programme exclusively. As an arts event, it has frequently provided a platform for expressing the artistic excellence of the host nation. However, in this function, the programme has rarely interacted with other dimensions of the Games, such as the education programme, ceremonies, or the sports events. This has prevented the programme from playing a central role within the Olympic experience and has often displaced cultural (and particularly arts) activity to the margins of the Games hosting process.

Moreover, the many variations in the format of this programme, from an arts competition to a four year cultural Olympiad, are another indication of its vulnerability. Changes in the structure, length or theme of the programme have normally been made at a superficial level. This has occurred without the ambition to overcome the entrenched problems and weaknesses of the programme, and without questioning what role culture can play in the context of an event as large and influential as the Olympics. Interestingly, the Olympic Winter Games and Paralympic Games, both exemplars of a smaller-scale Games delivery process, are placing greater emphasis on their cultural programmes to ensure they are more central to the Games experience. This provides an interesting referent for alternative Games cultural policy making.

After almost one century, the cultural programme has been unable to overcome the fundamental problems that affected it from its inception. With London 2012, comes the centenary of the programme and an opportunity to review its function and value within the Olympic Movement. However, without appropriate support within the Olympic Movement at large, it remains to be seen whether the programme can play a significant role beyond the constrained limits of its local host environment.

3   The Cultural Policy of the International Olympic Committee

More than 100 years on since the 1906 'Consultative Conference on Arts, Letters and Sport' that led to the establishment of Olympic Arts Competitions, the IOC maintains its commitment to ensuring the survival of the Olympic cultural programme as an event additional and complementary to the sports competitions. In 1993, this commitment led to the opening of a renovated and ambitious Olympic Museum in Lausanne, a venue that welcomes the display of arts and cultural elements related to sport and the Olympic Movement. Nevertheless, the ambiguous definition and variable nature of Olympic cultural programmes have limited the ability of local Games organisers and audiences to understand its function and purpose and question the extent to which it is integral to the Olympic Games celebration.

This chapter begins with a brief review of the elements highlighted within IOC official documents in reference to Olympic cultural activity. The second and third sections of the chapter analyse the position of cultural activities (and the cultural programme, in particular) within the structure and strategic agendas of the IOC. The main aim of the chapter is to provide a basis for discussing whether there is a defined cultural policy within the Olympic Movement or the IOC as its umbrella organisation. The period of time that is most relevant for this assessment is the lead up to the Sydney 2000 Games, as this helps explain the framework within which the Games operated and influenced the design, management and promotional structures that are analysed in detail in Parts II and III of this volume. Some of the IOC developments that followed the Sydney Games are also identified and discussed, so as to explain current Olympic cultural policy trends.

DEFINITIONS OF 'CULTURAL ACTIVITY' WITHIN THE IOC

The IOC (2009a) defines and lists the main missions of the Olympic Movement as follows:

- choice of the host city
- organisation of the Olympic Games
- promotion of women in sport

- protection of athletes
- development through sport
- promotion of sustainable development
- respect for the Olympic Truce
- promotion of culture and Olympic education

The latter mission, which has a mixed history in terms of visibility within key IOC policy documents and mission statements, is defined by the IOC in the following terms:

> The International Olympic Committee (IOC) has played an important role in the development of the culture and Olympic education agenda, by establishing a policy that seeks to provide greater resources to their promotion in and through sport at national, regional and international level, and particularly at the Olympic Games. This policy has two main objectives: [1] It strives to develop the link between sport and culture in all its forms, encourages cultural exchange and promotes the diversity of cultures; [2] It also aims to promote Olympic education and supports other institutions which prone the values of Olympism. (IOC 2009a)

The IOC goes on to frame these ambitions within the Olympic Charter Fundamental Principles, as discussed in Chapters 1 and 2, and then refers to the range of key stakeholders for culture and Olympic education initiatives, which include '[t]he Olympic Museum, Olympic Solidarity, International Olympic Academy, United Nations Educational Scientific and Cultural Organization, International Pierre de Coubertin Committee and Organising Committees of the Olympic Games' (IOC 2009a). OCOGs are the key stakeholder for the delivery of the Games cultural programme specifically.

Existing IOC regulations and guidelines emphasise that, to become an Olympic host-city, it is compulsory to organise and promote a cultural programme in parallel to the sporting competitions. As discussed in Chapter 2, these regulations appear in the Olympic Charter and in respective Games Candidature Procedure and Questionnaire documents. However, none of these regulations, guidelines and recommendations clarify the function and purpose of such a programme, nor indicate how its success or failure can be evaluated or studied by the IOC after its implementation. This has led to a series of problems, difficulties and dysfunctions that are affecting the preparations of current Cultural Olympiads as much as they affected prior Olympic Arts Competitions and Festivals. These circumstances are an indication of the ambiguity of the Olympic Movement's cultural policy. A study of the Movement's provisions for sustaining and protecting cultural activity should assist in identifying whether the Movement and, more specifically, the IOC as its leading institution, has a defined cultural policy framework.

Two months of research in 2001 at the IOC Olympic Studies Centre in Lausanne allowed a wide compilation of data, fundamentally archival and documentation materials, which indicate the position and potential prospects of cultural activities within the Olympic Movement. In this research, the concept of 'cultural activity' was understood in the sense suggested by the Olympic Charter in its fundamental principles, articles 2, 3 and 6, rules 31 and 32 and rule 44 (IOC 1999a).[1] That is, as all initiatives taken by Olympic related institutions or organisations which are aimed at least at one of the following purposes:

- emphasising the role that culture plays within the philosophy of Olympism and ensuring and association between culture and the Olympic Movement
- demonstrating existing parallelisms and synergies between culture and sport, culture and education or all three concepts together
- implementing cultural programmes in the context of other Olympic events

Thus, the concept of Olympic 'cultural activity' is not synonymous with the implementation of sports events, but only applied in the case of projects of other nature, notably, arts events, manifestations about the identities and values of specific communities and other creative endeavours complementary to sport. The research in Lausanne was aimed at studying the current involvement of the IOC to manage and promote cultural initiatives. In order to gather a representative and consistent perspective about this involvement, the research focused on analysing the position of cultural endeavours within the structures and policy agendas of the IOC. The outcomes of such assessment are detailed below.

CENTRALITY OF CULTURAL ACTIVITIES WITHIN THE IOC STRUCTURE

As the governing body of the Olympic Movement, the IOC describes itself as

> [a] catalyst for collaboration between all members of the Olympic Family, from the National Olympic Committees (NOCs), the International Sports Federations (IFs), the athletes, the Organising Committees for the Olympic Games (OCOGs), to the TOP partners, broadcast partners and agencies from the United Nations. (IOC 2009a)

In terms of organisational structure, in 2000, the IOC was structured in an Executive Board, 18 commissions and five special groups among which the Women and Sport Working Group and the Council of the Olympic Order (IOC 2000e). This structure has been maintained up to the time of writing, with only slight—but in some cases important—changes to the number of commissions and working groups. The Executive Board (EB) is the body with an ability to take key decisions about the main actions, activities and

Table 3.1 Composition of IOC Commissions in 2000[2]

Commission name	Num. EB members versus total members	% EB	Num. EB members and position in commission	Num. IOC members versus total members	% IOC members	% EB and IOC members combined
1. Juridical	5/7	71.5%	5: MBAYE, chairman; BACH, member; DEFRANZ, member; HODLER, member; POUND, member	6/7	86%	79%
2. Finance	1/8	12.5%	1: HODLER, chairman	7/8	87%	50%
3. Olympic Solidarity	3/27	11%	3: SAMARANCH, chairman; GOSPER & ROGGE, vice-chairmen of ANOC	21/27	78%	44%
4. Marketing	2/18	11%	2: POUND, chairman; BACH, member	13/18	72%	42%
5. Medical	1/15	6.67%	1: ROGGE, vice-Chairman	11/15	73%	40%
6. Athletes	1/17	6%	1: BUBKA, member	12/17	70%	38%
7. Ethics	2/7	28.5%	2: MBAYE, chairman; IGAYA, member	3/7	43%	36%
8. Sport and Law	5/15	33%	5: MBAYE, chairman; BACH, member; DEFRANZ, member; HODLER, member; POUND, member	5/15	33%	33%
9. Coordination summer Games	2/12	8%	2: ROGGE, chairman; DEFRANTZ, member	7/12	58%	33%
10. Coordination winter Games	2/19	10.5%	2: HODLER, chairman; IGAYA, member	9/19	47%	29%
11. Nominations	1/7	14%	1: MBAYE, chairman	3/7	43%	28%
12. Olympic programme	1/11	9%	1: ROGGE, member	5/11	45%	27%
13. Women and sport working group	1/20	5%	1: DEFRANTZ, chairperson	9/20	45%	25%
14. Culture and education	1/32	3%	1: HE, chairman	13/32	40%	22%
15. Sport for all	0/21	0%	None	9/21	43%	21%
16. Coubertin	1/7	14%	1: SAMARANCH, chairman	2/7	28%	21%
17. Radio and TV	1/24	4%	1: KIM, chairman;	6/24	25%	14%
18. Sport and environment	0/24	0%	None	6/24	25%	12%
19. Olympic collectors	1/10	10%	1: SAMARANCH, chairman	1/10	10%	10%
20. Press	1/28	3.5%	1: GOSPER, chairman	4/28	14%	9%
21. FIPO	0/4	0%	None	0/4	0,00	0,00
22. FINO	0/3	0%	None	0/3	0,00	0,00

Source: Author elaboration. Primary data obtained from the IOC (2000e).

programmes that are to be implemented at Games time. As such, the EB can be defined as the body that is most central to the operations of the IOC and, by comparison, the proximity of other commissions to the EB can also be taken as an indication of their respective centrality. An analysis of the membership composition of each commission provides a basis to determine their existing or potential links to the EB. Indications of these links have been found by comparing the number of EB members belonging to each commission. Indications of the centrality or the ability to influence IOC voting procedures have also been found by looking at the number of IOC members composing each commission by contrast to the totality of members. Find below a tentative table summarising the previous data.

As noted in Table 3.1 accepting that EB members are central to the operational structure of the IOC, the commissions with a greater number of EB members could be understood to have an advantage over the others in strategic terms. Also, arguably, commissions composed mainly by IOC members are in a better position to network within the Movement and protect their interests on occasion of the IOFC Session and other meetings. The correlation between the number of EB members and the number of IOC members by rapport to the total members of each commission could then be taken as an initial indication of their potential centrality and influence. On this basis, Table 3.1 suggests the following:

- the commission with the most central position within the IOC structure in year 2000 was the Juridical Commission. This commission is followed by the Commissions of Finance, Olympic Solidarity, Marketing and the Medical Commission
- commissions placed in a relatively central position are the Athletes Commission, Ethics, Sports and Law and the IOC Coordination for the Summer Games
- the above are closely followed in 'centrality' by the IOC Coordination Commission for the Winter Games, Nominations, Olympic Programme and the Women and Sport working group
- the following level of centrality is composed by the Culture and Education, Sports for All and Coubertin commissions
- at a lower 'centrality' level appear to be the Commission of Radio and Television followed by Sports and Environment, Olympic Collectors and the Press Commission

Naturally, the membership composition of each commission does not offer a complete account of the centrality of the matters to which each commission is assigned. For instance, the Commission of Radio and Television had a very low percentage of EB and IOC members in year 2000, despite the fact that television matters have become paramount to IOC operations. In order to understand this apparent paradox, it is important to note how Commissions relate to each other in their management of key assets. In the case of television matters, where negotiation of broadcasting rights are concerned, this task falls upon the relatively new Commission for Television Rights and New Media, which benefits from close connections with the Marketing and Finance Commissions. The Commission of Radio and Television is instead focused on overseeing the operational side of working with television industries in their coverage of the Games. Clearly, for the latter, this need not require such high level IOC involvement, while it requires the highest level of expertise in this particular professional skill base.[3] We must also take into account the role of bodies other than the commissions when trying to understand how the IOC functions. For instance, executive departments such as the IOC marketing department and, increasingly, the departments in charge of media relations, are central to its function. This explains the composition of the Press Commission, which shows the lowest rate of EB/IOC membership. Arguably, in this case, the participation of professionals from the media world has been deemed far more important than a predominance of IOC members. The particular case of the Commission for Culture and Education is another key example that suggests the need to contrast the above tentative data with a broader context.

The Commission for Culture and Education

The Commission for Culture and Education was created in March 2000 as a result of merging the existing Culture Commission (founded in 1968) with the Commission of Education and the International Olympic Academy (founded in 1967). After this fusion, the Commission was composed of thirty-two members, a number that has been kept from 2000 until the time of writing.[4] This makes it the largest commission of the IOC. Retaining 32 members has been considered by some as too large a number for the Commission to be as efficient as it could be expected. This challenge has been accentuated by the fact that only thirteen out of the total members were members of the IOC in 2000. This figure placed the commission in the fourteenth 'centrality' position out of the 22 groups presented in Table 3.1. By 2012, the Culture and Education Commission is composed of 35 members, none of which also operate within the EB and 18 are IOC members (over 51.4% of total membership). This places the overall 'influence' rating for the commission up to 25.7%.

Arguably, the abundance of members external or independent to the organisation can reduce the ability of the commission to network or influence other IOC members on occasion of IOC Sessions or other high-profile Olympic Movement meetings. However, as in the case of television and press operations, it could also be considered advantageous that there is such variety of members with influential positions in cultural and educational spheres, as this can facilitate the development of programmes likely to obtain support beyond the IOC. This was the case for the establishment of global events such as the World Forum on Sport, Education and

Culture which has taken place in collaboration with the United Nations since year 2000. Nevertheless, this suggests strengths outside the Movement rather than inside, and does not necessarily result in clear operational policies for culture at Games time. Indeed, such initiatives have so far not advanced the case for Cultural Olympiad activities, as will be explored in Part II of this monograph.

Perhaps the best asset of the Commission in terms of centrality within the IOC in the lead up to Sydney 2000 has been the continuity of its Chairman, Zheliang He, who fulfilled this role at the Culture Commission since 1995, moved on to chair the joint Culture and Education Commission from 2000 to 2009, and retains an honorary role to this day. He was also a member of the IOC Executive Board until 2003. This argument must be placed within the context of the Movement and the Commission's working agendas, which is analysed in the next section.

IOC Executive Provisions to Support Cultural Activities

Throughout his 20-year mandate, IOC President Juan Antonio Samaranch emphasised his interest in supporting the concept of culture, the arts in particular, within the Olympic Movement. In 1993, this support translated into the creation of the Olympic Museum in Lausanne, an institution equipped with the latest technology with which to preserve and showcase the history and prospects of the Movement, including information about sporting, cultural and educational achievements (Olympic Museum 2000). Nevertheless, the IOC headquarters do not hold a full time executive department dedicated to surveying, producing and/or assisting the implementation of Olympic cultural programmes.[5] For this reason, and taking into account that most IOC commissions only meet once or twice a year and have an advisory role exclusively, the Culture and Education Commission has very limited powers to ensure that the proposed cultural activities of Olympic Games hosts actually take place.

A general review of the structure and functions of IOC executive departments and services in the lead up and soon after the Sydney 2000 Games shows that, up to this period, there was no specific post dedicated to operationalise cultural programme needs at IOC level. This meant that the Sydney culture team did not have any day-to-day direct line of support within IOC headquarters. Instead, throughout this period, a range of IOC staff claimed to be aware of the cultural initiatives taking place and keen to promote them, but indicated that they could only do so on an ad hoc basis (2001, pers. comm., 5 & 24 Apr). For instance, the team in charge of publishing 'Olympic Review', the main regular publication of the Olympic Movement, are committed to ensuring the continuous appearance of news and background articles about cultural matters and the Olympic cultural programme specifically.[6] Moreover, occasionally, there have been issues fully dedicated to the subject such as 'Art and Sport' in April–May

2000. In 2001, the then IOC Secretary General also emphasised her interest to expand the operational positioning of cultural activities within the Movement and her willingness to contribute to 'the provision of greater support and resources in the near future' (2001, pers. comm., 5 Apr). However, these expressions of support have not been framed in a structure that allows their effective integration within the day-to-day operations of the IOC. Consequently, despite the high visibility of sport-inspired art pieces as key display objects both at the IOC offices and the Olympic Museum, the presentation of information about respective Olympic Games cultural programming, the Cultural Olympiad in particular, has generally kept a low profile within the IOC headquarters and, to this date, has no visible presence within the permanent Olympic Museum Games exhibition space.[7]

In 2006, a part-time post was created for the first time in an executive capacity within the IOC. The post is defined as *Head of Bid City Relations and OCOG Liaison for Culture and Education* and involves regular discussions with the team in charge of delivering the Games cultural programme. The London 2012 team is the first OCOG to benefit from this direct line of contact with IOC headquarters to address cultural matters. As such, to date, it is not possible to be conclusive about the impact or effectiveness of the IOC's executive involvement overseeing the cultural programme implementation. However, early observations and analysis of interviews with the current post holder (2009, pers. comm.,15 Dec) and London 2012 culture team representatives (2006, pers. comm., 8 Dec) suggest that this is a minor part of the role.

Given the growing convergence of cultural and communication policies and the ongoing challenge to ensure media visibility for the Olympic cultural programme, it is also relevant to examine the cultural involvement of other IOC departments such as Marketing and Communications and New Media. Tellingly, no clauses have been found within the documents and publications of the Marketing department that indicate a commitment towards assisting in the financing and promotion of cultural programmes. This corroborates the findings of previous research that suggest that the current Olympic worldwide sponsorship programmes do not consider the special needs of cultural activities but rather are focused exclusively on the support of Olympic sport (García 2001). The lack of explicit, IOC-sanctioned, Olympic marketing clauses for culture explains why the production of the compulsory cultural programme for the Games has been traditionally overlooked by global Olympic sponsors and OCOG marketing planners alike.

As is the case for Marketing, within the IOC Communications and New Media department, no evidence has been found of concrete structural provisions that guarantee the presence of cultural references within advertising campaigns, press releases, press conferences, image programmes, and so on. This resulted in a marked absence of IOC communications about the cultural programme well into the start of the 21st century. For example, up until 2002, the IOC website, which incorporates the website of the Olympic

Museum, did not include any section dedicated to explain the existence and history of Olympic cultural programmes.[8] Further, the 2000 advertising campaign 'Celebrate humanity', the first global promotional programme about the core values of the Games, did not incorporate any image or direct reference to Olympic moments other than sporting ones. By 2011, the IOC main website has been revamped into a more social-media friendly and easier to search environment which incorporates some clearer pointers into the cultural values and activities of the Olympic Movement, particularly within its 'Olympism in action' section. However, information about the Cultural Olympiad and its history remains very limited. While researchers can find references to Olympic cultural programmes within past press releases and official reports by Games organisers, no special emphasis has been made to ensure that these references are systematically included in standard IOC communications and they have not been incorporated to any purpose-built web-page. Consequently, it can be argued that, other than dedicated researchers introducing specific keywords, the general public can easily overlook the existence of Olympic cultural programmes and do not associate them with other Games imagery.

Beyond the Marketing and Communications departments, it is also appropriate to consider the priorities of the OCOG Relations department and their dedication, or lack of, to cultural matters. This department was particularly relevant at the time of the Sydney Games because it was in charge of surveying the implementation of the first ever 'Transfer of Knowledge' (TOK) programme in 2001, with some testing introduced during the 2000 Games and led by the Sydney Organising Committee for the Games. The TOK programme was originally devised to ensure that Games organisers collect as much information as possible about their experience and display it in detail in an official document that is to be available for future Games hosts. The implementation of such a programme has involved the development of a tightly controlled framework for Games monitoring and documentation. Thus, a further indication of the position that Olympic cultural activities hold within the IOC structure can be found by assessing how much emphasis or guidelines are provided by the TOK programme to survey the implementation of the Games cultural programme. For instance, if one were to ask cultural programmers within any host city, would they recognise having had some TOK from previous Games organisers?

An IOC source directly involved in OCOG relations and the implementation of the TOK programme in 2000 has acknowledged that 'the control of the cultural programme was not one of TOK's top priorities' at the time and that, traditionally, not much attention had been paid to study whether the cultural promises presented at the bid stage are put into place on occasion of the Games (2001, pers. comm., 20 Mar). This has been because '[cultural promises] do not imply major risks for the success of the Games if they go wrong. They are only a nice surplus if all goes well. They are part of the Games "success story"' *(ibid.)*. According to the same source, the TOK programme may help identifying the key problems that cultural managers face and may serve for future OCOGs to avoid making the same mistakes that have been usual in past Games. However, 'issues like security, transport and, indeed, the management of the sports programme are the real weight of the Games' (*ibid*) and are, therefore, the key aspects on which the TOK team focused their efforts to start with. This source pointed out that Games operational departments focus on the issues that are most likely 'to make a real impact on the public opinion' (*ibid*) and 'Olympic cultural activities other than sporting ones, have so far not proven to be a critical aspect for the general public'. In order to change this trend, this source agreed that it would be desirable that a position is created within the IOC to survey the specific needs of the cultural programme, claim information, promote cultural issues and ensure appropriate networking with the rest of existing departments. As noted earlier, such post was established in 2006 and, by the time of writing, the current version of the TOK programme— now termed Olympic Games Knowledge Management and directly managed by the IOC—incorporates explicit requirements to survey the cultural programme as part of a wider 'culture, education and live sites' brief. The implications of this development for the Games cultural policy is further discussed in the concluding chapter.

THE IOC'S CULTURAL AGENDA

A historical review of the composition and functions of the Cultural Commission, the organisation pre-dating the current Culture and Education Commission, reveals that its mission has been ambiguously defined over time, which has resulted in dramatic changes of approach depending on the preferences of the commission chairman. This has affected the coherence and sustainability of Olympic cultural programmes.[9] Wlodzimierz Reczeck, the first chairman, was committed to establishing networks with other Olympic Family members, notably National Olympic Committees (NOCs) (Reczeck 1970). Reckzeck also intended to establish stronger ties with other commissions, for instance, through the creation of an Information and Culture Commission in 1973 that combined the promotion of cultural initiatives with media relations (IOC 1978). However, few of these initiatives have been sustained. The Information and Culture Commission was disbanded some time after 1974 (*ibid*). Regarding the interaction with NOCs, the initiative to create Olympic cultural departments and cultural programmes around the world has been progressively abandoned, as noted below. National Olympic Academies have undertaken this function on some occasions but, most times, the notion of Olympic cultural programme has been blurred with the notion of Olympic education in ways that reveal weak structures and ambiguous definitions. These ambiguities have led to confusing strategies and a lack of cultural programme implementations.[10]

Pedro Ramírez Vázquez, chairman of the Culture Commission from 1982 to 1994, focused much of his work on the construction and promotion of the new Olympic Museum in Lausanne. Ramírez Vázquez was also supporting the creation of *Olympiart*, an arts award dedicated to 'an artist distinguished by the creation of works with remarkable aesthetic qualities . . . and his/her interest in youth, peace and sport' (IOC 1997c). The *Olympiart* prize was first awarded during the 1992 Games and has been kept as a quadrennial event, taking place on occasion of each Games edition up to the present. Beyond the Olympic Museum and *Olympiart*, it is difficult to identify other legacies of Ramírez Vázquez' mandate. Similarly to Reczeck, Ramírez Vázquez pursued the expansion of cultural activities within NOCs around the world, notably in the form of encouragement for the creation of national or regional Olympic Museums. However, as for the first Culture Chairman, many of his pursuits in this field have been progressively abandoned and, considering the subsequent agendas of the commission (IOC 1969–2000), it is apparent that they have had no strong support in following years.

Zhenliang He chaired the Commission from 1995 to 2009 and currently retains an honorary membership. During this mandate, the Commission has emphasised the organisation of international cultural forums and the establishment of special 'arts contests' (see IOC 2011b) as well as supporting some international festivals.[11] Key events organised or planned to date include the following:

- Forum on Sport and Culture in 1997 (IOC 1997e), which in 2000 became a biannual 'World Forum', as noted below
- Biannual World Forum on Sport, Education and Culture (fifth edition in 2006, Beijing, the sixth in 2008, Busan, Korea, seventh in 2010 in Durban, South Africa)
- Forum on the IOC and its Cultural Policy in 2000 (see IOC 2000f)
- Art and Sport Contest, launched in 2000 and taking place every four years coinciding with respective Olympic summer Games edition. This event did not have high visibility during the Sydney 2000 Games but it is gaining profile and attracting greater numbers of top IOC representative, as was shown in Beijing 2008 (*Olympiart*) and expected for London 2012
- Literature and Sport Contest, created in 2001 and repeated in 2005
- World Children Art Contest in 1997 and 2000
- Sport and Photography (no confirmed dates found)
- Sport and Singing (no confirmed dates found)

While the Arts and Sport Contest is progressively becoming a regular occurrence within the Olympic Games and providing an opportunity for IOC-led cultural activity to have a presence within the Games, the last four types of events have taken place infrequently and often without clear plans for continuity. This explains the lack of awareness and understanding of the IOC's cultural mission and dedicated cultural programmes by average Olympic audiences. This lack of consistency also explains the low levels of coverage in national and international media. The one event that has become more clearly established as an internationally recognised platform is the World Forum on Sport, Olympic Education and Culture, which is also supported by UNESCO and, in 2008, led to an 'Action Plan' including explicit recommendations to enhance the visibility of the Cultural Olympiad (IOC 2008b). The continuity of this event offers some grounds for the emergence of a more consistent Olympic cultural policy. However, there is no clear evidence that the recommendations and action plans produced so far are being transformed into actual guidelines within the IOC operational structure nor adapted for OCOG implementation.

The establishment of a joint commission encompassing culture and education has provided new possibilities for action together with new challenges. Structurally, the commission must find effective ways of managing its extensive membership size, in particular, providing reasonable mechanisms for members to find a common perspective and define their role and objectives clearly. For instance, the priorities of an institution such as the International Olympic Academy in Greece, which is represented by former Education Commission members, are rather different from those of an Olympic Museum, a national Olympic body, an OCOG or a school wishing to undertake Olympic education and cultural programmes. So far, the needs and aspirations of these diverse stakeholders seem to have been treated interchangeably, and this has resulted in decisions to support programmes and activities without an apparent clear rationale (see the Commission's advocacy pages online, IOC 2011b). This is an indication of an ongoing limitation in terms of sustainable Olympic cultural policy.

Cultural Commission, other IOC Bodies and OCOGs

The analysis of IOC archival material on the Cultural Commission from 1968 to year 2000 reveals that an aspect that had not been fully addressed is the role of this Commission to advise and support the cultural planning of respective OCOGs and the delivery of cultural programmes during Games time. The minutes of over 30 years of Culture Commission meetings include references to the presentations made by the teams in charge of designing Olympic Arts Festivals and, since 1992, summer Games Cultural Olympiads. These presentations have traditionally taken place in addition, or most times, prior to the presentation of abridged versions to the IOC Session. However, the verbal proceedings about this process within the IOC Cultural Commission archives shows that, generally, these updates have been approved without any major enquiry into the difficulties faced in the daily production of the programme (IOC 1969–2000). Furthermore, no evidence has been found of the contributions from the Cultural Commission to assist OCOG cultural organisers gather sponsorship funds or have a greater presence in the Games generic promotions, two of the areas that have traditionally presented the greatest challenge to cultural programme delivery. This situation, combined with the lack of recorded information on Olympic cultural programme delivery processes and the still vague specifications for current OCOGs to monitor and evaluate their approach to cultural and arts delivery,[12] suggests that each OCOG has had to operate in a vacuum, establishing priorities and facing ongoing challenges for resource allocation without an opportunity to learn from previous Games experience. The establishment of a part-time executive post for culture is supposed to address this caveat, with the team in charge of delivering the London 2012 Cultural Olympiad being the first to build on the potential benefits of increased IOC involvement providing advice and support towards cultural programme delivery. The effect of these new circumstances is discussed in Chapter 10.

Beyond the work of the Culture Commission, the joint Culture and Education Commission and the new executive post for OCOG culture liaison, recent initiatives that could open new paths for cultural collaborations between the IOC and respective OCOGs involve a trend towards regular presentations and exhibitions of cultural and arts materials from prospective Olympic host cities at the Olympic Museum in Lausanne. This initiative was successful in the case of Australia as, in the lead up to the Sydney Games, two major Aboriginal exhibitions were organised at the Museum to strong public acclaim (IOC Manager of Collections and Exhibitions 2001, pers. comm., 19 Apr). For the Winter Games of Salt Lake 2002, the Museum also organised an event in close collaboration with the official organisers of the Olympic Cultural Olympiad (*ibid.*). An expectation has since emerged within the Olympic Museum so that these initiatives and collaborations with Olympic host cities continue. In 2001, there was no evidence of a direct involvement of the Culture and Education Commission in this process, which could be explained by the major structural changes the Commission was going through at the time. Since then, the Commission as well as the appointed IOC-OCOG culture liaison have played a role surveying the appropriate application of this type of collaboration and this could be an early indication of a new dimension of Olympic cultural policy unfolding.

Cultural Programming Requests within the Agenda of IOC Sessions

IOC documents define the IOC Session as

> the general assembly of IOC members. It is the supreme organ of the International Olympic Committee, and its decisions are final. [. . .] If the Executive Board can be considered to be the 'government' of the IOC, the Session would be the 'parliament'. The Session may delegate powers to the Executive Board. With few exceptions all important decisions are taken by the Session, voting on proposals put forward by the Executive Board. (IOC 2000e)

The Session is structured in a series of more or less fixed components, including an official welcome and introduction by the President, reports by representatives of OCOGs in the lead up to respective Games and reports by each of the Commissions and Working Groups. An analysis of the Cultural Commission's interventions as recorded by Lyberg (1989, 1994) reveals that, frequently, presentations have been extremely brief, introducing projects that, despite being approved by the Session have rarely come to fruition.[13] On other occasions, proposals have been directly rejected. Examples of this include the proposed return to 'Olympic art competitions' (Lyberg 1989: 161; 1994: 56, 115) or the offering of 'art medals' for athletes with artistic aptitudes (Lyberg 1989: 178, 1994: 17). Tellingly, Lyberg does not always offer an account of the Cultural Commission presentations. When contrasting this fact with the original verbal proceedings, it has been found that either cultural presentations have not been recorded or the transcription records have been limited to a few paragraphs without attached annexes.[14] Furthermore, there are very few records of references to the cultural programme within the regular updates presented to the IOC Session by respective OCOGs. This strengthens the claim that cultural matters are not seen by the IOC as critical to the progress of the Games preparations. Furthermore, the lack of requests for this information by IOC members reinforces the impression that cultural matters are not placed in a priority position within the members working agenda.

An important exception to the above was the 100th IOC Session held in Lausanne in 1993, coinciding with the opening of the new Olympic Museum. The Session was entirely dedicated to discussing the links between culture, arts and Olympism. Important personalities from the world of culture and the arts were invited to speak to IOC members about three main themes: arts and Olympism, the cultural programmes of the Olympic Games and the reasons to open an Olympic Museum (IOC 1993). Building on the recommendations emerging from this Session, the Culture Commission committed to the regular organisation of special forums on sport and culture, as noted earlier, notably those in 1997 (IOC 1997e) and 2000 (IOC 2000f). The eventual establishment of a biennial World Forum on Culture and Education that has been sustained to this day, may indicate an implicit interest among members and related stakeholders for increasing the presence of cultural discourses and events within the Movement's agenda.

Further, there are considerable opportunities for the cultural programme to exploit the kind of exposure offered by online user generated content and social media, an area that has been explored mainly within OCOG environments, with Vancouver 2010 and London 2012 providing the best examples for online Cultural Olympiad exposure so far. At IOC level and within the Commission, the use of online environments to expand the visibility of cultural programmes is being explored mainly in the context of the new Youth Olympic Games programme, which was launched in 2010 and presented a cultural and educational programme fully integrated with the sports competition programme (see Wong 2011). It remains to be seen whether the strong cultural discourse and consistent approach to cultural policy put into manifest within the Youth Olympic Games transfers in any way into the operations and strategic agenda of the Olympic Games as well.

In order to showcase the effect of established Olympic cultural frameworks in the Games staging process, the remainder of the book offers a detailed assessment of a specific case study that has become a key point of reference in the lead to the London 2012 Games and is viewed as one of the most successful implementations of the 'Olympic experience': the Sydney Olympic Arts Festivals programme starting in 1997 and completed in year 2000.

SUMMARY

Over the years, the Olympic Movement has lacked a defined and consistent cultural policy. Although the Olympic Charter clearly states that Olympism is the result of combining sport with culture and education, this principle is often used as a philosophical aspiration, without being supported by an objective policy that helps directing the daily operations of the IOC. Starting with the President, key members of the IOC have emphasised their commitment to the above principle but, arguably, the lack of specific policies has prevented their action from being fully coherent and effective. This is reflected in the poor structural position held by the Commission in charge of protecting cultural activities and, particularly, by the non-existence of a dedicated executive body within the IOC headquarters, a situation that has only been partly addressed in 2006 by creating a part-time OCOG culture liaison post.

The Olympic Museum is an institution with considerable potential to assist in producing and promoting Olympic cultural activities and programmes. However, its mission has so far not been sufficiently coordinated with the mission of bodies such as the Culture and Education Commission. Beyond the role of the Museum as an exhibition space and venue for special events, the existence of an Olympic Studies Centre, safeguarding both historical and contemporary Olympic resources, suggests that the Museum could be a good context for an executive cultural and education department, but this has not been properly explored so far. Further, at IOC level, there are not specific provisions to support the work of the team in charge of designing, producing, managing and promoting the Olympic Games cultural programmes. The Cultural Commission has not been charged with surveying the implementation of OCOG programmes beyond the regular approval of summaries presented at annual meetings. Arguably, the creation of an executive post within the IOC dedicated to control and support the production of these programmes should prevent the repetition of problems and weaknesses that has been traditional in prior Games arts and culture festivals. Importantly, this post could ensure that other key departments at the IOC, such as marketing and communications, are aware of the cultural programme and ready to help attracting the attention of international Olympic sponsors and media. However, as yet, it is unclear whether the existing part-time post has sufficient capacity to fulfil these roles, or whether it would require additional administrative support to be effective. In any case, the current situation is an advancement from the period leading up to the Sydney 2000 Games, when no such post existed.

At the level of the Cultural and Education Commission, the emphasis on one-off events over the design of consistent policies has limited the long-term effect of activities and programmes up to the end of the 20th century. With the establishment of regular platforms such as the World Forum on Sport, Olympic Education and Culture there is an opportunity to amplify expectations among key stakeholders and expand the visibility of relevant cultural initiatives, particularly as they are more clearly linked to educational aspirations, which may offer a route to overcome the traditional 'Olympic sport—culture—and education' divide. Ultimately, this can assist in gathering greater attention by the media and the support of key actors in and out of the Olympic Movement.

In sum, working towards the definition of a clear cultural policy for the IOC and the Olympic Movement would help to maximise existing resources and coordinating the efforts and initiatives of bodies and individuals willing to support the promotion of culture and Olympism. The IOC is embedded in a rich cultural mosaic with a powerful network of institutions and personalities that could make a much greater contribution to emphasise and further develop cultural initiatives. Without a coherent cultural policy, culture is relegated to a secondary position, behind other concerns, such as finance, doping issues, sustainability challenges and so on. Yet, in most of these areas, culture could be seen as part of the solution to more effective Games delivery and as such deserves greater attention.

Part II

The Olympic Games Cultural Programme

Olympic Arts Festivals
in Sydney 2000

4 Defining the Vision

This chapter provides an overview of the rationale behind the Olympic cultural programme by contrasting the aspirations presented at the bid stage with the reality of planning and defining key deliverables once the Games have been awarded. The chapter starts by offering a perspective on the social, political and cultural context of Australia, host nation of the Sydney 2000 Olympic Games, and providing an overview of the country's cultural policy development. The chapter moves on to discuss the position of arts and culture within the Games bidding process. The last section describes the mission statements and key deliverables of the Olympic cultural programme as defined by the IOC and interpreted by the Sydney Organising Committee for the Games and compares this framework with the final programme design—four Olympic Arts Festivals—highlighting its chosen themes, key objectives and flagship events. This is followed by a brief overview of the vision and programming focus for Olympic cultural programmes after Sydney 2000.

AUSTRALIA IN CONTEXT: FOUNDATIONS FOR AN OLYMPIC BID

Australia is an island continent the size of the United States, excluding Alaska, with a population of approximately 21 million people, most of them living on the coast-line. Recent anthropological studies indicate that habitation in the country began between 40,000 and 60,000 years ago, with the settlement of Aborigines and Torres Strait Islanders groups. These cultures, comprising a range of 600 nations and 200 aboriginal groups, represented approximately 2% of the Australian population at the time of the Olympic Games (Australian Tourism Commission [ATC] 2000). Australia has experienced three major migrant waves since the first white settlement in 1788. The first wave, up to the beginning of World War II, was composed of English, Irish and Scottish settlers. The second wave began soon after World War II and ended in the late 1960s, and was mostly composed by peoples from Great Britain, Italy, Greece, Germany, the Netherlands and Yugoslavia. The third wave of immigration started in the 1980s and has brought into Australia, besides the ongoing flow of British migrants, populations from New Zealand, South Africa, Lebanon, Turkey, the former Yugoslavia, Vietnam, Philippines, Malaysia, Hong Kong and China (ATC 2000: 20). In total, since 1945, some 5.5 million people have come to Australia as new settlers.

In 1999, one year before the Games, 23.4% of Australians were born overseas (*op. cit*: 19). By the same year, despite the predominance of Anglo settlers, the growing diversity of new immigration waves had transformed the profile of the Australian population to the extent that nearly 28% of the total population was from non-English speaking backgrounds (Australian Bureau of Statistics 1999). Of this number, 19% of the population was from South and West Europe and a 4.5% from Asian countries (Department of Immigration and Multicultural Affairs 2000). Presently, over 200 different languages are spoken in Australia, which makes it, together with Canada, one of the most culturally and linguistically diverse nations in the world. These details are relevant when considering how a nation articulates itself at the time of bidding for an Olympic Games. For instance, in the bid to the 2012 games, both New York City and London emphasised their diversity and used the term 'World city' as a way of highlighting their internationalist credentials. Indeed, diversity and multiculturalism has become an increasingly dominant discourse within Olympic bids in the wake of Sydney 2000, as a way of demonstrating inclusiveness within an event that brings some 200 countries together. When examining the programme of an Olympic Games, representation of identities becomes crucially visible through the Games cultural mechanisms, such as the ceremonies and, increasingly, the cultural programme.

Politically, Australia is divided into six states and two territories, each of which has its own government. Canberra is the national capital and seat of the Federal government; the states are New South Wales, Victoria, South Australia, Western Australia, Tasmania and Queensland; and the territories are the Northern Territory and the Australian Capital Territory. The distribution of cities and population is extremely uneven. Five capitals, Sydney, Canberra, Melbourne, Brisbane and Adelaide are clustered in the South East of the continent, attracting up to 85% of international visitors (Bureau of Tourist Research 2000). They are at the forefront of business activity and the most visited cities in the country, only challenged by the tourism appeal of the coast in northern Queensland. The size and location of cities and states in Australia have influenced the way different segments of the population relate to each other. Arguably, this situation had an effect on the varying degrees of ownership felt about the Sydney 2000 Olympic Games and the will for respective regions to play an active role in defining the images of the country that the Games were to portray. For their distant location and relatively low international profile, the Northern Territory, Western Australia and Tasmania were the areas that profiled the least in the Games narrative, from the bid stage onwards; while Queensland

and Victoria were, after New South Wales, the two regions featuring most strongly. In this context, Cahill (1999) argues that symbolic activities such as the Torch Relay became an important catalyst to make every Australian feel part of the celebration. The Olympic cultural programme, with its flexible time and geographical frame, had the potential to be another relevant catalyst to expand a feeling of ownership and this was a core aspiration within the original bid, as discussed later in this chapter.

Defining Australia's Identity for the Olympic Bid

Australia is said to have had a 'long love affair with the Olympics' (Farrell 1999: 59) since it is one of the very few countries that, together with Greece, has attended every modern Olympic Games summer edition. Farrell goes on to argue that the 'Australian reverence' for the Games and sport in general is one of the reasons why, despite its remoteness and small population size, the country has been successful in hosting two Summer Olympic Games in the second half of the century, Sydney 2000 as well as Melbourne in 1956. For Farrell (1999), Australia's strong sports culture is inherent to the construction of its national identity. He explains it by reflecting on the country's colonial ties to the United Kingdom (and its sporting heritage), the convict nature of most initial settlers (leading to high radicalism and individualism, rooted in Irish traditions), as well as diverse theories of the 'practical man', which resulted in a rejection of European conceptions and colonial prejudices of respectability and in turn encouraged open air activities amongst other things. In his words,

> Like the modern Olympic Movement itself Australian identity is an evolving set of ideas. In each case, the great outdoors and a concentration on peaceful physical activity is central to the process of evolution. In each case the ideals being promoted are modern notions of a straightforward or practical kind, and largely pragmatic in application. (Farrell 1999: 60)

This conglomerate of influences has been transformed remarkably after World War II, due to the massive arrival of South European migrants, followed by the arrival of East Europe migrants in the late fifties and sixties and Asian communities from the late 1970s onwards. These recent waves of differing nationalities have modified completely the initial conception of an 'Australian' identity in the sense explained by Farrell.

As noted at the beginning of the chapter, the predominance of an Anglo-Saxon background is no longer so remarkable in Australia. This is particularly evident in capital cities such as Sydney and Melbourne, where new comers tend to concentrate. Sydney gathers migrants from some 215 different countries (Department of Immigration and Multicultural Affairs 2000) while, in Melbourne, sixty different nationalities are said to coexist

(ATC 2000: 20). In 1999, the Australian Bureau of Statistics counted some 160 different first or second-generation nationalities within the country and 200 different languages, excluding the aboriginal languages.[1] Consequently, the reference to Australia's multicultural components has become central to most government discourses. However, the country has still not reached any common agreement on how to respond to the challenges brought by the notion of multiculturalism in the definition of a national identity. This is partly due to resilient post-colonial roots which have not permitted a stabilisation of the identity discourse. In a joint personal interview, Professor Graeme Turner and Eric Louw explained that in seeking a reference to define their national identity, most Australian's began looking back towards Britain. 'the mother patria', while by year 2000 they were looking to the United States. They also noted the discomfort felt by Australians when attempting to represent their identity. In their view, the shift in the 1980s and 1990s towards multiculturalism as the main national identity discourse has been met with scepticism, considered just a 'fashion' by many, with its arguments 'reduced to the colourful appendix of events or promo[tions]' (2000, pers. comm., 25 Aug).

An event such as the Olympic Games acted as a catalyst to reconsider notions of identity if only, as argued by Berkaak (1999), to present an image to foreign audiences or, as stated by Louw, to act as a colourful appendix to its promotion. The role of sport in Australian traditions was certainly used as an ingredient of this image. However, the growing diversity of cultures and alternative traditions in the country indicates that other sources were necessary to construct a credible image of contemporary Australia. A revision of the evolution and influence of arts and cultural policy in the country offers some clues about the ability of policy-makers to play a relevant role in the definition of Australia's image to the world and the importance of the Olympic cultural programme in this process.

Arts and Cultural Policies: Conflicts of National Identity

In 'Arts Management in Australia', Radbourne and Fraser (1996) present a brief history of arts policy in Australia. The authors refer to the reconstruction period after World War I as the first time an Australian arts policy came under official scrutiny. According to the authors,

> public and political discussion about national identity was imperative in order to establish priorities in all facets of public life. The fact that Australians emerged from the war with a new confidence and sense of pride in their own rather than their mother country [Great Britain] had a bearing on arts policy and artistic endeavour. (p. 11)

The conscious break from a colonialist state of mind had great effects on the Australian artistic product. Early white settlers were self-conscious about the convict origin of Australia and the stigma deriving from it, at the same time as their dislocation from the intellectual and social culture of Europe. British expatriates felt ashamed at 'living as second-rate citizens in a country which was a poor masquerade of the mother country' (*op.cit.*, p. 12). This was the source of the much-discussed 'Australian cultural cringe' syndrome. Governor Macquaire—governor of New South Wales 1810–21—redressed the perceived lack of culture in the colony and employed a number of artists, including convicts, to assist him in his mission. Commercial theatre and variety groups expanded during the country's gold rushes. Soon after, the first state and national newspapers were founded. The latter would soon become known for their strongly nationalistic ideals.

Radbourne and Fraser argue that, despite these developments, being an agricultural community, Australians experienced the arts as a separate addition to life. Geographic isolation and the hard manual labour demanded by the harsh farming environment accelerated the process of separation of work and leisure that in other countries had only happened with the arrival of industrialisation. Consequently, participation in the arts was rare, as were the opportunities for it to take place at all. It was also 'self-conscious' either because standards were perceived as inferior or because 'it was unseemly to leave toil for such frivolity' (p. 14). As a result, 'the life of high culture and participation in the arts was not part of what social critics and historians have named the Australianist legend or the democratic tradition' (*ibid.*)

Rather than traditional elitist arts, affordable leisure time was developed in association with a strong unionism and later with support of the Australian Labour Party by means of their 'Art and Working Life' programmes. European intellectuals have commented on this situation, most times recognising the equitable progress of the labour movement and the spread out of material prosperity but criticising the slow progress of intellectual and moral pursuits (*op cit*: 16). In this context, Australian commentators such as Donald Horne have defined the term 'cultural cringe' as the 'depredations of a self-denigratory provincialism in academic, intellectual and artistic life'.

As a remedy to this cultural cringe, the beginning of the 20th century saw an emphasis on spreading the English education system within all universities, and training the speech and manners of all public personalities, from politicians to actors or media commentators. This resulted in what Radbourne and Fraser define as a movement towards 'being more English than the English', and included, among other things, an 'almost obsessional love for cricket which perplexed even their English rivals' (p. 17). However, the influx of non Anglo-Saxon immigrants after World War II caused a new awareness of other cultures in the country and changed earlier perceptions of national identity. As the authors put it,

> this pluralism has made 'Australian' difficult to define as has the more recent official recognition of Aborigines as the first Australians. Besides

the obvious artistic enrichment effected by a multicultural society, there remain large numbers of people adrift from their cultural heritage yet compelled to assimilate the dominant culture. (1996: 17)

Post-war reconstruction took place under the leadership of economist H.C. 'Nugget' Coombs, who founded the Australian Elizabethan Theatre Trust in 1954. The Trust was paramount to the foundation of an Australian cultural policy. This was because the institution's main objectives were to stop the belief that all cultural referents had to be brought from abroad and to promote the idea of theatre 'of Australians by Australians for Australians' (Australia Council 1994).

At this point in time there was still the belief that if the 'best' in the arts were to receive funding the effects would percolate down to society. However, new popular currents questioned this belief in the 1960s and 1970s who saw the idea as a 'misconceived anathema caused by middle class idealism' (Radbourne & Fraser 1996: p. 22). The increasing influence of the mass media, including television and advertising culture, set up new criteria for evaluating the role of the arts and anti-reactionary movements sprang up, often from a university campus base. As was the case in other parts of the world, the 1960s and 1970s were the time when civic and community festivals initiatives developed throughout Australia. By the mid seventies, there was an emphasis on multicultural or ethnic based events. In this context, the creation of a new organisation to overview national arts policy, the Australian Council, had to consider not only the aim to show Australian arts to Australians, but actively encouraging participation from a broad base.

The Australian Council was set up in 1975 and defined its main mission as promoting excellence in the arts; widening access; helping establish an Australian identity through the arts; and helping promote awareness of this identity abroad. The organisation was born within a highly supportive context for the arts, but changes in government structures led to severe reductions in funding and the start of what has been called an era of economic rationalism in public administration. Cultural matters had to face an economic analysis for the first time and many debates emerged. Craik (2007) has noted the arts groups that most benefited from such a rational or 'productivity' analysis were, once more, the main flagship companies. Nevertheless this generated controversies and enquiry reports were commissioned to justify the need for a wider support to cultural groups. As a result of some of these inquiries, the Australia Council returned to the initial commitment to assist and promote 'community arts' and secure community access to culture for.

As in so many other countries, the question of whether arts could be genuinely 'democratised' by arts policy changes has never been fully solved in Australia. According to Radbourne and Fraser (1996), 'it is clear that the very cultural diversity aimed at in access arguments can be lost if there is too much intervention in control of the arts' (p. 26). Consequently, the cultural and arts sector has been subject to constant modifications depending on the interests of the groups in power. As Radbourne and Fraser put it,

> The inadequate private patronage of colonial times was replaced early this century by vibrant support from dedicated amateurs in community organisations and professional entrepreneurs who imported shows as well as providing work for locals. Both groups then became lobbyist for government support as the private economy could no longer support artistic growth, and as the general desire became apparent for showcase art indicative of the nation. . . . Government support increased from the post-war years on, as did the policy control over it. Flagship funding and centralisation of institutions helped develop the showcase pieces desired, but soon a call for a more democratic and less centralised funding arose, reflecting a desire for democratic institutions from society in general. The main funding body responded by supporting diverse community arts at the grassroots level, as well as the major institutions, and by managing that support through the mechanisms of arm's-length funding and peer assessment. The resulting growth in myriad smaller arts organisations has now caused the Australian Council to encourage and support the industry and training of managers as well as providing grants for artists. State and local governments are increasingly taking up the call for this kind of individualistic funding. Separationist policy such as this will be important in creating the basis for self-funding independence. (1996: 28)

At present, the rationalist approach to the arts is still dominant in Australia as in most other countries worldwide. As discussed here and in subsequent chapters, this fact had repercussions for the way that the Sydney Olympic cultural programme was defined, structured and supported by key stakeholders. Some evidence of this is presented in the following section, which describes the process to prepare and gather support for the Sydney Olympic Bid and highlights the limited role given to the arts in this process.

BIDDING FOR THE SYDNEY 2000 OLYMPIC GAMES

Sydney was the third consecutive Australian city to present a candidature for hosting the Olympic Games between 1992 and 2000. Brisbane, capital of the state of Queensland and host-city of the 1988 World Expo, had bided for the 1992 Games; Melbourne, capital of the state of Victoria and host of the 1956 Olympic Games, submitted a bid for 1996. The failed but intense experiences of both Australian capitals were a critical point of reference for Sydney in its strategy to promote the candidature in 1992 (McGeoch & Korporaal 1994). Independent from these precedents, the interest of

Sydney to host the Games had a long history. Rod McGeoch, Chief Executive Officer of the Sydney Bid, has referred to Sydney representatives' initial discussions in 1970 about attempting to host the Games in 1998, Australia's bi-centenary year since the discovery and settlement by the British (*op. cit.*). Concern about the suitability of existing Sydney sporting venues and other infrastructures led to abandoning the project by the end of the 1970s. However, according to McGeoch and Korporaal, the interest to present a Sydney bid was kept throughout the 1980s at the time of the trials by Brisbane and Melbourne.

Farrell (1999) notes that the continued interest of Australia to stage the Games cannot be explained only by referring to the potential economic benefits and international exposure the Games are expected to bring to the host-city. Additionally, there is the strongly rooted passion for sports manifested by the daily practices of most Australians. Moreover, there is a wide spread acceptance and interest in the Olympic Movement demonstrated by Australia's consistent participation in the Games, despite the geographical isolation of the country. Most Sydney Olympic promotional material stated that Australia and Greece are the only two countries to have participated in every Olympic Games since their foundation in 1896.[2] This was a strategic selling point of the bid together with the argument that in Australia there was not any organised group or task-force opposed to the Games (McGeoch & Korporaal 1994). With regard to the latter, researchers and journalists have argued that, not even the Aboriginal communities, initially feared for potential boycotts, were strongly opposed to the Olympic Games per se (Thompson 2000). This has been explained on the grounds that the opportunity to participate and win Olympic medals had converted some members of this traditionally neglected community into Australian icons (Veal 1999, pers. comm., 15 Apr).

McGeoch and Korporaal (1994), list the promoted and perceived strengths of Sydney's candidature as follows: (1) a compact Olympic plan guaranteeing minimal travel to the venues for athletes, (2) the good Australian climate, (3) the country's political stability and security, (4) the massive community and government support, and (5) the fact that it was Australia's third consecutive bid. The authors also note that 'around 70% of the required sports facilities would be available prior to the IOC vote in 1993, regardless of winning the Games' which would be ultimate proof that Australia and Sydney could deliver (McGeogh & Korporaal 1994: p.38). All of these elements, together with Farrell's claims of Australia's perceived 'reverence for the Games' and sport (1999: 59) are indeed added-value assets that surely made a difference to secure IOC member's confidence and, ultimately, their votes. However, an additional mark of distinction was also Australia's peculiar cultural fabric, being a country that has attracted such diverse waves of immigration in the late part of the 20th century while retaining a millenary Aboriginal and Torres Strait Islander culture.

At this point, it is relevant to look more closely at how the arts and culture fitted into the original bid discourse for Sydney and Australia. This exercise suggests a divided approach to cultural promotion, which is indicative of a lack of coherence in the Games cultural policy framework.

Selling the Olympic Bid, Under-Selling Australian Culture?

In December 1992, the Sydney Olympic Bid Commission published a bulletin addressed to major Australian companies and governmental institutions in order to attract financial and political support nationwide. The Bulletin was called 'Fifteen good reasons to bring the Olympics to Sydney in 2000'. These reasons were listed as follows:

1. Sydney will stage the athlete's games
2. Sydney has the best climate in which to hold an Olympics
3. Sydney is one of the most beautiful cities in the world
4. The Sydney Olympics will reintroduce the Games to a major growth region
5. Sydney will pay for athletes and officials to come to Australia
6. Sydney is the best city equipped to cope with international visitors
7. Sydney Olympics 2000—prime time television
8. Australia has an outstanding Olympic tradition
9. Sydney is a safe city
10. Australia: stable and reliable
11. The people of Sydney want the Olympics
12. Sydney has plenty of accommodation for the 2000 Olympics
13. Sydney will be an environmental showpiece for the Olympics
14. Sydney's transport—up and running
15. Sydney will provide world class television coverage (Sydney Bid Ltd. 1992c)

This list does not include any reference to the cultural life of the city as a reason to bring the Olympics to Sydney. Instead, the focus is the city's sporting traditions and its commitment to support Olympic sport (list items 1, 5, 8, 11), Sydney's tourism and corporate appeal (4, 9, 10), the environment (2, 3, 13) and the existence of extensive and reliable infrastructures (point 6, 7, 12, 14, 15). This suggests that the bid organisers did not consider that an explicit mention to Sydney's cultural offer was either necessary or appropriate to gain the attention and support of local and national stakeholders. In another document destined to Australian corporations, the reason why 'Sydney is the best choice for the 2000 Games' was defined in these terms:

> Sydney will re-introduce the Games to a major growth region of the world. The Sydney Olympic Plan includes world standard facilities,

convenient transport, sound security and ample accommodation. The Games will reflect Australia's multicultural society and will include a sophisticated cultural programme. (Sydney Bid Ltd. 1992d)

On this occasion, there is a clear reference to cultural matters, by emphasising the importance of multiculturalism as the most characteristic aspect of Australian society. However, in the same document, the summary of key points justifying the connections between Sydney and the Olympics are told to be 'our love for sport and our tradition of a "fair go for all" that reflect the Olympic ideas of goodwill and sportsmanship' (*ibid*). This time, there is no reference to the supposedly exemplary and unique diversity of Australian cultures. Again, Australia's cultural traditions and potentials do not seem to have been seen as relevant enough to be placed at the centre of the bid local promotions. This suggests that cultural endeavours and the arts did not play a critical role in these first, short publications dedicated to promote the benefits of having the Olympics in Sydney among Australian stakeholders.

This impression is accentuated when one looks at the range of impact evaluation articles and reports published at the time. In 1995, the House of Representatives Standing Committee on Industry, Science and Technology published the results of an inquiry that analysed the opportunities for Australian industry arising from the staging of the Olympics; the impediments to the development of these opportunities and appropriate action which the Commonwealth government in Australia might take to maximise benefits (1995: i). Key areas of development were found to be promoting tourism, forging closer links between business and sport in Australia and in the Asia/Pacific region, and demonstrating the economic and social benefits of environmentally sound planning and development (*ibid*: vii). In this context, the Olympic cultural programme was seen as a junior partner, not necessarily critical to maximise trade, tourism, business and sport ventures.

A senior representative from the Australian Tourism Commission supported this suggestion by stating that in the late 1990s the arts were not yet a key selling point in the country and, as such, they had a secondary position in the promotional material and strategic tourist planning for the Olympics (2000, pers. comm., 3 Mar). This perspective is in stark contrast with the argument by Radbourne and Fraser that culture has become a commodity with important societal functions, including tourism attractions, in particular in countries with a growing international appeal such as Australia. In their words,

expressions of national identity in these countries will help reassert their differences to outsiders as well as to the people themselves. It is the responsibility of arts managers to keep informed about the dialogue of national identity and to prevent the distortion of images which can arise when market forces are unqualified by artistic integrity. With this safeguard, creators and consumers can benefit from discussions of national identity in arts policy and through art product. (Radbourne & Fraser 1996: 31)

The contradiction between the aspirations of cultural scholars such as Radbourne and Fraser and the strategic decisions of corporate planners, entrepreneurs and quango officials suggests a lack of confidence in the strength of Australian arts and culture at the time of the bid. At a later stage, this was reflected by the low levels of support provided by corporations and government to fund the Olympic cultural programme. Interestingly, the particularity and potential of Australia's culture was precisely one of the critical bid-selling point for international audiences, as is discussed in the following section.

DESIGNING THE OLYMPIC CULTURAL PROGRAMME

The previous section argues that Sydney's Olympic bid promoters emphasised the sporting, infrastructural and environmental strengths of Australia over its cultural assets in order to gather the support of national stakeholders. In contrast, the international media and IOC members in particular were attracted by the discourse of Australia's cultural promise. Within the bid international promotional literature, this gave rise to an emphasis on the concepts of multiculturalism and Aboriginal reconciliation as distinctive dimensions of Australia's cultural landscape. Thus, a cultural discourse—Australia's commitment to support its Aboriginal and multicultural populations—became a key selling point for the Sydney bid abroad.

This cultural discourse became central to the bid's international public and community relations strategy. It would take the form of music and dance displays during official visits to Australia by IOC members or accompanying Australian personalities in their promotional tours around the world. Furthermore, this discourse was also central to Sydney's proposed Olympic cultural programme and had a strong influence on its final design.

The Australian bid organisers claimed that the multicultural composition and, most importantly, the presence of Aboriginal cultures in the country, made Australia a unique place to explore exemplary ways in which the Olympic ideals of universal understanding could foster and promote the respect of human rights (Hanna 1999). Accordingly, the Sydney Bid group incorporated references to Australia's indigenous cultures within their promotions and emphasised the advances made by the Australian government to support them. An example of the prominence given to Aboriginal cultures is found in the public component of the bid presentation during the final week preceding the IOC definitive vote for the city to host the 2000 Games, hosted in Monaco in 1993. On the last night prior to the votes,

Indigenous musicians played outside the Hôtel de Paris with 'the haunting sounds attracting [IOC] members to [the Sydney 2000 Bid Committee's] hospitality suit'. (McGeoch cited in Hanna 1999: 28)

This cultural presentation has been criticised by Australian scholars such as Booth and Tatz who considered that Monaco might be 'flooded . . . with black dancers and performers, but as Aboriginal Commissioner Sol Bellear reminded us, they were tourist curiosities like koalas and kangaroos' (Booth & Tatz 1994: 6–7). Hanna has challenged this argument by claiming that 'although used in a token manner, the significant inclusion of Indigenous culture created the impression of a national culture that values the contributions of its minority groups' (Hanna 1999: 27) and this in turn could be considered a turning point for Australia's sense of responsibility towards these groups. Hanna goes on to praise the announcement of an 'ambitious Cultural Programme over the four-year Olympiad' (*ibid*). McGeoch notes that 'the Cultural Programme was used as an important part of the bid strategy; it was promoted at the July 1993 opening of the Olympic Museum in Lausanne [while] other cities, by contrast, focused primarily on the sporting festival' (McGeoch cited in Hanna 1999: 29). Donald McDonald, chairman of the Cultural Committee for the Sydney Bid and subsequent chairman of the Sydney Olympic Cultural Commission emphasised the unique characteristics of the Sydney proposal. McDonald argues that 'Sydney was the only city to have produced a special publication on the Cultural Olympiad and presented an extensive programme of activities to be held in the four years leading up to the Games' (*Arts Today* 1994). The 'special publication' McDonald refers to was a separate Olympic Cultural Bid book presented by Sydney as part of its Candidature Files, a gesture that distinguished it from all the competing bids. McDonald also claims that the use of the Sydney Opera House as the main cultural venue and the emphasis given to Aboriginal reconciliation were considered 'issues crucial' to the success of Sydney's bid (*ibid*).

International Expectations and Brand Perceptions

The emphasis on Aboriginal issues and multiculturalism within the Olympic project must be understood in the context of the particular climate of international expectations of the early 1990s, when addressing human right issues by Olympic bid cities was strongly valued. The Sydney bid was in close competition with the bid presented by Beijing, the candidate city that was considered by many as the real favourite (McGeoch & Korporaal 1994). The main limitation of the Beijing bid was China's dubious human rights record, a factor accentuated by the killings of pro-democracy demonstrators at Tiananmen Square in 1989. In this context, Sydney and Australia needed to address areas likely to raise similar international concern, and one of them was the perceived lack of appropriate government provisions for Aboriginal communities and Torres Strait Islanders. Accordingly, the promotion of a positive view on the Aboriginal and multicultural composition of the country became a priority for the presentation of Australian culture in the world stage and, as such, both themes were presented as central aspects of the country's cultural identity.

Another explanation for the emphasis placed on Aboriginal issues and multiculturalism relates to the pressures that event bid promoters face in order to present an image of the host-city and country that is clear, distinctive and easy to understand by international stakeholders. Sydney's choices can be compared with the decision of the Barcelona 1992 Olympic Games organising committee, which presented an image of the city modelled on its Mediterranean and European character. The use of simplified and unidimensional cultural themes to define the idiosyncrasy of a particular place can be interpreted in the frame discussed by Berkaak (1999: 68) when noting that 'an Olympic event is an opportunity to be focused on—with an assured benefit' (p. 68) and an opportunity for the host-city or nation to 'choose which aspects [it wants to] showcase to the world' (*ibid*). Furthermore, this selection responds to Moragas' (1992b) argument that, from a global media perspective, it is necessary for the Olympic city or nation to 'synthesize [its] complex reality in an image [or] brand image' (p. 32).

The use of Aboriginal reconciliation and multiculturalism as Australia's international 'brand images' was well adapted to the requirements of the mass media during the bid period. The presence of aboriginal troupes in Monte Carlo during the bid-deliberations in September 1993, and the touring of Aboriginal art exhibits such as the one presented in the Olympic Museum in 1993 and 1999 are two examples of cultural displays that were widely publicised and positively appraised by the international press. Further to these one-off successes, the promise of an Olympic cultural programme fully engaged with the same themes offered the host organisers a chance to develop these brand images in more comprehensive and representative ways. For Australia, the decision to keep the four-year Olympiad tradition increased the chances for the 'brand' to be integrated within national cultural policy frameworks. However, the political and social context of the country changed soon after winning the bid and the 'images' of multiculturalism and Aboriginal reconciliation were not as widely shared and acknowledged as the image of a Mediterranean Barcelona had been in Spain during the 1992 Games. This was evident in 1996, the year John Howard was elected Prime Minister, defeating Paul Keating's Labour government and ending an unprecedented thirteen years of Liberal-National Coalition opposition. Keating's progressive views on Aboriginal reconciliation had been a backdrop to the Olympic bid's aspirations and created an expectation, particularly within culture circles, that the Games would advance many pending Aboriginal causes. However, this was followed by a more cautious political environment under Howard, which meant that some of the aspirational bid promises had to be downplayed.

The disputed sense of identity in Australia over the Aboriginal and multicultural question became a cause of conflict and disagreement over the management and implementation of the Sydney cultural programme and was, arguably, a reason for the inconsistent government and commercial support that the programme received over the years, as will be discussed in following chapters. While I do not intend to develop an extensive inquiry into the contested notions of Australia's cultural identity, it is useful to note its drawn out history and that it became a focal point again during the Olympic Games preparations (see for instance Gibson 2001, Farrell 1999, Leishman 1999, McMill 1999, Munro 1999). Moreover, it is important to recognise the different terminologies at work here, where the term cultural identity can be understood as *national culture* or *imagined community* in the way argued by Stuart Hall (1992b: 274–323). Coming to terms with this different language is important so as to provide a background for the points made by Moragas (1992b) and Berkaak (1999) in a way that is reflective of the reality of Australia and the process to decide on the country's promotional images and the design of the Sydney Olympic cultural programme. This said, it is relevant to comment on some key features of the 'images' or 'concepts' chosen as paramount in the overseas promotion of Australia's culture. This will help to better understand the opportunities and constraints that surrounded them at the time of their promotion and implementation and will offer some basis for discussing the extent to which they responded to any defined local or national cultural policy.

Australia's Brand Images: Multiculturalism and Reconciliation

The emphasis on the concept of 'multiculturalism' or multicultural society by the bid organisers aimed to acknowledge the different first or second generation migrant communities that compose the current Australian demographics. Scholars such as Jakubowicz (1981, 1994) and Cunningham and Sinclair (2000) have discussed the uses and abuses of the term multiculturalism within the Australian government rhetoric of present times, a term that has been promoted for years as an official state ideology (Jakubowicz 1981). Cunningham (2000, pers. comm., 25 Aug) argues that the multicultural discourse in Australia has never been taken from a cultural policy perspective but only from the perspective of social policy. Consequently, Cunningham argues that, 'this discourse is focused on solving the social problems of immigration in terms of language, education, jobs, health services etc. but not in consistently promoting a presence of ethnically and culturally diverse people in the media or the arts world' (*ibid*). Thus, Cunningham concludes that, 'it is unlikely that relevant multicultural components are included within the Games cultural programme beyond its average use in the event promotional or marketing discourse' (*ibid*). Accordingly, in Cunningham's view, the use of a multicultural discourse in Sydney's cultural programme was not an effect of the host-city or Australia's priorities in cultural policy but rather a strategic decision associated with the country's policies in communication and international relations.

The second and most clearly emphasised image of Australia in the Sydney bid was the presentation of contemporary Aboriginal culture, which was promoted through the use of the term 'reconciliation'. Reconciliation was meant to signify the commitment of Australian society towards a full acceptance and acknowledgement of Aboriginal and Torres Strait Islanders cultures within its national discourse and sense of self. However, such authors as Tatz (1999) have rebated the use and meaning of the term reconciliation and have accused the Olympic organisations and those government bodies supporting them of masking an extremely delicate and largely unsolved issue behind a public relations rhetoric. According to Tatz, this game 'has always been conceived from a white sense of aesthetics' (*op. cit.*), which prevents the public from obtaining an accurate understanding of the situation. In the same line, Frankland (2000) states that the way Aboriginal questions were dealt with in Olympic discourses tended to be superficial and tokenistic. Frankland argues that they were aimed at exploiting their most appealing side for both governments and media to present a harmonic Australia to the world, but were not consistent in the process to create truly significant cultural projects and offer Aboriginal peoples a representative voice.

The lack of agreement that these brand images provoked among Australian scholars and government agencies did not prevent Games promoters and organisers from using the terms as core elements of their Olympic discourse for the enjoyment of foreign audiences. Nevertheless, as described earlier, the key words that were to be utilised to attract the investment and support of national stakeholders and promote the key benefits of Olympic project were terms such as 'trade' and 'tourism', which had little to do with cultural identity pursuits. This indicates a conflict between the image that was communicated abroad and the beliefs or aspirations of the Australian population, in particular, the corporations and other stakeholders that were to fund the Olympic hosting process. The following sections argue that the contradiction between what was sold or promised to international audiences and the interests of national audiences or stakeholders, resulted in the planning of a remarkably ambitious cultural programme which was to be produced with very limited formal support by Australian organisations.

From Bid Aspirations to Programme Design

The Olympic Arts Festivals are integral to the Sydney 2000 Olympic Games, showing Australians and the rest of the world the unique and varied qualities of our culture. . . . Sydney has chosen to present a series of four Olympic Arts Festivals over the four years of the Cultural Olympiad (1997–2000), each with a different theme and emphasis (SOCOG 1997–2000).

According to Donald McDonald chairman of the Olympic Bid Cultural Commission and, subsequently, of the Sydney Organising Committee for the Olympic Games (SOCOG) cultural commission, one distinguishing feature of the Sydney Olympic Bid in 1993 was the ambitious character of the proposed cultural programme (*Arts Today* 1994). Following earlier initiatives by Barcelona and Atlanta, Sydney promised to undertake activities for the entire period of the Olympiad in the approach to the Games (four years). The decision to do so with different themes and emphasis to reflect Australia's diverse cultural character was repeatedly defined as a key factor in winning the bid (Hanna 1999; McDonald in *Arts Today* 1994; McGeoch & Korporaal 1994). As such, Sydney promised to present a cultural programme that would incorporate a celebration of indigenous people in year 1997; a year-long nation-wide celebration of Australia's multiculturalism in 1998; a world tour of Australia's artists in 1999, and a major arts festival that would bring celebrated artists and artwork from around the world to Australia in 2000.

A senior representative of the Sydney Olympic Arts Festival (OAF) has argued that it is important to use the Olympics to project ambitious arts programmes despite the subsequent difficulties in implementing them. Thus, 'in the context of the Games, a four-year period is better than just three weeks, and national and international presentations, exhibitions and collaborations are more challenging and stimulating for the arts in Australia than a short Sydney-based festival' (1999, pers. comm., 15 Sep). Alternatively, another senior representative emphasised the relevance of the literature produced to explain and promote the festivals to justify his claim that 'the Sydney Olympic cultural programme will leave a long-lasting legacy' (1999, pers. comm., 23 Aug). In his view, the expectation that the Olympic Museum in Lausanne will keep a complete record of official documentation about the 1997–2000 OAF 'is a significant guarantee for the programme to reach international scholars and inspire future event organisers' (*ibid*).

In contrast, as discussed in previous chapters, there is evidence that the Olympic cultural programme is not a primary concern for the local organising committee for the Olympic Games. Likely reasons are the fact that the programme has traditionally maintained a low profile in terms of public recognition and thus, arguably, the media and average Games audiences have not developed an expectation of excellence in arts and culture during the Olympic period. For instance, in Sydney, the analysis of four years of press coverage on the OAF reveals that, despite the festivals receiving some negative criticism in the early years (prior to August 1997), in 1998 and the end of 1999, this did not have a major impact on Games related stories and only led to punctual controversy within media arts sections. In other words, the causes of such a criticism did not become a major controversial issue against the image of the Games and as such, remained unnoticed by the public (see more details in Chapter 9). This is indicative of the suggestion by IOC officials that the success of the Olympic cultural programme is not seen as a decisive factor for the success or failure of an Olympic Games in the way that the provisions for the sporting competitions, media, transport and security are (2001, pers. comm., 20 March). Consequently, the arts festivals are one of the first areas to be affected by budget cuts and re-allocation of resources in times of financial cut-backs.

The Sydney 2000 Games provides clear evidence of this challenge, as the programme suffered a radical budget cut soon after the Olympic candidature was won, being reduced from A\$51 million into A\$20 (Good 1999). This had a remarkable effect on the final design and production of the festivals. The team in charge of the cultural programme decided to maintain the four-year format and to attempt portraying the wide range of themes and emphases that were promised at the bid stage. However, many of the early proposals for implementation had to be cancelled. Furthermore, the lack of resources led to reallocating the responsibility for some of the designed Olympic cultural activities from the culture team to other departments within the organisation. The following paragraphs describe some examples.

Initially, the bid documents outlined the creation of an 'Olympic Village Cultural Programme' especially designed for the athletes but in coordination with the general Games cultural programme (Sydney Bid Ltd. 1992a). However, this programme was produced finally under the responsibility of the Olympic Village management in consultation with the Olympic Entertainment Committee, instead of the OAF programme. This resulted in a programme of activities that, although entertaining for the athletes, missed the chance to promote the cultural particularities of the host-city and country. According to one of the high profile Olympic scholars appointed (and accredited by the IOC) to observe the Sydney Games,

> the cultural programme in the Olympic Village was very poor, without offering any intellectual challenge nor many chances to enhance the athletes' awareness and understanding of the host culture . . . As an example, a particularly popular feature, as in so many prior Olympic editions, was the provision of gambling machines in the Village social club . . . The film programme for the Village was appallingly unrepresentative of the host country, offering an average selection of popular Hollywood movies and little else, instead of exploring Australian cinema. The provision of music entertainment was also rather average, consisting of standard [discotheque] music without much emphasis on local musicians and bands . . . Olympic athletes have the wonderful chance to interact with an incredible variety of world cultures and can surely discover the particularities of the Games host-city in their own way. Unfortunately, the programme of activities in the Olympic Village will surely not be one of their most inspiring sources. In Sydney, it is a programme designed to relax and provide fun, not a vehicle to enhance cultural understanding. (Müller 2000, pers. comm., 9 Sep)

Also, there were plans for establishing a liaison between the OAF programme and the arts and cultural activities scheduled for the Olympic Youth Camp programme,[3] an IOC required programme, which had been presented as a partner programme within the bid in response to the IOC 2000 Candidature Questionnaire (IOC 1992, Sydney Bid Ltd. 1992a). However, the plan was also cancelled at an early stage of the festivals design process. Subsequently, the cultural activities of the Youth Camp were organised in complete separation from the arts festivals and no direct association was made between the aspirations of the OAF and other Olympic youth programmes.

At another level, there was a plan for presenting symbolic cultural medals to acknowledge the most outstanding contributions of OAF participants (Sydney Bid Ltd. 1992). Nevertheless, in April 1998, the IOC Cultural Commission and Executive Board decided that the initiative should be replaced by the production of certificates commemorating participation. Arguably, this decision diminished the chances for the arts festival activities to attract press coverage and emphasise their association with the Games celebrations.

Planning the Programme

According to senior OAF staff (2000, pers. comm., 6 Oct) the planning stage for the Olympic cultural programme was surrounded by insecurity and permanent change in a context where the rest of the organisation, SOCOG, was just starting to take shape. By the end of 1994, at a time when the provisions for critical components of the Games such as the sports competitions, marketing and sponsorship were at their infancy, the team in charge of the OAF was fully operational. They had to undertake crucial decisions about the mission and key components of the cultural programme and present concrete proposals for events that were to take place three years prior to the Games, in 1997.

The same source (*ibid.*) explains that the lack of clear guidelines on the part of the IOC encouraged creativity but also presented a difficult challenge. This was because the team could not find a reliable point of reference to guide their decisions and avoid the conceptual mistakes of prior Games editions. As such, defining the final profile of Sydney's cultural programme was based mostly on the proposals made by the locally designated Olympic Cultural Commission,[4] a group of influential Australian personalities and experts in the cultural sector that had been assigned to advise on cultural matters since the bid stage. The executive OAF team had the difficult task to balance the ambitious proposals made by the Commission in is advisory capacity with the limited resources provided by SOCOG. Furthermore, they had to balance this situation with the growing suspicion that the OAF was not to receive the same financial and promotional support as other dimensions of the Games.

Below is a summary of the requirements that the IOC established for the design and implementation of a cultural programme in the lead to the 2000

Olympic Games edition, and the way these requirements were interpreted and adapted for implementation within the Sydney OAF.

Table 4.1 OAF Mission Statements and Key Deliverables (1997–2000)

Olympic cultural programme mission as defined by the IOC (Adapted from IOC 1997c: 56)
- Promote harmonious relations, mutual understanding and friendship among the participants and others attending the Olympic Games

Key deliverables as defined by the IOC (Adapted from IOC 1997c: 57)
- Include cultural events organised in the Olympic Village and symbolising the universality and the diversity of human culture
- Include other events with the same purpose held mainly in the host-city
- Cover at least the entire period during which the Olympic Village is open

OAF mission as defined by SOCOG (Adapted from diverse SOCOG fact sheets and press releases)
- Express to the world Australia's spirit of Olympic friendship and vitality (1998d)
- Demonstrate the unifying force of the Olympic Movement in blending sport and culture (1998d)
- Reflect Australia's diverse and dynamic artistic life and the powerful influences driving and shaping its cultural make-up, among them: indigenous cultures, geography and landscape, immigration and Australia's physical place in the world as a vast island continent of the Southern Hemisphere (1999f)
- Demonstrate the best of the arts in Australia and the Oceanic region to Australians and the rest of the world and leave a legacy of awareness of the wealth of talent Australia possess (1998d)

Key deliverables as defined by SOCOG (Adapted from notes in SOCOG 2000da–g: 6, *unpublished*)
- Establish an effective staffing team, highly experienced in project management of arts events, including artistic programme development, contract negotiation, production, operations, marketing and publicity and promotion
- Establish strong and effective links with key SOCOG programmes to ensure an integrated approach to the delivery of the festivals and the Olympic Games
- Establish strong and effective links with major arts organisations, arts companies and cultural venues, forming a partnership in the presentation of festival programming
- Develop and implement each of the four festivals for the four year OAF

Source: Adaptation by the author of IOC 1997c, SOCOG (1997–2000), SOCOG 2000d

The requirements presented in Table 4.1 led to the design of a four-year cultural programme with the following overarching mission statement:

> The Sydney 2000 Olympic Arts Festivals aim is to demonstrate the best of the arts in Australia and the Oceanic region to ourselves and the rest of the world and to leave a legacy of awareness of the wealth of talent we possess. . . . The festivals will reflect Australia's diverse cultural character and will look beyond Australia to involve many nations and peoples. (OAF Mission Statement, SOCOG 1997–2000)

The first arts festival for Sydney 2000 took place in 1997 and the final one in year 2000, alongside the Olympic Games sporting competitions and they were all branded under the generic name of Olympic Arts Festivals (OAF). Collectively, the different festivals were created to respond to the original OAF mission statement. However, each festival focused on a different theme and had a different emphasis. As such, each festival prioritised certain objectives over others, as the following list, produced building on OAF factsheets and strategic documentation, describes.

- people's awareness and understanding of the OAF concept and its mission (common goal)
- development of new opportunities, support to new works and emerging artists (common goal)
- establishment of legacies (common goal)
- genuine showcase of Aboriginal artworks (common goal, specific emphasis: *The Festival of the Dreaming*)
- manifestation of diversity to secure representation (common goal, specific emphasis: *A Sea Change*)
- national involvement, community participation (common goal; specific emphasis: *A Sea Change*)
- international scope and demonstration of excellence (specific emphasis: *Reaching the World; The Harbour of Life*)

Below is a brief summary of each festival's characteristics by title, time period, location, main themes, mission statements, defined objectives and programme of events. Additional details about the programme are included in the Appendix.

Clearly, Sydney retained an ambitious vision for its cultural programme and, by separating areas of emphasis across different festival years, it attempted to focus on different kinds on objectives and thus reach out to different kinds of communities at different points in time. The next chapters explain how the defined OAF objectives were eventually implemented in the context of SOCOG's internal management structure and the expectations and priorities of key programme stakeholders. As discussed throughout, there was a mismatch between the ambition and the actual resources

Table 4.2 OAF Length, Themes, Objectives and Main Components

Year, name, length and location	Theme / mission	Objectives	Programme components
1997 The Festival of the Dreaming, September to October (Sydney)	Celebration of the world's indigenous cultures, in particular those of Australian Aborigines and Torres Strait Islanders	*General:* expand a greater awareness and appreciation of Australian indigenous heritage. *Specific:* ensure indigenous authorship and control of the work presented	30 exhibitions, 14 dance and theatre productions, eight performance troupes, 50 films, a literature programme, three concerts and special commissions involving overseas indigenous artists. Every state and territory of Australia was represented.
1998 A Sea Change, June to October (national)	A 'snapshot' of Australia's diverse migrant cultures	Help people across the nation learn more about the arts in their country and demonstrate the importance of its geographic and cultural diversity; - Create a time-capsule of Australian culture in the end of the Millennium for generations to come	92 presenting companies and 122 dance, theatre, visual arts, literary, music and education events. *Highlights:* lighthouse and harbour concerts; touring exhibition *Sculpture by the Sea. Publications:*1998 Anthology of Australian writing and photography
1999 Reaching the World, November 1998 to January 2000 (international)	Events by Australian companies and artists touring throughout the year to countries in each of the five regions represented by the Olympic symbol	*General:* bring Australian arts and culture to the international stages; *Specific:* establish collaborations with foreign governments and arts organisations.	70 events travelling to 50 countries and 150 cities or towns including dance, music, theatre, visual arts, literature, films, architecture and design. Publication of *Australia on Show,* a guide to Australian Arts Broadcasting
2000 The Harbour of Life, August to October (Sydney)	The culmination of the Olympiad, 'a festival on a scale to match the grandeur of the Olympic Games'	*General:* define the finest elements of Australian culture; present a number of works on grand scale, unlikely to be seen again in a lifetime; establish artistic legacies	75 day-event focused in the Sydney harbour and Opera House— opera, theatre, dance and classical concerts; 30 visual arts exhibitions in key galleries and museums

Source: OAF web pages at SOCOG website and promotional literature (SOCOG 1997–2000)

available to operationalise it, which meant that not all objectives could be addressed with the same degree of success. Another underlying limitation of the OAF's vision as presented here was the lack of explicit emphasis on exploring synergies with the Olympic idea and the sports programme in particular. This could be considered one of the key limitations of Sydney's vision for culture as, even in the case when OAF components were acknowledged as successful (by the media or the general public) they were rarely associated with the Games.

BEYOND SYDNEY 2000

In line with Sydney's experience, candidate cities are increasingly utilising the cultural chapter within their bid documents as an opportunity to present the distinctive elements of their Games proposal and outline their more ambitious ideas. This is not evident in all candidatures, but it has been the case for all eventually successful host cities, consistenly so within Summer editions, and increasingly so for Winter editions. One of the main areas of growth within cultural bids, particularly for Western candidates, has been the emphasis on legacy as a key word and the association of the cultural programme with chances to expand the sustainability of Games developments. However, the survival of such promises within the eventual vision for the programme is not apparent. Changes in cultural programme leadership and lack of continuity in key local stakeholders support are the main reasons for this situation.

IOC guidelines for culture within Candidature Questionnaires did not show any significant change until the 2016 bidding process, as noted in Chapter 2. This has meant that the cultural programme definition framework for host cities up to London 2012 has been similar to that of Sydney. Further, the level of IOC operational support for the Cultural Olympiad has also remained equally ambiguous until 2006, well after the planning stages for the Salt Lake, Athens, Torino and Beijing Games. Consequently, these Games editions have built on the same Olympic cultural policy environment that surrounded Sydney 2000 and determined cultural programme priorities on that basis. It is my contention that this situation has continued to jeopardise the chances of the Cultural Olympiad to make a significant difference to the Games staging process.

Tellingly, Summer Games editions in Athens 2004 and Beijing 2008 have focused on traditional high arts and the showcase of flagship or iconic arts institutions, particularly during Games time. This has often implied an ongoing lack of linkage with the Games sporting components (both editions) and core Olympic narrative (Beijing). Winter editions have had more opportunities to grow and innovate in their programming when compared with their predecessors up to Nagano in 1988. This has been in part due to a previously unexplored focus on public space as a site for cultural celebration—from the mountains surrounding winter sporting resorts to the city as a hub for

partying (see García and Miah 2006) and also, largely, due to the emergence
and widespread usage of new technologies which are eventually becoming a
platform for artistic expression—this was at the heart of Vancouver 2010's
Cultural Olympiad Digital Edition (CODE) programme (see Job 2010). Ultimately, cultural programming within Winter Games counts on the advantage of complementing an event which operates on a far smaller scale than
the Summer editions and thus leaves more room for local stakeholders to
explore initiatives which help expand the Olympic experience.

Beyond a summer or winter trend, the vision for the cultural programme
has also been deeply influenced by locally or nationally based cultural policy trends at the specific time of Games hosting. In particular, it is possible
to detect marked differences between the cultural policies of Games hosted
in European latin countries such as Greece and Italy, Asian countries such
as China and Anglosaxon countries such as Canada, the US and the UK.
The latter, while showcasing some very important differences, are also similar in the sense that they have all been most directly influenced by Sydney
and inherited a lot of the expertise from Australia. Finally, within London
2012 cultural vision, an important advancement has been the clear emphasis on youth, the exploration of links with health and well-being and a very
strong emphasis on the synergies between the Olympic and Paralympic programme which had not been so clearly explored before (García 2012).

SUMMARY

Telling the story of what the Olympic Games meant to Australia in the context of a rapidly changing demographic, political, cultural and social heritage
was a challenge for Sydney's bid committee. Yet, the act of representation was
important for Australia to resolve through their Games and this is a common
process faced by any Olympic host city, region and country. To assist in this
process, an area that could have been a source for inspiration or guidance is
the arts and cultural sector. Nevertheless, the sector had traditionally operated in an exclusive close-circuit manner, often ignoring the changing realities of Australia and instead mostly influenced by the taste and aesthetics of
distant reference points in Europe and the US. As in other parts of the world,
some radical changes have taken place since the 1960s, involving the sector's
growing commitment towards supporting local community endeavours and
the creation of institutions fully dedicated to them. However, the emergence
of a national cultural policy discourse that embraces notions of multiculturalism and that offers genuine support to contemporary Aboriginal and
Torres Strat Islander expressions did not fully unfold until the very end of
the 20th century and, at the time of the Olympic bid, was still in its infancy.
The latest trend in Australia, as in so many other countries, is a rationalist approach to the arts, which implies an encouragement towards working
with the corporate sector and responding to the demands of the market. This
was particularly noticeable in the second half of the 1990s. Arguably, this

approach contributed to slowing the process towards making the cultural sector fully representative of the country's diverse minority cultural realities, and diminished its chances to take the lead in presenting a meaningful but complex image of contemporary Australia.

In this context, it is easy to understand that, at the bid stage, the Sydney Olympic promoters emphasised the corporate benefits of the Games among internal audiences rather than a cultural discourse. In this approach, the pride of sporting traditions and accomplishments is taken for granted, as it is clearly associated with the Olympic Games and the benefits that the event can generate. However, the role of the arts and culture as a catalyst to attract local Olympic support was less prominent. For the local and national corporations, the main reasons why Sydney should host the Games were its natural environment, its potential for infrastructure development and its sporting traditions. Moreover, the main benefits the Games would bring to the city were said to be opportunities for developing tourism, media coverage and trade opportunities in general. Thus, the promotion of Australian arts and culture was not a bid selling point at a national level, despite the willingness of cultural institutions to take centre stage.

In contrast, if one looks at Sydney's international promotional message for the bid, the emphasis was on cultural achievements and informed by cultural policy-makers. The bid promoters chose the country's multicultural profile and the claim of an advance towards full reconciliation with its Aboriginal peoples as Australia's international 'brand images'. The notion of multiculturalism and reconciliation dominated the tone of the bid public relations strategy and also guided the proposal for the official Olympic cultural programme. This programme was said to surpass the cultural proposals of other candidates and to offer a competitive advantage to Sydney's bid. Therefore, it could the argued that, at the bid stage, cultural policy had been able to inform and help defining the unique character of Sydney's Olympic project for external audiences.

However, soon after winning the right to host the Games, the organisation in charge of producing the event, SOCOG, cut the budget allowances for the cultural programme in half. With this decision, it was evident that the influence of cultural policy-makers was likely to be minimised throughout the Olympic preparations. The final design of the Olympic programme kept a strong commitment to sustain the ambitious promises made at the bid stage. Nevertheless, without appropriate resources nor clear commitment by local stakeholders to champion it, the programme could not play a defining role in the manner that had been claimed during the bid period.

In sum, the ambitious cultural and arts proposals presented at the Sydney bid stage were attractive to international audiences but not fully matched by the support available for the arts in the country, particularly once the Games were awarded. The proposal aimed at more than the stated interests of key Olympic stakeholders and thus, it set a series of aims and objectives that were difficult to achieve.

5 Managing the Programme
Internal Operations

To understand the potential for the Olympic cultural programme to play a distinctive role within the Olympic Games, it is important to have an overall view of the Games management structure and main strategic imperatives. This will help to evaluate the extent to which the day-to-day Games operations are informed by a coherent cultural policy. This chapter reviews the Sydney Organising Committee for the Olympic Games internal management structure as an exemplar of OCOG operations, and articulates the positioning of the Olympic Arts Festivals programme specifically. It starts by reviewing SOCOG's internal structure and ends with a review of the festivals' strategic management in terms of staffing, budgeting, marketing, promotions, and ticketing.

STRUCTURE OF THE OLYMPIC ORGANISING COMMITTEE

The Sydney Organising Committee for the Olympic Games was established on the 12th November 1993 as a statutory authority of the government, under an act of Parliament by the New South Wales (NSW) State Government. It originally comprised a board of fifteen directors representing the IOC, the Australian Olympic Committee, Federal, State and City governments and the business and sporting community of Australia. Under the terms of the Host City Contract, presented by the IOC upon award of the Games, SOCOG was responsible for planning, organising, managing and staging the Sydney 2000 Olympic Games. The Host City Contract had been signed initially between the IOC, the Council of the City of Sydney and the Australian Olympic Committee. SOCOG became party to it on 4 February 1994 and was to work closely with the three new special Olympic agencies that the NSW government had created. These agencies were charged with 'the construction of new, permanent venues and facilities required for the Games and [the] provision of support services such as transport, security and health care' (SOCOG 2000c: 9). The three agencies were the Olympic Coordination Authority (OCA), responsible for the construction of venues and facilities; the Olympic Roads and Transport Authority (ORTA), in charge of the delivery of transport services; and the Olympic Security Command Centre (OSCC), responsible for all Games security matters.

The OCA was the principal State organisation, acting within government and ensuring appropriate coordination of all other Olympic agencies and services in NSW. Federal Government had also an involvement in the Games staging process through the designated Minister for the Olympics, Michael Knight. The involvement of other Federal Government agencies was coordinated by a Commonwealth-State Secretariat in the Department of Australia's Prime Minister and Cabinet (SOCOG 2000c: 9).

Figure 5.1 shows SOCOG's corporate governance and interactions with its main external stakeholders as it stood in 1998 (SOCOG 1999 h: 10).

As reported in SOCOG 1998 Annual Report the organisation structure undertook significant modifications over the 1998/1999 financial year as it moved from a functional to an operational-based structure. The changes were ongoing during 1999 and the beginning of year 2000. From August 1999, a full year prior to the commencement of the actual Games operations that were to take place between the 15 September and the 1 October 2000, SOCOG moved into the Games time structure, a framework that consisted of two sub-structures working in parallel: a functional structure and a venue-based structure (SOCOG 2000c: 27). Figures 5.2. and 5.3 show the differences between both types of structure.

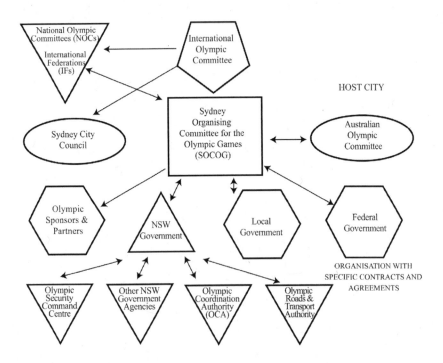

Figure 5.1   SOCOG corporate governance in 1998. Source: 1998 Annual Report, SOCOG (1999h)

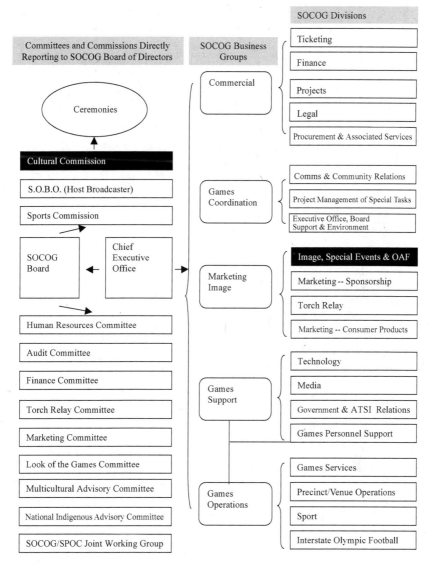

Figure 5.2 SOCOG structure by the financial year ending June 1998. Source: Adapted from SOCOG (1999h); OAF programme highlighted by author

and a venue-based structure (SOCOG 2000c: 27). Figures 5.2. and 5.3 show the differences between both types of structure.

Comparing both structures reveals a number of substantial alterations that took place throughout the Games hosting process, in particular, in the transition from a functional to an operational structure. The first major change was the creation of a new operational structure, and the disappearance of committees and commissions advising the SOCOG board,

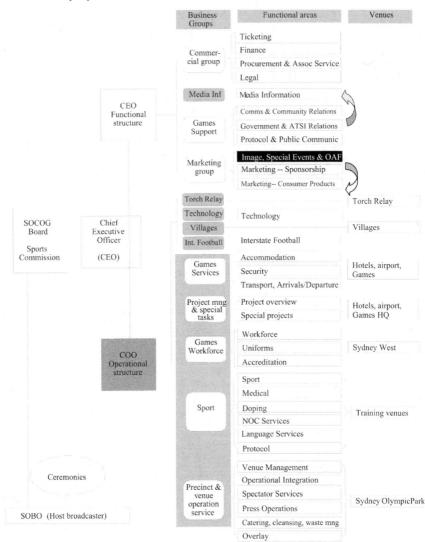

Figure 5.3   SOCOG structure during the Games in 2000. Source: SOCOG 1999k: 2; OAF programme and related highlights marked by author

including the Cultural Commission. However, during Games time, the functional areas remained comparable to how they had been set up by the end of 1998. The OAF programme was kept in a similar position throughout this process, remaining within the Image, Special Events and Olympic Arts Festivals division within the SOCOG Marketing group. The structural change most likely to have affected the liaison abilities of the OAF programme was the transfer of the programme and operations section of the Torch Relay division from the Marketing group within SOCOG's functional structure into an independent division within the Games operational structure. This is likely to have been a lost opportunity for potential collaborations between the OAF programme and the Torch Relay programme, a situation that has been common to most Olympic host processes. In parallel, within SOCOG's communications structure, a special Media Information division was created and separated from its initial placement at the Games Support group, and the Communications and Community Relations division was transferred from the Games Coordination group to the Games Support group. This allowed for greater interactions between the Communications division and the Protocol and Government Relations divisions at the time of the Games. However, as detailed in the next section, the OAF was not integrated within the Communications division and, as such, did not benefit from the potential increased liaison and visibility with the Olympic Protocol teams.

Final decision-making was the responsibility of SOCOG's Board of Directors, a senior group appointed by the Governor of NSW on the recommendation of the Minister for the Olympics and in consultation with the Australian Olympic Commission (SOCOG 2000c: 11). The SOCOG Board was responsible for the corporate governance of the organisation and guided and monitored the business and affairs of SOCOG on behalf of its stakeholders. The Board held monthly meetings with each working committee for the Games and with the Sports and the Cultural Commission, which had an advisory role. The operation and administration of SOCOG was the responsibility of the Chief Executive Officer and the senior management team, each of whom were in charge of one business group. In year 2000, the Board was composed of fourteen representatives from the three levels of Australian government (Federal, State and Local); the business community, and Australia's Olympic Commission in coordination with the IOC (SOCOG 2000c: 11). The main fields of expertise within SOCOG Board of Directors were sports administration, the Olympic Movement, commerce and public life affairs.

Beyond the separation of SOCOG basic structure into a functional and a venue-based sub-structure, an additional major change took place by mid year 2000 in terms of decision-making processes. After six years working as a separate and independent entity, SOCOG became part of a single team, the Sydney 2000 project. This reconfiguration integrated the Organising Committee with two of the NSW special agencies, OCA and ORTA. Confidential sources and personal observations at SOCOG have indicated that the integration of SOCOG within the more generic Sydney 2000 project had a major impact on the management of some SOCOG areas, such as the Communications programme, the Image programme and the Publications programme. However, such a change at the top level of the organisation did not affect the OAF programme structure and management. OAF senior staff have explained the lack of repercussions of such changes on the festivals management by referring to the complete separation of OAF operations, such as communications and marketing, from the rest of SOCOG programmes (2000, pers. comm., 22 Aug). The following section provides evidence of this 'separation' by describing the management structure of the OAF programme and the links established with other SOCOG programmes and functional areas.

STRUCTURE OF THE OLYMPIC ARTS FESTIVALS

The department responsible for the OAF was integrated within SOCOG's structure and was dependent on the decisions taken by the General Board of Directors (a case of 'Central Management' for the cultural programme, as described in Chapter 2). The OAF was defined as a 'programme' within the area of Image, Special Events and Olympic Arts Festivals and belonged to the Games Marketing division. Find a brief indication of the OAF staff structure in Figure 5.4.

The OAF programme structure was designed in the years leading up to 1996 and was fully operational by mid 1996. It acted independently from other functional areas of SOCOG such as the Media programme or the 'Look of the Games' programme, which were still in the planning stages at this time. The establishment of the Cultural Olympiad tradition has meant that the Olympic cultural programme is one of the first functional areas of an OCOG, together with the Handover Ceremony team, which is charged with the design and delivery of the 8 minutes presentation allocated to each Olympic host city in the context of the previous Games Closing Ceremony.

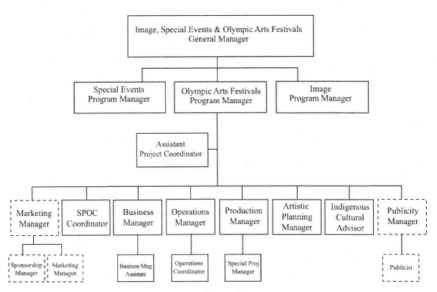

Figure 5.4   OAF staff structure. Source: SOCOG 1999g, Structure/Staff documents[1]

Table 5.1 OAF Team Job Descriptions

OAF General manager: In charge of OAF, Image and Special Events. Responsible for source programming for the festivals and evaluation of the Atlanta 1996 OAF programmes.
OAF Programme manager: Appointed in 1996. In charge of the general coordination of all four festivals. Responsible for establishing the overall staffing and operational structure of the programme. Evaluation of prior Olympic Cultural Programmes (Atlanta). Oversaw all liaison and provision of information across SOCOG.
OAF Area managers: Business, Operations, Production, Artistic Planning

- Business—Primary purpose: managing overall financial, ticketing and contractual requirements of the OAF and specific financial requirements of the Image and Special Events programme.
- Operations—Primary purpose: managing and implementing accommodation, travel, volunteers, security, catering, accreditation.
- Production—Primary purpose: identifying, planning and implementing all production and technical requirements relating to the presentation of projects and events. In charge of budget updates, contacting artists and companies, communication strategy. Link to SOCOG communications.

Artistic Planning—Primary purpose: ensuring overall programming across all art-forms for each festival. Link to festivals artistic director(s).
Programme Consultancies: Marketing, Publicity

- Marketing—Primary Purpose: managing overall marketing requirements including marketing strategies, marketing budget, marketing guidelines and kits. Managed branding and look approvals including design, production and distribution of all print materials, banners, videos and oversaw website content. Link to SOCOG sponsors and SOCOG Consumer Products and Licensing regarding cultural merchandise.
- Publicity—Primary purpose: developing and managing all publicity requirements including publicity strategies, plans and campaigns, publicity budget and events, media launches, press releases, media calls. Oversaw implementation of Cultural Media Press Centre during Games time. Liaison with media managers of national agencies and arts companies, liaison with national and international journalists.

Sub-area managers: sponsorship and marketing, special projects assistants, advisors and coordinators

- Project coordinator / programme manager: accountable to artistic director and arts companies to determine programming possibilities, develop and encourage projects.

(continued)

Table 5.1(continued)

- Business management: accountable to project business manager and ticketing coordinator.
- Operations coordinator: accountable to outside service providers, link to function command team at Olympic Headquarters during all stages of the festival.
- Production coordinator: accountable to Assistant Business Management, link to all relevant programmes and functional areas of SOCOG.
- Sydney Paralympic Organinsing Committee (SPOC) coordinator: link to SPOCfor planning Paralympic Arts.
- Indigenous culture advisor: accountable to Aboriginal and Torres Strait Islanders Committee.
- Ticketing coordinator: accountable to SOCOG ticketing services (appointed during Games time).

Specialists: publicist.
Respective Festivals Artistic Director(s): Responsible for developing the programme parameters, initiating projects and sourcing proposals, liaising with artists and arts companies and making the final selection of all programme content. Accountable to the OAF general manager but operating outside SOCOG's central management structure.

Source: SOCOG (1999g)

This means that cultural planning must start immediately after the Games are awarded and staff are appointed and delivering activity four years prior to the two weeks of sport competition.

Over the four year period, sixteen staff and several consultants were in charge of the Sydney OAF programme. Their most important role was to produce and promote the four festivals from 1997 to year 2000. Most of the team was also involved in the delivery of the cultural programme for the Sydney 2000 Paralympic Games. The production of *The Harbour of Life*, the final festival in year 2000, required the contracting of four additional staff. This comprised a second production coordinator and an operations assistant in support of the existing operations coordinator, and two ticketing coordinators to liaise with the main Olympic ticketing operations department. Additionally, an artistic director was appointed for each festival on the recommendation of SOCOG's Cultural Committee and Cultural Commission. Table 5.1 describes each OAF job function and the way these functions were supposed to link up with other SOCOG programmes and external groups. It is particularly important to note that the post of general manager was created in late 1996, soon before the start of the first festival. From 1994 to 1996, the post had been defined as OAF executive producer and involved a more active role shaping the content of the festivals as the post combined both an administrative and artistic function. The person appointed to this original post resigned in view of the ongoing budget cuts and disagreement over the vision for the Festivals in 1998 and 1999. This led to a redefinition of the role description which was to lose its artistic producer dimension and strengthen instead its administrative responsibilities across three different programmes: the OAF as well as Special Events and Image, which eventually also incorporated The Look of the Games programme.

All members of the OAF team were located in the same work area within SOCOG, sharing offices with the staff working for the Image programme and the Special Events programme. The office of the general manager was also located in the same space. Arguably, this physical concentration eased the interaction between the three programmes. Interestingly, no specific links, neither physical nor strategic, were established between the OAF and other programmes that also have a strong cultural focus, such as the National Education programme, the Multicultural Affairs services, the Torch Relay programme and the Olympic Ceremonies. The National Education programme and Multicultural Affairs services belonged to the Communications and Community Relations division and did not create any specific initiative or activity in conjunction with the OAF.[2] The Torch Relay programme, initially part of the Marketing and Image division, to which the OAF belonged (see Figure 5.2) was transferred to the Operations group at the time of its implementation in year 2000 (Figure 5.3) and did not develop any initiative in coordination with the OAF programme. Instead of ensuring some synergies, the organisation of cultural celebrations to accompany the passage of the Torch Relay was entirely the responsibility of the authorities of respective cities and towns. This resulted in a discontinuous programme of cultural activities, varying from spectacular cultural displays in some towns to the absence of special activities in other, mostly small towns (Purchase 2000). Finally, the Olympic Ceremonies were managed as a separate entity and reported directly to the SOCOG Board without interaction with other Games programmes. This managerial isolation prevented potential linkages or continuities between the cultural section of the Opening and Closing Ceremonies and the arts festival happening in year 2000.

Beyond the lack of interaction with other cultural and non-sports focused programmes the OAF was also affected by the absence of coordination between SOCOG's diverse programmes for communication and promotions—within the divisions of Marketing, Consumer Products and Media—and the OAF marketing and publicity services. As detailed in Chapter 7 (see Figure 7.1), specific programmes such as Ticketing, the Torch Relay, Volunteers, Test Events, Consumer Products and Olympic Football were considered individual marketing assets and managed by dedicated marketing managers in coordination with sponsors' account managers, and overseen by the Marketing and Image division general manager. In contrast, programmes such as the OAF were not directly related to mainstream Olympic marketing activities.

SOCOG's Marketing and Advertising programme team was responsible for developing the Sydney 2000 central brand campaign and for adapting the campaign main theme into the organisation multiple sub-programmes. The Marketing and Advertising team was also responsible for developing strategies for the official 'Sponsor Recognition' and 'Sponsor Presence' services.[3] This team was also in charge of developing marketing relationships and liaisons with national and international tourism boards, trade bodies, and other Olympic institutions such as the Australian Olympic Committee and the Sydney Paralympic Organising Committee (SPOC). However, none of these functions had a direct effect on the OAF, partially, because the OAF had developed its own brand theme under the advice of the Look of the Games committee, which was independent from SOCOG's Marketing programme. The only link between the OAF marketing services and SOCOG Marketing and Advertising programme was in terms of internal consultation. This consisted of instructions for the design of guidelines to allow co-sponsorship of events within the festivals, particularly where non-Olympic sponsors were involved. This was viewed as a significant opportunity by the OAF marketing manager (1999, pers. comm., 14 Sep) but it was not aimed at—and consequently did not assist—integrating OAF promotional messages within SOCOG's general Games messages.

Overall, it is difficult to identify a fixed style of management within the OAF, due to the lack of transparency and continuous change in the approach to design and implementation of SOCOG operations, which is common to most OCOGs. In the absence of published materials, most of the arguments presented in the following section are the result of direct observations within the organisation;[4] deductive analysis of personal interviews with managers and assistants; archival and documentary research, and content analysis of press clippings on the festivals.

STRATEGIC AND OPERATIONAL PLANNING FOR THE OLYMPIC ARTS FESTIVALS

The main strategic and operational planning roles within the OAF were the responsibility of the general manager and programme manager. The OAF general manager, who also oversaw the programmes of Image and Special Events, was in charge of supervising budgets, commercial opportunities and the programme's look or image strategies, which became named The Look of the Games. He was also in charge of liaising with SOCOG's Board, IOC members, sponsors, OAF presenting partners and government agencies, as well as making presentations at public forums and negotiating with arts companies. At the next level, the OAF programme manager was in charge of planning and monitoring the programme. This included strategic plan policies, operations plans, business plans, milestones and timelines. She also managed the planning, development and implementation of programme stems such as legal aspects, finance, programming, production, operations, marketing and publicity. The OAF programme manager also oversaw the provision of information across other SOCOG programmes, managed international liaisons and funding support with external agencies and oversaw the cultural media centre or 'Olympic Arts Festivals Media Office' during Games time. Within this context, it is possible to identify some trends in the way that the OAF programme was managed. McDonnell, Allen and Toole (1999) argue that an event management plan is usually broken down into two key processes: strategic and operational planning:

> in essence, strategic plans focus on setting long-term objectives and deciding on the strategies—the means and schemes—which will achieve them. Operational plans describe the specific steps needed to implement these strategies and establish quantifiable revenue and expenditure budgets. (p. 59)

A model for strategic planning involves the identification of current objectives and strategies. This results from analysing the opportunities and threats existing in the environment of a specific programme, and analysing the strengths and weaknesses of the resources available in the organisation. McDonnell et al. argue that these procedures lead to the reassessment of mission and objectives and the formulation of implementation strategies (1999: 60).

Looking at Sydney's case it is not possible to outline the exact process of development for the OAF strategic plan. However, the outcomes of such process are manifest in the mission statement and main 'deliverables' defined at the end of Chapter 4. Using the technique proposed by McDonnell et al., it can be argued that the definition of the festivals' mission and subsequent objectives was the result of balancing the cultural promises made at the bid stage—prior to 1993—with the opportunities and constraints detected within the Australian environment in 1997 (ie. potential to attract stakeholders support) and the strengths and weaknesses of SOCOG's corporate structure (ie. potential to effectively implement the strategy). After considering these decisions, it is possible to summarise the festival's implementation strategy or operational plan. McDonnell et al. (1999: 66–67) indicate that an operational plan consists of single-use plans for non-recurring activities, and standing plans for recurring activities. The first are designed to achieve particular objectives, and to comprise budget plans and project designs. The latter are designed to outline long term or generic policies, standard procedures and rules. In the case of the OAF, although the programme consisted of four festivals, the management team did not develop a fixed plan to be applied in all cases. Each festival had a different focus and emphasis and, as argued in the sections below, each of them relied on different resources. Therefore, the OAF operational plan consisted of single-use plans, one for each year or festival. As well, instead of policies and standard procedures, the programme focus was on the formulation of specific actions.

To facilitate assessment, the OAF operational plan can be sub-divided in three main components: budgeting strategy, marketing and promotional strategy, and sales or ticketing strategy. These three components are analysed in the following section.

Budgeting

The OAF four-year programme was formulated at the Sydney bid stage at the cost of A$51 million (Sydney Bid Ltd. 1992b). However, this budget was substantially cut once the plans for implementation began taking place. By 1995, the budget was cut to A$20 million (Good 1999). In subsequent years, the 'Olympic crisis' taking place from the end of 1998 to the beginning of 1999 and the resulting A$200 million sponsorship shortfall suffered by SOCOG,[5] led to major reductions in the funding for promotional campaigns and community initiatives. This affected the OAF by a further cut of A$2.3 million in 1999 (SOCOG 1999l).

The lack of official data on funding and budgeting makes it difficult to present a detailed description of the evolution of the festivals' budgeting strategy. Information on the strategy has been gathered through informal interviews with festival managers and the review of press publications. Table 5.2 shows a comparative description of figures as published by the press and publicly stated by SOCOG before the launch of the final festival, from 1993 (bid stage) to the 13 October 1999 (launch of *The Harbour of Life*). Table 5.2 shows some of the cuts announced in 1999, and Table 5.3

Table 5.2   OAF Budget Estimates as Published on the Press from 1993 to 1999 (in A$)

Pub Date	Total OAF Budget	Specific Festivals' Budget		Festival Length
1993	(Bid file) A$51m	The Harbour of Life (first draft)	A$10m	4 months
1995	(Press) A$20m	The Festival of the Dreaming	A$8m	20 days
1997		A Sea Change	A$1m	8 months
1998		Reaching the World	A$1.5m	13 months
1999	(Press) A$16.4m (SOCOG) A$19m	The Harbour of Life	A$4m	2 months

Source: Good 1999, various press articles

Table 5.3 OAF Budget Cuts as Announced in 1999 (in A$)

Pub date	Total OAF Budget
21 May 1999	SOCOG board publishes expenditure savings: A$2.7m cut out of OAF final budget
22 July 1999	SOCOG publishes the new revised Games budget: A$ 13.6m for the OAF

Source: SOCOG 1999e

shows the revised figures presented as 'definitive' in OAF documents by the 23 October 1999, after the launch of the final festival. More details about these figures can be found in Appendix 2.

In Table 5.4, the remarkable difference between gross and net costs for *The Harbour of Life* contrasts with the prior festivals. This was due to the expectation that the final festival would generate a high income. While a festival such as *Reaching the World* was not designed to provide any sales income, the final festival was supposed to pay off prior debts through box-office sales, national and international grants and special hospitality agreements. *The Festival of the Dreaming* attracted some income beyond SOCOG's core budgets through public sector grants (A$ 421,183) and box-office sales (A$ 430,083); *A Sea Change* had a A$200,000 grant from the government agency Arts Queensland.

In contrast with the regular budget variations suffered by the OAF programme, the budget allocation for other Olympic events such as the Opening and Closing Ceremonies remained unaltered since the bid stage (A$ 40m). Internal sources at SOCOG have argued that this was not the

Table 5.4 Budget Estimates by OAF General Manager at Final Festival Launch

Doc Date		Specific Festivals'	Gross Budget	Net Budget
11/11/1999	(Estimates)	Total OAF Budget	A$ 38.95 m	A$ 13.6 m
23/09/1999	(Actual figure)	The Festival of the Dreaming	A$ 5.6m	A$ 4.75m
23/09/1999	(Actual figure)	A Sea Change	A$ 2.8m	A$ 2.6m
23/09/1999	(Actual figure)	Reaching the World	A$ 2.25m	A$ 2.25m
11/11/1999	(Estimates)	The Harbour of Life	A$ 28.3m	A$ 13.6m

Source: SOCOG (1999d, 1999e)

case for other cultural and community related programmes such as the Torch Relay and, more noticeably, the Olympic Education National Programme which, as in the case of the OAF, had their funding cut considerably prior to their final implementation. The case of Opening and Closing Ceremonies can be seen as exceptional and is explained by the fact that they belonged to a separate division (Ceremonies division), which was directly accountable to the SOCOG Board and the IOC. As such, it can be inferred that the ability of respective programmes to retain their budget allocations was in part influenced by their structural position within the organisation.

Extrapolating to other Games experiences, while the total budget for hosting the Games grows exponentially from one city to the next, the budget for the Olympic cultural programme has been significantly reduced since the Barcelona Cultural Olympiad in 1992. This has been so despite the fact that the scope and length of the programme (four years of local and national celebrations) has remained the same. Again, this makes a case for studying the major obstacles towards the official Olympic cultural programme evolving and growing in parallel to other components of the Olympic Games.

Interestingly, after Sydney 2000, both Athens 2004 and Beijing 2008 secured considerably higher budgets for their cultural programmes. In the case of Athens, the Cultural Olympiad was established as a separate organisation entirely funded via the Hellenic Ministry of Culture through the specially set Hellenic Culture Organisation, which acted independently from the Athens Organising Committee for the Games. In the case of Beijing, final figures have not been released but the cultural programme was directly funded by the Chinese Government in conjunction with the Beijing OCOG (BOCOG) and encompassed the programming of all major cultural organisations in Beijing during 2008 plus five years of pre-Games festivals, leading to one of the largest listings of Olympic cultural activity ever presented at Games time (see BOCOG 2008). The latter does not imply that the programme was in any way more central

Table 5.5   Budget for 4-Year Cultural Olympiads 1992–2004[6]

Games Edition	Reported Budget in Original Currency	US$	A$
Barcelona 1992	PTS 6,515m	U$ 71m	A$ 98m
Atlanta 1996	U$ 25m	U$ 25m	A$ 33m
Sydney 2000	A$ 28.3m	U$ 16.5m	A$ 28.3m
Athens 2004	EUR 143m	U$ 173	A$ 247m

Source: COOB 1993, ACOG 1997, SOCOG 1999d, Panagiotopoulou 2008

to the Games experience than was the case in Sydney as, in fact, there is evidence to the contrary (see Garcia 2008 for a critique of Beijing's cultural programme implementation). However, this situation is indicative of the remarkable differences in levels of funding allocation for Olympic cultural activity when host Governments see the programme as a top priority and the OCOG does not need to rely on private funds to sustain its cultural budget. The changing trends post Sydney 2000 and early indications of funding priorities in the lead up to London 2012 are discussed in more detail in Chapter 10.

Marketing and Promotions

The OAF marketing and advertising strategy was managed through a marketing consultancy team contracted to work within the Sydney Olympic headquarters. The marketing management and strategy involved the development of marketing guidelines and marketing kits for each festival; the design, production and distribution of all print materials, banners and videos; liaison with artists and arts companies to address the threat of 'ambush marketing',[7] liaison with SOCOG sponsors and creation of opportunities for other official commercial partners; development of look (ie. visual design), venue and site signage including posters, banners and way-finding; and revision of the content of the OAF sections within SOCOG's webpage. The marketing manager was also in charge of media promotions; preparing media schedules and advertising placement; assisting in the organisation of each festival launch for the media, VIPs and general public; preparing ticket pricing proposals; facilitating box-office reports, and finally liaising with SOCOG Consumer Products and Licensing regarding cultural merchandise such as pins, posters, caps and T-shirts.

The OAF marketing strategy became operational by the end of 1996 in order to support the first festival in 1997. The arts festival campaign was preceded by the *Olympic Journey*, which was the first large marketing exercise undertaken by SOCOG. The *Olympic Journey* was an ambitious nation-wide celebration of parades, exhibitions and public gatherings designed to 'unite, inspire and embrace all Australians in the spirit of the Olympic ethos' (SOCOG 1999i: np). The 'journey' lasted six months starting June 1997 and brought Olympic memorabilia, interactive exhibits and athlete parades to diverse locations throughout the country. The event created a significant media opportunity to promote the Olympic ideals and provide information about the Sydney Games. However, it did not include any link or reference to *The Festival of the Dreaming*, which began in September 1997.

Similarly, in following years, other Olympic activities highly marketed by SOCOG general communications programme did not offer a platform for the promotion of the arts festivals. This was the case for the *Sydney Spirit Art Student Prize,* which was part of the National Education Programme in 1997, 1998 and 1999. It was also the case for the Torch Relay celebrations and the Community Hospitality Programme in year 2000. In general, contrary to the expectations set up by the OAF programme manager, most marketing efforts to promote the OAF were designed, produced and implemented in isolation from the rest of SOCOG marketing and promotion activities. The following paragraphs offer a brief description of the marketing efforts taking place to support each of the arts festivals.

In 1997, *The Festival of the Dreaming* utilised a broad range of communication channels in Sydney to promote the festival concept and branding identification. These included Sydney city decoration; transport advertising; TV and press advertising, and flags and posters in all participating venues, libraries, schools, cafes and shops. According to both the OAF marketing manager and the OAF programme manager, the campaign resulted in a high level of public awareness and recognition of the main imagery—an eye looking from behind a piece of corrugated iron—and the slogan: 'Intimate. Contemporary. True'. According to the festival artistic director, the poster of the festival also played a relevant role in terms of public identification

Figure 5.5 Festival of the Dreaming. Poster designed by Adrian Adams. Reproduced courtesy of the International Olympic Committee.

and was critical for the transmission of the programme character and fundamental aims:

> This poster is about Aboriginal art today. It's not always predictable didjeridoos, boomerangs, or dot painting. This is the contemporary nature of what we are—vibrant, creative and richly talented across all the arts. . . . This is a symbol of the future . . . [this says] we are looking at you, for the first time we're not being interpreted, we're telling you how it is. (Roberts cited in Hanna 1999: 66)

The design of the festival poster required prior approval by SOCOG Cultural Commission because it juxtaposed images that made political references to Indigenous oppression (Hanna 1999: 67). According to the festival artistic director, the gaze of an eye at the centre of the poster encapsulated the key to the festival, as it blurred the notions of a critical, confronting, condoning and curious approach to the spectators. The challenging look of the eye was intended to encourage viewers to participate in the poster and be part of the communication process, which proved very successful throughout Sydney and the state of New South Wales (*ibid*).

A Sea Change was presented to the media in May 1998. In order to promote the festival, a national 48-page guide listing all events and venues was created in accordance with the strategic aim to 'help people across the nation learn about the arts in their country' (SOCOG 1999a). One and a half million copies of the guide were distributed nationally, either through participating arts companies or through the press and newsagents.[8] Additionally, the OAF team designed a comprehensive series of web pages within SOCOG's site, listing all festival events and offering detailed information on all participating arts groups.[9]

The 1998 festival did not have a budget to fund a nation-wide promotional campaign. To compensate for this and maximise the coherence of communications of all participating venues, the OAF marketing services created a marketing guide that was made available to each venue hosting a festival event. The guide was a 22-page document called 'The Official Marketing Kit' for *A Sea Change* (SOCOG 1998d). It included brief information about the festival marketing objectives; communication channels to be used; the national advertising campaign, which was fundamentally placed in local newspapers and radio stations; the logo usage guidelines and applications, and a list of all available marketing materials. The latter included the official 48-page programme, the official souvenir poster and an over-print poster, radio tails and television tails where it was possible to add the name and details of specific projects and venues. Finally, the marketing strategy was accompanied by the circulation of a contemporary 'Anthology of Australian writing and photography', a book commissioned and published by the OAF, which was promoted as the fundamental bearer of the festival philosophy and principles. This book was distributed in most

Australian schools and public libraries as part of the festival educational plan and was to remain the clearest legacy of the event.

The festival for 1999, *Reaching the World,* was promoted mainly through brochures adapted to the place where each event was taking place in different venues around the world. Australian Foreign Embassies and Consulates assisted in the festival promotion in coordination with the Australian Tourism Commission in countries like the United States and United Kingdom. However, after the official media launch of the festival in November 1998 and the distribution of the festival official poster, there was not a

Figure 5.6   Book publication for A Sea Change. Cover design by Adrian Adams. Reproduced courtesy of the International Olympic Committee.

synchronised campaign taking place, neither through advertising nor public relations. Instead, two glossy documents were created and distributed to a selected range of audiences. The first document was the publication of a comprehensive guide to all the programmed events happening around the world with detailed information on the presenting companies and arts groups. The second document was a special commission titled 'Australia on Show', a publication documenting a wide range of Australian arts materials of interest to broadcasters that was promoted and distributed to broadcasting companies from Europe, America, Africa and Asia (SOCOG 1999c).

In contrast to prior festivals, *The Harbour of Life* in year 2000 was supported by a carefully planned and properly budgeted promotional campaign. The campaign started on 17 October 1999, soon after the official launch of the festival that took place on the 13th October of the same year at Sydney Superdome in Olympic Park. An important marketing decision was to change the name of the festival, from *The Harbour of Life* (as it had been referred to since the bid stage) into *Olympic Arts Festival*, thus appropriating the generic OAF term and reinforcing the Olympic association. A second marketing decision was not to make many references to previous festivals or the concept of a four- year Cultural Olympiad. The latter was justified as a 'marketing priority' by OAF senior staff (2000, pers. comm, 14 Aug) because, in order to maximise ticket sales, it was considered more relevant to ensure the identification of the 2000 festival and its association with the Olympic sporting competitions, than the promotion of continuity with regards to the Cultural Olympiad concept. During the Olympic period, a key element assisting in the promotion of the festival and its association with the Games was the city-wide placement of signs linking the five Olympic rings with the word 'arts', a design that had not been used in any of the prior festival years.[10] This is a key example of the advantage of having a general manager charged with the arts programme as well as the image programme, in particular, The Look of the Games. The communication benefits of such association are discussed further in Chapters 6 and 7.

In general, the promotional approach taken for the final festival revealed an emphasis on marketing objectives—ie. market targets such as ticket sales—over communication objectives—ie. expanding awareness and understanding about what the festival stood for. This was not the case for the prior festivals, as the expected lack of financial profits led to prioritising general communications over marketing efforts. This resulted in campaigns that were fully committed to supporting the ambitious conceptual promises of the bid stage, but lacked a clear focus. The OAF budget limitations had also a remarkable effect on the 1997–1999 communication campaigns. These limitations obliged the festivals to depend on free publicity or press coverage to effectively reach the public. In contrast, *The Harbour of Life* or *Olympic Arts Festival* in year 2000 was the only festival to count on a comprehensive marketing strategy and promotional campaign, as discussed in full within Chapter 7.

Ticketing

The OAF ticketing strategy varied from festival to festival. As already stated, while the three initial festivals were not expected to cover costs, the 2000 festival was designed to create some profit based on ticket sales as a main funding source. The tickets for *The Festival of the Dreaming* were managed through the services 'First-Call' in Sydney and 'Ticketek' in New South Wales, the usual entertainment ticketing network. *A Sea Change* and *Reaching the World* relied on the ticketing strategies of each participating venue. As such, none of them had a unified sales strategy. Conversely, the final festival in 2000 was supposed to sell tickets within the main Olympic ticketing system strategy. The expectations were that a joint Olympic ticketing strategy would increase the chances of achieving an association between the arts and sporting Olympic events and that the OAF would benefit from the main Olympic sales strategy.

Being part of the main Olympic sales strategy was supposed to ensure the appearance of references to the OAF in all ticket souvenir brochures and the distribution of arts tickets at all Olympic box-offices and general Games ticket marketing. Nevertheless, this strategy had some negative impacts. For example, the festivals were more likely to be perceived as a second choice in relation to the sporting events. This was assumed because a significant number of Australian tickets for the OAF were expected to sell after refusal for a first choice sports competition.[11] Further, the integration within SOCOG general ticketing strategy slowed down the production of the formal OAF programme, which could not be available until June-July 1999. International agents complained or were affected by the delay in publishing details on the programme and, in many cases, were not able to prepare Olympic tourist packages that incorporated a reference to the arts events. In addition, the so-called 'ticketing fiasco' that inflamed Australian public opinion from October to November 1999, endangered the OAF expectations of benefits from shared ticket marketing. Soon after the first Olympic sports ticket allocation ballot was published in October 1999, a general inquiry revealed the existence of a 'Premium Ticket Programme' consisting of ticket packages offered to individuals at inflated prices. A total of 400,000, tickets, including some of the most high profile sold out events, had been put out of the reach of the general public. The Olympics Minister, SOCOG Chief Executive, SOCOG group general manager, a SOCOG board member and ticketing subcommittee chairman were processed during the following months by a NSW parliamentary committee.

To counteract potential negative effects, a 'ticket crisis' document was prepared by the OAF team to prove the transparency and fairness of the arts festivals ticket allocation. In the document, the OAF department stated that 78% of the tickets were publicly available for Australian audiences (OAF senior staff, 1999, pers. comm., 11 Nov). In an interview conducted in November 1999, OAF senior staff acknowledged that the impact of the

Games ticket fiasco might prevent some people from booking tickets so far ahead in time—especially as all booking forms looked like the ones for sporting competitions. However, he relied on 'the quality and uniqueness' of *The Harbour of Life* programme to overcome the scandal frenzy and finally get 'the attention and interest the festival deserves' (*ibid*). The same OAF source accepted that criticism was justified on account of the 22% ticket hold having been made on the classical operas and star concerts that would be on stage during Games time. He explained the decision had been made to guarantee that international visitors who might not come back to Sydney had the chance to see a major event in the Sydney Opera House. In his words, '*The Harbour of Life* will begin a month prior to the Games with a more diverse and unique offer to Australia and it is then when national residents and Sydneysiders in particular will have complete priority' (*ibid*). However, the content analysis of media coverage on the

---

Table 5.6   Ticketing Strategy for The Harbour of Life Olympic Arts Festival 2000

First round: Prior to October 99—No specific information on the Festival programme was available.
- *May 30th 1999*—Publication of the official Olympic Bookings book. It included a page referring to the OAF but without details on programme contents and schedules. The OAF team justified this by saying it was too soon to sell arts events and because of the huge demand expected for Olympic sports.

Second round: After October 1999—Complete information on the Festival was made available.
- *October 1999 onwards*—Special ticket booking publication in Sydney and Melbourne papers *The Sydney Morning Herald* and *The Age* and mail out to all people who had booked sports tickets since May. The central Olympic ticketing system would advise those who had missed out on tickets for their selected sports events to reallocate their money to arts events (and other sports alternatives) instead of getting a refund.
- *December 1999*—Tickets on sale.
- *January 2000*—Alignment of OAF tickets within SOCOG ticketing system.
- *February-March 2000 onwards*—Access to OAF tickets through the telephone.
- *June 2000 onwards*—Box-office. Different sites around Sydney including all Olympic ticket-venues would have OAF tickets available. Cultural sites as Sydney Opera House would sell OAF tickets but no Olympic sports tickets.

Source: OAF team notes Sep.1999

festivals reveals that these arguments were refuted and criticised by the Australian press during year 2000 (see Chapter 9). Regardless, the OAF team was prepared to implement the 'joint-ticketing' Olympic strategy as initially planned and, by September 1999, had the strategy implementation scheduled as noted in Table 5.6.

The implementation of this strategy suffered many alterations during year 2000. After the alignment of OAF ticket sales with the general Olympic ticketing system at the end of December 1999, the OAF team found out that the coordination of all tickets within SOCOG was too difficult and resulted in slow processing and distribution. During February and March 2000, when OAF sales were made available on the phone, customers complained about the lack of training and information of SOCOG general sales operators with regard to the arts festivals. To solve the situation, the sale of OAF tickets was brought to a halt during April 2000 in order to transfer the overall management from SOCOG to the art-ticket network, 'Ticketek'. In May 2000, sales were made fully operational again, this time without any link to SOCOG sports ticket sales. May was also the month when sales were available on the Internet. The plan to open box-offices by June 2000 was kept as initially planned and promoted as such by May 2000.

Overall, the OAF ticketing experience exposed the many challenges resulting from trying to integrate an ambitious cultural programme within the far larger framework of Olympic sport programme priorities. Such an integrated ticketing approach has not been attempted in any subsequent Olympic Games editions.

BEYOND SYDNEY 2000

From a management point of view, there seems to be an ongoing division between a focus on integrated operations within the OCOG and a mixed model of management, combining a team located within influential government culture departments and liaising staff at the OCOG. Sydney followed an integrated model, and this has also been the case for Salt Lake City 2002, Vancouver 2010 and, in different ways, for Beijing 2008. Mixed models have been the preference for London 2012 and Torino 2006, as they have provided shared responsibilities for culture between the OCOG, government agencies and specially appointed quangos. Athens presented a completely different approach, establishing a separate and publicly managed organisation for the Cultural Olympiad, funded by the Hellenic Ministry of Culture.

The case of London 2012 is particularly interesting because this is the first Games to establish a nationwide Cultural Olympiad delivery structure involving special appointments in the form of thirteen full time regional creative programmers. These programmers operate in parallel to the OCOG and are only partially funded via the central Games budget. This gives an opportunity to introduce greater fluidity and flexibility in the management of activities throughout the country and could be considered the most appropriate model yet to enable significant Olympic-related cultural programming outside the host city. However, it also increases the risk of marginalisation from the main Games narrative and operations (García 2012).

Overall, regardless of the management model chosen, ongoing issues have been the continued lack of synergy with other Olympic programmes. This situation is exacerbated by the common practice to second staff from cultural government organisations on a short-term and rotating basis, thus not giving them time to fully come to terms with the overarching OCOG structure and identify opportunities for programme collaboration. Further, as in the case of Sydney, subsequent editions have relied on separate marketing and ticketing arrangements, which often focus on distinct, already established arts audiences rather than average Olympic audiences. Such an approach to marketing encourages the perception that the cultural programme is not part of the Games. Finally, despite an ongoing aspiration to establish nominal links between the Culture, Education and Ceremonies programme (particularly in the context of OCOG integrated models) these keep failing to materialise in specific joint activity. The most common trend is to present these three programmes as interrelated at the bid stage, develop them under the same management umbrella at the early stages of Games planning and then progressively separate them and make their implementation completely independent from each other so that, by Games time, they have no specific commonalities compared with any other Olympic programme.

London 2012 offers the additional challenge of having to find a route to ensure synergies between its regionally managed UK-wide four-year programme, and its OCOG-led and (mainly) London focused Games-time programme. Despite continued effort to protect communication channels by committing to monthly team meetings between the core OCOG team and regional programmers, pressures to ensure media attention and provide world class entertainment during the Games fortnight points at a preference for separate management and promotional structures, to the detriment of the visibility and Olympic association of the great majority of non-London based cultural activity.

SUMMARY

The team in charge of the OAF programme was part of the complex management structure within SOCOG. The programme was located in an influential division, Marketing and Image, which incorporated a wide range of programmes charged with the delivery of marketing matters, advertising, design and other promotional devices. However, the OAF did not establish direct links with the Games mainstream marketing and promotional structure, relying instead on its own separate sub-team.

In general, the OAF management structure was rather marginal within SOCOG's structure. Beyond the lack of interaction with marketing, the arts festivals were isolated from other programmes with a clear focus on cultural matters and an emphasis beyond sport. Notably, there was not a proper interaction with programmes that had or might have developed some common aims and objectives such as the Torch Relay, the Education programme, Community Relations and the Ceremonies programme. Furthermore, there was not a direct interaction with the committees in charge of addressing and collaborating with Aboriginal and multicultural communities in particular. This prevented the OAF from gaining profile within some widespread and outreaching community and educational initiatives such as the *Olympic Journey* and *Share the Spirit Student Art Prize*.

The programme's internal operations relied on very limited resources. Its budget was severely cut on repeated occasions, which diminished the ability to commission new work and develop appropriate communication programmes. This was accentuated by the OAF managerial isolation, which prevented the programme from building on the image and implementation successes of other programmes and from the appeal of the Olympic project in general, with some notable exceptions. Paradoxically, the one area where integration was attempted, ticketing, ended up failing and led to a last-minute separation of OAF tickets from Olympic sport tickets.

This situation suggests that the volume of mainstream Games operations is at odds with the requirements to deliver a successful and relevant arts programme and requires further consideration in order to maximise the benefits of managerial synergies while avoiding conflicts of interest.

The next chapter explores the operational needs and challenges emerging out of the OCOG's external operations programmes, in particular, the relationship with key stakeholders.

6 Managing the Programme
External Operations

Chapter 5 provides an insight into the internal structure and operations of the Olympic Arts Festival programme and its links with other programmes and divisions within the Organising Committee for the Olympic Games. Yet, a complete vision of the way the programme is delivered requires a complementary insight into the external management structures or, more specifically, the strategies that are used to engage existing and potential stakeholders of the Olympic project. An analysis of the relationship with Olympic stakeholders based in the host city and nation is relevant because these are key actors with an ability to influence the shape and scope of the Games and indeed, its cultural policy.

In present times, it is possible to identify three main types of Olympic host stakeholders, though clearly in each of these categories, there are overlapping roles and interests: (1) *the public sector* which, in Sydney 2000, beyond underwriting the Host-city contract, was involved in the two Olympic organisations acting in parallel to SOCOG: OCA and ORTA; (2) *the corporate sector* or Olympic sponsors, a critical source of funding for the Games since 1984; and (3) *the media*, without which, the Games would not be the global mega-event it has become today. For the OAF, a fourth area can be identified, namely the *cultural sector* or, more often, the arts community of the local host. This chapter summarises the external management strategies developed by the OAF team in order to approach existing or potential Olympic stakeholders in each of these areas.

ARTS COMMUNITY: THE ROLE OF SOCOG'S CULTURAL COMMISSION AND PUBLIC CULTURAL ANNOUNCEMENTS[1]

From the time SOCOG became operational in 1994, the organisation supported the development of strategies to approach the cultural sector, the arts community in particular, and to receive advice on how to design and implement the OAF programme, including staff appointments (often seconded from relevant arts institutions) and the design of an appropriate operational structure for arts delivery and promotions. On the same year, a Cultural Commission for the Olympic Games was established with an expected life-period of 6 years that would take it until the end of the Games. The appointed chairman was Donald McDonald, general manager of the Australian Opera since 1987, chair of the Australian Broadcasting Company (ABC), SOCOG board member and former chair of the Olympic Bid Cultural Committee. The Commission was originally composed of six SOCOG Board members and one SOCOG employee, charged with the preparation of a Cultural Implementation Strategy and overseeing the adaptation of the bid cultural proposal into a feasible arts programme. In 1995, SOCOG created a Cultural Committee also chaired by McDonald. The Committee comprised eight members representing a range of Australian arts organisations. It was decided that each member would chair an 'Artform Committee' in the areas of dance, theatre, opera, music, visual arts, indigenous arts and community liaison. These committees were composed of up to twelve members representing artists and arts organisations, and were established to put forward ideas and suggestions appropriate for the OAF. However, by 1996, the Cultural Committee and Artforms Committees were disbanded. This coincided with the resignation of the OAF first appointed executive producer and was framed by other major changes in the OAF structural composition. The Cultural Commission was re-established to secure appropriate liaison between the arts programme and SOCOG board but only at an advisory level and without the same degree of interaction with the wider arts community.

From 1996 onwards, the Commission's main task was to advise the Australian government on all aspects of the Cultural Olympiad or OAF and position the festivals in the community. Members met monthly and worked as a subcommittee of SOCOG. The Commission could influence the festivals' programme design but did not have the power to modify the final decisions made by the appointed artistic directors. OAF senior staff have indicated that the critical role of the Commission was its ability to lobby at SOCOG board level on controversial decisions (1999, pers. comm. 11 Nov). In June 1999, an important contribution by the Commission was to obtain the permission for OAF marketing staff to seek funds from non-Olympic sponsors provided that they were not direct competitors of the official commercial partners (in Sydney, the Team Millennium Partners). This is a significant achievement within the Olympic hosting process, given the tight control over commercial associations with the Olympic brand, as discussed in more detail later.

In the approach to the 2000 Games, artists and journalists stated unofficially that they were concerned about the possibility that Commission board members used their power of influence to benefit the organisations they represented. While the Commission members denied this, most of the institutions represented by the Arts Committees in 1996 and the Cultural Commission in its early stages had some level of involvement in the OAF programme from 1997 up to year 2000. However, the Commission membership changed drastically over time and ended by being composed mainly of SOCOG board members, who were not directly related to any arts institution (see Appendix 3).

There are no publicly available documents explaining the policies or principles followed to determine the festivals' contents. The only available documents outlining policies and criteria for the design of the programme consist of broad references to the commitment to follow the parameters set in the bid cultural proposal,[2] as well as the stated vision of respective festival artistic directors (see SOCOG 1998a, 1999a, 1999b, 1999c, 2000b). This is an established approach in most arts festivals around the world, which tend to be determined by the vision of their artistic lead, however, in the context of a one-off mainstream event of the magnitude of the Olympic Games, the expectation for total transparency and broad consultation in decision-making is high, and its absence is a factor that causes controversy and attracts criticism by members of the arts community, especially if they feel excluded from the process.

Sydney did attempt a public consultation during the initial inception of the OAF programme under the guidance of the first appointed OAF lead, acting as an 'executive producer'. Public invitations to artists and cultural institutions to present expressions of interest started in 1995 under the supervision of the Commission chairman, McDonald. These public invitations continued for some years, supported by the Cultural Commission and the festivals' respective artistic directors, as well as the OAF programme manager and the OAF general manager that replaced the first executive producer at the end of 1996. In 1995, the Australian press published a range of articles and advertisements calling for artists' proposals to participate in the OAF. In interviews with the press, McDonald stated that 'inclusion' was the key word (*McArthur Chronicle* 1995). In his discourse, while admitting that the Olympic Cultural Commission was not a funding or producer body, McDonald remarked that it offered artists the opportunity to be included and publicised within the Olympic arts programme.

However, by the end of 1996, major changes within the OAF team and delivery structure following on the resignation of its first appointed executive producer had some negative effects on the relationship between SOCOG and local as well as regional artists.[3] According to artists and arts institutions representing a range of community and minority initiatives, the encouraging promises of the immediate post-bid period were not transformed into a 'real' invitation to Sydney's diverse arts communities for inclusion in the programme.[4] This was felt to be the case despite the acknowledgement that some artists, Aborigines in particular, were offered great opportunities to be seen in mainstream stages both nationally and internationally.[5] Furthermore, artists from states outside New South Wales claimed not to have received sufficient information about their chances to take part in the event nor to receive support to put on new shows or exhibitions especially designed for the Olympics (Arts Queensland 1999, pers. comm., 25 Aug). This was felt to be a betrayal of the original bid vision for the OAF.

Despite the increasingly divided opinion within the arts community, by 1997, SOCOG approved the implementation of a 'Cultural Ambassadors Programme' to cover the four years of the Olympiad and encourage greater involvement by Australian arts organisations. The aim of this initiative was expressed in the following terms:

> to extend the brand of the Sydney 2000 marketing initiative domestically and internationally . . . foster closer relationships with flagship Australian arts organisations . . . [and] allow for performances and entertaining opportunities flowing back to SOCOG for Olympic partners, IOC members and special guests. (SOCOG 1997b)

The stated aims for the Ambassadors programme reinforce the impression that SOCOG's strategy to liaise with artists and arts institutions was mainly directed towards flagship artists and companies and less so towards community and minority arts groups. In subsequent years, the OAF general manager has justified this approach by emphasising the importance of the Olympic period as an opportunity for Australia to feel comfortable celebrating its elite artists in the same way as it was ready to celebrate its elite athletes. It is a move that he has termed 'the cry of elitism' (Hassall 2008: 310):

> . . . our most revered citizens are our most accomplished sports people. . . . Unfortunately, when an Australian artist triumphs abroad . . . there is not quite the same level of elation or public recognition. Nevertheless, the arts were able to take this duality of support and use it to our advantage during the Olympic Games cultural programme. For the first time in my memory, we could unashamedly promote the "elite' amongst our visual and performing artists. One of the challenges for our cultural programme was to resist the temptation to be all things to all people. There were many competing pressures on our programme. Whereas we would not think twice about presenting the finest athletes in the sporting events, we had a long battle to present only the best artists in the cultural programme. This was not to the detriment of inclusivity however. (Hassall 2008: 310)

Striking the right balance between an aspirational programme that would showcase the best of Australia's artistic offer and reflect the vision of respective artistic directors, at the same time as sustaining a commitment towards broad consultation and inclusion of the many voices representing the country's diverse artistic community was not easy to achieve and led to ongoing tensions with the arts community. This is a recurrent situation in the context of one-off large-scale cultural events, which are perceived to be a defining moment for the host city or nation (see Garcia 2004b). In Sydney, an attempt was made to overcome such challenge by setting up four festivals with different remits, as noted in Chapter 4, and also by designing the original OAF team structure to be led by an 'executive producer' that was to be supported by 'festivals producers'. Such delivery structure aimed to guarantee the continuity of all four festivals and ensure ongoing consultation with cultural stakeholders for any major decision.[6] Nevertheless, by the end of 1996, this formula had proven unsustainable in the context of SOCOG due to the lack of appropriate funding and the need to downsize the two middle festivals as well as avoiding branding conflicts. The producer delivery model was thus substituted by an, arguably, more agile structure where a general manager would oversee the work of directors and programmers without interfering with their artistic choices—including their criteria for inclusion and exclusion of acts—but retaining control of major operational issues such as marketing and public relations. The ultimate model for the OAF arts stakeholder liaison can be considered more effective in the context of an Olympic Games hosting process, but also less sensitive to local arts communities needs. This was particularly the case for the final and more spectacular festival in year 2000, as it was the one expected to have the best chance of defining 'Australia's place in the world as we approach the 21st century' (SOCOG 1997–2000) to a world-wide audience.

In 1998, the lack of open interactions with artists and arts organisations provoked abundant criticism by other festival directors such as David Blenkinsop (director of the Perth Festival during 22 years), Jonah Jones (former OAF executive producer), Rob Brookman (Adelaide Festival director in 1992) and Anthony Steel (Sydney Festival director 1995–97). Key names in the Australian arts world would coincide in their rejection of the SOCOG model. They would often concentrate their complaints on the role of the festival artistic director instead of SOCOG as a whole, perhaps indicating that they did not think it correct to attribute responsibility to define the state of Australian arts on one person alone, particularly if this person was uncompromising in defining a preferred vision for this event. From 1998 to 1999, the arts community's criticisms of SOCOG's arts management model had reached most Australian papers. In particular, it was notable how many articles were published highlighting the views that diverse arts leaders had against the OAF artistic director for 2000:

> [The OAF2000 artistic director] is an extraordinary marketer [and a] leader in raising sponsorship and gathering political support [but] what puts him on the periphery of the arts industry is that he doesn't talk to people. He does not work with people. (*The Weekend Australian* 1998, p. 23)

The effects of such disagreement over the best approach to manage external relations from the arts community point of view are discussed in more detail in Chapter 8.

Public Sector: Government Relations Strategy

As discussed in Chapter 5, the analysis of SOCOG's functional structure suggests that the OAF was not strongly related to—nor supported by—the main Olympic programmes dedicated to interacting with the public sector, including those programmes focused on the areas that were most central to Sydney's cultural vision at the bid stage, multiculturalism and Aboriginal reconciliation. SOCOG's Government Relations programme and Aboriginal and Torres Strait Islander (ATSI) Relations programme emphasised Aboriginal concerns and interacted with Australian federal, state and local government bodies for the supervision of transport, venue management, taxation, international accreditations, security and other related issues in a way that was sensitive to ATSI communities' needs. However, these programmes were not designed to engage with or champion artistic initiatives specifically. This was despite the fact that during press conferences and other public events, the programmes' respective leaders would repeatedly emphasise that cultural issues such as community and multicultural understanding were strongly supported, in line with the main ambition for the OAF programme. Internal sources at SOCOG indicate that a series of cultural and community related Olympic programmes had a major presence in both the Government Relations and ATSI Relations agenda. These were the Torch Relay programme, the Community Torchbearer Nomination process, the Volunteer Recruitment programme, the Look of the Games, the Pre-Games Training programme, and the Ticket Pricing and Ticket Marketing processes. In contrast, the official Olympic cultural programme was not considered a priority area and, consequently, the arts festivals depended on the networking ability of the appointed artistic directors and Cultural Commission members to approach and get the support of public institutions on an ad hoc basis. This was by no means a straight forward task, particularly given the degree of pressure on existing resource allocations. An added challenge, according to OAF representatives, was the perception that the arts were not seen as a priority at governmental level. Leo Schofield, director of the final OAF festival in 2000 put it this way:

> Our biggest challenge is to make governments understand the value of a culture to the country. The French governments understand perfectly, so do the Germans, so do the Koreans and the British. They see it as a source of prestige to the state, but we don't seem to see it that way. (Schofield 1998)

OAF senior staff have acknowledged the enormous difficulties faced by the OAF programme to lobby for government involvement (1999, pers. comm., 15 Sep and 11 Nov). Despite the generous support received for the implementation of the 1997 Aboriginal and indigenous festival, the OAF was not framed by a specific strategy to approach government bodies until September 1998, and this was aimed exclusively at getting funds for the final festival in year 2000. Consequently, a relevant number of the partnerships developed with public bodies were the result of those bodies' own initiatives and policy interests rather than an OAF lobbying achievement.

Two significant examples of the kind of partnership experience referred to previously involve the State of Queensland and the City of Sydney. In the case of Queensland, arguably the State (outside of New South Wales) providing the greatest level of support to the OAF in 1998 and 1999, the main reason for this involvement has been explained on the grounds that the arts festivals were expected to have a strong tourist appeal and bring a sense of Olympic ownership beyond New South Wales (Arts Queensland 2000, pers. comm., 25 Aug). In the case of the City of Sydney, official presenter of the OAF in the year 2000, the only festival to directly benefit from this partnership was *The Harbour of Life*, while none of the three initial festivals, having a focus beyond Sydney city district, received any relevant financial or promotional support. This suggests that the collaboration was led by the Council's pre-existing interests rather than an OAF-led strategy. *The Harbour of Life* was focused on the Sydney Opera House and harbour, the heart of the City of Sydney's cultural precinct, which could provide international benefits and spin-offs directly to the council. For example, the Olympic festival outdoors programme became mainly a showcase of the City of Sydney Public Art scheme.[7]

The main purpose of the OAF strategy to lobby government for support in 2000 was to secure grants from Australian and international government agencies to minimise the financial and programming risks of projects produced by the arts festival team. OAF senior representatives have explained that a key factor of the strategy was to seek support for specific projects rather than the festivals at length (1999, pers. comm., 23 Aug). Another factor was to allow the grants to be made directly to companies, as this was likely to be the preferred option for the funding agencies and would minimise OAF administrative responsibilities. This is indicative of the difficulty to establish Olympic-specific cultural policies and the ongoing challenge to attract special government funding to protect the vision of an Olympic cultural programme.

Initially, the OAF government funds strategy sought a support of approximately AU$2.5 million. Overall, six Australian government bodies and four international bodies were approached to support a mixture of established art pieces and new work that was to premiere at the OAF. Meetings were held from September 1998 and advice of confirmed support was received by mid 1999. In exchange for government support, the OAF offered a package of benefits including hospitality and logo identification/presence, aligned to the level of support provided, the project supported and the parameters of the benefit packages being offered to corporate sponsors. Table 6.1. indicates which national and international government agencies were initially approached and the approximate amounts that were requested in relation to specific festival components.

OAF senior representatives have indicated that most of these agencies confirmed funding, which was the core income source for the 2000 festival.

Table 6.1   The Harbour of Life 2000—Government Funding Strategy[8]

Australian Government Bodies	Proposed Events to Support	Total Requested
Federal: Australia Council	*Concerts*: Australian Youth Orchestra; *Dance*: Meryl Tankard Premieres: *Theatre*: Australian Theatre for Young People; *Dance*: DV8	A$ 260,000
Federal: ATSIC	*Dance*: Bangarra Dance Theatre, new work	A$ 50,000
Federal: Festivals Fund	*Theatre*: Don Quixote	A$ 50,000
State: NSW Ministry	*Concerts*: Sydney Symphony Orchestra, Gotterdamerung; *Theatre*: Don Quixote, Sydney Theatre Company, New Australia Play; *Film*: Australian Film Festival Premieres: *Dance*: Bangarra Dance Theatre; *Theatre*: Australian Theatre for Young People	A$ 260,000
State: Victoria Ministry	*Concerts*: Melbourne Symphony Orchestra	A$ 180,000
Local: City of Sydney	*Opera*: Deustchland Symphony Orchestra, Parsifal *Dance*: Australian Ballet/Opera Gala	A$ 300,000
European Union	*Concerts*: European Union Youth Orchestra	A$ 50,000
German Government	*Dance*: Pina Bausch *Opera*: Deustchland Symphony Orchestra, Parsifal	A$ 200,000 A$ 800,000
British Council	*Dance*: DV8, new work	A$ 100,000
United States Government	*Dance*: Bill T. Jones	A$ 150,000
	TOTAL	A$ 2,500,000

Source: Adapted from SOCOG (1997c)

The dedication of the OAF team to secure government funding for aspirational new pieces as well as internationally renowned and established art companies is a clear indication of the commitment to present an Olympic cultural programme of international significance, as proposed within the original OAF vision. Nevertheless, the ongoing need to act on a one-to-one basis rather than receiving central support from SOCOG suggests that the OAF was subject to reactive rather than proactive strategies for government involvement. This compromised the programme's ability to advance new cultural policy goals building on the Olympic momentum.

Corporate Sector: OAF Sponsorship Strategies

The OAF programme team structure included a marketing manager to liaise with Olympic sponsors and, more specifically, to create strategies and opportunities for engagement with the Australian based sponsors, the so-called Team Millennium Partners. The OAF general manager would also approach corporations via corporate presentations and functions organised with the assistance of the Special Events programme, which he also oversaw. Each of the festival's artistic directors would often take part in these presentations and functions, particularly in the lead to the final festival in 2000.

In 1995 the OAF team produced a 'Sponsor Information Kit' that was distributed among existing and potential Olympic sponsors. The kit included information about the history of the Games as a cultural and educational event and about the IOC requirements in regard to the production of an Olympic cultural festival. In 1995, the OAF was defined as a 'Cultural Olympiad', the terminology used for the Barcelona 1992 four-year programme, and this was the term used throughout the kit as well (SOCOG 1995: 4). The kit offered a full description of the member composition of SOCOG's then called Cultural Committee and announced the plans to create SOCOG's Cultural Division by the end of the year. This first document, a highly descriptive fact-sheet, was followed in 1996 and 1997 by promotional brochures inviting corporations to have some financial involvement in the festivals using standard marketing terminology.

By the end of 1995, SOCOG started negotiations with Fairfax, one of the main press publication companies in Australia, for it to become a Team Millennium Partner. Fairfax was in charge of four major newspapers so, following SOCOG sponsorship guidelines, it was awarded the title of Olympic media partner. Further, besides the average packages offered to Millennium Partners, Fairfax was offered the ownership of a series of 'core proprieties'; this consisted of an association as 'Presenting Partner' with a number of SOCOG specific programmes, such as the Torch Relay or the OAF. In exchange, SOCOG requested a series of 'media assets' to be provided by Fairfax. This consisted of advertising space, supplement publications with Olympic information and assistance in publishing documentation about all the agreed core proprieties. By mid 1996, Fairfax had agreed to become Sydney Team Millennium Partner for the period of 1997–2000 and SOCOG initiated discussions so as to define the core proprieties the company would be more interested in owning. In the end, it was decided that Fairfax would own the right to be associated with the OAF and that its Sydney paper, *The Sydney Morning Herald*, would be the official presenting partner of the four festivals. This agreement involved a commitment in terms of value in kind support but no cash funds. Consequently, the SMH role was to secure a minimum amount of publicity support for each festival. This included a specially designed logo attached to all published articles about the OAF during the 1997 and 2000 festivals; the publication of special newspaper supplements prior to each festival; assistance to publish brochures and booklets, and the provision of daily advertising space for the 1997 and 200 festivals.

Further to these initial negotiations, sponsor kits and corporate presentations, it was not until 1998—with the final and most box-office oriented

festival in view—*The Harbour of Life* or *Olympic Arts Festival 2000*—
that a detailed corporate sponsorship strategy was created. Thus, none of
the pre-2000 festivals had secured significant sponsorship deals. Funds for
The Festival of the Dreaming in 1997 had been essentially donated by public bodies or taken from the OAF budget, while the 1998 and 1999 festivals
did not have any special sponsors beyond the already existing agreement
with the *Sydney Morning Herald*, a grant by Arts Queensland in 1998
and some branding support from the City of Sydney in 1999. In contrast,
for year 2000, the aim was to attract additional private funds that would
allow putting into place special productions during Games time and an
appropriate promotional campaign to secure extensive awareness among
Australians and international visitors.

When the strategy was first designed in August 1998, it expected to
raise AU$6 million through the sale of sponsorship packages. Leo Scho-
field, OAF 2000 festival's artistic director, would be in charge of making
the necessary presentations to potential sponsors. However, by 1999, the
outcome of such negotiations was not clear. As a journalist put it,

> Schofield's programme for next year's 12 week event [OAF'2000] . . . is
> likely to be dependent on the goodwill of local companies, his success
> at raising sponsorship and overseas government's contributions in get-
> ting productions to Sydney. It is the goodwill factor that might be the
> hardest to find in competitive Sydney. (Usher 1999: 21)

The sponsorship packages requested A$3m for the status of 'presenting
partner' and A$800 for the status of 'cultural partner' in exchange for a
selection of tickets to festival events, special functions at the Sydney Opera
House and other venues, and appropriate sponsor logo recognition. In contrast, Olympic sponsors uninterested in the OAF argued that in the context
of the Olympic Games, where the association with sport prevails as 'top-
of-mind for most audiences, media and corporate guests', the high rates
demanded in exchange for a package of cultural hospitality made the deal
resemble patronage or donation rather than a win-win business partnership
(Telstra Olympic Manager 1999, pers. comm., 2 Sep). Alternatively, corporations who might have preferred access to arts rather than sports hospitality tended not to be Olympic sponsors in the first place and, therefore,
were denied commercial access to the OAF. This situation suggests that
some of the major difficulties faced by the OAF team in order to secure corporate sponsors are the requirements outlined in IOC and, consequently,
SOCOG marketing regulations, which are designed to protect and support
the sporting competitions rather than the cultural programme.

The prohibition of corporate support from non-Olympic sponsors was
re-negotiated by SOCOG's Cultural Commission in 1999. Subsequently,
from June 1999, it was agreed that the OAF was allowed to seek cultural
partners outside of the Olympic sponsorship pool as long as these corporations product or service category did not conflict with any of those

represented by the Team Millennium Partners. This led to agreements with arts and entertainment companies that would cover the expenses of specific performances in exchange for name recognition in the official OAF programmes. As OAF senior staff noted, this benefited both the OAF and the arts company (2000, pers. comm., 6 Oct).

Another important difficulty for the OAF to approach corporate sponsors is the IOC demand that both Olympic and non-Olympic sponsors remove all commercial signage from any designated Olympic venue (see Chapter 7). This presented particular conflicts in the case of the OAF, as most, if not all, festival cultural venues had their own on-going partnerships with corporate sponsors, who in turn requested their logo to be appropriately acknowledged at all times. Additionally, the OAF programme required, by its very nature, the development of partnerships with cultural organisations external to SOCOG, which meant that the programme could not be totally framed by the current IOC sponsorship guidelines the way it happens with the sporting programme. This accentuated the conflict over brand recognition and signage. Consequently, the OAF team required extensive negotiation within SOCOG's areas of Finance, Risk Management, Legal, Sponsorship and Communications, as well as with arts companies, venues and artists, in order to ensure that the IOC guidelines were respected at the same time as they were implemented with appropriate flexibility. The OAF general manager, the OAF programme manager and the OAF marketing manager undertook this task, particularly in the 1999 to 2000 period.

Another challenge arising from the signage ban for the OAF's sponsorship strategy was the high investment needed to capitalise on the Olympic association beyond the initial purchase of sponsorship rights. In short, as IOC regulations prevented the use of commercial branding in Olympic venues, Olympic sponsors were compelled to promote their Games association through alternative media, which meant extra investment and strategic efforts. As such, one sponsorship relations manager at SOCOG noted that, 'sponsors tend to focus on the most visible and publicly expected facets of the Games such as the ceremonies, torch relay and key sporting competitions, including star athletes or teams, and are generally insensitive to the OAF's appeal' (1999, pers. comm., 1 Sep). Furthermore, the prohibition to showcase sponsors' brands in Olympic venues has traditionally provoked a risk for 'ambush marketing' strategies by non-Olympic sponsors, which can be especially difficult to monitor in the context of cultural venues.

Ambush marketing is defined by the IOC as all intentional or unintentional attempts to create a false or unauthorised commercial association with the Olympic Movement or the Olympic Games (IOC 2000a).[9] As a direct effect of that threat, in order to protect and justify the value of the partners' Olympic rights, the SOCOG Sponsorship division followed strict IOC regulations to fight this possibility. The measures taken by SOCOG created an extra concern for many companies supporting projects or funding venues somehow associated with the Games without having the right to be official Olympic partners. Indeed, this was the case of most long-term arts and cultural venues sponsors in Sydney. Olympic arts venues for the 2000 festival such as the Sydney Opera House, the Art Gallery of NSW, the Australian Museum or the Powerhouse Museum were supported by a majority of corporations not involved in Olympic sponsorship deals. These corporations might not have had any interest in being associated with the Games. However, they were affected by SOCOG regulations if the arts group they sponsored was included in the OAF programme. Taking into account that most Olympic arts productions were not exclusively funded nor curated by SOCOG, the resulting 'acknowledgment' conflict became a major issue. The resulting situation is discussed in more detail in Chapter 8, which outlines the OAF stakeholders' point of view.

MEDIA: OAF PUBLICITY STRATEGY

In an interview held in September 1999, the OAF publicity manager expressed confidence in the likely media impact and success of the *Olympic Arts Festival* for the year 2000. In her words, 'the department has had four years to build the event and we have learnt from the difficulties faced in previous festivals' (1999, pers. comm. 1 Sep). National and international media had been approached since 1995, with a special emphasis on the Australian press and specialist magazines. From 1997, contacts with broadcasting corporations had been made through the festivals' respective artistic directors. In particular, Australian public networks—ABC and SBS—had been very supportive. In the run up to the final 2000 festival, there were plans for the creation of a Cultural Command Centre and Cultural Media Centre to assist the provision of Australian arts information and festival contacts to both local and international media during Games time. These did eventually materialise in the form of an OAF Media Office within the so-called Sydney Media Centre, as discussed later.

The OAF publicity strategy was the most significant dimension of the OAF external relations strategy. This was due to the non-existence of a consistent budget to produce formal advertising campaigns prior to year 2000. As such, there was a great dependence on 'free' media coverage for most events to get known and the distribution of media releases became a key factor. From 1997 to 1999, most publicity efforts focused on the distribution of media releases about the 'Olympic Arts Festivals' concept, then about the theme and programme of each festival and, in the last instance, about specific arts groups and shows. A similar amount of press releases was prepared and distributed each year. The distribution was done at the official media launch of respective festivals and, subsequently, by fax or post to Australian arts journalists and to selected international media.[10] However, the media impact of each festival varied considerably.

In 1997, the OAF publicity team worked full time from May to late October to provide information on *The Festival of the Dreaming* and the process resulted in abundant coverage by most Australian media, especially Sydney based. To explain the massive coverage of the festival, the OAF publicity manager has acknowledged the importance of political issues related to the state of the Aboriginal population in Australia and emphasised that in 1997 there were not many Olympic related news to compete with. In contrast, both *A Sea Change* and *Reaching the World* had a very poor media presence despite the intensive mail-out of press releases to national and international journalists. The Olympic editor of the *Sydney Morning Herald* (SMH), the leading paper in the city, tried to justify this by pointing out that the year-long multiform concept of the 1998 and 1999 festivals was 'confusing'. In his opinion, 'these festivals could not possibly catch the attention of the media as much as other Olympic happenings such as transport upgrading, venue design and building and, indeed, IOC related issues such as the Olympic crisis happening at the time' (1999, pers. comm., 13 Oct).[11]

According to the OAF publicity team, by year 2000 it became clear that the poorly funded OAF publicity strategy alone could not guarantee a wide media presence for each festival. The content, purpose and placement of the festivals played a fundamental role in attracting the media. In this sense, *The Harbour of Life* was expected to be the festival that the public would remember and associate with the Olympics, and the festival attracting greater coverage by all Sydney and Australia major press and broadcasting media, as was indeed the case (see Chapter 9). The publicity team also expected that the OAF would play a greater role in year 2000 in other Olympic channels such as Olympic sponsors' corporate magazines and SOCOG publications—ie. Education programme materials or the special year 2000 Olympic family communications intranet 'Olympic Info'.

Table 6.2 includes a draft of the planned publicity strategy for the year 1999–2000 as sketched by the OAF publicity manager in 1999.

Generally, in order to approach the media through means other than press releases, the OAF needed to build on interest from other mainstream Olympic channels because the department did not have the resources to put on special community, public and media relations activities on its own. Therefore, an important task of the OAF publicity consultancy was to secure the inclusion of references to the OAF throughout SOCOG publications and media programmes. However, a great limitation was the lack of a centralised information database. This prevented an effective control and awareness of all communication materials distributed by the different SOCOG areas.

As an example of the above, key media publications such as the official 'SOCOG Media Guide', which was reviewed and updated regularly, did not always offer accurate information about the arts festivals. For example, in its Games time edition, the Media Guide failed to provide a correct update of data about the 2000 arts festival. The Guide for January 2000 noted the change of name of the 2000 arts programme from *The Harbour of Life* to *Olympic Arts Festival*. However, the issue distributed in September 2000 (arguably the issue that would reach the greatest range of media)

Table 6.2   Publicity Strategy for The Harbour of Life or OAF'2000

1. Leading to the event . . .
OCTOBER 1999—main point to promote: Olympic association
Planned activities:

- Announcements: Artistic director addressing Foreign Correspondence Association and potentially the National Press Club.
- Official launch (13 Oct 1999): 700 journalists over the world invited. Expected attendance: 300. Journalists will be provided with press kits -all information on the event. TV and photo opportunities.
- Official programme publication (15 Oct): booklet insert in SMH and The Age.
- Official programme mail-out: 3000 copies to media agencies and relevant government organisations such as the Australian Trade Commission, Tourism NSW etc.

FEBRUARY TO JUNE 2000: main point to promote: Leo Schofield's [arts director] festival.
Planned activities:

- Phone bookings.
- Individual booking details collection.

2. During the event . . . *(expectations)*
AUGUST 2000: main point to promote: curtain raiser of the Olympic Games competitions. Planned arrangements and expected support:
Press coverage.

- Fairfax- *SMH:* (official presenter) daily major review page; photo coverage.
- *The Australian:* (Team Millennium Partner) secure good news stories.

TV coverage

- *Seven:* (Team Millennium Partner) make arrangements to get 'vignettes' in the middle of sporting coverage. Concerns: The channel is generally focused on sport and entertainment and is mainly concerned with sporting competitions coverage.
- *ABC:* (Public broadcaster. Status as 'cultural channel' in Australia. SOCOG media partner) secure broad coverage, long format report in programmes such as 'The Arts Show', 'Arts Today'.

Radio coverage
- *ABC:* (as above) secure broad coverage, long format reports and programme discussions.

Strategy to ensure references to the OAF throughout most Olympic publications:

- OAF monthly publication on the evolution of the Festival.
- Delivery of kits to key areas: Education and Olympic Info intranet, communications, marketing.
- Olympic Sponsors magazine: ie. flying company *Ansett:* very good coverage in their *Airlines* magazine.
- Official Supporters magazine (Fairfax and City of Sydney) internal magazines and publications.

Source: Notes by the author based on sketches by OAF publicity manager, September 1999

went back to referring to the festival with its previous name without noting the remarkable changes that the festival concept had undergone after 1999 (see SOCOG 1999i, 1999j, 2000a).

In year 2000, the amount of OAF media information on display increased dramatically. Besides the mail-out of regular press releases, a Cultural Media Centre was created with the name 'Olympic Arts Festivals Media Office' within the Sydney Media Centre (SMC). The SMC was a media centre for journalists who were not accredited by the IOC to cover the Olympic sport competitions. It was run by several government agencies with a focus on the promotion of business, tourism and cultural stories. The SMC required a separate registration process to gain access but was far less limiting than the official Olympic media centres (which involve strict guidelines in exchange of access to Olympic venues and athletes) and was open to all journalists, including freelancers (see Miah García 2008). The OAF media office was planned in conjunction with *ausarts2000*, a project run by the Australia Council and was promoted at *ausarts2000* website and at a range of other government newsletters and web-pages including the Australia Council, the Australia Tourist Commission and the New South Wales Government. Both the SMC and the Sydney Opera House (the venue for all performing arts events during year 2000) held a number of press conferences to present the OAF to the international media. Additionally, in order to link with the Olympic accredited media, a small office providing information on the festivals was placed at the Olympic Main Press Centre in Olympic Park. Other media initiatives to support the OAF included SOCOG's website, which contained an 'archives' page with links to press articles about the OAF, and the incorporation of sixteen OAF press releases within the 'Olympic Info' intranet. The latter was a computer network set up during Games time to provide detailed information about the Games organisation, especially about sports competition schedules and immediately updated competition results.[12] The inclusion of OAF information within the 'Olympic Info' service can be seen as an important achievement because the net was specially targeted (and only available) to the IOC invited Olympic family members, including all accredited media. 'Olympic Info' computers were located at all Olympic venues in the 'restricted entry' areas dedicated to the media and Olympic family. These computers were also located at all Olympic media terminals such as the Main Press Centre and the International Broadcast Centre and at official accommodation venues such as Olympic Family hotels, the Olympic Village and the Media Village.

However, in contrast with the situation at the SMC, the presence and visibility of information about the OAF within the Olympic official or accredited media centres was poor. The OAF office at the Main Press Centre was under-resourced and registered such a low activity that the staff contracted to attend enquiries were gradually transferred to the SMC. By the second week of the Games, the office was left unattended, only provided with some brochures about the *Olypic Arts Festival 2000* and a note encouraging interested journalists to visit the non-accredited media centre. Furthermore, the International Broadcasting Centre, home for the television right-holders and radio stations, did not hold any information or reference about the Olympic cultural programme.

BEYOND SYDNEY 2000

Since Sydney 2000, the main strategic advancement to engage stakeholders has been in terms of media communication platforms. After Sydney's successful delivery of a non-accredited media centre with space for dedicated cultural programme information, this has become an established practice in every subsequent host city, both in Winter and Summer editions. Interestingly, this progress has been mainly led by local or national agendas (ie. developing medium to long term tourism and wider business opportunities) rather than Games related agendas. In parallel, these centres have also attracted growing numbers of alternative media with a particular interest in socially and culturally sensitive story angles. By Beijing 2008, however, this operation became centralised and managed via the organising committee, which made it an environment at times even less accessible than the official Olympic media centres (Miah Garcia 2008). The official cultural programme also featured within this environment, but the kinds of journalists invited to access the venue and engage in the stories were less diverse than had been the case in previous non-accredited centres and less focused on cultural and arts coverage (op.cit.). In the lead up to London 2012, the city has established a 'London Media Centre' with backing from a public-private partnership funded by the Mayor of London and commercial partners. The focus is clearly on promoting business and tourism opportunities with a strong corporate angle.[13] At the time of writing, it is still unclear whether the Cultural Olympiad and related cultural and arts programming will feature high in the Centre's agenda, although London 2012 sources have indicated that an additional media centre will be created to promote the Games-time arts festival and related cultural stories (2012, pers. comm., 16 Jan). It is also unclear whether small independent publications and bloggers may be given access to such facilities, as had been the case up to the 2006 Winter Games. As an alternative, a social-media led movement called #media2012, has been established with the aim to capture Cultural Olympiad and other non-sports oriented Olympic stories without any dependency on formally regulated media structures but aiming to secure some kind of formal relationship with Olympic culture stakeholders that may otherwise struggle to secure media visibility.[14]

Strategies to engage other stakeholder have remained variable. The public sector was a priority stakeholder for Athens and Torino, to the point that the cultural programme was led by the municipality (Torino) or the national ministry (Athens) rather than the OCOG. Athens is an extreme case as the cultural programme was entirely overseen by a specially appointed agency, the Hellenic

Culture Organisation. Other host cities, however, have not developed any kind of government-oriented strategy for culture, as was the case in Salt Lake City.

The arts community tends to be disenfranchised, with the kinds of criticisms noted for Sydney being replicated in almost every subsequent Games edition. In London, the existence of regional creative programmers has meant that there is a far wider range of opportunity to fund and engage local arts communities. However, these links have often been disregarded as non-Olympic enough (because they have not involved the use of clearly recognisable Olympic branding in the years leading to 2012) or have ignored the Games link altogether. Paradoxically, in the UK, there is also the perception that creative programmers have been more proactive with the arts community when based outside of London, while the two programmers based at the host-city are said to have less free reign to encourage new arts activity and little capacity to satisfy the levels of demand for communications and engagement emerging out of London's extensive creative sector (London 2012 creative programmer 2008 pers. comm. 15 Dec. and 2009, pers.comm. 10 Jul).

Finally, sponsor relations have kept fluctuating, depending on the OCOG's vision—which often correlates with its geopolitical context. As such, North American hosts have always developed special strategies to engage private groups, be it independent donors (Salt Lake City) or corporations (Vancouver) while corporate involvement has been practically unnoticed within southern European countries (Athens, Torino) and Asia (Beijing). London has followed Sydney's model signing in various corporate sponsors in the form of 'Premier Partners' for the cultural programme, as well as relying on public funding.[15] However, the main innovation to maximise stakeholder involvement has been the creation of a non-conflicting brand, 'Inspired by 2012', which is designed to tag cultural activity and identify it as part of the 2012 Games umbrella, without clashing with the commercial interests of Olympic global partners. It remains to be seen whether this alternative form of branding may become a viable way forward to increase the visibility and Games association of cultural activity. So far, ongoing challenges remain the requirement to avoid any for-profit link (which is increasingly difficult for growing numbers of cultural practices, as they try to align themselves with creative industries activity and attempt to become financially viable without dependence on public subsidy) and the possibility that the Olympic association remains weak, particularly from an international point of view, given the removal of the Olympic rings and the term Olympic. Clearly, such branding strategy is mainly dedicated to domestic partners and audiences.

SUMMARY

OCOGs tend not to establish distinct stakeholder involvement strategies to support the cultural programme. This is accentuated by the fact that there is often a gap between the expertise and networks established to support the bid (at the time of maximum ambition for culture) and the confirmation of full time positions to operationalise the programme. Rather than strategies being OCOG-led, respective cultural stakeholders try to figure out a way to link into the Games depending on other ongoing agendas. As a result, the cultural programme is one of the areas most reliant on secondments from cultural agencies. This allows rationalisation of resources and synergies with established local or national cultural policies, but limits the continuity of vision, priorities and understanding of the specific needs for the programme in a Games context.

As noted in Chapter 5, the Sydney OAF programme was managed in isolation from most mainstream Olympic activity. This resulted in a replication of resources (separate marketing and media relations planning for the OAF) and lack of visibility within key SOCOG strategies and operational programmes. A further negative effect of the programme's managerial isolation was that it weakened its chances to establish a strong strategy to approach and lobby external stakeholders. SOCOG had specific programmes to approach government, sponsors and the media respectively. However, the OAF was not part of these programme's agenda and rarely did it benefit from the agreements that SOCOG established with these groups.

This situation was particularly poignant in the case of sponsors, because the Olympic sponsorship strategy was designed in a way that clearly benefited the sporting competitions at the expense of those Olympic programmes that did not yet have an established public profile. In the case of the media, the OAF developed an extensive publicity strategy and succeeded in being part of key media contact points such as the Sydney Media Centre and the 'Olympic Info' system during year 2000. However, the OAF was not clearly integrated within the mainstream Olympic media relations programme and, further to its marginal position in the lead up to year 2000, at the time of the Games, its presence in the official Olympic media centres—the Main Press Centre and the International Broadcasting Centre—was almost non-existent.

On the whole, the lack of strong and centrally coordinated strategies to approach stakeholders indicates that the cultural programme was not well placed to secure optimal positioning to meet its original objectives. Instead, its success depended on the willingness and particular interests of respective partners. This suggests that SOCOG's management structure did not respond to or support a defined cultural or arts policy. Decision-making was based on economic imperatives with a view to supporting tourism, business and sporting achievements rather than guaranteeing a coherent cultural strategy. This situation limited the ability to capitalise on resources and ultimately, reduced the impact and sustainability of the OAF programme.

7 Marketing and Communications

This chapter explores the key principles that underpin current Olympic global communication and marketing strategies and reviews SOCOG's specific implementation model in the lead up to and during the 2000 Games. The aim of the chapter is to contextualise the promotional strategy of the Sydney OAF and to identify established Olympic communication parameters that have yet to be adapted to the characteristics of a cultural programme. This analysis highlights ongoing tensions that reveal the need to develop clearer coordination between global communication marketing imperatives and locally sensitive cultural policy requirements within the Olympic Games staging process, a theme that continues to challenge recent Games.

The chapter begins with an overview of Olympic global marketing policies and programmes as defined by the IOC, with an emphasis on the framework that informed the Sydney 2000 Games. Section two describes the procedures SOCOG followed to implement the IOC communication and marketing policies, and section three provides an overview of the communication strategy and operational plan for the OAF final festival, focusing on the rationale for its distinct iconography. The chapter concludes with a discussion about the degree to which general Olympic marketing and communications guidelines in Sydney were consistent with the strategies applied to the cultural programme.

Most of this chapter is based on direct observations, personal interviews and the analysis of internal documents accessed over two years of research and work placements at SOCOG in 1999 and 2000. Given the unique nature of my internship and the level of access provided to rarely documented event hosting processes, it has been deemed valuable to provide as much detail as possible about my original sources to support my analysis as well as provide future reference points about materials no longer accessible.

IOC MARKETING AND COMMUNICATIONS: GUIDELINES AND APPLICATIONS

The main reference document on the marketing policies and programmes of the IOC is the 'Olympic Marketing Fact File', which is updated on a regular basis (see IOC 2011). The 1998 'Olympic Marketing Fact File' (IOC 1998a) was the document to frame and inform key marketing and communication operations for the Sydney 2000 Games and is thus the main reference point for this chapter. This document explains that Olympic marketing is composed of a series of revenue generating programmes covering broadcast rights, sponsor partnerships, licences, ticket sales, coin programmes and philatelics. In the 1990s, the IOC distributed 93% of the final revenue among Olympic Family members, which comprise OCOGs, National Olympic Committees (NOCs) and International Sports Federations. Such division has remained stable to date, with 90% going to Olympic Family members and 10% retained by the IOC (IOC 2011a). The revenue is also used to finance the Olympic Solidarity programme, which supports developing nations in order to promote sport and assist Olympic athletes in their travel expenses to attend the Games.

Within the Olympic Marketing programme, the sale of television rights to broadcast the Games is the largest component and represented close to 45% of the total Olympic revenue in 1998, 51.2% in 2000 (IOC 2000a: 3), 53% by the end of the Athens Games in 2004 (IOC 2008c) and 47% by the end of the Beijing 2008 Games (IOC 2011b). The Olympic Sponsorship programme is the second largest component and, by 2000, it represented approximately 33.5% of total revenue (up to 44% by 2008). This programme is organised in three levels: the IOC world-wide programme or TOP (The Olympic Partners), the OCOG national programme (which in Sydney was named 'Team Millennium Partners' or TMP) and the NOC national programme. Each sponsorship level offers the participant corporations the exclusive right to use images and Olympic brands or symbols in different marketing regions for limited periods of time. At another level, the Licensing programme is also a relevant component of Olympic marketing dedicated to the commercialisation of products officially considered under license by the host OCOG, NOC and IOC.

One of the main aims of the IOC Marketing Department is the implementation of long term marketing programmes inspired in the success of activities developed by each OCOG to avoid recreating a new marketing structure for each Games edition. With this in mind, to assist in the coordination and assimilation of the central IOC marketing efforts, in 1998 the Marketing Department created a 'Marketing Communications Manual,' which would act as a key communication policy reference for OCOGs. This manual resulted, for the first time in an OCOG, in the creation of a Marketing Communications programme within SOCOG to inform the 2000 Games.

One of the most distinct dimensions of this new communications policy document was the explicit request by the IOC that all OCOG marketing communications become 'intimately familiar with the operations and programmes of other OCOG departments [as well as] the IOC' (IOC 1998b: 46). Areas that were emphasised for Sydney and which have remained priority areas for marketing coordination hence, included the following,

- *IOC Image Programme*: This programme encompasses all marks, imagery and official designations such as the Olympic rings, motto, anthem, film footage and photography
- *Broadcaster Relations Programme*: This programme oversees all broadcast rights agreements, to ensure rights holders are clearly identified and their programming and public announcements well negotiated. The latter implies the requirement that Olympic broadcasters give preference to partners (Olympic sponsors) rather than to non-partners in the distribution of advertising time during Games time
- *The Licensing Programmes*: This includes the Games mascots programme and Olympic Marketing Partner premiums regarding the use of licensed products such as pieces of clothing and commemorative souvenirs
- *The Ticketing Programme*: The association with this programme is required at two levels. First, at the level of the TOP Partner recognition programme, which has the responsibility to ensure that the back panel of each ticket bears the corporate logos of TOP partners. Second, at the level of Media Education and Public Relations programme. This programme, is responsible for combining any information on ticket availability details and statistical information with information on the partners on the course of any media event or press conference
- *The Look of the Games Department*: This department manages the logo and basic design elements of a given Olympic Games, and ensures consistency of use with all OCOG Marketing Communications department materials
- *The OCOG Media and Community Relations Department*: Coordination with this department is considered essential to maintain consistency and reduce redundancies in the OCOG's information output. The interrelation between both programmes plays a role in the definition of promotional strategies for the Games in general and might affect the design of the Cultural Olympiad strategy

Further recommendations include the organisation of 'Partner Workshops' twice per year in order to present updated information on the OCOG marketing plan to the IOC, and the need to consider the so-called 'IOC Promotional Programming and Public Service Promotional Announcements' which, in 2000, consisted of a contract agreement with Olympic broadcast right holders that obliged them to air IOC Public Service Announcements to promote the Olympic Movement. This included the first generic Olympic advertising campaign produced by the IOC under the slogan 'Celebrate Humanity'.[1]

SOCOG MARKETING AND COMMUNICATION PROGRAMMES

In order to implement the IOC's policies for marketing and communications, SOCOG established a communication structure for operations comprising more than thirty separate responsibility areas with at least four layers of management. The complexity of these operations was accentuated by the ongoing changes taking place within SOCOG's internal structure, which, expectedly, also led to changes in the function and location of the divisions or groups in charge of marketing and communications. The need to undergo significant structural changes over a concentrated period of time is a situation common to all OCOGs and this has been recognised by the IOC, which provides ongoing support to ensure a smooth transition and minimal disruption to the perceived coherence of general Olympic and Games specific communications. Coming to terms with this turmoil is essential for Cultural Olympiad programmers, with the additional challenge that they tend to require a different timeframe and greater flexibility in communication agreements with non-official Olympic partners.

For the purposes of simplification, this section describes the state of communication divisions and programmes as it was in year 2000, at the time when SOCOG operated under its Games time structure.[2] As explained in Chapter 5, during that period, SOCOG was divided into two parts: a functional structure and an operational structure. SOCOG's functional structure was also divided in four major management groups, each of which played a critical role in securing the correct implementation—operations—of the Games. Critically, communication or marketing related programmes existed within all of them, in line with IOC requirements. Three groups were fully dedicated to promotional or communication tasks: the Marketing and Image group, the Media Information group and the Games Support group. Table 7.1 provides a simplified listing of the marketing and communications related programmes in these groups.

The Sydney 2000 communications plan aimed to achieve maximal integration during Games time. The process to integrate all or most communication channels involved a series of special initiatives or priority communication agendas. SOCOG internal documents (2000d) describe three of these agendas in the following terms:

- *Involvement/Come to the Games*: aimed at generating public enthusiasm and maximising involvement. The OAF was one of the programmes identified as relevant to achieve this goal. Other priority programmes were Ticket Marketing, Torch Relay Media and Marketing, the Volunteers programme, Aboriginal and Torres Strait Islander Relations, Multicultural Affairs, National Education programme, Sponsor Hospitality and Consumer Products
- *Structural objections*: aimed at counteracting negative Games time logistic pre-conceptions that could inhibit public involvement. Programmes that were sensitised towards this issue and led to special communications were Transport, Accommodation and Security in particular

Table 7.1   SOCOG Marketing and Communications Programmes in 2000

SOCOG Functional Structure

Marketing Group

Management Group / Division	Games Time Functional Area	Programme
Olympic Arts Festivals and Image	Look of the Games Cultural Programme / Entertainment	Image OAF Special Events
Sponsorship	Sponsorship	Sponsor Hospitality Sponsor Servicing
Consumer Products	Merchandising	Olympic Stores Consumer Products, Licensing and Concessions
Marketing	Marketing	Marketing Communications Marketing and Advertising Media Partners

Games Support Group

Management Group / Division	Games Time Functional Area	Programme
Government Relations / Protocol	Aboriginal and Torres Strait Islanders Relations Government Relations Government / VIP Protocol	Aboriginal and Torres Strait Islanders Relations Federal Government Relations International Relations NA

(continued)

Table 7.1 (continued)

Communications and Community Relations	Communications	Communications Services Community and Public Relations Corporate Communications Multicultural Affairs National Education Publications

Media Information Group

Management Group / Division	Games Time Functional Area	Programme
Media Information	Media Information	Media Information

Commercial Group

Ticketing	Ticketing	Ticket Marketing

SOCOG Operational Structure

Operations Group

Management Group / Division	Games Time Functional Area	Programme
Torch Relay	Torch Operations	Torch Relay Media and Marketing
Sport	NOC Services	NOC Services
	IOC Relations and Protocol	IOC Relations and Protocol

Source: SOCOG 1999k: 1–4

- *Games time public communications*: aimed at providing spectator information, public information, wayfinding and communicating instructions to deal with incidents. Priority programmes were the Publications, Advertising, and Media programmes

The definition and wide promotion of these communication agendas allowed 'an organised way to timeline the big picture of the Games experience, prioritise communication requirements and maximise synergies between the communication areas' (SOCOG 2000d: np.). To service these agendas, SOCOG centralised the authoring and distribution of most of its Public Information documents such as press releases and fact-sheets, along with a Public Information database and calendar. For the latter, this involved compiling video-tapes and documentation from all high-profile speeches, public relations exercises, sponsor and media events, call centre services and other Olympic Information centres. These processes took place during the Olympic period in September 2000. In contrast, from 1993 to 1998, there was a lack of centralisation of information and a lack of interaction between programmes. Up to year 2000, as discussed in Chapter 5, this situation prevented the integration of information about marginal or non-sports related programmes such as the OAF within the general Olympic marketing and communication strategies. This is an indication of the isolation within which the OAF programme was managed and promoted. The effects of this lack of integration are discussed later on in this chapter.

In order to offer a specific example about how marketing and communication strategies were designed and implemented at SOCOG and to offer a point of contrast with OAF arrangements, the following sections outline the approach to managing Sponsorship programmes, and the main functions and components of the Marketing division and Communications and Community Relations division respectively.

Sponsorship Programmes

As noted in previous sections, a key characteristic of the Olympic sponsorship policy is the emphasis on exclusive negotiations, so that only one company by product category can become the official sponsor of the Games. SOCOG created eight main 'cluster definitions', from food and beverage to natural resources, sports equipment and media, and only approached organisations that represented specific exclusive categories within these broader definitions. The sale of sponsorship rights for the Sydney 2000 Olympics delivered approximately 40% of the OCOG net revenue to stage the Games, compared to 44% by 2008. Following the policies of the IOC Olympic marketing programme, SOCOG raised this revenue by selling intellectual property, accommodation, tickets and hospitality in exchange for cash, products and services from the sponsor organisation.

The Sponsorship programme ran a series of market research projects to investigate potential sponsorship opportunities, around which it then designed a sales strategy. The strategy involved the creation of a specific vocabulary—e.g. all sponsors would be known as 'partners'—and a detailed outline of levels of sponsorship, which included cash investment, value in kind (VIK) and cause-related marketing opportunities.[3] Depending on the levels of sponsorship, companies would have varying levels of access to associations with the range of Sydney 2000 intellectual properties. Intellectual properties included the use of the names and images of the 'Sydney 2000 Olympic Games', the 'Sydney Organising Committee for the Olympic Games', the 'Australian Olympic Committee' and the 'Australian Olympic Team'. Depending on the amount of investment, the use of intellectual properties would be allowed in one or other media. For instance, at the lowest level of investment, companies were allowed to incorporate the logo of the agreed intellectual property into company stationary products. At the highest level, companies were allowed to incorporate the logos within their television commercials.

In Sydney 2000, the top level of Olympic sponsorship was called 'The Team Millennium Olympic Partners'. This was the first time in the history of Olympic marketing that the traditional TOP programme, comprising the Movement world-wide sponsors, was combined with the Games major domestic sponsors as a single entity. Olympic sponsors within this group had access to the best Olympic packages of intellectual properties, hospitality and so on. The only difference between the rights of TOP versus domestic sponsors was that, while TOP sponsors could promote their Olympic associate world-wide, domestic sponsors could only use their privileges within Australia. On a second level, there was the 'Supporter' programme. This programme granted, in Australia exclusively, a limited set of rights and benefits. The most valued was the right to utilise the Sydney 2000 branding emblems in the broadcast media. Finally, on a third level, there was the 'Provider' programme, which had different sub-levels in terms of sign and imagery usage. This level mainly consisted of organisations associated with operational goods and resources.

The use of VIK investments is one of the key resources for the preparation of the Olympic Games, particularly at a local level. Consequently, SOCOG was dedicated to exploring the best VIK opportunities. For example, a feature of the Sydney 2000 Sponsorship programme was the establishment of official sponsorship with national media organisations, which would become 'Media Partners'. As already stated, this resulted in the involvement of the two main Australian publication companies (Fairfax and News Ltd) as official Olympic partners and assisted in the development of a national media network, which could communicate key Sydney 2000 messages through the press. In exchange for their investment, organisations acquired a set of rights and benefits defining their association with the Olympic Movement or the Olympic Games in particular. The sliding scale of rights and benefits was proportional to the sponsorship investment and was termed the 'value chain'. SOCOG internal documents state that sponsorship rights included access to Olympic emblems, designations, symbols and imagery for use in conjunction with business activities. Approved designations varied from generic ones such as 'Official World-Wide Sponsor for the 2000 Olympic Games' to more specific ones like 'Official Presenter of the Olympic Arts Festivals'. Approved symbols included official pictograms, and imagery elements included the use of the colours and patterns of the official Look of the Games.[4]

There were some Olympic marketing properties that were developed with the dual purpose of offering sponsors incremental marketing opportunities and for creating a secondary revenue stream for SOCOG. These were known as 'complimentary properties' or 'core assets' (SOCOG 2000d) and included the *Olympic Journey Tour* 1997, the OAF 1997–2000, the National Olympic Education programme, the Volunteers programme, the Test Events programme, the International Youth Camp and the Olympic Torch Relay (*ibid*). Each 'core asset' property had its own Olympic emblem, which enabled sponsors to market themselves in association with that property. In many cases, the marketing opportunity was the result of a sponsor becoming the 'presenting sponsor' of one of SOCOG's operational programme. This was the case for the *Sydney Morning Herald*, which became official sponsor of the OAF.

Marketing Division: Functions and Strategies

In common with most Olympic Games hosting processes, the complexity and high fluctuation of SOCOG communications structure made it difficult for Olympic marketing plans and strategies to be fully centralised. Rather, they depended on several programmes placed at different divisions and management groups. However, following the requests of the IOC marketing department and its published manuals, SOCOG developed a specialised marketing programme to respond to the multi-programme marketing requests of the organisation. This resulted in the creation of two specific programmes within SOCOG Marketing group: the General Marketing and Advertising programme and the Marketing Communications programme.

The Marketing Communications programme was a first-time initiative by SOCOG, created to follow the guidelines of the new 1998 IOC Manual. The programme was initially set up as part of the Marketing and Image group to provide a link between marketing and media programmes in SOCOG. Among other things, it focused on assisting the negotiation of media assets with Australia media sponsorship partners, such as Fairfax and News Ltd. The programme was supervised by the General Marketing and Advertising programme up to August 1999 when, along with the overall change of structures leading to Games time operations, Marketing and Communications became a sub-programme of the Media Programme within SOCOG Media group.

'General Marketing and Advertising' was the programme overseeing most marketing initiatives and was in charge of designing marketing guidelines that ranged from the description of general sponsorship and core asset 'value chains', to detailed guidelines about the usage of mascot imagery. The structure of this programme displayed in Figure 7.1.

Figure 7.1 conveys a direct relationship between the Marketing and Advertising programme and SOCOG's core revenue-based marketing programmes, such as Sponsorship Sales. It also indicates the role of the programme to supervise all marketing activities associated with Ticketing, Torch Relay, Volunteers, Test Events, Consumer Products and Olympic Football—all of them denominated 'core assets' for marketing purposes. Finally, the figure reveals a strong interaction between the programme, external advertising agencies and media partners working in collaboration with SOCOG. The interaction of the Marketing and Advertising programme with media partners was particularly significant because 'it involved the negotiation of sponsorship agreements for a myriad of valuable media assets' (SOCOG sponsor relations 1999, pers. comm., 1 Sep). Representatives from the SOCOG sponsor relations team

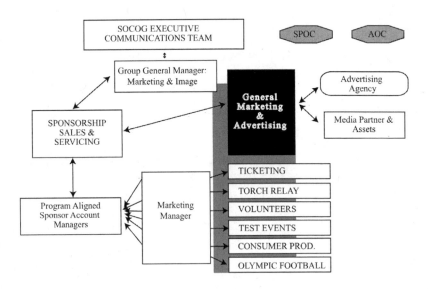

Figure 7.1　General Marketing and Advertising Structure in SOCOG. Source: SOCOG 2000d-Marketing Communications

assert that these negotiations led to establishing relationships across all media groups, from television, magazines and newspapers (all of them Team Millennium or TOP partners) to radio, cinema and outdoor media (all of them Supporters) (see Table 7.2).

The management of media assets was overseen by Marketing and Advertising and budgets were allocated on a programme-by-programme basis. According to the Sponsorship-Media partners management team, revenue generating programmes such a Ticketing received the largest allocations, which implied a strong presence in all sorts of media. In contrast, programmes such as the OAF were not seen as revenue generators and, therefore, had very limited allocations. The terms of the negotiation of assets varied by media type. Internal documents at SOCOG reveal that certain limitations included the time when the media could be used, as not all years of the leading period between 1997 and 2000 were of the same interest for partners. There were also important restrictions regarding the inclusion of logos and corporate branding external to SOCOG. The latter made it more difficult to establish messages that related to SOCOG's advertising programmes, which were directly supported by Games sponsors such as the Torch Relay and Ticketing programmes. This, as already indicated, was one of the key elements (and challenges) of the negotiation for the placement of OAF advertising.

Another key role of Marketing and Advertising was to guide and coordinate SOCOG's main advertising campaigns. According to SOCOG internal sources, the organising committee took a proactive approach towards setting the Olympic communications agenda. The objective was to set a strategy that maintained a significant level of positive Games support and pride.

Table 7.2 Involvement of Media Groups as Olympic Partners

Category	Sponsorship Level	Partner
Television	Team Millennium	Channel 7 and Prime (regional affiliate)
Magazines	Team Millennium (TOP)	Time/Sports Illustrated
Newspapers	Team Millennium	Fairfax News Limited
Radio—commercial	Supporter	Talk Australia Network Sky Radio Network
Radio—non commercial	Supporter	Australian Broadcasting Corporation
Cinema	Supporter	Val Morgan
Outdoors	Supporter	Buspak

Source: SOCOG Sponsor relations manager 1999, pers. comm., 1 Sep

This was particularly relevant at the time of the IOC scandal that occurred in the early part of 1999.[5]

SOCOG's main brand advertising campaigns were ongoing from 1997 up to year 2000 and had two main stages. The first was from 1997 to 1998 with a celebratory style and the second was from 1999 to 2000, which had a sales orientation:

- January 1997: 'The Journey Begins'. This first campaign involved a series of television and radio commercials running between 15 and 30 seconds. The commercials covered venue constructions, environment issues and athlete preparations. They were a continuation of the bid communications that had made popular the slogan 'Share the Spirit'. This slogan would be developed in all following advertising communications
- Christmas Day 1998: 'Share the Dream—Share the Spirit'. This was a second campaign including four different television commercials, some running 60 seconds and some 45 seconds. The first commercial was entitled 'Remember When', and was aimed at the domestic audience's pride in winning the Olympic bid by capturing the moment of the victory both in Australia and overseas. The last three featured athletes training overseas and one national athlete training in Australia
- 1999 onwards: The third campaign introduced new advertisements, this time focusing on revenue programmes such as Ticketing and Consumer Products

Within the celebratory style campaigns, the series portraying athletes training were the most broadly distributed. This was the case for Games advertising within Australian television, radio, cinema, magazines, street billboards and promotional materials presented at overseas Australian embassies and diplomatic outposts of the Australian Department of Foreign Affairs and Trade. Internal sources indicate that they were so successful that they were also considered for inclusion within the IOC international marketing programme. This situation provides a further example of the popularity of sporting traditions in Australia and the pride attached to the achievements of athletes. As argued in subsequent chapters, this diminished the chances for non-sporting messages to prevail within SOCOG's communication agenda, particularly the local arts and culture elements.

Further to the interaction with media and other partners and the design of advertising campaigns, another main function of the Marketing and Advertising programme was to ensure sponsor recognition and sponsor presence strategies. The aim was to guarantee the visibility of references to Olympic partners throughout SOCOG communications and to avoid confusions with non-sponsors. In that regard, there were a series

Figure 7.2   The Look of the Games. Reproduced courtesy of the International Olympic Committee.

of commercials addressing the question of 'ambush marketing' in order to get the domestic market to 'look for the Games symbols as used by official Games sponsors' (SOCOG 2000d: np).[6] Also, in addition to traditional media support, SOCOG pursued active sponsor recognition in the following areas:

- SOCOG publications such as 'News Relay', 'Sydney Spirit', primary ticket publications, Volunteer publications, SOCOG Annual Reports
- Press kits to all visiting media
- SOCOG Internet site
- SOCOG stands in Australian events such as the Royal Easter Show
- Stands in information centres by sponsors such as the Westfield Information Centres, AMP Tower Screen etc
- SOCOG headquarters
- Australian Olympic Committee publications, headquarters, functions

In terms of sponsor presence, there was a specially designed Look of the Games imagery that included references to sponsors. A prominent example of this was the flag poles placed throughout Sydney main streets and avenues during September 2000 (see Figure 7.2).

Communications and Community Relations Division

SOCOG's Communications and Community Relations division (CCR) evolved from a single communications coordinator in 1994 to an entire division in charge of eight different programmes by 1999. The primary goal of the communications function was 'to ensure the distribution of information to the general public, local and international media, and government, business and community organisations' (SOCOG 2000d). As a first public communications initiative, by late 1995, the Public Relations area of the division incorporated a 'Speakers Group' to coordinate all briefings by SOCOG staff and volunteers directed to community and government groups. With time, public relations initiatives would be directly addressed to Olympic partners, media, key stakeholders and key community groups, such as Australia's diverse ethnic communities and school children. Aboriginal groups were another differentiated communication target. This community was addressed by SOCOG's Aboriginal and Torres Strait Islander Advisory Committee, which was under the responsibility of the Government Relations division.

In 1997, the CCR division took a more concrete form and integrated several communications specialists, including two Public Information officers, a Multicultural Affairs manager, and a manager for the 'Olympic Communicators' Speakers Bureau'. In that year, key events conducted by the communications team were the *Olympic Week*, *SOCOG call centre* and the first stages of the National Education programme. In contrast, the

Communications programme was not involved in supporting *The Festival of the Dreaming* with any sort of community or public relations event. Furthermore, plans for subsequent years were to support community initiatives such as the *Olympic Ambassadors Programme, Olympic Neighbours* and *Welcoming the World* but not the OAF as such.

After 1997, the CCR mission statement read that it was 'to inform and inspire all Australians to embrace the spirit and ideals of Olympism and to engender and build their support for the Sydney 2000 Olympic Games' (SOCOG 1998c: 3). According to SOCOG, the strategic plan resulting from this statement was inspired by the pillars of the Olympic Movement. At this stage, SOCOG defined them as 'sport, education (youth),[7] culture, environment and equality' (1998c: 4). The aim of the strategic plan was to secure the association of these ideals with each of the fundamental components of the Sydney 2000 Olympic Games. In 1998, these were listed as 'Sports, Volunteers, Olympic Torch Relay, Ticketing, Education, Environment, Olympic Arts Festivals and Sponsors' (*ibid*). With this in mind, a three-year communication plan was established under the following themes:

- 1998: *The year of awareness*—focused on 'creating national and international awareness of the Sydney 2000 Olympic Games' and launching the Games central pillars
- 1999: *The year of involvement*—focused on 'encouraging national community involvement and participation'
- 2000: *The year of support and ownership*—focused on 'creating international and national support, excitement and ownership of the Games' (1998c: 4–5)

The target audience and geographical areas of the plan were described as follows:

> [*Target Audience*:] the general Australian public, community and sporting groups, school students, Australian youth, business and tourism groups, venue-host councils and their communities, sponsors and media'. [*Geographical areas*:] Sydney, regional New South Wales, national and international through Department of Foreign Affairs and Trade and the Australian Tourism Commission. (SOCOG 1998c: 5)

To accomplish these objectives, the CCR division was structured, by 1999, in eight different programmes, each of which addressed a different target:

- *Corporate Communications* coordinated the public delivery of SOCOG key messages and ensured public communications synergies among Olympic right holders (Olympic Inc. group, including OCA and ORTA) and other partner organisations such as tourism and commerce agencies;

- *Community and Public Relations* was dedicated to raising awareness of the Sydney Games among all Australians and supported SOCOG marketing and sponsors with community based activities and links to community media;
- *National Education Programme* was set up to reach 'over three million Australian students from kindergarten to Year 12' (*op. cit.*: 13). To achieve this, the programme organised a national student art prize, distributed educational and entertaining materials to all schools and created a specially designed Internet site
- *Multicultural Affairs* was a programme focused on encouraging the involvement of multicultural communities in key Games related areas and provided input to all SOCOG programme areas 'to ensure access and equity for Australia's diverse society in relation to the Games' (*op. cit*: 14)
- Finally, the *Communication Services* programme consisted of three sub-programmes: Public Information Coordination, Publications, and Research and Information, all destined to coordinate, support and complement other communications programmes and other SOCOG divisions

As a whole, the CCR division was an area of SOCOG composed of programmes which were strongly interlinked and linked to other non-divisional programmes, such as Marketing in the case of Corporate Communications, or Media Information in the case of Community and Public Relations. The different communication teams shared responsibilities within common communication projects such as the publication of 'Share the Spirit', which was one of the longest lasting and most widely known of SOCOG periodicals. Another example was the design, planning and implementation of *Welcoming the World*, an initiative designed to enhance the Olympic experience of overseas visitors, which involved corporate networking, ethnic community support and children's participation. Also incorporated in these communication projects was the creation and distribution of information systems, such as the placement of computer terminals or 'Infopoints' for Olympic Family members, the establishment of call centres, and the placement of information booths in popular shopping centres and Australian major public events such as the *Royal Easter Show* or *Australia Day*. However, the CCR did not include specific programmes to support the OAF which, instead, relied on its own separate communications and marketing strategy.

THE OLYMPIC ARTS FESTIVALS COMMUNICATION AND MARKETING STRATEGY

The above sections indicate the complexity and scope of SOCOG marketing and communications structure. In this context, the OAF had a marketing and communications plan set up by its own separate marketing consultancy and related to other SOCOG promotions only tangentially. Arguably, this led to a sense of isolation and minimised the presence and influence of OAF communication initiatives over other Olympic communications, but it also provided a sense of independence and greater flexibility that facilitated decision-making and adapting messages and techniques to more specific audiences.

This section provides an overview of the promotional strategy established for the final Sydney *Olympic Arts Festival* in 2000, which was the only OAF event supported by a detailed marketing and communications plan and separate branding.[8] The section presents detailed information on how the festival iconography was developed, how target audiences were defined in the context of the wider Games hosting process and what media were utilised to reach out to them. The exploration of the festival promotional strategy offers an insight into the possibilities for a more coherent interaction between cultural and communication policies within a sports mega-event.

Communication Objectives

The festival for year 2000 intended to be 'the culmination of the Olympiad, a festival on a scale to match the grandeur of the Olympic Games' (SOCOG 2000b). The main aims of the festival were to define the finest elements of Australian culture; to present a number of works on a grand scale 'unlikely to be seen again in a lifetime'; and to establish artistic legacies (*ibid*). These culturally informed aims were to be transformed, in communication terms, into the following objectives:

- to reach all Australians and ensure international coverage
- to secure the association of the arts festival with the Olympic Games
- to maximise the visibility of OAF events during the Olympic period, and
- to emphasise the uniqueness, great scale or high standards of the work and artists presented (OAF marketing manager 2000, pers. comm., 22 Aug)

To understand how the communication objectives were transformed into operational messages, target audiences and campaign coverage, it is necessary to consider the relevance of marketing principles in the 2000 festival. In contrast with the 1997–1999 period where 'there had not been financial or profit expectations but only the expectation of legacies in terms of co-operation and acknowledgements by general Olympic or OAF stakeholders' (*ibid*), the final festival was set up to recover most of its investment through ticket sales. Consequently, the planning and implementation of a detailed marketing strategy became as relevant as the planning and implementation of a culturally informed communication strategy. Ultimately, the festival marketing objectives became a key driver for the design of its cultural and communication objectives which, at times, led to some contradictions with the original OAF vision and mission statement.

Concepts and Iconography

As discussed in Chapter 5, in an effort to secure maximum visibility and a clear differentiation of the *Olympic Arts Festival* in year 2000 from other arts festivals in Australia, the OAF marketing team was fully dedicated to maximising the association of the 2000 arts events with the Olympic Games celebrations. As such, the team dismissed all communication elements that had led to confusions about the 1997–1999 festivals. According to the festival artistic director, *The Harbour of Life* was to be the 'Olympic' festival by excellence (Schofield 2000, pers. comm., 9 Mar). This was imposed as a critical need from a marketing point of view because it was the festival that required major ticket sales, and the target market needed to be an 'Olympic market' rather than a typical arts market in August and September 2000 (OAF marketing manager 2000, pers. comm., 22 Aug). From the perspective of image and communications, the emphasis on the Olympic association was also critical because this was the one festival that would coincide with the sporting competitions and was aimed at showcasing events on a 'big scale' to match the grandeur of the Games (Schofield 2000, pers. comm., 9 Mar).

However, this marketing and sales imperative also led to overlooking the communication requirements of the OAF as a four-year Cultural Olympiad. According to the bid mission statement, each OAF festival was supposed to balance its respective thematic focus with the themes explored in other editions, so as to ensure an acknowledgement of the wider vision for the Olympiad. Nevertheless, as noted in Chapter 5, the festivals in 1998 and 1999 had a very low communication impact and the success of the Aboriginal festival in 1997 was too distant in time. Furthermore, none of the previous festivals had succeeded in leveraging an Olympic association. Thus, the feeling of a communication failure and the pressures of marketing to ensure that the final festival was a financial success, led the 2000 artistic director to undertake major modifications of the festival concept and imagery.

The two major modifications affecting the communication of the final festival were the adaptation of its name and the development of a new visual identity, including a new logo and colour patterns. After more than six years referring to it as *The Harbour of Life*, the festival's rebranding as the *Olympic Arts Festival* implied an appropriation of the concept that, so far, had been used as a generic term to denote the four festivals of the

Olympiad or *'Olympic Arts Festivals'* in plural. Journalists, arts institutions and opinion leaders required a period of transition to understand and assimilate the change of name. However, immediately after the formal launch of the final festival and announcement of the new brand imagery in October 1999, the OAF team eliminated references to *The Harbour of Life* in the festival promotional material. This rapid transition was not fully assimilated by all stakeholders and in year 2000, only months after the formal announcement of a name and imagery switch, there was still over 10% of media coverage calling the festival by its previous title. Furthermore, a range of SOCOG publications in year 2000 referred to the festival as *The Harbour of Life* rather than its new title, a clear indication of the lack of coordination between the OAF and other SOCOG communication programmes. Among them was the 'Sydney 2000 Media Guide', a general reference document widely distributed among international media at the peak Olympic period in September 2000 (see SOCOG 2000a: 77). This resulted in some title confusions and inconsistencies within the press, as noted in Chapter 9.

The aim to maximise visibility, recognition and clear Games association also implied the progressive suppression of all references to the prior festivals, so that no ambiguities were introduced. The *Olympic Arts Festival* (from now on, *OAF'2000*),[9] would be thus publicly introduced as a festival in its own right and not as the culmination of the Olympiad, as originally envisaged. In this context, brochures, merchandise, pocket guides, advertising posters, mail-outs, special promotions and most information kits would not include information about the 1997, 1998 and 1999 events. Furthermore, the SOCOG website substituted the extensive information hosted on the web pages of the three prior festivals with a succinct summary page that did not link to any additional information.

Development of a Strong Imagery: Olympic Art

Another fundamental component of the new communication strategy was the development of a comprehensive *'OAF'2000* look' or design plan. This led to a transformation of the festival iconography which was meant to enable a noticeable 'step forward to secure the high impact of the promotional campaign' (OAF marketing manager 2000, pers. comm., 22 Aug). The first component of the new look strategy was a series of posters and decorative motifs displayed on occasion of the festival's official launch in October 1999. They were coloured in bright orange and deep purple, the new festival colours, and featured the superimposed shadows of a female silhouette intertwined with computer graphic designs made out of thin lines, the latter being an abstract reference to the sails of the Sydney Opera House. This choice differed from the imagery of prior festivals, which had

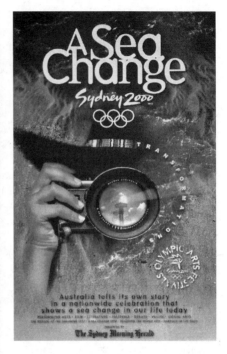

Figure 7.3   Central imagery for each of the four Olympic Arts Festivals. Credit: 1997 to 1999 Posters designed by Adrian Adams, 2000 poster by Emery Vincent. Reproduced courtesy of the International Olympic Committee.

been represented by clearly figurative images. For example, *The Festival of the Dreaming* consisted of an Aboriginal eye looking behind a plaque of corrugated iron. For *A Sea Change*, the imagery entailed a photographer surrounded by sea images and for *Reaching the World*, it consisted of a girl jumping over the faded image of planet Earth.

The breadth of this book does not allow for a detailed analysis of the images shown in Figure 7.3, but it is worth noting the change of approach for the final festival in regard to its visual iconography. The strong visibility of the festival colours were described by the OAF programme manager as 'paramount for the impact of the extensive outdoors promotional campaign put in place in August 2000' (2000, pers. comm., 6 Oct). In fact, a major component of the campaign was the display of over five hundred banners showcasing the *OAF'2000* orange and purple motifs throughout the city of Sydney, a first for an Olympic cultural programme. The use of *OAF'2000* banners throughout the city was made possible by the dual role of the OAF general manager as the person in charge not only of the OAF but also the highly successful Look of the Games programme. This situation is indicative of the relevant synergies that can be established between the cultural and wider communication agenda of the Games, which can be a crucial route towards greater visibility and clearer identification with the Olympic narrative.

Beyond the choice of colours and background features for generic *OAF'2000* promotions, the communication plan focused on highlighting the Olympic character of the festival. This was achieved by including the image of the five Olympic rings in all print materials (such as flyers, posters,

Figure 7.4 OAF'2000 city banners imagery. Reproduced courtesy of the International Olympic Committee.

Figure 7.5   OAF'2000 billboards in 2000. Reproduced courtesy of the International Olympic Committee.

bus-shelter advertising) and by linking the word 'Olympic' to each of the art-forms composing the festival programme. The 'Olympic' wording was divided into seven main categories: Olympic Theatre, Olympic Opera, Olympic Music, Olympic Sounds, Olympic Dance, Olympic Film and Olympic Epic. Furthermore, in the case of outdoors advertising, an alternative 'Olympic' series was created, this time associating arts images with sports-related concepts. Some examples were the image of one of the festival's orchestra accompanied by the phrase 'Olympic coach', and the image of a group of dancers under the phrase 'Olympic training'. Other billboards created an association to terms that were popular within Olympic sport coverage such as using the phrase 'enhanced performance', which is reminiscent of the term 'performance enhancement', a common topic of media discussion in relation to issues such as doping in sport (see Figure 7.5).

The combination of the Olympic rings and the word 'Olympic' resulted in the creation of a new logo for the 2000 festival that substituted the generic OAF logo utilised since 1997. The new logo (shown in Figure 7.6), composed of the Olympic rings plus the word 'arts', played a fundamental role in the street direction displays set up throughout Sydney during August and September 2000.[10]

This logo was displayed at all central squares and streets of the city to indicate the placement of the closest venue for the arts festival. On many occasions, the logo shared space with the generic Sydney Olympic 2000 logo—which indicated the direction towards sports competition venues—and the logo of the *Live Sites!* outdoors entertainment programme.[11] These three logos were also utilised in most of the city guide maps distributed to tourists.

Figure 7.6 The evolution of the OAF logo (generic 1997–1999; specific 2000). Reproduced courtesy of the International Olympic Committee.

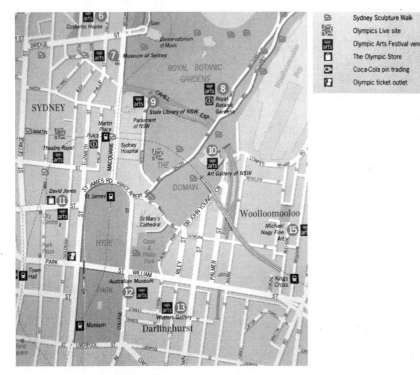

Figure 7.7 Sydney maps in August 2000, including the OAF'2000 and LiveSites logos. Source: 'OlympicArt' visual arts brochure, SOCOG (2000i). Reproduced courtesy of the International Olympic Committee.

Table 7.3 Evolution of the OAF'2000 Design Plan

- October 1999: *OAF'2000* media launch—presentation of new name and festival imagery
- October 99–January 2000: promotion of chosen colours: orange-purple (key concepts: esoteric, clear, direct)
- June 2000: emphasis on the Olympic rings and the word Olympic preceding event genres (eg. Olympic Music, Olympic Theatre)
- June–July 2000: show specific advertisements: use of the Olympic rings and the word 'Olympic' in these adverts
- August 2000: main outdoors campaign—orange and purple flags; wayfinding on display throughout Sydney—Olympic rings + arts logo

Source: Sketches by OAF marketing manager (2000, pers. comm. 22 Aug)

Figure 7.6 shows an image of the OAF generic logo and the *OAF'2000* logo. According to the OAF programme manager, the latter achieved a much wider recognition than the prior one (2000, pers. comm., 6 Oct). Arguably, a key reason for this was the greater simplicity and directness of the *OAF'2000* logo. Other factors relate to the levels of direct promotional support available to each of them. During the 1997–2000 period, the use of marketing and advertising was practically non-existent. In contrast, the *OAF'2000* logo had the advantage of being supported by a strong promotional campaign and of being displayed throughout the city of Sydney as a 'way-finder' sign acting in parallel to the widespread Look of the Games city dressing devices.

The design plan for the new *OAF'2000* imagery evolved from the end of 1999 up to mid year 2000. The different stages are summarised in Table 7.3.

Target Markets and Sales Strategy

The 2000 arts festival was designed to maximise sales income in order to recuperate losses from prior arts festival investments. This led to the development of a detailed ticketing strategy and the implementation of a large advertising campaign, which focused on the promotion of tickets for shows happening from August to early September 2000 (the 'pre-Games period'). The *OAF'2000* marketing plan indicated that up to 71% of the festival revenue was expected to be earned through ticket sales during the pre-Games period, when there would be no clashes with the top Olympic sports events (SOCOG 2000e). Key events on promotion were the *Symphony for a thousand*, performed by a thousand musicians at the Sydney Superdome in Olympic Park and a weekend package of world music called *Hemispheres*. Both events were designed to attract a wide audience combining both existing arts audiences in Sydney and new audiences such as 'Olympic ticket holders who wished to complement their sporting events with entertainment' (*ibid*).

The sales strategy faced the many changes affecting the ticket sales implementation, which, as noted in Chapter 5, ranged from modifications in the operational system,[12] to modifications in the delivery system.[13] These changes, and consequent complaints by the public, brought some negative publicity by mid year 2000. However, this was counteracted by the promotion of a specially designed *Olympic Arts Festival* music CD in May 2000 and the launch of the most popular events for the pre-Games period, including *Hemispheres* (launched in June 2000), the film festival *Sunscreen* and the free visual arts programme, both launched in July 2000.

The OAF team decided to focus on the local market during the pre-Games period and this resulted in promotional strategies directed mainly towards audiences in Sydney and New South Wales, followed by the State of Victoria—Melbourne in particular, Canberra, and the city of Brisbane in

Queensland. States further afield such as Adelaide, Western Australia, the Northern Territories, regional Queensland and Tasmania were excluded from this first batch of promotions. This was justified on the grounds that it was unlikely that the population from these areas would be interested in 'yet another arts festival in Sydney', especially as, ' . . . [t]he distances are far too large and in many of these areas there is not a strong tradition of inter-state travel for arts purposes' (2000, pers. comm., 22 Aug).

Further, the pre-Games sales strategy excluded international audiences, which, instead, were reached through the Internet, NOC newsletters and the in-flight magazine of Ansett Australia (Sydney 2000 official airline). International sales agents received some information on the *OAF'2000*, but this was only the case in selected countries and did not complement the far wider international sales strategy for Olympic sport events. Moreover, information was not distributed internationally until mid year 2000, after most Olympic tourist packages had been organised and promoted, so this limited prospective visitor opportunities to plan for OAF events. For example, one of the international Olympic scholars appointed as Games observer by SOCOG considers that the German market was not informed about the existence of the OAF.[14] In his view, the average German Olympic tourist had not planned to attend arts events on occasion of their trip to the Sydney Games but many, if suitably informed, would have been interested (2000, pers. comm, 9 Sep).

Overall, the communications campaign tended to give priority to the local arts audience target over other 'Olympic audiences' such as Olympic (sports) ticket holders. Evidence of this is given by the placement of the festival advertising and promotions, which responded to the profile of average arts audiences in Sydney. For example, the distribution of promotional materials and advertising placements was done primarily in arts venues, the arts pages of the papers and arts company programmes. Furthermore, direct mailings were sent to arts subscribers and outdoors advertising was located in upper and middle upper class suburbs, which are traditionally identified as a primary arts target.

Communication Plan: Target Audience and Campaign Coverage

The target audience for the 2000 festival was wider than any previous Olympic arts programme and included established local and national arts audiences as well as general Olympic audiences at a national and international level. Both the festival artistic director and the marketing manager noted that their priority target was the average arts audience in Sydney, then the state of NSW and the rest of Australia. The latter were mainly based in capital cities from states close to NSW in the East coast, such as Melbourne in Victoria, Brisbane in Queensland and Canberra, the Australian capital. The marketing team prepared arts promotional packages placed on press media distributed in these areas. In Sydney, press and magazine advertising was complemented by arts company programmes and the distribution of flyers, brochures, decorations and promotions within typical arts attendant neighbourhoods in the city's medium to high-income boroughs.

A secondary target was defined as those Australians who had applied or were interested in Olympic tickets but may not be arts event regulars. In order to reach out to potential audiences that had the so-called 'Olympic experience' as their main motivation, the OAF team focused on promoting individual events expected to have a popular appeal, rather than the generic festival concept. This included events such as the *Symphony for a Thousand* to be played at Sydney Superdome or family shows such as the acrobatic display of the Flying Fruit fly Circus. For these sorts of promotions, the OAF relied on the support of SOCOG general communications, particularly the information displayed on the Olympic ticket bookings brochure and SOCOG Internet pages.

Overall, the target audience for the festival was divided into four main categories and several essential media were identified as key to reach them. The two groups above were defined as the 'national' target and were reached via press and direct media, as well as national tourism groups such as the Australian Tourism Commission (ATC) publications and commercial tourism agencies.[15]

Besides the national target, the *OAF'2000* had an international target as well as tourism groups and other more specific target groups, such as students and the staff of Olympic stakeholders. As noted, the budget to reach international audiences was very limited. For the most part, it was dependant on free-of-charge support from Olympic bodies such as National Olympic Committees (NOCs), the in-kind support of Olympic sponsors such as the flying company Ansett Australia and the use of Internet pages at the website of SOCOG and other Olympic institutions.

Tourism groups were treated as a separate category because a majority of the Olympic audiences were expected to be either national or international short-term visitors. According to OAF senior staff, these visitors were likely to have an interest in attending the city cultural venues as part of their tourist experience, in particular, the Sydney Opera House (1999, pers. comm., 6 Aug). Consequently, the OAF team prepared advertisements focused on the promotion of the venue itself rather than on the festival programming. This was done with the support of the Sydney Opera House Tourism department and was accentuated by the promotional initiative of numerous flying companies that showcased videos about the site in all their flights destined to Sydney.

Under the category 'other groups' were included school and university students and the staff of Olympic stakeholders. To reach school students, the OAF marketing team distributed flyers about selected events in all NSW schools. To reach secondary and university students, there was a distribution of flyers and posters about youth events such as the two scheduled film festivals and a popular music concert. Workers at SOCOG and Olympic

Table 7.4   OAF'2000: Media Distribution Plan

February–May 2000: newspapers (Fairfax), magazines (Time Inc), radio

- Content: blocks of the festival (genres): music, theatre and listings of the complete programme

June–July 2000: main newspapers campaign (Fairfax), magazines, radio
- *Newspaper area*: NSW focus (Sydney, Newcastle) + national; other states (Brisbane, Melbourne, Canberra)
- Content: Show specific advertisements (daily)

August 2000: main outdoors campaign, newspapers, television, radio
- *Flags* (City of Sydney sponsorship): 500 in city centre (where most OAF venues were located)
- *Bus shelters*: Sydney city centre, Sydney North Shore (middle- upper class areas, arts audiences)
- *Bus advertising*: city routes, 40% Sydney North Shore (most upper and middle upper classes)
- *Newspapers*: Fairfax (daily advertising 'What's on', plus festival updates & reminders)
- *Television*: *Channel 7* (Australia Olympic broadcaster), *SBS* (Australia multicultural channel)
- *Radio*: *2UE* (Olympic supporter), *Triple J* (non commercial radio)

September 2000: no more outdoors flags, only newspapers and some magazines
- Content: focus on promotion of the Sydney Opera House

Other media:
- *In-flight advertising* (*Ansett, Airline United, N7, Lufthansa*): focus on the Sydney Opera House.
- *Cinema*: 300 theatres throughout Australia
- *Ethnic media, youth media, other niche media*: niche advertising- show specific depending on audiences
- *Internet*: SOCOG webpages. Other web pages: *City Search* (Fairfax agreements), *Sydneytribe.com, juice.net* (youth site advertising), *Universal Music* Online CD competition
- *Printed material*: brochures (one by genre—Olympic Music, Olympic Theatre etc); pocket guide to festival (the most widely distributed information document); guide to the arts exhibitions. This material was distributed in all cultural venues, at all functions. Also placed at City of Sydney stands, Olympic stands, media centres, Olympic and media villages, Olympic Park and so on.

Source: Sketches by OAF marketing manager (2000, pers. comm. 22 Aug)

sponsor staff were treated as a separate target group to be reached through internal corporate magazines. This group benefited from special promotions to events, particularly, ticket reductions or free tickets to events that had not sold out. These strategies were used to raise the awareness about the shows and encourage others to attend them via word-of-mouth.

Media Distribution Schedule

The *OAF'2000* was the first OAF event to be supported by a comprehensive media distribution plan. Media placements did not follow directly after the festival media launch in October 1999, which included the presentation of a 43-page programme schedule. This was to avoid any direct clashes with the promotional campaigns of other established Sydney festivals and events during this period, such as the city's traditional Christmas promotions, the New Year's Eve preparations, the Sydney Festival in January 2000 and the Mardi Grass parade in February. As such, the *OAF'2000* media campaign did not start in full until the end of February 2000. Table 7.4 provides an overview of its main components and evolution throughout year 2000.

The support of Fairfax and the *Sydney Morning Herald* as presenting partners was paramount to enable the extensive press campaign described in Table 7.4. As a complement, the City of Sydney, which became the second *OAF'2000* official presenter, made possible the large outdoors campaign put in place in August. However, the final festival was not fully integrated within the general Olympic communication campaign, which was focused on sport. The interaction with other Olympic initiatives was reduced to the distribution of printed material at Olympic venues, such as all media facilities and Olympic family official accommodation venues, but high visibility was rarely achieved within these environments. Visibility was much higher within established arts environments, again demonstrating that the main target audience were arts rather than Olympic communities of interest.

Print Media Placements

Fairfax papers were the principal media for the distribution of OAF promotional material and all placements were provided at no cost as part of SOCOG value-in-kind negotiations. Advertising and promotions placed in Fairfax papers included all major selling elements within the festival programme and basic information features, such as the announcement of ticket sales and ticket availability. Table 7.5 provides a version of the Fairfax weekly placement schedule:

In terms of magazine placement, two of the most important contributions came from *Time* and *Who Weekly*, both of which belong to *Time— Sports Illustrated*, a TOP partner that is defined as the 'official publications company of the Olympic Games' (IOC 1998a). The promotional space provided by these magazines was also free of charge for the OAF. Additionally,

Table 7.5 Fairfax OAF'2000 Media Placements

Fairfax (VIK) Promotional placements	Feb	March	April	May	June	Jul	Aug	Sep
First Ticketek launch– Telephone sales	x	x x						
Second Ticketek launch; live sales			x x	x				
CD Release				x				
Commence shows—specific ads (daily)					x x	x		
Hemispheres launch					x			
SMH—Spectrum wrap (4 pages)						x		
Visual Arts Programme Launch						x		
Lead-up to the festival advertising						x x x		
Spectrum full page colour launch festival							x	
Hemispheres—							x	
Festival advertising—directory (daily)							x x	x x x

Source: SOCOG 2000f (unpublished)

advertisements were placed intermittently from the end of February to mid July (an average of one advertisement a month). After mid July, in the case of *Who Weekly*, ads would be placed in all issues up to the end of September. *Time Australia* published one advertisement per issue from mid July to the second last week of August. There were other sorts of magazines placing paid or VIK advertising. Most of them were in-flight magazines from Olympic partner or supporter companies such as Ansett Australia—Team Millennium Partner—and Lufthansa—supporter. Most of these placements were also offered in-kind and were concentrated during the Olympic period, September 2000, with a focus in promoting the Sydney Opera House.

Other print media placements included a range of niche media such as minority ethnic papers, popular suburban press and youth or 'street press' publications. In the case of the ethnic media, a total of six papers were selected, five of which were from Asian based communities. Not surprisingly, all of these advertisements were 'show specific' and the shows promoted were all composed by Asian troupes such as the Asian Youth Orchestra, Taiwanese dancers Cloud Gate, a film festival on Japanese 'anime' cartoons (*Japanime*) and a Korean Arts exhibition at the Powerhouse Museum. Other niche media included magazines and tabloids distributed among middle and middle-low class audiences in the Sydney suburbs. The tabloid including a major number of advertisements was the *Sydney Star Observer*, which placed one in every issue almost without interruption from the end of April to the end of August. Events promoted in those magazines and tabloids were, largely, those with a more popular appeal such as cabaret style shows and shows by the highly popular Sydney Dance Company and Australian Ballet. Finally, in the so-called street press, two kinds of advertisements were placed in a total of four titles comprising youth magazines and student publications. One advertisement promoted the weekend of world music concert *Hemispheres*, and another promoted the Japanese cartoons film festival *Japanime*.

Outdoor Media Placements

Beyond newspapers and magazines, the outdoor campaigns implemented during August 2000 were paramount in ensuring the public presence of the festival for locals and visitors at a critical time in the Games build-up period. This was the first time that an Olympic cultural programme built on the official Look of the Games programme, an opportunity that was made possible by the dual role of the OAF General Manager, who also oversaw the Look programme. Five hundred flags—donated by the City of Sydney—with the festival logo were placed at Sydney major transit and commercial streets as well as at key squares, avenues and meeting points in the city centre, including Sydney Harbour and the Opera House. However, the flags for this event were taken away on 1 September (12 days before the opening ceremony of the Olympic Games) and were replaced by flags referring to the Olympic Games in general, with sport themes exclusively. Some flags displaying the *OAF'2000* logo were kept in front on the Sydney Opera House for an extra week in September. However, these were also changed once the Olympic torch arrived in the city and the Olympic rings were lit up over the Harbour Bridge.

Other outdoor elements such as bus shelters and posters were kept during the first week of September but were less visible than the flags. Bus shelters displayed genre specific references—Olympic Music, Olympic Theatre—while posters, placed in cafes, universities and cultural venues were show specific.

Audiovisual Media Placements

The festival was also promoted on the radio, through *Radio 2UE*, which was a SOCOG media partner that provided value in-kind space in exchange for diverse agreements with the Olympic organisation. Coinciding with the Fairfax newspaper promotions, *Radio 2UE* released information on Ticketek live sales and the festival musical CD. From the beginning of June to mid September, just before the start of the Games, most advertising was dedicated to specific high profile shows such as the *Symphony for a Thousand*, diverse operas, theatre events and ballet. These promotions were run intermittently from June to August and on an ongoing basis from the first August to mid September, which became the festival's peak period in terms of awareness and local interest in Sydney. An important complement to this was the placement of 'ticket give-away promotions', which took place during three weeks in July and three weeks in August. Another radio station providing advertising space was the non-commercial radio *Triple-J*, which supported the *Hemispheres* concert and promoted the event intermittently from the last week of June up to the concert weekend, on the 9th and 10th of September.

Cinema placement at Val Morgan theatres was the other relevant in-kind contribution to the promotion of the *OAF'2000*. Val Morgan was the official sponsor of the Australia Olympic Team and a SOCOG provider. The cinema company showcased slide advertising about the festival in 300 cinema theatres nationally. The placement was made uninterruptedly from the last week in March up to the end of August 2000.

The use of television was not as frequent as other media. After a failed attempt by SOCOG's Cultural Commission Chairman to create a national cultural channel to broadcast all OAF events, the team focused instead on placing a few but supposedly high impact television adverts. *Channel 7* from the Seven Network, the official Australian broadcaster of the Olympic Games and Team Millennium partner, displayed a generic spot promoting the *OAF'2000* as a whole, and a show-specific spot about the *Flying Fruit Fly Circus*. In SBS, the multicultural broadcaster in Australia, the OAF team inserted a spot about Taiwanese dancers *Cloud Gate Dance*

Theatre. Finally, the OAF team made a special agreement with *Channel V,* a local broadcaster, in order insert weekly promotions from mid June to mid September 2000 and complement them with a competition and prize draw about the festival. Tellingly, *Channel 7,* despite providing 23 hours a day of official Olympic broadcasts, did not provide space for OAF activity live coverage or reviews and only featured paid adverts as was the case for non-Olympic broadcasters.

Other Media: Direct Advertising, Direct Mail, Special Promotions, Internet Placements

An alternative to advertising media was the production of print materials directly distributed in public spaces, among them City of Sydney information boots; cultural venues, hotels and tourist agencies, and Olympic sites in general, including ORTA venues. As had been the case with the 1997 festival, the OAF team produced a wide range of brochures, flyers, posters, cards and pocket guides. General information and programme brochures were distributed in March and April 2000 as a complement to the promotion of ticket sales availability through the Ticketek system. These brochures were placed partly as an insert within Fairfax newspapers and partly in the above mentioned spaces, arts venues and education centres in particular. In May, specific art forms or genre flyers were made available. There were flyers promoting 'Olympic' dance, theatre, music, stage, opera and open events. In June and July, flyers became show specific to promote *Hemispheres,* the *Film Festival* and the *Flying Fruit Fly Circus.* A more detailed flyer about the weekend concert *Hemispheres* was created and distributed in August and the week prior to the event. As a complement to the flyers, a set of promotional postcards was put on display from July to mid September. These cards were also show-specific about the very same events promoted in posters and flyers: *Hemispheres, Japanime, Cloud Gate* among others. In mid July, at the time when the visual arts programme had been officially launched, a special 'Visual Arts' brochure was distributed. Finally, at the end of July, a 'Pocket guide' to the festival was put on display and was to become the most widely available reference about the Olympic arts events.

The print materials were distributed at public spaces as well as sent through direct mail and adapted to the profile of their mail targets. Two thousand schools from NSW received flyers about the *Flying Fruit Fly Circus* show; senior cardholders were sent information about the Melbourne Symphony Orchestra or the Asian Youth Orchestra; Ticketek theatre list receivers were sent theatre flyers. The OAF team did also build on the mailing lists of participant cultural organisations such as the Sydney Opera House and the Art Gallery of New South Wales.

Another alternative was the implementation of special promotions with Olympic partners. The chain of shopping malls *Westfield* (Team Millennium

Figure 7.8   OAF'2000 brochures, flyers and pocket guide. Materials published by SOCOG in 2000. Reproduced courtesy of the International Olympic Committee.

Partner) supported a number of initiatives including artist appearances in the two last weeks of August and first week of September. *Ansett Australia* (flying company, Team Millennium Partner) agreed to display OAF video promotions and brochures in May, June and July. *Traveland* (Tourism agencies) prepared promotional packages for tourists to visit Sydney and attend the festival. *Universal CD* (musical stores) also organised in-store promotions of the *OAF'2000* official CD.

Finally, detailed information about the festival and specific shows was placed at selected Internet sites. The OAF programme was hosted at the SOCOG website within its 'About the Games' section. Although SOCOG's homepage did not include direct links to the OAF, the festivals were presented as a key feature in the 'About' section and had three different dedicated links. The first was titled 'Olympic Arts Festivals' and provided information about the 1997–1999 festivals as well as a detailed 2000 festival programme; a second one titled 'Tickets' provided the full 2000 programme schedule and a booking service; finally 'Press Reviews' provided a selection of articles published on the festivals. The OAF was also promoted through *CitySearch*, one of the principal web-based entertainment engines in Australia in this period, supported by Fairfax. Other sites used for promotion were mainly youth-based, including *Sydneytribe.com* and *juice. net*. The events most widely promoted in these sites were *Hemispheres* and *Japanime*, from June to the first week in September 2000.

Campaign Issues

One of the main constraints for the appropriate implementation of the *OAF'2000* communication and marketing strategy was the budget limitation and, consequently, the need to rely on VIK media placements. Fairfax provided this kind of support extensively. However, VIK agreements with other sort of media, of international outreach in particular, were more precarious and often unsuccessful. As there was no budget for international advertising, reaching out to international audiences was mainly the responsibility of the OAF publicity department in conjunction with the Australian Arts Council programme *ausarts2000*,[16] rather than the OAF marketing department.

In terms of city presence, the City of Sydney was a key stakeholder providing extensive VIK support, but this was only the case in August 2000, at the time of the OAF outdoor flag presence, and not during the Olympic Games competition period. This was also the case for most print material placements, as the information booths that had been provided by either the City of Sydney, the State Rail Ferries and Buses company or ORTA stopped being available by the beginning of September. Consequently, *OAF'2000* had an opportunity to have a visible public presence in Sydney during August 2000, but in September, beyond the placement of wayfinding logos, the outdoors city presence was almost non-existent. This diminished the chances to reach out to international visitors and tourists staying in Sydney during Games time, in particular those not reading the arts section of Australian papers, where the daily event directory and show specific advertisements provided by Fairfax would concentrate.

Further, the support of SOCOG media partners was dependant on the needs and priorities of the sports ticketing programme and other sports related marketing departments at SOCOG. This was a common situation with Olympic sponsors, who were not requested to support the Olympic arts programme specifically as part of their SOCOG or IOC arrangements. For example, *Time Inc.* would not sacrifice a potential space to promote the sporting competitions so as to guarantee the presence of Olympic arts adverts and this led to many lost opportunities for *OAF'2000* promotions. The relationship with other established marketing partners such as Universal Music, EMI Music and non-commercial radio stations was similar. In most cases, promoting the *OAF'2000* programme would come second to the support for Sports programmes or the Torch Relay programme and would rarely be considered as a key asset to promote in conjunction with the above. This hierarchy was reinforced by the communications policy at SOCOG Communications and Community Relations division, as none of its communications programmes included clauses to liaise or secure the promotional presence of the OAF in the key events or functions they managed.

Finally, a significant issue for the promotion of the OAF was the lack of control over SOCOG's website and the strong dependence on the interests of the electronic server, TOP partner IBM, to display information and links to *OAF'2000* or previous OAF event years. Although the OAF had a central presence in the 'About the Games' section of the web, SOCOG's homepage did not display any link or specific reference to the arts festivals. This would have prevented many web users from knowing about the OAF. By the year 2000, it was noticeable that SOCOG's website homepage excluded references to the OAF, even at the time of the *OAF'2000* formal opening in August. In part, this was due to space limitations and a preference on the part of the web managers to display the countdown to the Games official Opening Ceremony in September and to promote sports ticket sales and Olympic merchandise. Further to this, IBM stipulated in its contract that online pages displaying *OAF'2000* events within SOCOG's web environment could not include links to the venues where they were taking place or the companies delivering them. This limited the amount of Olympic arts information available online and the attractiveness of the pages providing such details. In general, these Internet limitations were a missed opportunity for the national and, particularly, international promotion of the OAF, considering the low or no-cost implied. This is a situation that has changed considerably in more recent editions of the Games, as discussed below.

BEYOND SYDNEY 2000

While marketing and communications has remained a challenging area for the Olympic cultural programme, there has been some noticeable advancement in areas that were just at their inception in Sydney, such as culture or arts-focused city dressing initiatives and the use of online environments, both of which provide a platform to diversify Games narratives. Other areas, such as cultural branding iconography, have also progressed in interesting ways, if not always leading to greater recognition by mainstream Olympic audiences.

The emergence of a Look of the City programme as a complement to the IOC-sanctioned Look of the Games programme has been an important platform for cultural programme representation. Athens 2004 and Torino 2006 experimented with variations of this programme as an opportunity for Games-time public art interventions. In Athens, the programme was managed by the OCOG under the title *Catch the light* and ranged from building wraps to interactive sculptures dedicated to showcasing contemporary visions of Greece and Greek creative practices. In Torino, the programme was a direct response to the Look of the Games aesthetic, which dominated within sporting venues, involving instead stylised representations of

Torino cultural icons displayed over large city wraps, all coloured red. The Torino Municipality also managed a parallel art and light public display that contributed to creating a festive as well as arts-sensitive atmosphere. Vancouver highlighted its cultural programme via a more traditional Look of the Games route, the innovation being the wide range of city banners displaying the term 'Cultural Olympiad' and the amount of time they were on show within the city centre: over three years before the Games and throughout the sporting competition period.

In terms of titles and iconography, the term Cultural Olympiad has become increasingly popular, being the official name of choice for every Games edition except Beijing (which opted for 'Cultural Festivals' instead). London has decided to use a dual name: Cultural Olympiad for the four-year country-wide programme, and the London 2012 Festival for specially curated Olympic cultural activity in 2012, with a special emphasis on London during Games time. Distinct culture logos and related visuals have also become a common practice, at times created in line with other Olympic branding (eg. Beijing, Vancouver) in other cases completely different and unrelated (Torino, Athens). In parallel, it is also increasingly common to create a wide range of programme sub-brands, with different degrees of Olympic-related rhetoric around them. In Vancouver, the *Cultural Olympiad Digital Edition* (CODE) became one of the most widely known programme components throughout Canada; Torino used the term *ItalyArt*, Athens presented at least four parallel culture brands during Games time, while London has one the most complex cultural Olympiad related naming structure yet, due to the different degrees of synergy or separation between official and 'fringe' programmes run by the OCOG and 13 different regional programmers. Naturally, generating a coherent media communications strategy encompassing all of these variations is no easy task and, for the most part, ensuring the Olympic association for all of this cultural activity remains an unmet challenge.

The other communication area showing considerable development are online environments and this has had a particularly strong effect on the cultural programme as, for the first time, communities of interest around the Cultural Olympiad, no matter how small, can identify each other and share ideas and experiences from one Games edition to the next. OCOGs, as well as the IOC, are progressively embracing social media platforms, from differing blogging structures to Twitter, Flickr or Facebook environments. This has allowed the cultural programme to have a greater presence within official communication channels, though this has also been the case for all the other, traditionally most popular programmes, such as the torch relay, sporting events and so on, which still means that cultural activity may be easily overshadowed. Indeed, the big difference is that any interested party proactively seeking information about the cultural programme can find it and follow it, something that was harder to achieve at the time of Sydney 2000.

In contrast with these advancements, there has been no significant change in the hierarchical management structure for marketing and communications delivery, as already noted within Chapter 6. This means that, regardless of the increasing sophistication of design and imagery features, the cultural programme still struggles to secure funding, Games time visibility and clear association with the core Olympic brand.

SUMMARY

Olympic marketing and communications is a priority area for the IOC and for respective organisers of the Olympic Games. The IOC provides strong leadership in the definition of marketing and communication policies through the regular update of reports and fact-sheets and the willingness to guide the development of new areas, as was the case with the creation of an 'Olympic Marketing Communications Manual' for OCOGs in 1998. The IOC focuses on managing the worldwide dimension of Olympic communications. As such, it is directly involved with the management of global programmes such as TOP, the negotiation of broadcast rights and now Internet rights, and the distribution of generic advertising campaigns about the ideals of Olympism. This means that the design and management of local campaigns to promote specific messages about individual Olympic Games editions is mainly the responsibility of respective OCOGs.

The structure of marketing and communications at SOCOG in the lead up to and during the 2000 Games exemplifies the need to reconcile the global aspirations of the IOC with the more specific, locally based needs of an Olympic Games. The drive to find such a balance is evident when looking at the ambitious task definitions of its sponsorship, marketing and communications programmes. Within the sponsorship programme, SOCOG had to respond to the requirements of TOP partners at the same time as the needs of domestic partners despite the fact that they provided very different levels of support and had different communication agendas. The marketing programmes had to reach local audiences while securing a worldwide impact that was coherent with the IOC strategies. Further, SOCOG was also expected to cover the needs of a wide range of local communities while, at the same time, achieving the integration of all OCOG communications within a joint Olympic promotional plan.

Underpinning SOCOG's main decisions to implement Olympic marketing and communications was the objective to ensure the success of the Games as a global media (sporting) event. Traditionally, this core ambition has led to imbalances in the levels of support provided to different Olympic dimensions, and this was certainly the case in Sydney as well. While iconic Olympic programmes such as the Torch Relay, Ceremonies and Sports were centrally placed in the main agendas of either marketing or communication divisions, the OAF and associated needs were rarely mentioned within

SOCOG's communication and marketing strategies. Arguably thus, the global aspirations of the IOC have resulted in a strong emphasis on marketing imperatives (responding to worldwide commercial partner demands) at the expense of communication policies that could assist in leveraging the meaning and implications of an Olympic cultural programme. This has led to a situation in which the promotion of the Olympic cultural programme operates almost in total isolation from the rest of the Olympic marketing and communication structure.

IOC staff have at times indicated that it is best not to have a say in the promotional priorities of Olympic cultural programmes as this could be insensitive to local idiosyncrasies. However, in Sydney, the lack of IOC requirements and SOCOG's limited interference on OAF-specific decisions did not empower those local stakeholders most likely to have a strong cultural agenda and aspirations to ensure a sustainable Olympic arts legacy.[17] Instead, the establishment of a OAF brand and communication priorities relied mainly on the vision of respective artistic directors and the programme marketing manager who, by year 2000, were more concerned with ensuring the commercial success of the final festival (as a one-off arts event) than maintaining a coherence of vision with the three prior festivals (as an ongoing Cultural Olympiad). This is an issue that keeps placing major challenges to subsequent Olympic hosts, as has been made evident in the experience of London 2012 (García 2012).

In sum, there is little evidence of appropriate coordination between communication, marketing and cultural policies within OCOG operations. Indeed, up to the Sydney 2000 Games, there has been a clear dominance of marketing imperatives that do not fully consider the potential of cultural promotion and local representation to enrich the Olympic narrative. As such, the application of cultural policy principles has tended to be relegated to a secondary position and traded off by short-term commercial imperatives. This has limited the ability to optimise arts engagement and establish cultural legacies as a central dimension of the Olympic Games staging process. This lack of synergies is gradually being recognised by the IOC, since it is seen as limiting the potential to create meaningful and distinct 'Olympic experiences'. Prospective organisers are starting to notice that a full realisation of the 'Olympic experience' should account not only for the memorable moments that may emerge out of world class sport competition, but also absorb the unique, locally rooted, cultural context of respective host cities. This requires a revision to current IOC marketing and communications guidelines so that the apparent excessive compartmentalisation of Games promotional operations is replaced by a more holistic approach which fully integrates sport with culture and education, as aspired to within the Olympic Charter.

8   Stakeholder Contributions

This chapter provides an analysis of the approach taken by key institutions and corporations to engage with the Olympic cultural programme. The institutions analysed here belong to four main categories: the public sector, the private sector, the arts community and the media. Each category has been identified as a key interest group with a potential to contribute to and/ or gain benefit from an association with the Olympic cultural programme and a potential to influence the Games' cultural policy. As such, as already discussed in Chapter 5, institutions belonging to each category can be considered key stakeholders of any given Olympic cultural programme.

The chapter explores the interests and expectations of each stakeholder in the context of the 2000 Olympic Games and their reasons to support or avoid supporting the Sydney Olympic Arts Festivals specifically. The analysis of public sector involvement looks at the correspondence between cultural policy choices and level of involvement with the OAF at local, state and federal levels. The study of relationships with the arts community looks at ways in which artists and art institutions engaged in the OAF and their ability to inform or influence the shape of the programme. Analysing the approach by the private sector helps to determine whether the programme had a market or corporate appeal and whether corporations had an interest in contributing to it. Finally, the study of the opinions by the local and national media and their interest in covering the festivals offers some indication of the programme's ability to capture public interest and its chances to project specific images about the event host community and its cultural values.

Most of the situations analysed in this chapter could apply to Olympic Games hosting experiences other than Sydney 2000 and are representative of the ongoing challenges as well as opportunities in Olympic cultural programming.

THE PUBLIC SECTOR

Chapter 4 noted that towards the end of the 20th century, Australia's cultural policy, in line with other parts of the world, has been dominated by a rationalist approach to the arts. At the time of the Sydney Games, there existed a general retreat from cultural public funding that was initially heralded by the report 'Creative Nation' (Department of Communication and the Arts 1994)—claimed to be the first official cultural policy document in the country—and was subsequently reinforced by the 'Nugent Report' (Nugent et al. 1999) which became the first of the so-called 'Review-Cycle' into Australia's arts sectors. The government's discussion resulting from such policy documents, the 'Nugent Report' in particular, led to a situation where arts organisations were encouraged to diversify funding sources and develop self-sustainable projects, less dependant on public subsidy. Tucker and Philips (1999) note that this also led to organisations avoiding economic risks and giving preference to projects that were easier to market or commercialise. Other authors note that this environment led to a 'shift in focus to audience development away from product development', which require strong marketing skills (Rentschler et al. 2006) and that this pressure favoured major arts companies ('elite nurturing') over small-organisations (Craik 2007: 19). The cultural policy approach that framed the development of the Sydney OAF from the mid 1990s must be understood in this context. That is, Australia's governing bodies supported the OAF with a view to maximising the festivals' potential to create trade opportunities such as attracting cultural tourism and the corporate convention market.

The Australian government also considered the Games to be an opportunity to re-define the image of the country and expected the cultural programme to assist in refuting the stereotype of a post-colonial white Australia to promote, instead, an image of tolerance and pride in diversity. In this sense, a second strand in the cultural policy approach of governing bodies involved supporting arts and cultural initiatives to promote ideas of reconciliation and multiculturalism. Both types of cultural policy priorities (economic rationalism and diversity promotion) are reflected at most governmental levels, be it within local, state or federal structures, as discussed in the following sections.

Local Government

The City of Sydney (CoS) was associated with the OAF in a range of ways: the Lord Mayor was a board member of the Olympic Cultural Commission; CoS was official sponsor of *Reaching the World*, and in 2000, CoS became official presenter of *The Harbour of Life* or *OAF'2000*. The threefold association of CoS with the Olympic cultural programme offers some indication of how local government used the OAF as part of the city's cultural policy strategy. Interestingly, CoS concentrated most efforts in supporting the festival in year 2000 (see below), while its involvement in prior festivals was merely nominal or non existent, as in the case of *A Sea Change* in 1998. This suggests that the notion of a four-year Cultural Olympiad was not considered a strong strand for CoS' cultural strategy. Instead, the interest was focused on the short period leading to the main event, the

Olympic sporting competitions in September 2000, when the attention of the international media and external visitors would be at its peak.

The agreement to become official presenter of the *OAF'2000* resulted in CoS' operational authorship of all outdoor arts and entertainment programmes for that year as well as A\$2.25m value in kind support in the form of OAF banners in main city streets and squares, bus advertising and brochure placement in official booths (CoS executive director of major projects, 2000, pers. comm., 8 Oct). *OAF'2000* events created in partnership with CoS were the following,

- *The Sculpture Walk*, a permanent public art project by CoS featuring outdoor sculptures at Sydney Botanic Gardens and other popular city locations;
- *Sunscreen Sydney 2000*, an open air film festival designed in collaboration with Tourism NSW and two entertainment corporate groups, and
- the *Olympic Park Exhibition*, a miniature display of the 2000 Olympic venues held at Sydney's Customs House Exhibition Centre

In addition to these OAF projects, an Olympic Project was created within CoS Major Projects division to coordinate the relationships between CoS, SOCOG, the Olympic Roads and Transport Authority (ORTA) and the Olympic Coordination Authority (OCA). This project was, however, not directly linked with the OAF. According to the executive director of major projects at CoS,

> this arrangement was planned to provide a mechanism for crowd management during major events happening in year 2000 such as the New Year's Eve celebrations, Sydney Festival and Australian Day festivities in January 2000 and, most of it all, to avoid congestions during the Olympic Games period, from the 14th September to the 1st October 2000. (1999, pers. comm., 20 Aug)

During the Olympic period, the project took the form of the so-called Olympic *LiveSites*. This was an entertainment programme distributed in six popular locations at the city centre and taking place 'at times when Olympic venues were filling and spilling at the same time and when transport would be at its most stressed' (CoS executive director of major projects, 2000, pers. comm., 8 Oct). The *LiveSites* programme comprised live Olympic coverage displayed at giant screens by Olympic official broadcaster *Channel 7* and, on prime locations, it also included live concerts, acrobatic shows, mime shows and street theatre. According to the policy officer in the Cultural Affairs and Protocol unit at CoS, her department actively programmed to link some events with the city's Olympic *LiveSites* plan during the Olympic period but maintaining its own purpose and annual objectives. In her words,

Our unit is keeping its on-going programme and utilising it again during the Olympic period. [The aim is to provide a balance to] the high end indoor programme designed by SOCOG [on occasion of the *OAF'2000*]. The Cultural Partners who have been working with City of Sydney since 1997 have developed programmes for the City's Olympic *LiveSites* [. . .] serving a more 'local' Sydney audience with an entertainment value for visitors from overseas as well. (1999, pers. comm., 16 Aug).

The *LiveSites* programme was one of the most popular initiatives during the Sydney Olympic Games, attracting large crowds of local residents, national and international visitors. Interestingly, despite becoming a key site for cultural exchange, the initiative was not part of the *OAF'2000* programme and did not include any officially branded joint project. In fact, it could be argued that the popularity and visibility of the *LiveSites* limited the impact of many OAF Games-time activities that year, as the latter were mainly presented indoors and were perceived to be of a less 'festive' nature. This led many journalists, tourists and Sydney-siders to believe that the main cultural programme for the Games was in fact the *LiveSites* and not the OAF programme (see Chapter 9).

As a whole, the importance of CoS involvement in the final Olympic arts festival cannot be denied, but it should be understood in the context of other plans and activities for year 2000, where the Olympics and the OAF in particular were not the only priority. An analysis of documentation and project manager claims suggests that CoS' interest in *The Harbour of Life* or *OAF'2000* was not as much the exploration and promotion of the city's cultural values and assets specifically but rather the projection of a commercially competitive, contemporary and lively image of central Sydney to attract foreign visitors and corporations. This affected the nature and emphasis of the Olympic outdoors activities or *LiveSites* which, though being highly entertaining and widely popular, were poorly related to the bid promise of a multicultural, all embracing and representative cultural celebration.

State Government

At state level, the provisions and schemes of respective governing bodies were quite varied and, often, lacked appropriate coordination. Expectedly, New South Wales was the state providing the greatest support scheme for the OAF. However, its contribution was well below that of local and federal government. In most cases, it was limited to indirect funding and in-kind support. Queensland was the second most supportive state and the only one to offer a direct grant to the 1998 nation-wide festival, *A Sea Change*.[1] Other states offered minor support, mostly in the form of promotional assistance through tourism bodies. As for Queensland, their support was focused mainly on the 1998 festival, as it was the event that brought activities to each Australian state and territory. Representatives from the Australian Tourism Commission and OAF senior staff have indicated that other states and territories did not follow a clear plan of action to support the Olympic cultural programme because they had not expectations that it would lead to tangible benefits (2000, pers. comm., 3 Mar; 1999, pers. comm., 11 Nov).

In New South Wales, the main state contributions towards the OAF were in communications and advocacy terms, by including some mentions in government newsletters and brochures, and the provision of links to the festivals web-page from government websites. For example, the NSW Ministry for the Arts mentioned the OAF in its 'Cultural Grants: year 2000 guidelines by the NSW Arts Advisory Council' (1999). The Ministry did not provide direct funds for the Olympic events, nevertheless, it urged applicants for cultural grants to 'take the *2000 Harbour of Life Festival* into account when planning their activities for 2000' (p. 66) and added,

> The Arts Advisory Council may give priority in its funding recommendations to proposals which, in its opinion, accord with the objectives of the Olympic festivals and the arts policies and priorities of the New South Wales Government. (*Ibid*)

Further, Tourism NSW provided some indirect support by financing the Sydney Media Centre, a joint government initiative, where the *OAF'2000* media information desk was based throughout Games time, and by contributing to the official film festival, *Sunscreen Sydney 2000*. These few initiatives suggest that NSW government agencies focused on supporting the final festival in 2000 but overlooked the festivals in 1998 and 1999.

Overall, Australian state agencies supported the OAF mainly by providing some platforms for ad-hoc communications, however, it is not possible to identify broader strategic thinking to ensure clear links between OAF opportunities and medium to long-term cultural policy objectives that could ensure a sustainable festival legacy. This situation is in line with previous Olympic cultural programmes and one of the ongoing challenges for the Cultural Olympiad today, as will be discussed in the concluding chapter.

Federal Government

At the federal level, support by arts funding authorities was low up to year 2000. The Australia Council (AC), the Commonwealth government's principal arts funding and advisory body, provided funds for each of the four festivals and helped in their promotion through continuous references in its main newsletter 'ArtForce'. However, the AC did not create any special Olympic fund or promotion scheme to encourage participation in the OAF.

Instead, assistance was given to specific projects on an individual basis following AC existing policies and guidelines.

The AC offered a direct grant to the *Festival of the Dreaming* in 1997 through the 'Aboriginal and Torres Strait islander Arts Board' and the Visual Arts/Craft fund (SOCOG 1997a: 18) however, it had a very low involvement between 1998 and 1999. The AC created a 'Major Festivals Initiative' in 1999,[2] but this grant was dedicated exclusively to the established city Festivals in Perth, Adelaide, Melbourne and Sydney and did not include any reference to the four Olympic festivals. Further, AC created a A$10m three-year special package to assist Australian groups touring overseas during year 1999 (*The Advertiser* 1999), but did not actually provide any direct assistance to *Reaching the World*, which was the Olympic festival dedicated to overseas touring as its main mission. Thus, it can be concluded that while the AC acknowledged the opportunities that the international exposure of the Games might bring to the arts, up to year 2000, it did not use the OAF as its preferred medium nor did it use it as a vehicle to apply or expand cultural policy initiatives.

In contrast, in year 2000, AC initiated an ambitious project to support the promotion of Australian artists and institutions in parallel to the celebration of *OAF'2000*. The project was called *ausarts2000* and lasted from May 2000 to the end of October 2000. The project was developed in partnership with the OAF and comprised the creation of a comprehensive website and a shared information office at the Sydney Media Centre. According to the *ausarts2000* general manager, the project focused on ensuring that the OAF and the overall Olympic experience provided long term legacies for the arts. As such, it was used to complement the more commercially oriented (i.e. ticket sales) efforts by SOCOG staff.

> *ausarts2000* is not about putting on or funding an event, but about reaching, getting the most in terms of international exposure, encouraging collaborations with other companies in the future and maximising the potential to tour and export Australian arts (2000, pers. comm., 4 Oct).

The initiative was positive for the OAF, as it provided a share of promotional resources and staff expertise and provided further publicity opportunities within the international media. Moreover, the initiative assisted those companies involved in the OAF to explore new opportunities after the Games were over, via the development of post-festival evaluation strategies.

Other federal bodies were supportive of the OAF but only as part of their ongoing commitment to Australian arts. The following details have been extracted from a letter addressed to the author responding to the inquiry: 'Commonwealth Government Support for the Olympic Arts Festivals'. The response was written by the general manager, Arts Branch—Department of Communications, Information Technology and the Arts (DCITA).[3]

Table 8.1   Commonwealth Government Support for the Olympic Arts Festivals

The Australia Council has funded companies participating in *The Harbour of Life Festival* (HOL), including:

> Australian Ballet
> Bangarra Dance Theatre
> Bell Shakespeare Company
> Company B Belvoir
> Flying Fruit Circus
> Sydney Dance Company
> Sydney Theatre Company

The Commonwealth provides direct funding to some companies scheduled in HOL:

> Sydney Symphony Orchestra
> Melbourne Symphony Orchestra
> Opera Australia

The Department of Foreign Affairs and Trade (DFAT) has developed a media strategy to promote Australian culture and the arts throughout the Olympics and has plans to distribute international promotional material about *The Harbour of Life*. DFAT and SOCOG agreed to collaborate to deliver *Reaching the World* in a range of markets. Both organisations have jointly funded a South American tour of DFAT's Aboriginal Art Exhibition, *Seasons of Kunwinjku*. DFAT has initiated some exhibitions illustrating and promoting Australian cultural diversity, *Richness in diversity: people of Australia*, and Australian sporting excellence, *Australia- our Sporting life*.

Source: DCITA (1999, pers. comm., Aug).

The letter does not indicate that there was any direct fund or programme to assist in the implementation of the OAF programme. Rather, funds were given to individual projects that suited existing Department guidelines. Consequently, the OAF was not allocated federal funds to initiate new projects or explore the possibility of developing new cross-institutional partnerships. This reinforces the impression that the Australian government and arts funding bodies did not use the OAF as a forum to explore new artistic proposals but rather showcase well-established cultural assets.

Finally, some non-arts led federal organisations offered various levels of support to the OAF at national and international level. Most of these bodies put an emphasis in supporting notions of 'reconciliation' with Aboriginal peoples and in portraying a positive image of other highly politicised issues such as the notion of 'multiculturalism'. These include the Department of Foreign Affairs and Trade (DFAT), the Australian Tourism Commission (ATC) and the Aboriginal and Torres Strait Islanders Commission (ATSIC). The most common form of support was the inclusion of references to the OAF within their printed promotional literature and in their web-sites.

International Governments

International government agencies played a relevant role in both the 1997 indigenous festival and the final 2000 festival. For *The Festival of the Dreaming*, international bodies providing major support were the Arts Council and the Lottery Grants Board of New Zealand, the Australia-Korea Foundation, the Australia South Pacific 2000 Programme, the Injalak group, the Canada Council, the Canadian Department of Foreign Affairs and International Trade, and diverse embassies, in particular, the Canadian Consulate which hosted a reception to welcome Canadian artists (SOCOG 1997a: 18–19). The involvement of these bodies entailed supporting the participation of indigenous artists from their respective countries in the Australian festival.

In year 2000, international bodies providing support to the *OAF'2000* were the German government through the Goethe Institute in Australia; the British Council and the Royal Festival Hall in London; Creative New Zealand; the government of the Hellenic Republic; the Embassy of Japan and the Japan Foundation; French institutions such as the Paris Council, the French Embassy and the region of L'Île-de-France; the Netherlands Chamber of Commerce and the Rijksmuseum from Amsterdam, and some institutions from the United States such as the Hancher Auditorium at Iowa City and the Myer Foundation. The support provided by most of these institutions consisted of funding arrangements for events originated in their respective countries (SOCOG 1999b).

Government Joint Initiatives

The previous points indicate how, up to year 2000, the approach of most Australian government bodies to support the cultural programme was vague and rather limited. To explain this, Louw and Turner have pointed out at the conflict that took place in terms of 'ownership' of the Games (2000, pers. comm., 25 Aug). The Games had been awarded to the city of Sydney, so they were designed to be the responsibility of the state of NSW, and the federal government was to have only a secondary role in terms of decision-making and resource allowances. According to Louw and Turner, this led not only to a lack of coordination between state and federal bodies, but also to a certain sense of competition among the various states that also wanted to benefit from the Games, but which had priorities and interests that differed from those in Sydney and NSW. On some occasions, this led to what could be considered a defensive posture on the part of SOCOG or NSW. This is best exemplified in their relationship with Queensland, a state that was proactive and interested in taking part of the Olympic project but was not encouraged to have the degree of involvement it would have expected. The low contributions of federal arts funding during the first three years of the Olympiad could also be interpreted as a measure to avoid conflicts among states.

However, in preparation for the Olympic Games period in September 2000, local, state and federal bodies joined their efforts in a common initiative that was to be one of the greatest catalysts for the promotion of the OAF. This was the creation of a non-accredited media centre, the Sydney Media Centre (SMC). This Centre had the mission to serve all media, regardless of whether they had been officially accredited by the IOC to access Olympic venues,[4] by providing stories about Australia not specifically related to the Olympic sport competitions or any other areas protected by IOC copyright. The SMC was run by Tourism NSW and the Department of State and Regional Development (state bodies), in conjunction with the Sydney Harbour Foreshore Authority (local government), the Australian Tourism Commission, and the Department of Foreign Affairs and Trade (federal government). Tourism, trade and culture were focal points of most press conferences at the SMC and, in terms of culture and the arts, the final arts festival, *OAF'2000* was a key beneficiary.

The most remarkable examples of SMC events created to promote the OAF specifically were the *OAF'2000* inaugural conference in July 2000; two press conferences held in September by two of the festival's major stars (French ballerina Sylvie Guillem and Italian tenor Andrea Bocelli), and a conference held by *OAF'2000* artistic director Leo Schofield in conjunction with representatives of Tourism NSW. Additionally, the OAF held a media information office at the SMC in partnership with *ausarts2000*, the ambitious programme established by the Australia Council. This was one of the key communication achievements of the OAF, but one that makes it manifest how the cultural programme tends to operate as an aside rather than central component of the Games experience.

THE ARTS COMMUNITY

As it tends to be the case in the lead to each Olympic Games edition, soon after the Sydney bid award and the feelings of euphoria that took over Australia, a large number of national press articles conveyed negative comments about the Games by artists and arts institutions. The initial hostility of the arts community towards the Games might have been accelerated by the strong presence of articles in business journals featuring projections for sponsorship distribution figures. In such publications, it was emphasised that there would be an increasing rate of sports sponsorship over arts sponsorship from 1997 until the end of the Games. For example, *The Australian Financial Review* stated that, 'unfortunately, in 1996–97, corporate sponsorship of the arts generated only A\$29.2 million compared with the A\$281.9 million generated by sports' (28 May 1999: 14). In *The Sydney Morning Herald* a series of articles expressed the concerns of Margaret Seares, Chairman of the Australia Council, about the difficulties that the art community was facing to compete with the Games for sponsorship (see 14 March 1997: 29).

The negative image of the Olympics among arts opinion leaders immediately after the Games award explains some of the initial difficulties faced by OAF managers to get their festivals acknowledged and embraced by potential cultural stakeholders. Arguably, the possibility to participate in the OAF and establish a direct link with SOCOG should have enabled a change in this trend. However, other relevant issues to consider are the actual possibilities that arts organisations had to get involved, the quality of the communication and relationship between them and SOCOG, and the outcomes and benefits brought by such an experience. This is analysed in the following sections.

SOCOG and the Arts Community

A content analysis of press publications from 1993 to 1997 suggests that, prior to the first press announcements made by SOCOG culture team, most Australian arts organisations were unaware of the Games cultural programme and considered the Olympics a threat rather than an opportunity for the arts. In contrast, according to OAF senior staff, once artists and arts groups learnt about the existing plans for a series of Olympic arts festivals, an important number of them showed an interest in being involved (1999, pers. comm., 15 Sep).

From 1995, the year of the first formal Olympic culture press announcements, SOCOG received a large number of cultural proposals from organisations across the arts spectrum. However, ongoing budget limitations and poor resources allocation meant that most proposals had to be rejected during 1998 and 1999. Proposals that were particularly affected were those from community artists without an established professional profile and/or the possibility to self-finance. Furthermore, according to representatives from a range of community arts groups, the bureaucratic apparatus implicit in all negotiations with SOCOG prevented many small organisations from approaching the OAF in the first instance. A NSW Community Arts Association spokesperson has stated,

> The relationship with the people in charge at the OAF department has been very good, but SOCOG in general has not proven to be an approachable organisation from the community point of view. Community artists have not really felt invited to participate. The deadlines

and conditions have been designed for extremely organised, business like companies or on-going projects not needed of initial support. The opportunity to create new, grassroots artwork is missing. *(*1999, pers. comm., 13 Sep)

In effect, arts community leaders and other arts groups that felt excluded from participation in the OAF have suggested that the most successful way to ensure inclusion in the festivals was lobbying and profiting from personal contacts with SOCOG decision-makers (personal communications with the NWS Community Arts Association 1999, 13 Sep & Casula Powerhouse 1999, 14 Sep).[5] By mid 1999, according to the former director of Sydney's major multicultural festival, *Carnivale*, and member of SOCOG's Multicultural Advisory Committee, artists representing minority groups felt that the work that was being showcased in the OAF did not adequately reflect the Australian arts reality of 1999 (1999, pers. comm., 13 Sep). The leaders of other well established cultural institutions such as the Casula Powerhouse in Sydney, have corroborated such perception (1999, pers. comm., 14 Sep).

Implementing the Olympic Arts Festivals

In order to maximise the visibility of the OAF during Games time, organisers decided to concentrate all performing and most outdoor art activities around the Sydney Opera House. This met strong criticism from major arts companies from 1998 onwards, as they perceived such approach as the 'appropriation' of the Sydney Opera House from August to November in year 2000. Expectedly, criticism was stronger amongst companies that had not yet been appointed to be part of the event. Nevertheless, some companies with an international profile that were later invited to take part in *OAF'2000* argued that participating in this festival would not make a great positive difference for them either. Even though they accepted that the Games are a unique event with an extraordinary appeal, they felt that the OAF was not going to increase the profile of their performance in any significant way, because the uniqueness of the Olympics was not associated with the arts. A common commentary amongst arts companies was that 'any visitor coming to Sydney for the first time will try to go to the Opera House. You do not need an Olympic Arts Festival to get that.' (2000, pers. comm., 5 Oct) Consequently, in the lead-up to the Games, most participating OAF flagship companies tended to focus their concerns on the conflict created for their long-term sponsors, whose logos were to be banned from all Olympic venues and leaflets during the Games, rather than on the long term benefits of their Olympic involvement.

Generally, both elite and community artists felt sceptical about the impact and benefits of the OAF up until the start of the Games. Levels of scepticism surrounded each of the four festivals, regardless of their apparent external success. *The Festival of the Dreaming* left an unprecedented legacy for Aboriginal artists and organisations that were empowered to gain visibility and claim a position within Australia's most high profile arts environments. However, according to Colin Tatz, director of the Australian Institute for Holocaust and Genocide Studies 'considering the low basis the festival was starting from, its success in terms of public impact did not necessarily imply a success in terms of community representation' (1999, pers. comm., 4 Oct). In contrast, one might argue that the fundamental achievement of this festival was the decision and drive to make it happen in the first place. Regardless of the many important achievements, contents, presentation styles and promotional strategies did not receive the unanimous support of Aboriginal elders, Land Council representatives and other indigenous people outside artistic circles as some were still concerned with the dominant trend towards a 'white sense of aesthetics' to allow an acceptance of Aboriginal ways of life and creative expression. This is an ongoing area of debate.

Further, participants and observers of the 1998 and 1999 festivals wondered what *A Sea Change* or *Reaching the World* were supposed to achieve and complained about the minimal outcomes brought by the experience (personal communications with *Carnivale* 1999, 13 Sep; NSW Community Arts Association 1999, 13 Sep; Casula Powerhouse 1999, 14 Sep). These were the two festivals most commonly perceived as having failed to deliver on their promise, due to their lack of visibility and extremely low resources to produce new and innovative work.

The Harbour of Life or *OAF'2000* also met with the disapproval of a wide range or artists and organisations. The process of negotiation with SOCOG disappointed many ethnic and community arts institutions as they felt excluded from the event. Many people among these groups indicated that observing how the event was planned and managed accentuated their scepticism about the chances that an Olympic arts festival could ever involve non-mainstream organisations as certain 'elitist approaches' seemed endemic to their organisation (*Carnivale* 1999, pers. comm., 15 Nov). In addition, mainstream arts institutions participating in the event were also divided in their consideration of the benefits brought by holding an exhibition or performance during the Olympic period. The sections below describe these impressions in further detail, making a distinction between the experience of ethnic community arts groups and mainstream or flagship arts organisations.

Ethnic Arts Community Voices

As stated above, the existence of the OAF did not stop a relevant part of the arts community from feeling that the Olympics were a threat to innovative and representative cultural manifestations. This feeling was expressed from the moment when Sydney won the bid in 1993. However, in many cases, it was strongly accentuated after the experience of the initial festivals and the preparations for the final one in 2000. At the time of *The Harbour of Life* or *OAF'2000*, the worst impressions were found amongst multicultural arts representatives and small companies from suburban Sydney. The latter claimed to be doubly disappointed: firstly, for the impossibility to be an active component of a festival 'exclusively designed to showcase high art' and, secondly, for their exclusion as potential venues or receptacles of the event (Casula Powerhouse 1999, pers. comm., 14 Sep). Cases deserving special consideration were said to be the suburbs of Auburn (whose council incorporates Homebush, site of the Olympic park), Parramatta (adjacent to Homebush and a demographic centre of Sydney) and Liverpool (host of some sporting competitions). Despite their geographical proximity to the principal sporting competitions, none of these suburbs hosted events taking part in the *OAF'2000* and that was felt to be a major missed cultural opportunity.[6]

Sydney's multicultural arts representatives denounced what they saw as a lack of genuine interest in embracing the existing diversity of the city, despite its being a focal point of the OAF mission statement. To substantiate this impression, the former director of Sydney *Carnivale*,[7] the most comprehensive multicultural festival in Sydney that, throughout the 1990s, was held annually in the period chosen for the 2000 Olympic Games, repeatedly denounced the disinterest by SOCOG in integrating *Carnivale* as part of *The Harbour of Life* (1999, pers. comm., 13 Sep). After mixed discussions on the matter, the decision was to postpone the festival until the Olympics had finished. The festival was finally held during the Paralympic Games but it was not allocated any special Olympic or Paralympic fund.

Interestingly, the Premier of NSW, Bob Carr, proposed the creation of a street festival to be held during the Olympic period with the aim of reflecting aspects of Sydney's multicultural society at a grassroots level. The NSW Ethnic Council obtained a grant for this and local ethnic councils were invited to present proposals (McMill 1999). However, *Carnivale* was not included in these negotiations. Furthermore, this street festival initiative was not designed to interact or collaborate with the OAF. The *Street Festival* project was ultimately designed without the involvement of established ethnic and multicultural arts groups and focused on folkloric and community celebrations rather than artistic expression. Consequently, this festival did not provide a platform for the participation of multicultural artists and arts institutions in Sydney.

The frequent confusions and misunderstandings between different factions of Sydney's ethnic arts community and government bodies suggest that the city lacked a consistent multicultural arts policy in the lead up to the Games, and this resulted in frequent clashes between organisations within the otherwise proudly titled 'diverse cultural Sydney' (Collins & Castillo 1998). The perceived lack of genuine multicultural representation within the OAF and *OAF'2000* in particular, seems to have been a direct effect of this situation.

Mainstream Arts Venues

Mainstream institutions and venues participating in the *OAF'2000* were not as critical of the event as the ethnic arts groups, but they were not unanimously positive either in the period between 1993 and September 2000. Although most institutions saw a clear benefit in the potential media exposure that an Olympic-related event would bring to them, there were also doubts about the long-term legacy and sustainability of such exposure.

The Sydney Opera House was one of the key venues for the festival in August 2000 and the sole OAF performing arts venue during Games time in September 2000. The venue became the flagship of the *OAF'2000*. Consequently, its management team worked throughout year 2000 to maximise the opportunity. The 'Opera House 2000' was a public relations programme which started with the New Year's Eve celebrations, a time when the Opera House rooftop was used as a background for an acrobatics show and spectacular fireworks display. The 2000 programme continued throughout the Sydney Festival in January 2000 when, in addition to the festival regular music and dance programme, a special roof light design show was performed on a nightly basis. These were some of the activities that were to be repeated and expanded during Games time in order to attract massive public attention and emphasise the key role of the building in Sydney's lifestyle. In fact, close to all the *OAF'2000* outdoors events took place in the Opera House forecourt. This was the case for the Torch Relay Opera Gala on 14 September, featuring the opera singer Andrea Boccelli and attracting media coverage throughout the world, as it was just one day before the Opening Ceremony (see Hassall 2008: 309). Other forecourt events included the staging of a free Tainui Dance show featuring Maori dancers from New Zealand and the nightly lighting of the Opera rooftop. According to the Sydney Opera House Media Relations officer, these events, combined with the international dance, music and opera programme taking place indoors, ensured the protagonism of the venue throughout Games time. As such, it provided great opportunities for national and international media coverage (2000, pers. comm., 5 Oct).

The exterior image of the Sydney Opera House had certainly a significant presence in all Games media coverage. However, most international media focused on the venue as an architectural icon within Sydney's skyline rather than refer to or praise its cultural programming or, indeed, its role as a flagship for the *OAF'2000*. Further, a significant amount of Games-time media footage around the Opera House was related to the range of sporting competitions happening in front of it, rather than the cultural events. These comprised the Olympic sailing contest, the men and women triathlon and the men and women marathon. Additionally, the Opera House had a privileged status in most Olympic ceremonial events, from the arrival of the torch to Sydney—involving lighting one torch from the top of the roof sails—to the Games Closing Ceremony Fireworks Spectacular. The latter were the two most widely recognised Olympic cultural events to happen in the area, far more visible than any OAF activity.

Further to the above, the involvement of the Opera House in the official Olympic cultural programme brought some challenging consequences. The most noticeable example was a significant increase in ticket prices that, arguably, limited the chances for average audiences to attend indoors events during Games time.[8] Many shows were almost sold out, which suggest that the cultural programme was certainly successful and met high demand levels (a positive contrast with previous arts festival Games editions, such as Atlanta in 1996). Yet, unofficially, some observers have suggested that most of the shows were sold out because of Olympic sponsor functions and other pre-arranged Olympic Family evenings, rather than as a result of massive general public demand. Indeed, this brings into question the extent to which the Sydney Opera House ticketed programming played a significant role for the general public during the Olympic period.

In addition to the Sydney Opera House, the only arts venues with a strong presence during Games time were Sydney's main visual arts galleries and museums. Together, these presented one of the most extensive visual arts programmes ever delivered within an Olympic cultural programme (Kidd 2000, pers. comm., 30 Sep). This was the result of many years of planning and joint thinking. The Art Gallery of New South Wales, the Australian Museum, the Australian National Maritime Museum and the Powerhouse Museum, among others, met at a special session with the OAF programme manager to discuss the opportunities the Olympic period could bring them and share programming priorities. Interestingly, the Evaluation and Visitor research manager at the Powerhouse Museum noted that, 'each of these institutions [had] a very different opinion about how to maximise the Olympic experience . . . [which ultimately] provoked great difficulties to create joint projects and partnerships among them' (2000, pers. comm., 4 Oct). She offers some views on the approach of each institution present at this original meeting. To start with, for the Australian Museum, the Games were seen as an event that would not increase visitors to the venue. Instead, it was considered that it would diminish visitation patterns due to the venue being located away of the main Olympic sites—i.e. sporting venues and entertaining sites such as the *LiveSites*. Consequently, the Museum decided not to create any special exhibition. Rather it decided to host a low budget display of pictures with some potential to be linked to an Olympic theme. In contrast, both the Art Gallery of New South Wales and the Powerhouse Museum considered the Olympics as a good opportunity to host some major hallmark exhibition and reach as many local and international visitors as possible. As such, the Art Gallery presented a wide range of prestigious exhibits: *Papunya Tula,* a highly praised Aboriginal exhibit; *Australian Icons* an exhibition presenting some of the greater Australian names in painting; and *The Dead Sea Scrolls* a rare and internationally renamed collection. The Powerhouse Museum also presented three major exhibitions, all from overseas countries: a world first import of Greek antiquities; a collection of Korean art works, and the *Codex Leicester* by Leonardo da Vinci. Catering for the local population, the Powerhouse Museum also presented a display of items from the Opening Ceremony and other Sydney Olympic memorabilia. From a different perspective, the Australian National Maritime Museum considered the Olympic Games as a great chance to get some extra revenue. The Museum is located in the Darling Harbour, an area that hosted the second major Olympic competitions site after Olympic Park. It also hosted two of the six Olympic *LiveSites* and is one of the most popular nightlife areas in the city. Consequently, the approach of the Museum to the Olympic period was to present some spectacular exhibitions and,[9] importantly, rent space for Olympic sponsors and athletes functions. The latter proved to be the most lucrative strategy.

The visual arts institutions participating in the OAF final festival were very proactive and took complete control of the works presented, from the initial selection and design, to the final promotional strategy, with the OAF team assisting only in terms of branding and publicity management (2000, pers. comm., 14 Aug).[10] Beyond programming, this also involved the design and development of an ambitious visitor research project by the Powerhouse Museum and the Australian National Maritime Museum. As these institutions are located in the surroundings of Sydney Darling Harbour, which became an Olympic sports site and a major Olympic entertainment location, both museums were interested in seeing whether the Olympic experience would bring any change to the profile of tourist and local visits to their venues in the near future. The visitor research project started a year prior to the Games and aimed to compare qualitative and quantitative data collected intermittently from visitors attending exhibitions from September 1999 up to September 2001. This was one of very few initiatives providing evidence about how the Olympic Games can impact on the cultural venues of the host-city and the results (Scott 2005) have made a valuable contribution to improve understanding of the role and potential of the Games cultural programme.

THE PRIVATE SECTOR

The private sector tends to be one of the most difficult stakeholders to secure as funder and supporter of the Olympic cultural programme due to the Olympic branding restrictions noted in Chapter 7. In Sydney, the main corporate sponsor of the OAF was the *Sydney Morning Herald* (SMH), which acted as the OAF exclusive official presenter from 1997 to 1999 and kept its commitment in the year 2000, this time accompanied by the City of Sydney. As already stated, the association of the paper with the festivals was the result of negotiations between SOCOG, Fairfax and News Ltd., the latter two being Team Millennium Partners. The SMH Olympic Programme

Sponsorship manager, argued that, 'the involvement of the paper with the OAF was a self-evident move [because] the SMH positions itself as the "leading arts supplier" in Sydney and addresses upper and middle-upper urban socio-economic groups' (1999, pers. comm., 23 Aug). As Olympic sponsor, key benefits sought by SMH representatives in line with the sponsorship managers of other Sydney Millennium Partners were 'partnership opportunities' with other sponsors; 'Image/recognition', as the company associated with the Games is perceived to lead its product category; 'competition', that is, preventing product competitors from obtaining an association with the Games; and 'internal rewards' such as tickets and related hospitality packages for company VIPs and staff (personal communications with SMH sponsorship manager 1999, Swatch Public Relations Manager 1999, Telstra General Manager—Events 1999). In its publication 'Marketing fact file', the IOC adds some other possible benefits to the previous list:

> *Brand equity:* 'Sponsorship of the Olympic Movement can increase goodwill and esteem toward a sponsor as the ideals and spirit of the Olympic Games are associated with the sponsor's brand'; *Business objectives:* 'Sponsorship of the Olympic Movement can enhance core business objectives such as revenue goals, share goals or brand awareness'; *Brand repositioning* and *Showcasing:* 'the Olympic Games [. . .] provide unmatched opportunities for sponsors to showcase technology, products or services'. (IOC 2000a: 6.8)

In the case of the OAF, the SMH considered that the major benefit of the sponsorship arrangement was the opportunity to use the Sydney Opera House as main venue for the group business-to-business functions in the year 2000 (1999, pers. comm., 23 Aug). This association also allowed the creation of a special 'subscriptions offer' consisting of the provision of tickets to the OAF for SMH subscribers. The SMH Sponsorship manager stated that the support provided to *A Sea Change* and *Reaching the World* did not result in significant outcomes, especially as both festivals were happening outside Sydney in areas where the paper has no distribution. However, she emphasised that the SMH benefited from their continuous OAF support. In her words, 'the reason to keep our commitments as official presenter has been the guarantee to receive top priority for hospitality packages in the Sydney Harbour and Opera House in year 2000' (*ibid*).

In contrast with SMH, Telstra, an Australian telecommunications company with a strong tradition in supporting the arts, did not show any particular interest in having an official association with the OAF. According to the company's Group Manager- Sponsorship and Olympics, it was not expected that an association with the OAF would offer any special surplus in terms of Telstra's cultural profile. Being official sponsor of the *Adelaide Festival*,[11] and sponsoring the Australian Ballet and the Australian Opera amongst others, Telstra had already a wide access to top range cultural

Table 8.2 Olympic Sponsors' Involvement on Cultural and Entertainment Programmes in 2000

TOP Sponsors (World-wide)	Cultural /Entertainment Programme	Description
The Coca Cola company	*Coca Cola* Olympic Club Sydney & *POWERADE* Training Camp	Offer 300 teenagers from around the world with the opportunity to experience the Games
McDonald's	Olympic Youth Camp	400 teenagers from around the world share two weeks of cultural exchange and Olympic excitement in Sydney and Australia
Panasonic	Olympic *LiveSites!*	Six giant screens displayed in six popular city locations to showcase Games coverage
Samsung	World of entertainment at the Olympic Rendez-vous@Samsung	Cultural performances celebrating diversity by folkloric groups at *Samsung* tent, Olympic Park
UPS	Aqua Spectacular	Nightly laser and water show in Darling Harbour
Visa	Olympics of the imagination arts contest	A world-wide arts contest for kids between 9 and 13 years old from 25 countries. 36 winners attend the Games

Team Millennium Partners (National)	Cultural /Entertaining Programme	Description
Swatch	Olympic *LiveSites!*	Six countdown clocks, one at every site
AMP	Torch Relay Sponsor	Funds and promoted the relay in Australia
Holden	Hospitality Community Project Concert at the Domain (2000)	Assistance to the Chinese community Sydney Symphony Orchestra open air free concert
Westfield	The Olympic Journey (1997–1999) Hosting the Kids 2000 Olympic Arena	Olympic-related activities, especially for children
Westpac	2000 Pacific School Games Westpac Olympic Youth programme National Education Programme The Olympic Journey (1997–1999)	Youth-oriented educational Olympic programmes

Sydney Olympic supporters	Cultural /entertaining programme	Description
Nike	Kids interactive sport park Radio Free Sydney	Entertainment park at the Domain and Fox Studios Underground radio station featuring athletes' interviews combined with youth-oriented house, techno, acid jazz and World Beat music

Source: Author's elaboration based on IOC 2000a: 6.12–6.21 and sponsors media news releases

venues and a clear profile in the area. The company association with the Olympics was aimed at the celebration of Australia and, in this context, Telstra 'gets better value by assisting the national teams in popular sports as swimming or the Sydney to Hobart yatch race' (1999, pers. comm., 2 Sep). Telstra might have expected to be associated with the OAF in any case, as it was both an Olympic sponsor and the patron of several companies involved in the arts festival. Their position as sponsor of the *National Aboriginal and Torres Strait Islanders Award*, which was held at Sydney Customs House as part of the *OAF'2000*, provided Telstra with a good opportunity in this regard. Further, the company was introduced as the event's presenter in the venue and in *OAF'2000* promotional materials.

Besides SMH, the only other special collaboration of an Olympic corporate sponsor with the OAF was *Energy Australia*, a company that was Team Millennium Partner within SOCOG's national programme. *Energy Australia* agreed to sponsor the evening light show designed by Marc Newson which had the sails of the Opera House as its backdrop. The show took place from the opening night of the *OAF2000* until the end of the Games and was called *Energy of Australia by Marc Newson*, thus securing high sponsor recognition.

In contrast, the *Seven Network*, official Olympic broadcast right holder in Australia, Team Millennium Partner and, coincidentally, the main sponsor of Opera Australia at the time of the Games, did not have any official involvement in the OAF. Neither did it offer any coverage, vignettes or inserts about the cultural programme during its daily Games coverage. According to the *Seven Network* communications manager, the only OAF event receiving some coverage was Andrea Boccelli's *Torch Gala*. In her words, this was because 'Seven is a commercial TV station associated with sports and entertainment but not dedicated to the coverage of arts events and activities' (2000, pers. comm., 2 Oct). In her view, Australian public broadcasters such as ABC and SBS were the most appropriate media outlets to fulfil this role.

Other Olympic sponsors invested or offered in-kind support to events that were not strictly related to sports. However, rather than supporting activities taking place within the official Olympic cultural programme or OAF, they preferred to sponsor events that were part of the city outdoors programme, such as the *LiveSites*, a range of youth and community based initiatives, and events organised by the sponsor itself. Table 8.2 lists some of the cultural or entertainment programmes external to the OAF in which Olympic sponsors were involved.

Other sponsors providing extra funds and assistance to the Olympic *LiveSites* project were *Coca Cola* and *Kodak* (TOP); *AMP* (Team Millennium—national), and *Cadbury's* (Provider). Such trend towards cultural activity and entertainment support but ongoing distance from the OAF is evidence of the difficulty that the official cultural programme faces in demonstrating that it can be an internationally significant dimension of the

Games experience. Branding issues, combined with lack of international media presence are at the heart of this problem and have been a constant in Games edition up to the 2000 Sydney Games. The end of this chapter discusses emerging opportunities for change in subsequent Games editions.

THE MEDIA

The Sydney 2000 Games presented the unique situation of two publishing companies being Team Millennium Partners. According to SOCOG Sponsor Relations manager, the marketing negotiations of SOCOG with Fairfax and News Ltd. did not affect the papers editorial freedom, but helped maximise the quality and quantity of Olympic coverage and the publication of special supplements on their respective 'core properties.' (1999, pers. comm., 1 Sep) News Ltd. 'owned' as core properties the right to associate its national paper, *The Australian,* with Olympic ticketing and the Torch Relay. Fairfax 'owned' the right to denominate the *Sydney Morning Herald* (SMH)—Sydney's main broadsheet—the 'official presenter' of the four Olympic arts festivals. Fairfax also 'owned' the exclusive right to present official information about the Education programme and the Volunteer programme through the *Sun Herald,* its national tabloid.

A content analysis of the OAF press coverage from January 1997 up to October 2000 reveals a disproportionate predominance of SMH publications over the rest of Australian national and local newspapers. However, the coverage was not evenly distributed during the four years of the Olympiad and SMH was not always the leading publication in offering information about the festivals. In 1998, at the time of the nation-wide festival, local and regional press coverage in the areas were activity was taking place was more comprehensive than the official presenter's Sydney-based coverage. Moreover, from January to June 1999, when the OAF went overseas, coverage was almost non-existent in all Australian papers. From August 1999, SMH would, again, be the leading paper offering information about the OAF. However, most of the articles were dedicated to the preparations for the *Harbour of Life* or *OAF'2000,* rather than to the 1999 international festival, *Reaching the World.* The imbalance in the coverage of different festivals suggests a failure to communicate the four-year or Olympiad concept, as well as attract and influence public opinion. Nevertheless, from the perspective of the media, the main problem was that individual festivals, particularly in 1998 and 1999, did not provide sufficient stories with a newsworthy angle.

It is a common assumption amongst media and public relations managers that basic ingredients making a story appealing to the media are bad news, sensationalism, uniqueness or a 'human touch' (Cutlip, Center & Broom 1994). Arguably, the 1997 festival succeeded in attracting the interest of the media through the arguments of uniqueness and human touch.

The festival was considered unique since it claimed to be the 'first of its kind' in Australia (i.e. the first large festival fully dedicated to the celebration of Aboriginal cultures). It also provided a clear human touch by emphasising that it offered a platform for accelerating the long and difficult process of reconciliation in Australia. In 2000, an appealing ingredient of the *OAF'2000* might have been associated with the notion of sensationalism, as it incorporated a series of large-scale events such as the *Symphony for a Thousand* at the Superdome and the visit of renowned international stars such as Andrea Boccelli. In contrast, according to both the Olympic and the arts editors of *The Australian,* Australia's main national newspaper, the festivals in 1998 and 1999 were not supported by arguments that were clear and strong enough to gather the attention of the media. This led to a loss of momentum in the middle of the Olympiad (1999, pers. comm., 28 Sep; 2000, pers. comm., 13 Sep).

During an informal interview, SOCOG Communications and Community Relations general manager suggested that the use of 'cultural ambassadors' in parallel with the 'sports ambassadors' represented by popular athletes under SOCOG's coordination would have increased the public appeal of the OAF. Indeed, the notion of 'cultural ambassadors' was part of the OAF communication strategy since 1997 and included major arts groups such as the Sydney Symphony Orchestra. As such, the apparent lack of awareness about this initiative might indicate that the selected 'ambassadors' were not popular or appealing enough for the general public and Olympic interested audiences (1999, pers. comm., 17 Sep). SOCOG's Communications general manager has informally commented 'what a frenzy it would have been raised if Australian stars and icons such as Elle McPherson or Nicole Kidman had advocated for the OAF' (*ibid*). The emphasis on Australian entertainment icons was precisely at the heart of the Olympic closing ceremony, starring the top model Elle McPherson and Australian pop star Kylie Minogue. These views are a reminder of the ongoing tension between mainstream Olympic communications, which tend to place an emphasis on popular, celebratory and iconic moments or individuals, and the preferred approach of cultural programme communications, which tend to focus on subtler messages, often targeted at specific interest groups rather than a generic mainstream public.

From another perspective, the Olympic editor of *The Australian* noted that a major limitation for the OAF to attract good and abundant publicity was the conventionalism of most events during *A Sea Change, Reaching the World* and the programme announced for *The Harbour of Life* or OAF'2000 (1999, pers. comm., 28 Sep). She has argued that the definition and programming of these festivals was neither controversial nor challenging enough to compete with the appeal of other Olympic happenings. Furthermore, she predicted that during year 2000, the large amount of 'unique' sporting moments originated by the Games 'will easily overshadow the "once-again" performance of a classic opera or ballet if it does not incorporate attractive and niche added values' (*ibid*). Despite these concerns, *The Australian* took into consideration the need to provide coverage about the *OAF'2000* during Games time and to associate it with the rest of Olympic activities. The paper's arts editor secured an arrangement with the Olympic editor to guarantee that all coverage of *OAF'2000* was included in the special separate Olympic section of *The Australian*, which was published from 15 September to 1 October 2000. In an informal interview held after the end of the Games, the arts editor commented that stories and reviews about the OAF appeared every second day during Games time. Moreover, two one-page feature articles were published, one prior to the Games and another one after the end. Additionally, the Olympic edition of the paper included a daily page featuring a Sydney diary of events, which listed most if not all *OAF'2000* events happening on the day (2000, pers. comm., 5 Oct). In contrast, in the lead up to the Games, the OAF was treated as any other Australian festival because, in words of the arts editor, 'it was necessary to make a balance between a Sydney focus and a focus on activities happening in the rest of the country' (2000, pers. comm., 13 Sep).

In terms of volume of coverage, the SMH was by far the paper delivering the largest amount of stories about the OAF. This can be interpreted as a direct result of it being the official presenter of the festivals. However, it is necessary to consider other elements, as the policy for arts coverage in Australia varies strongly from paper to paper. SMH and *The Australian* were the two mainstream papers with a stronger dedication to cover the Olympics. They also had a similar vision about their approach to cultural programme coverage. Nevertheless, in 2000, while the SMH had a policy to include up to three daily pages about culture and the arts, *The Australian* published arts pages only every other day. This explains the marked difference in percentage of articles dedicated to the OAF in *The Australian* (13% of all OAF articles reviewed) and SMH (39%).

The arts editor of *The Australian* has explained the paper's approach to cover the OAF (2000, pers. comm., 13 Sep). *The Australian* offered a wide coverage of *The Festival of the Dreaming* and was constant in reporting the evolution of the *OAF'2000* since its official launch in October 1999. From that date to March 2000, most articles were dedicated to summarising the highlights of the festival programme and to report criticism by some companies and artists disappointed with the contents, ticket prices, the cancellation of some events and/or SOCOG's way of dealing with it all.[12] From July to September 2000, articles were less critical and focused on announcing the forthcoming opening of the festival and highlighting the confirmed programme of events. The editor acknowledged that, in general, there were not many front cover stories about the OAF. Rather, highlight articles, artist profile stories and, during the time of the festival, a wide range of review articles tended to dominate. In the editor's opinion, the lack of cover or editorial stories for the final festival was the result of 'a programme which had very few pieces telling "stories" or having an edgy side' (*ibid*). Further to this, the added challenge was that the festival was happening at the same time as other Olympic events that were clearly perceived as more newsworthy.

> *The Festival of the Dreaming* offered a more attractive concept from a journalist perspective. [. . .] The [*OAF'2000*], besides not being insightful enough, has had to compete with the torch relay and the sporting competitions, events containing highly appealing motifs that have in the end taken over most space in the papers. (2000, pers. comm., 13 Sep)

From a different perspective, in 2000, SMH updated the editorial strategy put in place during *The Festival of the Dreaming* and created a distinctive OAF logo to accompany most reviews and cover articles on the 2000 festival. The paper published stories about the *OAF'2000* on a daily basis from 18 August—official opening of the festival—to the end of the Games. The content analysis of all press coverage reveals that the paper published an average of four *OAF'2000* articles a day during the Olympic period. However, not all articles were marked as OAF reporting and, as it had been the case in 1997, many did not mention that the story or specific event being reported was part of the official Olympic festival. This fact might have, once more, affected the potential association of the cultural events with the Olympic Games, more so as SMH maintained the OAF coverage within its traditional arts and culture pages while its Olympic section focused on the sports competitions. The only non-sporting news included in the paper Olympic section were the articles dedicated to the Torch Relay and Ceremonies. All the same, it is worth noting that, after the end of the Games, the paper web site provided links to most articles about the OAF within the archives of its *Olympics Extra* section. This is indicative of the lack of coherence in Olympic cultural programme media reporting and the still unresolved tension between the appropriateness of framing it as an arts or Olympic story.

BEYOND SYDNEY 2000

The relationship between the Olympic cultural programme and its key stakeholders has remained uneven in subsequent Games editions. Observations and interviews at every Games from 2002 to 2012 reveal that an important point of distinction exists between countries whose approach to cultural policy is dominated by public sector investments and those which prioritise or have a more established tradition of involvement of private partners within the arts and cultural sphere. In the first, governments tend to take the lead and become the main stakeholder, using the Games cultural programme as a platform to advance local or national cultural policy agendas which, since 2000, have mainly revolved around projecting—or branding—the host city as a 'creative city' (Landry 2000). In the latter, private organisations prevail, at times demonstrating great entrepreneurial ability to raise the profile of Olympic cultural activity but often failing to secure an overarching coherence to sustain emerging initiatives or involve other stakeholders.

Government organisations were clearly the dominant partners for both Southern European hosts, Torino 2006 and Athens 2004, and are playing a critical part in the context of London 2012. Torino's main programme, *ItalyArt*, had a national theme, but was led by the Municipality which viewed this as an opportunity to position Torino as a leading arts and creative centre. In Athens, the Cultural Olympiad was a national priority of the Hellenic Ministry of Culture, which diverted considerable resources and created a special organisation, the Hellenic Culture Company, to lead the Olympiad's strategic vision. Athens is perhaps the clearest example of strong government involvement to define an *Olympic* cultural policy (rather than just grow existing local or national policies for culture more generally). This was made manifest in the ambition to establish a permanent Cultural Olympiad Foundation with an international remit and backing from UNESCO.[13] The main limitation in these approaches has been the ongoing difficulty to set a precedent that could be built on by subsequent host cities and become embedded in the Games hosting process. Opportunities for this to change may emerge out of the Vancouver 2010 and London 2012 editions, both of which used government support to establish not-for-profit and legacy-oriented initiatives aimed at enhancing the sustainability of cultural as well as educational programmes inspired by the Games.[14] The IOC has shown an interest in these approaches and offered recommendations for their continuity, given the growing dominance of legacy concerns, a situation that was just at its inception at the time of Sydney 2000 (see Moragas et al. 2002).

The private sector had a stronger presence in the two North American host cities, particularly in Salt Lake City 2002, which relied mainly on private donors to fund its Cultural Olympiad. Vancouver 2010 followed Sydney's model with Bell as their official 'presenting sponsor'. In Europe, London 2012 has also built on this approach and, although mainly relying on public funds, it has named British Telecomm and British Petroleum as 'premier partners' of the Cultural Olympiad, making them lead a number of programmes, including two in association with the National Portrait Gallery, both of which touch on notions of identity. These corporate links suggest that domestic sponsors can see the value of associating themselves with the cultural programme, particularly in the context of programmes likely to capture the general public's imagination, such as nation-building identity exercises.[15] However, as in the case of Sydney, the large majority of global corporate sponsors (TOP) tend to use their Olympic affiliation to create their own cultural programmes, for which they retain total creative control and which they can transfer from Games to Games, rather than committing additional funding to Games-specific Cultural Olympiads. The most noticeable area of growth has been the development of 'plaza' environments throughout the host city, at times maintaining Sydney's denomination- *LiveSites* (London), in other cases termed 'sponsor plaza' (Athens, Torino) or cultural squares (Beijing). In all of these cases, there is a limited or no presence of the official Games cultural programme and the activities focus instead on general entertainment.[16]

The experience of the arts community tends to follow similar patterns regardless of locality. Artists and arts institutions tend to engage with the opportunity to link to the Games at the bidding stage, when advisory groups are open to ideas and making their best to secure public support. However, scepticism and, at times, hostility, ensues when it becomes apparent that funding is very limited and branding demands high, with the latter often resulting in exclusion from official programming. Community arts groups tend to be the most critical of the Olympic cultural programme, feeling disenfranchised and disadvantaged. Such feelings are as strong within the host city as in other parts of the host country. In Vancouver / Canada and London / UK this has led to a range of arts initiatives that use the Olympics as a platform to highlight and denounce Games-related issues, from housing evictions to the perceived corporate dominance in official cultural narratives (see Jeffreys 2011).[17] Other criticisms, mainly voiced by established arts institutions, include the perception that the official cultural programme does not provide sufficient room for innovation or a 'cutting edge' approach (pers. comms, Athens Gallery Director 2004; Citta di Torino Culture Commissioner 2006; London 2012 Creative Programmer 2009). Some view this to be a result of the pressure to ensure that a wide range of audiences, beyond the arts realm, and from very different national backgrounds, feel engaged and are able to understand and appreciate what is on offer. Given the ongoing tensions between official organisers and arts communities, and the frequency of rejections due to the need to protect the interests and expectations of ever growing numbers of stakeholders outside the arts and cultural worlds, one may argue that some of the most interesting, challenging and innovative cultural and arts experiences inspired by the Games happen at the fringes, rather than within the official cultural programme.[18]

Finally, in the case of the media, major technological developments have had an impact on opportunities for culture stakeholders engagement. This has been particularly noticeable since Vancouver 2010, which was the first Games to plan for and welcome social media contributions from the outset and attracted a wide range of alternative online media environments reporting on very specific areas of interest, such as the Cultural Olympiad. The existence of specialist or niche media reporting on non-mainstream areas of the Games is not new, however, the ease of access for national as well as international communities of interest is a new phenomenon that is potentially giving greater weight, visibility and longevity to these media stories and offers a distinct route for Olympic cultural programme communications. Mainstream or traditional media, however, continue to struggle with the Cultural Olympiad concept as a core Olympic story and rarely see it as a source of national or international news beyond punctual event launch announcements which mainly happen during the pre-Games period. In the absence of special agreements, such as the 'official OAF presenter' role for SMH in Sydney, it is rare to see media partners providing dedicated coverage on the cultural programme with explicit reference to the Games link. This is even more noticeable for broadcasters. For London 2012, the BBC is the host broadcast Olympic rights holder and it will also be a special contributor to the Cultural Olympiad programme, via its *Olympic proms* programme.[19] Despite these links, BBC executives still claim that it is difficult to present the Cultural Olympiad as a nationally relevant Olympic story unless it can provide spectacular activity on the scale that the public expects of the Games (BBC Sports, pers. comm., 2008). As noted in Chapter 7, this tends to result in a distinct brand and communication strategy for Games-time cultural programming, which is often focused on big iconic acts and international stars, at times to the detriment of an overarching four-year Olympiad vision. Athlete biographies remain a broadcaster favourite to cover the 'human touch' angle as opposed to the kinds of arts-led community initiatives that prevail within the official cultural programme. These stories tend to be covered at a local level only, often without stressing Olympic links, particularly when occurring away from the Olympic host city.

SUMMARY

The involvement of different stakeholders in supporting and/or influencing the Sydney OAF programme evolved from 1995 and throughout the four-year period of the Olympiad. For the most part, stakeholders saw an interest in the first festival, became vague or reticent to support the two central ones, and increased their contributions in time for the final events in year 2000. Despite the fact that the *OAF'2000* attracted the largest amount of resources, on average, perceptions about the 1997 festival were more positive than the 2000 festival.

Government bodies were divided in their interests and expectations towards the OAF. Local and state bodies seemed to interpret the festivals as an opportunity to expand tourism and trade opportunities. As such, their focus was the final festival, *OAF'2000*, as it was expected to be the event gathering most media attention and reaching an international audience. Their policy was dominated by a rationalist and market-oriented approach to the arts. Alternatively, the approach taken by federal bodies such as the Arts Council suggest a greater interest in revisiting notions of Australian culture and fighting established stereotypes. As such, their emphasis was in exploring and supporting the notions of multiculturalism and aboriginal reconciliation that had been presented since the bid stage as Australia's 'brand images'. This made the AC particularly supportive of the first festival but also the final one, for its potential international projection. Both governmental approaches had common goals and used similar techniques in their support to the OAF but, arguably, the first welcomed the use of pure entertainment and spectacle in general whilst the second tended to put the emphasis on maximising representation and a shared vision in Australia's cultural discourse.

The Australian arts community has expressed mixed feelings about their OAF experience. After their original scepticism towards the bid, many arts groups felt encouraged by the artistic challenges and energy resulting from the first festival in 1997 and developed greater expectations for the years to come. However, the lack of resources available for 1998 and 1999 was a disappointment for a large section of this community, multicultural and ethnic groups in particular. The frustrations surrounding the two middle festivals led to a renewed sense of scepticism towards the OAF as a concept and set the tone for the final festival or *OAF'2000*. The 2000 festival was regarded by a broad range of artists and arts institutions as an elitist and unrepresentative event, unable to assist changing stereotypes about Australia and unable to bring new legacies to the cultural sector nationally. Consultation with members of the arts community in 1999 and 2000, including some groups that were active participants in the final festival, suggests that many of them did not feel they could influence the format of the programme. Furthermore, many have stated that, for the most part, the programme did not offer them an opportunity to progress or explore new fields. Despite such perceptions, the festival attracted considerable media coverage and helped advance Australia's international projection, thanks in part to its association with the Australian Council funded *ausarts2000* programme.

Representatives from the corporate sector have declared that it was difficult for them to see the OAF as an investment that would be as profitable as other components of the Games. The strict Olympic marketing regulations can be seen as determinant of this circumstance. However, explanations are also evident via the ambiguous and, at times, exclusive character of the programme itself. Olympic sponsors have suggested that the OAF—the *OAF'2000* in particular—did not engage with a wide enough audience and could not make a difference in the way that other activities such as the ceremonies and free street entertainment can. Thus, they tended to see greater benefit in developing an association with the sporting competitions, Olympic ceremonial events or their own specially designed community entertainment programmes.

Finally, the media understood Sydney's OAF as an interesting addition to the Games but one that lacked the public interest and uniqueness that distinguishes other Olympic programmes, from infrastructural developments to, indeed, the sport competitions. During the interviews, journalists, press editors and broadcasters noted that, in their view, the OAF programme was not challenging nor daring enough, with the only exception of the 1997 festival. They all agreed that the concept of an indigenous festival in a grand scale was impacting and relevant to Australia, two ingredients that are necessary for a good news story. However, that momentum was lost in subsequent festivals, a factor which was accentuated by the growing presence of other more easily recognisable Olympic news as Games time approached. The final festival, despite the wide coverage offered by major papers such as the SMH and *The Australian*, was not seen as an event as distinctive as the 1997 festival and was not seen as a festival capable of engaging the average Olympic fan nor the Australian population at large as it was perceived as less accessible and 'entertaining'.

In sum, there is no strong evidence that the involvement of OAF stakeholders led or contributed to strengthening the Games cultural policy framework. Their interests were disperse, as were subsequent delivery procedures and final outcomes. The search for spectacle and media appeal was mixed with the ambition to guarantee diverse local representation and reconciliation. Ultimately, it can be argued that programme stakeholders were unable to prevent the imbalances and limitations caused by the vulnerable position of the OAF within SOCOG.

Overall, in Sydney and beyond, cultural programme stakeholders operate according to very different agendas and do rarely work towards a collaborative or joint vision that can be sustained beyond Games time or transferred from one Games to the next. Nevertheless, the aspiration to use the Games as a platform to promote creative practices has gained momentum since Sydney and this has led to greater involvement and coherence of vision by public bodies, which see in the cultural programme an opportunity to advance cultural policy agendas and demonstrate a link between culture, sustainability and long term event legacies. This has certainly been the main area of growth and opportunity for the cultural programme to demonstrate its relevance to Games partners and the Olympic Movement at large. Corporate stakeholders have, so far, not been completely in tune with this, and tend to focus on their own entertainment programmes. The media remain divided in their relationship with the programme but the growth in the range and accessibility of user-led social media environments is providing greater visibility to cultural stories all the same. The greatest stakeholder tension remains with the arts community, as both independent artists and arts organisations struggle to relate with Games organisers, given their perceived lack of sensitivity towards cultural ambitions and the ongoing clash with Olympic branding restrictions. As argued throughout the rest of this monograph, this is all indicative of ongoing contradictions within the Games cultural policy framework both at a local (OCOG) level and at the international (IOC) level. The issues raised here and in previous chapters are revisited and recommendations put forward within the concluding chapter.

9   Media Coverage

One of the greatest challenges to the perceived relevance of the Olympic cultural programme is its apparent lack of media appeal. This is in stark contrast with the transformation of the Olympic Games into the most successful global media event of our times. A study of the kinds of media narratives generated by the cultural programme provides a basis to understanding how the programme is positioned within the Games hosting process and how this reflects the event's cultural policy framework.

This chapter presents a selection of findings resulting from the content analysis of four years of Australian press coverage on the Sydney OAF (1997–2000), which broadly spans over the full period of the Cultural Olympiad. This content analysis exercise, conducted at the end of year 2000, helps identify which elements of Sydney's Olympic cultural programme were considered news-worthy and whether they were interpreted as a significant component of the Games experience. This analysis also provides a measure of the effectiveness of the programme to project the images and values it originally intended, as discussed in Chapter 4.

METHODOLOGY FOR THE CONTENT ANALYSIS

The press clippings used for the research presented here were provided by SOCOG's Record Services with consent of the OAF publicity department. The only exception were the clippings for year 2000, which at the time of the research data collection had not been stored yet and so, were directly provided by the OAF publicity department.

The selection of clippings was undertaken by 'Australia Media Monitors', an independent company contracted by SOCOG to follow up all media coverage on the Sydney Olympic Games from 1993 to the end of year 2000. The OAF publicity department received a daily pack of articles dedicated to the Olympic arts programme and cultural events, which were consequently classed by date and filed at SOCOG's Record Services after a year of reception.

In total, the analysis presented here covers thirty-one Australian newspapers—from national to state, regional and local papers, both broadsheet and tabloids—and includes 693 articles published over the four-year period of Sydney's Olympiad. These articles are fully representative of the period in terms of thematic variety and presentation formats. This is guaranteed by the 'Media Monitors' service, as it followed exactly the same selection procedures for each day of the period and included all the most relevant and widely distributed papers in Australia.

For the purpose of this content analysis, the 31 papers were categorised under 18 titles. To reduce the number of categories, papers which had Sunday variations have been understood as one single publication. For example,

Table 9.1 List of Analysed Papers, Area of Distribution and Publishing Company

Paper Name	Distribution Area (acronym in brackets)	Publishing Company
The Australian + The Weekend Australian	Australia wide	News Ltd.
Australia Financial Review	Australia wide	Fairfax
Bulletin	Australia wide	
Sydney Morning Herald	Sydney, New South Wales (NSW)	Fairfax
Daily Telegraph + Sunday Telegraph	New South Wales (NSW)	News Ltd.
Sun Herald	New South Wales (NSW)	Fairfax
The Age	Melbourne, Victoria (VIC)	Fairfax
Herald Sun + Sunday Herald Sun	Victoria (VIC)	News Ltd.
Canberra Times	Canberra, Capital Territory (ACT)	Canberra Times Group
Courier Mail + Sunday Mail	Queensland (QLD)	News Ltd.
The Advertiser	South Australia (SA)	News Ltd.
Examiner	Tasmania (TAS)	Examiner Group
Mercury + Sunday Tasmanian	Tasmania (TAS)	News Ltd.
Daily Advertiser	Western Australia (WA)	
Sunday Times	Western Australia (WA)	News Ltd.
The West Australian	Western Australia (WA)	West Australian Newspapers Holding
Other local or regional papers	Various territories	Various news groups

Source: Australia Media Monitors and individual papers website

the *Courier Mail* and *Sunday Mail* were gathered under the common name 'Courier Mail'. As well, all papers with a local or regional character, either suburb based, village based or specific community based, were gathered under the common name of 'Local- regional' papers.

The papers composing the research sample belong to all states in Australian geography. Table 9.1 lists the name of each paper and relates it to the area or state were the paper is distributed.

In terms of area distribution, three of the papers were distributed Australia wide, three belonged to the state of NSW with capital Sydney; three were based in Western Australia with capital Perth; two in the state of Victoria with capital Melbourne; two in the state-island of Tasmania; one in the Australia Capital Territory and one in South Australia. An area not mentioned in the above listing is the Northern Territory. Papers belonging to the Northern Territory exclusively had a limited distribution and have been grouped under 'other local or regional' newspapers.

In terms of publication companies, the two major publication groups in Australia are Fairfax and News Ltd. and both were Team Millennium Partners. Of the papers examined, seven belonged to News Ltd., whose principal newspaper is *The Australian*, distributed nation wide, and four to Fairfax, whose principal newspaper, *The Sydney Morning Herald* (SMH), was official presenter of the OAF. The content analysis had a special interest in contrasting the amount and tone of the articles published by Fairfax with those of News Ltd. and to further contrast it with articles by other publication companies and regional or local papers. This was to determine the extent to which Fairfax and News Ltd. coverage was affected by their Olympic sponsorship deal with SOCOG. In particular, there was a close analysis of the coverage by the SMH, as the paper is based in Sydney and was the official presenter of the four festivals. The research hypothesized that this would be the paper offering the greatest volume of coverage on OAF events.

Following established content analysis techniques, the main categories of analysis presented here are as follows:

- date (differentiating year and month from January 1997 to September 2000)
- title of publication (18 separate newspaper titles)
- festival the article refers to (either one of the four festivals or the OAF as a whole)
- way the article refers to the festival (word or terms used by journalists, categorised into 13 categories)
- reference or not to the OAF (core reference, reference in passing or no reference)
- key subject (classified in three main thematic areas and 25 sub-themes)
- tone of article towards key subject (positive, negative or neutral)

The following sections offer an overview of the main findings, organised in six main areas. The first, volume of coverage, places an emphasis on the chronological evolution of coverage throughout the four years of the Olympiad. The second section focuses on the variations of coverage depending on the Festival and the levels of recognition of respective titles and event denominations so as to determine which festival identities or brands became more clearly recognised or appealing to the media. The third section focuses on the issue of Olympic Games association specifically, analysing the percentage of articles about the OAF that mention the term 'Olympic' explicitly. Sections four and five touch on the thematic emphasis of coverage and attitudinal tone, identifying which 'key subjects' attracted the highest volume of coverage and the extent to which these were associated with respective festivals. In particular, it has been deemed important to assess whether the topics promoted as part of the original and evolving OAF vision have been identified and expanded on by journalists and whether they have been treated with a positive, negative or neutral tone. Finally, section six offers a brief overview of coverage sources in order to identify the most dominant newspapers and assess whether certain festivals where more appealing than others depending on the typology and location of newspapers.

In order to simplify graph production, the names of specific festivals have been replaced by the following acronyms: FD: *Festival of the Dreaming* (1997); ASC: *A Sea Change* (1998); RW: *Reaching the World* (1999); HOL-OAF: *The Harbour of Life / The Olympic Arts Festival* (2000); CO-OAF: *Cultural Olympiad / Olympic Arts Festivals* (1997–2000).

VOLUME OF COVERAGE ON OLYMPIC ARTS FESTIVALS ACTIVITY

As it has been discussed in previous chapters, the levels of media attention about the OAF varied year on year. The cultural programme was presented as a highlight at the bid stage in 1993, and the first festival in 1997 was heralded as a major step forward for Australia and the recognition of its Aboriginal and Torres Strait islander populations. The figures below clearly indicate the changing cycles of media attention, from a strong build-up in 1997 to a marked peak in the Olympic year, and also make manifest the difficulty in attracting attention towards the intervening 1998 and 1999 festivals which, as discussed in Chapter 7, where not supported by consistent marketing strategies nor significant programming budgets.

Figure 9.1 shows that media coverage was at its peak during year 2000, the Olympic year. This dominance is even more remarkable if one considers that the articles compiled from that year for the purpose of this content analysis were published between January and September 2000 (over 9 months), while articles from prior years had been published along the complete twelve-month period (see the monthly distribution in Figure 9.2).

In contrast with the high rate of publications in 2000, there was a progressive decrease of articles from a peak in 1997 to a minimal media presence in 1999. Interestingly, year 1998 does not present such a great contrast

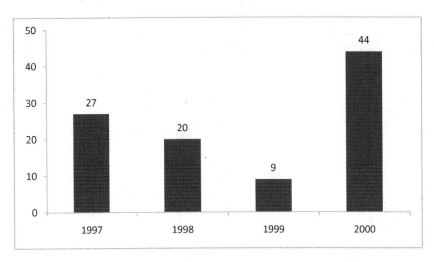

Figure 9.1   Percentage of articles by year.

comparing to year 1997 in terms of coverage. However, this is not necessarily an indication of specific coverage about the 1998 festival and activities taking place that year. Instead, as shown in Figures 9.3 and 9.4, this is evidence that during the second year of the Olympiad, the media were interested in exploring a wide range of OAF issues, including a reflection on the four-year Olympiad concept and projections towards the cultural programme for the Olympic year.

The most interesting finding in Figure 9.2, showing the distribution of coverage per month, is the nearly exact proportion of articles published in September 1997 (when *The Festival of the Dreaming* was taking place) and articles published in August and September 2000 (two months when *The Harbour of Life* or *OAF'2000* was taking place). The similarity of the proportions indicates that, over these three months, publications about the OAF happened daily. A review of the festivals' marketing, sponsorship and publicity agreements, indicate that this daily presence took place, essentially, because of the role of the *Sydney Morning Herald* as presenting partner.

Other interesting data are the smaller peaks in publications over July 1997 (contrasting to June and August 1997), May–June 1998 (contrasting with March and April 1998), October–November 1998 (contrasting with September and December 1998) and October 1999 (contrasting, remarkably, with September and November 1999). Each of these dates corresponds with the month when each respective festival had its media launch: *The Festival of the Dreaming* was launched in July 1997, *A Sea* Change in May 1998, *Reaching the World* in November 1998 and the *OAF'2000* in October 1999. This confirms the impression that the official launch of the festival was key to gather media coverage, especially for the period between 1998 and 1999.

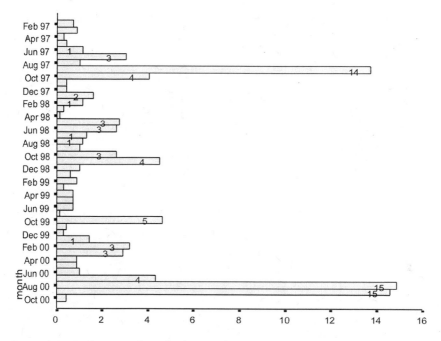

Figure 9.2   Percentage of articles by month.

Finally, it is worth noticing the peaks taking place in October 1997 and February—March 2000. Arguably, the peak in October 1997 was due to publications of reviews and cover articles evaluating the first festival once it had finished and was generally considered a success. The peak over February and March of 2000 can be explained on the grounds of them being the months when the *OAF'2000* tickets went on sale, which is confirmed by analysing subject coverage by month.

COVERAGE BY FESTIVAL

At this point, it is relevant to assess which festival titles attracted higher levels of recognition and how references to specific festivals varied over time. The articles included in this analysis, although covering OAF activity, may not have made any explicit reference to festival titles—focusing instead on specific arts activities and ignoring that they were part of an overarching festival programme or indeed, associated in any way with the Olympic Games. Figures 9.3 and 9.4 show which festivals provided content that was most attractive to the media and Figures 9.5 and 9.6 show how this content was framed by journalists.

Figure 9.3 shows which festivals received most coverage regardless of year of publication. These percentages reflect the amount of articles dedicated to

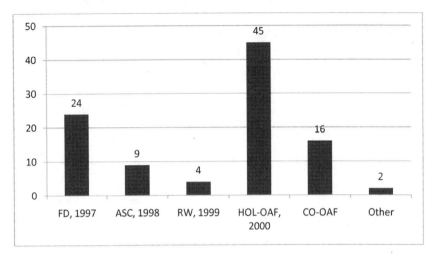

Figure 9.3 Percentage of articles by festival.

events that were part of respective the festivals, independently of their key subject or the denomination the journalist gave to the events or activities described. The festival receiving most coverage was the final *OAF'2000*, attracting close to half of the total number of articles. *The Festival of the Dreaming* was second, gathering a 24% of the total, followed by articles dedicated to the OAF as a whole or the notion of a Cultural Olympiad (16%). Articles within this category have been identified as those that did not describe or review events from a particular festival. Rather, they did one or several of the following: offered a perspective on the Olympiad; discussed the role or vision of the OAF or Cultural Olympiad concept; referred to the history of the Olympic cultural programme; analysed the components of the programme, and/or compared one festival with one or more of the others.

The label 'other' refers to articles about festivals and events that were not part of the OAF but included some sort of indirect references to the OAF. This was the case for articles dedicated to other Australian festivals (e.g. the *Sydney Festival*, the *Adelaide Festival*), or to other cultural, festive or educational Olympic events (e.g. *The Olympic Journey*, *Share the Spirit* student arts prize).

Figure 9.4. shows how references to activities within different festivals have evolved over the years. The percentage of articles dedicated to programming within *The Festival of the Dreaming* and *The Harbour of Life* (HOL) or *OAF'2000* were clearly dominant on the respective festival years in 1997 and 2000.[1] However, *A Sea Change* was only slightly predominant in 1998 and articles dedicated to *Reaching the World* events were a minority even in 1999, which is indicative of the challenge to attract Australian media interest for events happening overseas. Interestingly, both *The*

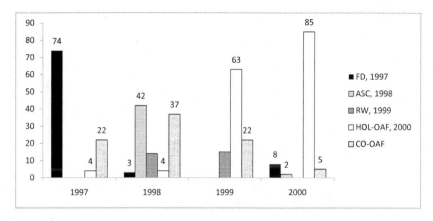

Figure 9.4 Percentage of festival mentions by year.

Festival of the Dreaming and HOL-*OAF'2000* had some articles dedicated to them every year of the Olympiad, which supports the view that these were the most successful and widely recognised components of the Sydney OAF. Further, HOL-*OAF'2000* was the focus of 63% of articles published in 1999, which is indicative of the OAF's dedicated publicity campaign to promote the final Olympic festival since June 1999 and the event's official launch in October.

References to the OAF in general or the concept of Cultural Olympiad also took place every year, with a special emphasis in 1998. However, they were almost non-existent in year 2000. Considering that the category Cultural Olympiad- OAF (CO-OAF) comprises articles referring to either the festivals' four-year period or explaining the links between arts and the Olympic Games, such a distribution in time could be understood as evidence that journalists maintained an interest in linking specific year on year activity with the notion of a four year programme up until 1999, but that SOCOG's decision to change strategy and appropriate the generic OAF denomination to promote the final 2000 festival exclusively from June 1999 onwards, led to the eventual disappearance of media references to a wider Cultural Olympiad concept.

Other Games host cities, such as London 2012, have also been keen to change promotional tactics about the cultural programme during the 'official' Olympic year and downplay references to a four year Cultural Olympiad or any arts activity taking place in the lead to the Games fortnight. This is often justified on the grounds that it creates confusion for the media and the general public and that there is a need to focus on high profile cultural activity within iconic host city venues to complement the Olympic sports programme rather than maintain the type of campaign required to promote more widely inclusive and geographically disperse activities. The downside of such an approach is a lack of consistency in media messages

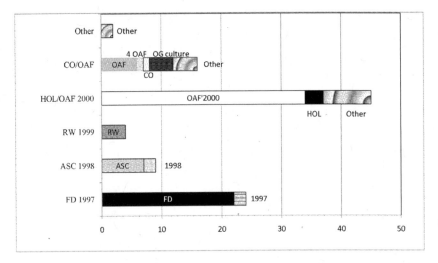

Figure 9.5　Percentage of articles about specific festivals and chosen denomination.

about core Cultural Olympiad aspirations and the perception by a range of interested stakeholders that the Olympic cultural programme usually fails to deliver on its original bid aspirations. Such tension is explored further later on in this chapter (see sections on 'Key topics' and 'References to the Olympic dimension' of the OAF).

Figure 9.5 is indicative of the level of recognition by journalists of official festival branding when reporting on OAF events. It compares the percentage of articles dedicated to each actual festival (titles on the left column) with the way the festivals or their events were being described by the media (principal denominations, presented as subgroups within each festival).

The 2000 *Olympic Arts Festival* was the festival attracting the largest amount of coverage (45% of all analysed articles) and was mostly referred to by its official final title or a close approximation (34% of all articles, 75% of 2000 festival articles). In contrast, only 3% of published articles referred to it as *The Harbour of Life*. This is significant, given that this title had been used since the bid stage in 1993, while *OAF'2000* was a name appropriated in October 1999. This is indicative of the success of the final festival marketing campaign and the appropriateness of changing the festival name into what would be most clearly perceived and assimilated by both media and the general public. Interestingly, however, 18% of articles about the 2000 festival programme (8% of all articles) referred to it with other names or did not give it a festival name at all. This was mainly the case of coverage about international star performances which the media felt needed little introduction, such as the widely anticipated concert by opera singer Andrea Boccelli.

The lack of articles specifically mentioning *The Harbour of Life* as a key feature is an indication of the difficulty to establish and promote new concepts that have no obvious link to a given Olympic narrative. This was also the case for *Reaching the World*, which was only mentioned in 4% of cases and was overlooked by the press even at the time when it was taking place in 1999. *A Sea Change* attracted greater media attention and was identified as such by 7% of all articles, which may be indicative of SOCOG's or the OAF team success establishing a link between the Olympic Games and Australia's multiculturalism. Nevertheless, the festival remained unmentioned or was referred to simply as the festival or events 'happening in 1998' in 22% of 1998 festival related stories.

Contrasting with the two middle festivals, *The Festival of the Dreaming* attracted a quarter of all coverage (24% of articles) and it was referred to by its official name in 91% of cases. This can be largely explained by the success in establishing a distinct brand for this festival, regardless of its Olympic association. In fact, as discussed in the next section (figure 9.7b), a majority of articles about this festival ignored the Olympic link.

It is also interesting to observe the variety of forms that were used to explain the generic OAF or Cultural Olympiad concept. Up to 6% of articles were dedicated to the OAF in general and used this title specifically, with an additional 2% referring to the existence of 'four Olympic Arts Festivals' explicitly; 4% referred to the relationship between culture and the Olympic Games, either by writing about 'Olympic Games festivals', 'Olympic cultural events', 'Olympic arts' or 'sport and arts' events; and 1% did mention the phrase 'Cultural Olympiad' specifically.

Further, other sorts of event, not actually linked to the OAF would, at times, be denominated as such. This was mainly the case for the entertainment programme set up by the City of Sydney during Games time, the *Live Sites*, which, as discussed in other chapters, was often perceived as the main Olympic cultural programme and confused with the OAF.

Overall, up to 14% of all articles gave the OAF or their events different names or did not address them with any particular name, focusing instead on the titles of specific performances or artist names. Most of these articles (presented as 'other' in the right hand column) referred to the OAF'2000 programme or were about the *Live Sites*.

REFERENCES TO THE OLYMPIC DIMENSION
OF THE CULTURAL PROGRAMME

At the heart of the Olympic cultural programme communication challenge is the traditional lack of association with the Games. The following figures provide an indication of the degree of centrality of Olympic references within articles about Sydney OAF activity, from 'core' references, that is, articles including explicit discussion about the Olympic cultural framework, to references only in passing ('only ref') or no reference at all.

In Sydney, media coverage about OAF activities was evenly divided between articles that located references to their Olympic nature at the heart

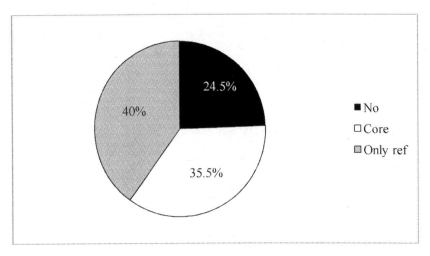

Figure 9.6   Percentage of articles referring explicitly to the Olympic context/OAF.

of the story, those mentioning it in passing, and those ignoring the link altogether. Although it is apparent that three quarters of analysed coverage was in some way framed by an OAF reference, it is not possible to conclude that clear Olympic associations were prevalent within Australian media narratives about the cultural programme. This is because, within the 40% of articles tagged as 'only ref', mentions of the OAF would often be placed exclusively at the foot of the article as part of a standardised background information section. This was particularly the case for arts reviews and highlight listings, which account for the majority of articles. Further, most of the articles analysed here were located within specialist sections of the papers, such as the arts and entertainment pages, and it can be inferred that they were mainly addressed to an interested and locally-based arts audience rather than national or international Olympic visitors. As such, it is likely that the Olympic link was not the main motivation to produce the article and attract readers' interest.

The way journalists referred to the OAF varied depending on the year and depending on the festival to which the article was dedicated. This is shown in Figure 9.7.

Figure 9.7a shows the distribution of types of references by year. An expectation might be that references to the OAF would increase the closer the article was published to the Olympic Games period. Indeed, this trend is apparent to some degree, as the percentage of core references rises from 17% in 1997 to 48% in 2000. However, the peak of 'core' references did not happen during the Olympic year but in 1999 (53%). This can be explained on the grounds that 1999 was the year when the final festival was launched to the media, which involved the publication of many articles explaining the ambitions and background of *OAF'2000*. 1999 was also a year when

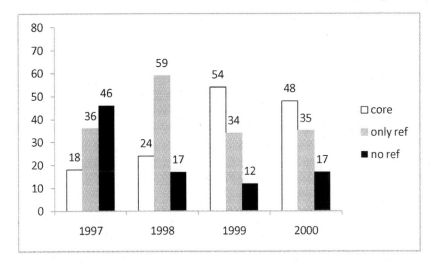

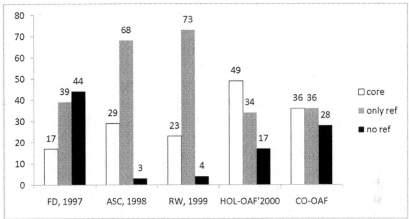

Figure 9.7   (a) Centrality of OAF references by year, and (b) by Festival (in %).

the media focused on re-visiting and explaining the concept of a four year OAF or Cultural Olympiad.

Although the trend of references in 2000 was similar to that of 1999, during the Olympic year there was a higher proportion of articles that did not make any reference to the OAF. This can be explained by looking back at Figure 9.4 (festival mention by year). In 1999 a great number of articles were dedicated to the generic OAF-CO concept. However, in year 2000, the majority of articles were exclusively dedicated to the events or artists taking part in *OAF'2000* and, as shown in Figure 9.7b, within such articles, the title or nature of the festival they were part of was not mentioned in 17% of cases (that is, articles focused on specific events without referring to their broader festival context).

The most remarkable trend, however, takes place in 1997, when almost half (46%) of articles did not make any reference to the OAF or any Olympic link. This can be attributed to the fact that most articles were dedicated to reviewing specific events within *The Festival of the Dreaming* which, as highlighted in Figure 9.7.b, did not incorporate any reference to the OAF in 44% of cases. This suggests that the 1997 festival was perceived to have significance in its own right and, thus, did not require the OAF or Olympic Games association to attract media attention.

KEY TOPICS ASSOCIATED WITH
OLYMPIC ARTS FESTIVALS ACTIVITY

Another way of understanding what makes the media interested in Olympic cultural programming is to identify the key topics that tend to be at the heart of related coverage. In the analysis of Sydney OAF coverage, a series of topics were identified and are presented below. Prior to interpreting the data, it must be noted that only one key subject has been identified per article. This means that only the most relevant or noticeable theme every article has dealt with has been coded. Relevance has been identified by focusing on predominance within article heading or first paragraph (see Reason & Garcia 2007 for additional detail on media analysis methodology). It is in this context that it must be understood why figure 9.8 shows that only 3.5% of all articles dealt with Aboriginal issues when, in fact, nearly all articles about *The Festival of the Dreaming* (24%) touched on some kind of Aboriginal issue. The 3.5% indicates the percentage of articles which focus essentially on the discussion about political, economical or social conflict related to Aboriginal and Torres Strait Islander peoples. In other cases, when the main focus has been to discuss the type of show presented or the artists performance, despite the mention to Aboriginal issues, articles have been classified under the subject of 'highlights', 'reviews', 'OAF stars' or as appropriate to each case.

Figure 9.8 shows which elements or themes were most central to the articles analysed. Overall, it is possible to identify three main thematic areas: articles discussing themes related to the OAF mission (OAF themes) which amounted to 25.8% of the total; articles about managerial issues (22.4%) and articles focused on event specific topics, such as event reviews and highlight listings, which were the most dominant area (45.8%).

As noted above, a remarkable majority of articles focused on either providing a generic overview and listings of festival highlights (23%) or reviewing specific events (18%). This can be explained on the grounds that most articles were published within the arts/entertainment section of newspapers. This type of coverage, although potentially beneficial for the artistic credibility of respective festivals if presented positively, has a potentially negative effect on the promotion and understanding of the OAF and what

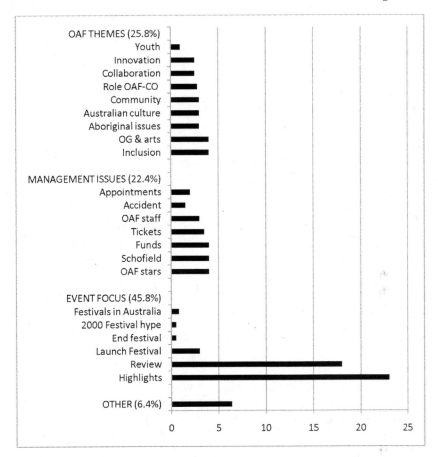

Figure 9.8 Percentage of articles by key subject.

it stands for as an Olympic cultural programme. This is because a focus on highlighting or reviewing events in a conventional arts critic sense does not always lead to mentioning the name of the festival events are framed by, nor to communicating the notion of a larger multi-annual programme such as the OAF. Thus, such an emphasis is likely to overlook the association of specific events with the wider Olympic project and, by implication, the events' ability to reflect the cultural policy choices of the host-city in the Games context.

Beyond this clearly dominant approach, journalists focused on a wide diversity of themes, evenly distributed in two main thematic groupings. Firstly, there are topics related to the management and implementation of the festivals. These include, in percentages of 4% to 4.5%, the subject of 'funds' implying the use and distribution of funds to support the festivals; 'tickets', referring to ticket sales or ticketing conflicts; 'Schofield', comprising those articles dedicated to the artistic director of the final festival, a well-known personality in the arts circles of Sydney and Melbourne; and articles dedicated to the biography or a personal interview of some of the 'stars' participating in each of the festivals. Secondly, gathering between 3% and 3.5% of articles, the most frequent subjects are 'venue conflicts', which are those articles mentioning the negotiations to use or renounce to use specific venues; 'OAF staff', signifying those articles mentioning the role or function of managers, assistants or directors (other than Schofield) within the OAF team; and the subject 'accidents', meaning articles describing difficulties found in the production or staging of shows. Most articles classified as 'accident' referred to the collapse of the grades where the audience was placed during a theatre show of *The Festival of the Dreaming*.

Other topics relate to the character of festivals' programme, including commentary on the social or cultural value of the themes and type of events presented. Most of these themes are related to the overarching OAF thematic ambitions, as presented in Chapter 4. Among these, gathering between 4% and 4.5% of articles, we find the topic of 'inclusion- representation' referring to the festivals ability to be culturally representative or inclusive of Australia's diverse arts communities. We also find the topic of 'Olympic Games and arts' referring to the relationship between the arts or cultural events and the Olympic sporting events. Secondly, gathering between 3% and 3.5% of articles we find the subject of 'Australian culture', which refers to articles commenting on the festival's success or failure to showcase Australian artists and works, regardless of their cultural background. In this percentage group there is also the subject of 'community', referring to the chances for participation or access to events for the wide Australian community, from children and students to regional populations and grassroots artists. Moreover, 3.5% of articles focused on the discussion about 'Aboriginal issues', with an emphasis on the event's or festival's political, economical and/or social dimensions (a preferred term in this context was the notion of 'reconciliation' and discussion on the event or festival's ability to advance towards it). Around 2% of articles discussed 'collaborations', meaning the ability of the festivals to encourage new partnerships among artists, companies or institutions. Finally, 'innovation-new ground' consists of those articles dedicated to analysing the level of creativity and originality of the events or shows presented within the OAF.

Figure 9.9 shows the percentage of articles addressing specific themes in the context of respective festivals. An interpretation of the figure helps understand the extent to which the festivals were successful in promoting media coverage of specific themes and gives and indication of the issues that the media considered to be more central to each festival. In this sense, it is relevant to distinguish the subjects that are reflective of the OAF mission statements and festival themes, from the subjects that emerged out of what was deemed newsworthy by respective papers.

As already noted, subjects reflective of the OAF original mission have been categorised as 'Aboriginal issues', 'Australian culture', 'collaborations',

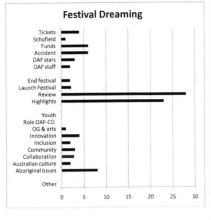
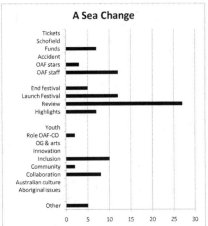
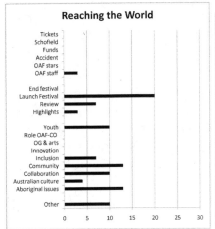
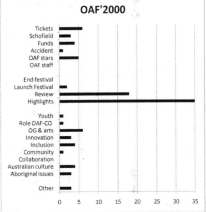

Figures 9.9a–d Percentage of key subjects by festival.

'community issues', 'inclusion-representation', 'innovation- new ground' and 'role of the OAF- CO'. References to 'Aboriginal issues' were made largely during *The Festival of the Dreaming* and *Reaching the World*. While it was to be expected that this issue would be central to the 1997 festival, it is interesting to observe that it was also extremely dominant within coverage for *Reaching the World*. This might be an indication of the efforts during the 1999 festival to assist Aboriginal artists and shows that had been successful in 1997 to tour in overseas countries.

The subject 'Australian culture' was treated on occasion of all festivals except *A Sea Change*. This suggests a clash between the media or general public perception of what Australian culture is and the theme for the 1998 festival, which was, precisely, the exploration of Australia's diverse cultures and their continuous transformations. In contrast, the subject is central to 4% of articles about the *OAF'2000* and 3% of articles about *Reaching the World*. Interestingly, most of the articles dealing with this subject had a negative tone (see section below). As such, it could be inferred that the two latter festivals were subject to criticism due to the perception that they did not fully succeed offering a renewed perspective about Australian culture. From this point of view, the lack of references to this subject during the coverage of *A Sea Change* may suggest that journalists did not find reasons to criticise the festival on this matter.

The distribution of the subject 'collaborations' reinforces one key argument discussed in prior chapters. It was essentially addressed during *A Sea Change* and *Reaching the world* (approximately 10% of total of subjects related to each festival) and not mentioned in any of the articles dedicated to *OAF'2000*. Given that most articles on this matter are positive (see Figure 9.10), this indicates that both the festivals in 1998 and 1999 were appreciated for their emphasis on providing room for partnerships and collaborations among companies. It also reinforces the view that *OAF'2000* was not perceived as a collaborative festival focused as it was, instead, on fulfilling the vision of its director and, in line with its defined mission, presenting work on a grand scale with an emphasis on international rather than local networks.

The subject 'community' was treated most thoroughly during *Reaching the world*. Considering the scarce amount of coverage on this festival, the finding indicates that most articles about the festival were motivated by the emphasis on activity dedicated to school children and other outreach events. The inclusion of non-professional and community based activities was considered one of the festival strengths for promotion. Furthermore, during 1999, 'community' references, together with 'Aboriginal issues', was one of the key reasons for press publications. It is also worth mentioning that most papers publishing articles on the 1999 festival were local or regionally based.

The subject of 'inclusion—representation' was the focus of 10% of articles dedicated to *A Sea Change*. This could be interpreted as success in terms of promoting the main theme of the festival, though Figure 9.10. 'Tone by subject' indicates that the majority of articles treating this subject were making negative references to these issues. They were critical about the real chances the OAF was providing for meaningful cultural representation. However, a more detailed analysis of these findings reveals that the majority of articles that were critical about this matter were not linked to *A Sea Change* but rather to *OAF'2000* or the concept of OAF-CO in general.

Interestingly, the subject 'innovation—new ground' was mostly discussed in the context of *The Festival of the Dreaming* and nearly 100% of the time, the theme was treated positively. Thus, we can conclude that 1997 was considered successful for opening new ways of developing artistic expressions in Australia. *OAF'2000* was the other festival gathering a relevant proportion of articles discussing 'innovation'. However, the latter have mostly been negative or critical articles, thus suggesting that journalists considered the character of *OAF'2000* as more conservative or conventional than the 1997 festival.

Notably, references to the 'role of the OAF' or the Cultural Olympiad concept were rare in the context of festival- specific coverage. This fact reinforces the impression that most articles about specific festivals obviated explanations about their Olympic character and explains the reduced amount of articles treating the OAF or Olympic arts theme as a core element. Further, this provides some evidence of the ongoing challenge to communicate the notion of an 'Olympiad' and make it news-worthy, given that media coverage on the Olympic cultural programme tends to be motivated by the artistic merit of individual components rather than any intended Olympic rationale.

This argument is further reinforced when looking at the second (and clearly most prominent) group of themes on the Sydney OAF. As noted earlier, the most popular subjects were in fact not related to the OAF mission statement or respective festival themes and emphasis. Rather, journalists and arts editors were more interested in publishing articles that 'reviewed' or 'highlighted' components of the arts programme, the coverage of the 'festival media launch' and issues related to controversies that arose from the arts programme (eg. funding, ticketing, accidents). Other subjects that attracted media attention included those which can be defined as human interest stories, articulated within the analysis as stories dealing with 'OAF stars' or celebrities, OAF staff 'appointments' or 'OAF staff' points of view.

Highlights and reviews have already been defined as the main focus of most published articles for all festivals. The listing of 'highlights' was the main focus of articles dedicated to the *OAF'2000* (a total of 35% of all articles) closely followed by *The Festival of the Dreaming*. However, 'reviews' were dominant in articles about the 1997 festival (28% of articles) and, interestingly, about *A Sea Change* events, but not so much in the case of the final festival (18% of articles). The existence of abundant reviews about *A Sea Change* indicates that the media perceived that the 1998 festival was more relevant for the Australian public than the festival in 1999, which, by comparison, received a very low percentage of reviews. Despite not being able to have an impact across Australia, *A Sea Change* was celebrated locally and regionally, as any other local festival or event.

The subject 'launch festival' refers to each festival media launch, which tended to take place four months to one year prior to the opening of the event. Such moments were paramount to the coverage of the middle festivals, occupying 12% of the total of articles dedicated to the 1998 events and, remarkably, 20% of articles about the 1999 festival. The launch events were organised by the OAF team as a key component of their marketing and publicity strategy. They guaranteed a media presence of the festival's overall programming and, in most cases, reference to the festival's purpose. The duration between the festival media launch and the festival opening explains the existence of coverage about 1999 events in year 1998 and the significant predominance of articles about the *OAF'2000* in 1999 (see Figure 9.7). The media launch of *A Sea Change* took place during the same year that the festival took place, which explains why there were no articles about it in years other than 1998.

The findings reveal that the subject of 'funding' was pertinent to all festivals, except for *Reaching the World,* which did not get any coverage on this topic. This points to the fact that there was no investment or funding strategy for 1999 events. As was mentioned in Chapter 5 *Reaching the World* was the only festival that did not receive any purpose-built funds or grants, relying instead on the value-in-kind support of the *Sydney Morning Herald* as presenting partner and the basic support of SOCOG.

Finally, 'ticketing' was a focus of coverage for *The Festival of the Dreaming* and *OAF'2000* exclusively, as these were the only festivals that relied heavily on ticket sales. As indicated in the following section, nearly all articles that dealt with ticketing issues were negative, thus indicating that the subject is one of the main sources of bad impressions about either of the two festivals.

ATTITUDES TOWARDS OLYMPIC ARTS FESTIVALS STORIES

In order to understand how the above subjects were treated by journalists and thus likely to be perceived by the general public, it is paramount to contrast key subjects with the tone of the articles. Overall, coverage on the OAF was 39% positive, 45% neutral and 16% negative. Taking into account that the two subjects more frequently treated were festival highlights and festival reviews, the prevalence of positive articles can be explained on the grounds that most specific events reviews were positive and the dominance of neutral articles mainly relates to the large numbers of purely descriptive articles listing festival highlights.

The subjects attracting the largest percentage of positive coverage were discussion about 'community' engagement, 'OAF stars', the 'launch' of festivals and event 'reviews'. Other subjects, such as 'highlights', 'Aboriginal issues' and 'OAF staff' were viewed either in a neutral way or a positive way. Clearly, thus, the treatment of Aboriginal issues and community participation were the two most successful original OAF aspirations from a press point of view.

Subjects that were mainly covered in a negative tone were mainly related to management issues, but there are also some noticeable cases within the other two thematic groups. From a management point of view, 'ticketing' was the topic generating the largest percentage (and volume) of criticism, mainly due to the perception of high pricing, delays or losses in the sales process, and confusion about SOCOG's sales system. This was followed by 'accidents' within the staging of shows, and 'funds', which in a majority of occasions would be referred to as 'insufficient'.

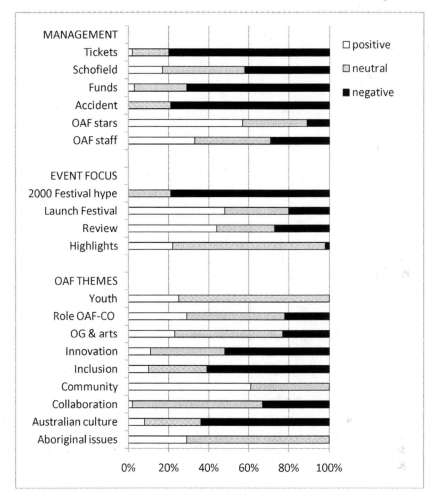

Figure 9.10 Distribution of attitudes by key subjects (in %).

In relation to the OAF original mission, the theme gathering the largest proportion of negative analysis was 'Australian culture', which often was considered missing or very scarce within OAF programming, particularly during *OAF'2000*. The OAF was also criticised for failing to fully address 'inclusion- representation', a topic that reflected the strong opinions and disappointment of artists and institutions based in suburban Sydney and other Australian ethnic or multicultural communities. These groups did not consider that they had had a chance to take part in *OAF'2000* and were very vocal about it in 1999. References to 'innovation- new ground' were also mainly negative, as journalists felt that the OAF failed to be sufficiently cutting-edge, relying instead on established acts.

Finally, criticism of the '2000 festival hype' consisted of comments about the great amount of events planned for year 2000 that were expected to compete with the OAF or be a drain on public resources at a time of high event-related expenditure.

VARIATIONS IN COVERAGE BY PAPER

The *Sydney Morning Herald* (SMH) was, by far, the paper dedicating the largest amount of coverage to the OAF, totalling 39% of all articles. This can be partly explained on the grounds that SMH was the official OAF presenter and offered daily reviews and listings for OAF activity, particularly in 1997 and 2000. This was followed by *The Australian*, the country's main national paper, which published 13% of articles. The noticeable difference in coverage between the two major Australian papers can be better understood if we consider the role of the publication companies they belong to, Fairfax and News Ltd. Significantly, *The Daily Telegraph*, a NSW paper published by News Ltd., gathered 11% of publications. This places News Ltd. in a much closer position to that of Fairfax. Yet, *The Sun Herald* is a tabloid paper of Fairfax also published in NSW, which adds an extra 5% presence to Fairfax within the OAF coverage arena. In total, if percentages of each different paper are calculated in the function of the publication company they belong to, Fairfax papers accumulate 50% of publications throughout the country, while News Ltd. accumulate approximately 33%. This leaves other publication companies gathering around 17% of articles. With these data in view, it can be argued that the coverage by Fairfax and News Ltd. did not differ as strongly as it might appear at first view. Both were Olympic media partners and both offered support to promoting SOCOG media assets.

An analysis of the percentage of explicit references to the OAF by paper indicates that the distribution of references is very balanced in all cases, to the extent that it is not possible to find a clear correlation between a paper, publication company or editorial line and the approach of articles towards the OAF concept.

It is not possible either to identify any remarkable pattern or correlation between the type of paper or publishing company and the tone or articles. The only point worth noticing is the dominance of a negative discourse by papers such as *The Advertiser, The Australian Review, The Canberra times* and *The Courier Mail,* and the limited presence of positive coverage by papers such as *The Age* and *The Sun Herald.* These papers were distributed at a national level, or in states other than NSW. This might indicate some correlation between distribution area and tone. Arguably, papers distributed in Sydney and NSW incorporated a greater number of articles covering day to day news such as event reviews and festival highlights, two subjects that were mostly treated in a positive light (see Figure 9.10 tone by subject). In contrast, papers distributed in other states might have had a predisposition to publish articles about conflicts and controversies.

In terms of volume of coverage about individual festivals, generally, papers offered some coverage about each of the four festivals. In most cases, papers emphasized *The Festival of the Dreaming* and HOL-*OAF'2000*. Notably, SMH dedicated 59% of articles to the final festival in 2000, *The Age* dedicated 50% and *The Australian*, *The Courier Mail*, *Daily Telegraph* and the *Sun Herald* dedicated between 43% and 45%. Alternatively, *The Australian Financial Review* and *The Canberra Times* dedicated 50% of their coverage to the aboriginal festival in 1997.

In contrast, some papers did not offer any coverage about the major festivals of 1997 and 2000 and focused, instead, on minor festivals or the generic concept of OAF-Cultural Olympiad. *The Examiner*, a paper from the state of Tasmania, dedicated all coverage on the OAF to *A Sea Change*. This can be explained by the fact that the 1998 was the only festival occurring in the state and the event was highly praised. The *Daily Advertiser*, a paper from Western Australia, dedicated all coverage to the generic OAF-CO concept. Finally, *The Sunday Times* dedicated 50% of its coverage to the generic OAF-CO concept and 50% to other festivals and events that the paper associated, mistakenly, with the OAF.

Interestingly, the only trend common to all papers was the dedication of articles to the generic OAF-CO concept. This reveals a shared interest in explaining that the Games have a cultural component and suggests that, despite not being a dominant theme, this issue had an appeal for the media. The challenge for cultural programmers is thus not to lose momentum and to ensure that all cultural activities invite the media to sustain references about the nature of Olympic cultural programming.

SUMMARY

The primary objective of this chapter has been to determine the perceived relevance of the Olympic cultural programme as an element of the Olympic Games. Given the positioning of the Olympic Games as a 'media event' first and foremost, the apparent lack of media appeal of the Olympic cultural programme is indicative of its limited impact to date and its low significance in the context of local and, particularly, global Olympic narratives.

It has not been possible to analyse the full range of Olympic related stories published in the lead-up to and during the Sydney 2000 Games competition fortnight. Nevertheless, it is apparent that Olympic Arts Festivals coverage was of marginal interest to the media when compared to, for example, sporting stories or the various controversies surrounding the Games preparations (from ticketing scandals to budget cuts or infrastructure development delays). In the period analysed, Australian papers published a range of Olympic stories every single day and by year 2000 and, indeed, during the Games period, these would multiply frequently into entire editions or supplements. Yet, in such editions, articles about the OAF were present in a very small proportion. This proportion can be inferred by the consideration that, at the peak of Sydney 2000 press reporting, coverage about the OAF reached a maximum average of five to six articles a day across all Australian papers, while other Olympic stories would occupy, at times, full newspaper editions ranging from 20 to 30 pages each. As such, rather than offering a strict comparison with other Olympic stories, the relevance of the cultural programme can be inferred by analysing how journalists referred to and interpreted the function of the different festivals. For this, it has been of particular importance to examine whether the cultural programme was identified as a component of the Olympic Games and/or associated with other elements of the Olympic experience.

In general, the media coverage of Sydney's OAF reveals that there was limited value attributed to its relationship with the Games. Although three quarters of all articles analysed made some sort of reference to the association of the programme or specific festivals with the Olympics, only 16% emphasized the tradition of such a programme within the Games and its value as an intrinsic component of the Games. This means that the rest of references were limited to mentioning the name of respective festivals (notably, the *Olympic Arts Festival* in 2000), which frequently was made in the form of an end-note, together with the date and location of specific events. Furthermore, during the Olympic period—at the time of greater press distribution—only 2% of articles were explicitly focused on explaining the role and aspirations of the Olympic cultural programme, while 98% of OAF coverage treated the activities covered as standard arts events, without particular emphasis on their Olympic motives or associations.

When looking more closely at the differing impact and perceived significance of individual festivals, it is useful to consider the amount of coverage dedicated to each of them. In terms of volume of coverage, the final 2000 festival clearly dominates, as it was the key feature of 45% of all analysed articles. *The Festival of the Dreaming* followed with 24% of articles while the 1998 and 1999 festivals had an extremely low coverage—9% and 4% respectively. As already noted, the remainder 18% of coverage focused on generic Cultural Olympiad overview stories or other established Australian festivals. However, further analysis reveals that, despite the higher amount of coverage and despite the frequent reference to the word 'Olympic' in relation to the *OAF'2000*, there was a very low percentage of articles about this festival that offered background notes about its function and ambitions as part of the Games. Instead, the focus was on the programme's specific arts content. This was even more noticeable in the case of *The Festival of the Dreaming* which, despite being the festival to receive the most positive reviews and the one celebrated as a ground-breaking experience in the Australian arts world, it was practically not associated with the Olympic experience. Notably, 44% of articles about this festival did not include any direct reference to the Olympics nor to the fact that the activity being reported was part of a four year Olympic Arts Festival programme.

Beyond articles that were specifically about individual festivals, the generic concept of the OAF was dealt with in 16% of the total press coverage, within which the history and function of the cultural programme is emphasized. Thus, the generic OAF programme had greater chances to be perceived as a relevant component of the Olympics, rather than any individual festival. An analysis of the discourse utilised within this 16% of articles reveals that 50% of them did so by reviewing the evolution of the Sydney OAF and its mission specifically. Moreover, 25% of articles were dedicated to explaining the links between culture and the Olympics and the other 25% was divided between explaining the concept of a Cultural Olympiad through history and emphasizing that Sydney was presenting a four-year programme. This reveals an interest in explaining the case of Sydney in particular, over an interest to communicate the sense of the programme throughout Olympic history.

A second issue addressed with this content analysis has been the ability of the cultural programme to project the images and values intended in its mission statement and defined objectives. In general, when contrasting the festivals' objectives with the themes that were predominant in the press coverage, the level of achievements was medium to low. Chapter 4 offers a list of the programme key objectives. They are defined as (1) genuine showcase of aboriginal cultures; (2) manifestation of diversity, inclusion, representation; (3) international scope—showcase of excellence; (4) national involvement—community participation; (5) people's awareness and understanding of the OAF concept; (6) development of new opportunities, and (7) establishment of legacies.

A measure of success for this is the revision of themes that appear most frequently in the press and the tone (positive, negative, neutral) with which they are treated. On this basis, the OAF was particularly successful in 'showcasing the work and ambitions of aboriginal cultures', as this theme was treated as a central or secondary theme in a high percentage of articles and it was treated in a positive tone in 40% of occasions. Remarkably, the other 60% of articles treated it in a 'neutral' tone, thus, there was not noticeable criticism—no 'negative' approaches—on this issue. The second relative achievement was the portrayal of an 'image of excellence', as the amount of articles dedicated to praise the artists and institutions that were part of the programme was relatively high and 55% of them treated this theme positively. Finally, the issue of 'community participation' was treated positively in 60% of articles. However, the press was very critical about the 'lack of collaborations' between the OAF and other institutions, in particular, from states and territories other than New South Wales. In this sense, the OAF did not entirely succeed in portraying participation and national involvement as a key element of the festivals' experience.

Another issue that the OAF failed to project was a sense of 'developing new opportunities.' This is evident in the 2.5% of articles that treated the theme of innovation within the programme, of which 80% referred to it by criticising its absence. The second, most poorly projected issue was the idea of 'manifesting diversity, inclusion and representation.' 4% of articles discussed inclusion issues within the OAF, with 60% criticising the lack of sensitivity for these matters. Thirdly, 60% of articles dealing with the issue of 'presenting Australian culture', criticised the OAF for failing to achieve so. Finally, the content analysis reveals that the OAF did not succeed in promoting the idea that the festivals would leave long-term legacies, since the issue of 'legacies' was not the main theme of any articles.

A final element that can be concluded from this content analysis is the poor ability of the festivals to have a media appeal and respond to the demands of communication specialists. The findings indicate that the OAF had a relatively low media appeal and that journalists treated it as another 'standard' arts event, rather than a distinctive component of the Games experience. The treatment of the OAF as a standard arts event is evident in the predominance of articles dedicated to cover its highlights or programme agenda, and the predominance of articles reviewing particular events in the manner that is common in the arts section of most papers (these two approaches combined range up to 41% of all analysed articles).

Furthermore, the low media appeal of the festivals is evident in the lack of noticeable controversies and stories considered worthy to occupy the papers front pages or editorial pages. The media was attracted by the controversies surrounding the festivals' funding process and the ticketing scandals. There was also an interest in analysing the political implications of the cultural programme contents in areas such as the showcase of aboriginal cultures and the representation of Australian culture. However, these aspects were not dominant (only up to 21% of all analysed articles) and were overshadowed by either the highlights and arts review approach (41%) or the treatment of other generic themes about the design and purposes of the festivals (38%). As explained in the above paragraphs, the latter contributed to explaining the nature of the festivals and to projecting (either positively or negatively) the images it intended. However, this tended to be relegated to the papers' arts sections and, as explained by the editors of a major newspaper such as *The Australian*, it was not considered particularly newsworthy in the context of other Olympic stories (pers. comm. 1999, 28 Sep; 2000, 13 Sep).

Part III

Towards a Culture-Led Olympic Games?

10 The Future of Cultural Policy at the Olympic Games

This book has reviewed the positioning and application of cultural policies to inform the production of the Olympic Games cultural programme. The Olympic Games offer unique grounds to explore this question as it is a mega-event that operates at the interface of extreme global as well as local cultural imperatives. The official Olympic cultural programme is the most suitable element of the Games for this interrogation as it is ideally placed to address and balance these often conflicting demands.

Previous chapters have analysed the evolution of cultural policy discourses and their link to mega-event hosting processes, de-constructed the existing definition of Olympic cultural programme, analysed the levels of cultural provision within the structure and agendas of the IOC and studied the conditions and strategies that lay behind the design, management and promotion of a paradigmatic case, the Sydney Olympic Arts Festivals, as a programme which has had a noticeable influence on subsequent Games editions. This final, concluding chapter, is structured to respond to the main areas of exploration identified at the outset of the book. This will be achieved by separating the conclusions into four sections, each of which addresses one of the book main areas of enquiry:

1. How is an Olympic cultural programme informed by the cultural policy of the Games global network?
2. How is it informed by the cultural policy of the local host?
3. Is the Olympic cultural programme able to play a relevant role in defining the Games' cultural dimension?
4. Is it perceived as a core component of the Olympic Games?

The chapter concludes by outlining key cultural policy tensions in the Games hosting process and suggests a way forward.

THE CULTURAL POLICY OF THE OLYMPIC MOVEMENT

This book started by interrogating the historical and internationally outreaching framework within which Olympic cultural programmes operate.

This has involved an analysis of the notion of cultural programme as understood within the Olympic Movement; a review of past programme implementations and an assessment of the IOC provisions to sustain cultural activity. This analysis provides a strong basis to critique the IOC's policy for culture and leads us to conclude that there is no such a thing. Despite some efforts to establish an Olympic cultural policy discourse (IOC 2000f) this has remained a nebulous area that has failed to materialise in effective guidelines for operations, particularly within the Olympic Games hosting process.

Chapters 2 and 3 have shown that the definition and purpose of an Olympic cultural programme is inconsistent and that the programme has traditionally been weakly positioned within Olympic Movement structures and IOC operational guidelines. This has been largely due to an entrenched tendency to present the discourse for culture in out-of-date and over-simplistic terms and a failure to update its operational framework in tune with the continuously evolving Games business model.

The apparent resistance to change the discourse for culture could be explained on the grounds that it touches on the modern Games founding rhetoric as defined by Pierre de Coubertin at the end of the 19th century. At that time, cultural practices were typically understood as artistic expressions, with an emphasis on the traditionally denominated 'high arts' such as painting, sculpture, music, theatre, dance, literature and so on. Since then, while notions of culture and the remit of cultural policy have evolved and become more inclusive, the Olympic cultural programme has remained strongly attached to this initial conception. In contrast, other Olympic programmes have adapted to the Games changing reality in order to retain a connection with contemporary issues. This is particularly evident for Opening and Closing Ceremonies, which have evolved to move beyond relatively fixed patriotic pageants to become the largest global media event, and in so doing, balance their role portraying established Olympic traditions with broadcast-friendly showcases of respective hosts' cultural icons.

A further consequence of the lack of a clear definition for the cultural programme has been the difficulty establishing an effective operational framework for delivery and ensuring a full integration in the Games celebration. Respective OCOGs have had to justify the presence of such a programme in their own terms rather than count on the IOC as a global long term supporter. As such, depending on the agenda of the OCOG, the programme has been seen as an element central to advance the Games host narrative—from a Nazi propaganda tool in the Berlin 1936 Games to the showcase of avant-garde and youth culture in Latino America during Mexico 1968 or the presentation of post-Franco Spain in Barcelona 1992—or as a purely complementary element with barely any influence on the Olympic experience. Regardless of the approach taken by the OCOG, the implementation of the programme has encountered similar problems at each Games edition. The most frequent of these include the lack of synergy with other Games components, limited financial resources, branding clashes with Olympic right-holders and lack of support to ensure local as well as international media appeal. As a result of these challenges, regardless of the quality of the actual activity being presented, the programme has not been able to raise a profile and stand out as a significant dimension of the Games experience.

The ambiguous definition of the cultural programme is an indication of the IOC's fragmented cultural discourse and the limited confidence it has on the Cultural Olympiad as a platform to convey key Olympic values. References to the importance of culture in the Olympic Movement are a constant within the IOC and Olympic Family members' rhetoric. However, the use of the term culture does not respond to any explicit set of premises and as such it has no weight to guide action. Furthermore, Chapter 3's analysis of the structure and agenda of the IOC suggests that, up to Sydney 2000, the protection of its official cultural programme or Cultural Olympiad was not a priority for the IOC. The commission in charge of cultural matters appears to be one of the less influential commissions in the movement hierarchy and has traditionally operated on an ad-hoc basis. As such, the IOC provisions for culture have not been attached to any defined policy but rather to the punctual decisions of individuals with the ability to influence the Executive Board at particular times.[1]

The IOC has not followed a consistent cultural policy strategy, built on a commonly agreed definition of culture and aimed as a guide for cultural action. As discussed throughout, this has been particularly damaging for the cultural programme. In contrast, there are other elements of the Games that enrich its cultural dimension and are protected by specific policies and guidelines. This is the case for the Olympic properties (including the 'Olympic symbol' or five rings, the anthem, motto, flame and torches) and ceremonies. These elements have traditionally been kept separate from the cultural programme and related activities and are not the responsibility of the IOC cultural commission. Instead, they were gathered under the denomination 'Olympic protocol' up to the Sydney Games (IOC 1999a: 67–73) or regulated by the 'Protocol Guide' (IOC 2007). Furthermore, over the years, the IOC has developed extensive policy guidelines in the areas of communication and marketing. These policies have proven extremely successful at a global level, in particular, the worldwide guidelines for the TOP programme and the selling of broadcasting rights. However, as discussed in Chapter 7, these regulations do not extend to the cultural programme.

In this context, it can be argued that, if the IOC had been as consistent with its cultural policy as it has been with its Olympic protocol, marketing and communication policies, the Olympic cultural programme could be playing a more central and coherent role than has been the case so far. However, for this to happen, the cultural policy of the IOC and, by extension, of the Olympic Games, must ensure a clear coordination of all the elements that are part of the Games' cultural dimension. What is at stake here is to fully acknowledge that cultural activity (and by implication, contemporary cultural expression) is not just a secondary element of the Games but a component that is as important as the established elements within Olympic protocol and the key to establish a direct dialogue with younger generations as well as local Games stakeholders not familiar with the Games international heritage. Linking up the cultural programme with more media-friendly components, such as Opening and Closing Ceremonies, would allow the latter to better contextualise their content and message, while raising the profile of the former.

Unless greater synergies are established between these components, the notion of an Olympic cultural programme will remain ambiguous and its potential unfulfilled. To achieve this, the cultural programme must evolve from the limited function of an out-dated and often isolated 'arts component,' into an overall programme of activities that is clearly linked with the sports, education as well as the ceremonial and symbolic protocol programmes.[2] Furthermore, the IOC must embed the cultural programme within its communication and marketing framework. This links back to the exposition made in the introductory chapter, where it was argued that a way of ensuring the global impact of cultural policies is to intertwine them with communication and media policies.

In sum, if the IOC aspires to protect the cultural programme as a relevant component of the Olympic experience and add credibility to the Games cultural dimension, it must take on a stronger role to guide the programme's implementation. This requires a careful re-consideration of what is understood as culture in the Olympic context and the definition of a consistent cultural policy to guide action. This cannot be the sole responsibility of the OCOG at a local level but be supported by the IOC and involve its global partners. To be *effective*, this policy needs to be co-ordinated with existing policies in the areas of communication and marketing. Further, to be *meaningful*, it must be integrated with the policies currently framing highly symbolic areas such as the programmes overseen under the 'Olympic protocol' guide.

THE CULTURAL POLICY OF THE GAMES LOCAL HOST

The second area of enquiry considered how an Olympic cultural programme is informed by the cultural policy of the local host. To address this question, the book has looked at the tradition of cultural policy in Australia in the lead up to the Sydney 2000 Games and has contrasted it with the country's socio-demographic trends, sporting traditions and related elements that may have influenced its sense of identity and cultural aspirations. Subsequently, the process to design the cultural programme has been analysed, paying special attention to its evolution from the generic proposals made at the bid stage to the specific definitions prepared by the team in charge within the Olympic organising committee once the Games were awarded to Sydney. This leads to the conclusion that local cultural policy aspirations played an important role at the bid stage to attract international interest, but this original vision was not fully supported by local stakeholders and was poorly operationalised once the delivery team was in place. These gaps and contradictions provide evidence of the ongoing limitations of implementing a coherent cultural policy discourse in the context of a mega event if there is no clear synergy between local and global policy guidelines.

The review of Australia's current socio-demographic and cultural trends reveals that, at the time of bidding for the Games, policy-makers were trying to come to terms with a national identity discourse, but struggled to find an obvious common ground given the rapid growth in the diversity of ethnic backgrounds and cultural traditions of the population. The passion for sport had long been considered a tradition that unifies interests and aspirations across the country. However, it has become increasingly apparent that this tradition alone could not solve the country's growing identity tensions, particularly given that many sporting practices are heavily linked to the Anglo-Saxon background of the first immigrant wave and could be put into question by a section of the new-coming multi-ethnic population.

Arts and creative practices could be considered an important source of new identity discourses and this was an area that some of the Olympic bid team influencers were keen to explore. However, the conservative approach to cultural policy-making that was common for most of the 20th century had also failed to assist Australians to find a common language that could be claimed as representative of all population groups. This was mainly due to a long maintained focus on supporting an outdated concept of culture modelled on classic western European notions of the high arts. In line with other parts of the world, since the 1960s, the perspectives of cultural policy have diversified and have been, for some years, centred on a discourse that debates notions of multiculturalism. All the same, this discourse has been criticised by some as being a tokenistic exercise lacking real content. Further, in common with other countries, the trend in Australia's cultural policy over the 1990s was an emphasis on a rationalist approach to the arts with a focus on diversifying sources of funding and addressing the demands of the market. This re-energised segments of the cultural sector and made them more competitive, but it also brought the risk of slowing down the process to undertake a comprehensive revision of the country's contemporary cultural discourse and its emerging, more diverse and inclusive, cultural aspirations.

The decision to bid for the Olympic Games for the third consecutive time was a sign of the country's determination to find a place in the global sphere. The process was a catalyst to negotiate a common identity discourse and overcome past limitations within a concrete timeframe, if only to present a coherent and contemporary image of Australia to the rest of the world. Given the ongoing tensions and disagreements about the most appropriate discourse, it was to be expected that the design and communication of the Olympic bid followed a dual approach that was not always easily reconciled. Local audiences—potential Games stakeholders in particular—were animated by an economic discourse that was clearly focused on emphasising the benefits of the Games in terms of tourism development and business growth. In this discourse, culture played a minor role and the influence of cultural policy makers was apparently minimal. In contrast, foreign stakeholders were attracted by a discourse whose most distinct trademark was an emphasis on portraying cultural issues. This discourse built on an approach to cultural policy that celebrated Australia's cultural diversity and led to the formulation of multiculturalism and aboriginal reconciliation as the two main premises representing the country's cultural character and immediate aspirations. These premises were also at the heart of the proposed Olympic cultural programme.

Thus, the Sydney Games' cultural discourse and its proposed cultural programme were informed by a strong and coherent notion of cultural policy during the bidding process. However, as noted, this discourse was mainly aimed at international stakeholders and was often overlooked in the bidding discussion with local partners. The contrast between the local Games selling discourse and its presentation to international audiences suggests that the process of deciding Australia's cultural image may not have been the result of an open consultation and was not likely to be fully owned by local and national partners. This does not diminish the value of the defined cultural discourse and the two main 'brand images' resulting from it (celebrating multiculturalism and aboriginal reconciliation). Expectedly, these images and the important concepts they involved were widely shared throughout Australia. However, the possibility that the images were designed without the direct involvement of many of the Games key stakeholders (from the arts community to businesses and the media) is an indication of the many difficulties that existed at the time of implementation.

Indeed, from the time the Games were awarded to Sydney in 1993, the coherence of the Olympic cultural discourse began to diminish. With the creation of Sydney's Organising Committee for the Olympic Games (SOCOG), the priority discourse and key guiding policy for designing and delivering the Games moved on to immediate economic and corporate interests over broader long term cultural policy goals. The proposed key cultural messages or 'images' were maintained as guiding concepts. However, the operational structures for their implementation were fragmented into a series of programmes and working groups that acted almost in complete isolation from each other thus preventing their full effectiveness. Notably, the promised—and extremely ambitious—four-year Olympic Arts Festivals programme was separated from SOCOG's various community programmes which, in turn, also tended to operate in isolation from each other. For example, the Community Relations programme was separated from the programmes addressing multicultural and Aboriginal communities specifically. The Education programme was also separated from each of the previous programmes. Furthermore, the teams in charge of implementing the most well-recognised Olympic protocol programmes (the Torch Relay and the Opening and Closing Ceremonies), which act as the main platform to communicate the Games cultural and symbolic message locally as well as internationally, were designated as separate elements and, as such, also operated independently from the cultural programme. In this context, maintaining the coherence of the Games' cultural discourse became a great challenge. The cultural programme was one of the areas most clearly weakened by these circumstances, not only through its isolation, but also due to the lack of resources. This conditioned the final shape of the OAF programme which, despite some successful components, was not able to play the kind of transformative role that it aspired to at the bid stage.

In sum, from the moment that the Games are awarded, the Olympic cultural discourse and its cultural programme in particular, tends not to be directed by a strong host cultural policy. Games cultural bids have often been informed by influential commissions or advisory boards with ambitious visions for culture, but these groups normally dissolve or have diminishing opportunities to shape the day-to-day decisions of an OCOG. A further challenge is the tendency to narrow the scope of cultural commission responsibilities, which, as has been the case throughout most of the 20th century, are focused on elite arts matters rather than a wider concept of culture offering clearer Games synergies. This is mainly the result of unstable local cultural policy frameworks. While international stakeholders can appreciate the symbolic aspirations of bidding candidates, they are not in a position to overview the final implementation. As such, despite their potential, Olympic cultural programmes often become localised affairs with minimal influence over the Games global narrative.

CULTURAL PROGRAMMES AS A PLATFORM TO DEFINE THE GAMES CULTURAL DIMENSION

The third proposed area of enquiry was the extent to which the Olympic cultural programme is able to play a relevant role in defining the Games' cultural dimension. This issue is reviewed in Chapters 5, 6 and 7, which explore the working conditions of the cultural programme in the context of other Olympic preparations, such as the OCOG's structures of management and the promotional devices set up for the programme in terms of marketing and communications. The main conclusions of this assessment is that the cultural programme tends to have a marginal structural positioning within the Games hosting process, even when it is fully integrated within the OCOG, and that it cannot benefit from effective Olympic branding due to major clashes with the current global Olympic marketing guidelines.

As noted in Chapter 5, the Sydney OAF had a marginal managerial position within SOCOG, which led to low resources and influence within the organisation. The OAF was integrated within a tightly structured and business-oriented organisation and was part of one of the organisation's most prominent business groups, Marketing and Image. However, the programme did not benefit from the potential advantages of such a relationship. Rather, it was affected by some of the more negative aspects of being integrated within a much larger organisation. These aspects are all interrelated and can be summarised as: isolation from mainstream operations, low priority and visibility within the Games hosting process, weak link to key Olympic stakeholders and limited know-how. The latter is particularly telling as it has in turn led to replicating the same problems in subsequent Games editions.

Isolation from mainstream operations: All OAF services, including the marketing and publicity consultancies, were located in the same area (physically as well as operationally) within SOCOG's headquarters and structural diagram and separated from the Games main marketing and publicity operations. This aimed to increase the unity and consistency of the OAF project but also reduced the opportunities for OAF marketing and publicity consultants to interact with the overall Games marketing, communications and community relations programmes. An example is found in the constant budget reductions, which minimised the possibility of long term planning for the festivals and affected negatively the contract and production relationships of the OAF with other arts organisations. Further evidence is found in the delay for publishing the time-schedule for buying tickets to the *OAF'2000*, which had remarkable repercussions in the distribution of Olympic cultural offers through overseas tourism agencies.

Low priority and visibility: The OAF was not perceived nor treated as an essential Olympic programme. In contrast with the Ceremonies programme, which had its own designated Division, reported directly to the SOCOG Board and maintained its budget allocation along the seven years of preparations for the Games, the cultural programme was vulnerable to last-minute changing resources-allocation and was affected by each of SOCOG's budget reduction agreements.

Weak link to stakeholders: Government, sponsors, media and arts organisations were not equally and substantially involved in supporting the OAF. The OAF team was not given the means to develop strong and sustainable relationships with stakeholders and was not offered consistent support by SOCOG's Government, Sponsorship or Media Relations programmes. This resulted in a limited ability to negotiate and be proactive, relying instead on respective Games stakeholders' interests and having thus to juggle their often competing agendas.

Limited know-how: Sydney's OAF management limitations were inherited from Atlanta and other previous Olympic host cities. The transient nature of an Olympic committee plus the OCOG short-life cycle and reduced public accountability up to the major IOC shake-up in year 2000 led to the paradoxical need to keep 'reinventing' the process of staging an Olympic event after more than one hundred years of operating.[3] This fact has been accentuated in the case of the Olympic cultural programme as, to date, this is a programme that is not defined in detail nor protected by IOC regulations. There is a potential for change with the implementation of the IOC 'Transfer of Knowledge Programme', which was tested in Sydney for the first time. SOCOG was requested to monitor its key programmes and provide detailed reports to the IOC to inform subsequent host cities. The information collected and transferred on the cultural programme was, however, very limited, and this has led to the ongoing replication of the most common managerial challenges, as identified here.

From a promotional point of view, despite the success of generic Olympic communications and marketing programmes for the 2000 Games, SOCOG did not achieve wide awareness about the Olympic Arts Festivals amongst Olympic audiences. This was partly a result of management and structural limitations, as noted above, but also due to the non-inclusive nature of current Olympic sponsorship and broadcasting policies as defined by the IOC. This leads to three important observations.

First, the financial contributions of The Olympic Partners (TOP) and Host City Partners (in Sydney, Team Millennium Partners) are rarely extended to the Olympic cultural programme, while their exclusive branding rights prevent other long-term art sponsors from providing corporate funding. The lack of funding support by official Olympic sponsors tends to be justified on the grounds that the cultural programme is perceived as one of the least cost-effective aspects of the Games, unable to compete with the high symbolic appeal of the torch relay or the family appeal of the nation-wide schools education programme. This is due to its poor media profile and the impression that its primary target market tends to be highly selective and out-of-touch with the general Games public. Ultimately, the underlying challenge is one of conflict between the priorities and expectations of Olympic corporate sponsors, as they see their Games involvement in line with other sport industry sponsorship programmes, rather than resembling an arts or cultural sponsorship deal. The high investment required for their Olympic association does not leave much room for experimental or specialist audience activities as is common in arts sponsorship agreements. Even if some of the official Olympic corporate partners may also be long term contributors to arts activity, in the context of the Games, they are only interested in activity that can reach to a mainstream audience and provide high returns for their investment and, to date, the cultural programme is not perceived as any such activity.

Second, the global Games exposure resulting from the lucrative Olympic broadcasting rights do not provide direct leverage for the Olympic cultural programme. To date, specific clauses to guarantee the coverage of cultural activities associated to the Games have not been established, despite punctual attempts to overcome this challenge. In Sydney, the chairman of SOCOG's Olympic Cultural Commission proposed the creation of a national cultural channel to broadcast all OAF artistic activities. Nevertheless, from 1997 to 2000 there was no progress on this direction and, during the period of the Olympic competitions, references to the OAF on television were almost non-existent.

Third, the OCOG mainstream Olympic promotions, publicity campaigns and community event programmes tend not to be coordinated with the cultural programme. The Sydney OAF had its own marketing and publicity department, working independently from the Communications and Community Relations department. This arrangement might have been a logical decision considering the specific needs of an arts festival compared with the sports events. However, it relegated the OAF to a secondary place within the general Games marketing campaign, which received a higher allocation of resources.[4] Another point worthy of remark is the way the Games official website is designed. In Sydney, one of the first Games to present a comprehensive online platform, the pages providing information on venues, Olympic time schedules or the history of Olympism did not include any reference to the OAF, and at the time of the official launch of respective arts festivals, SOCOG home page did not highlight the event in any differentiated form. This has also been the case in subsequent, more sophisticated web environments, particularly in Athens, where the Cultural Olympiad had its own separate web environment without a direct link from the official Games website. With the advent of ever more personalised social media platforms, official Games sites are providing a growing number of references to the Cultural Olympiad—however, the programme still tends to have a low profile within the main Games information and overview sections and is still virtually absent from the official Games narrative within the IOC site.

Further to these limitations, the study of the campaigns put into place to promote respective Olympic arts festivals provides evidence that Olympic arts marketing tends to prioritise different target audiences building on core messages that are often disconnected from the main Games narrative. In Sydney, the promotion of the sports competitions and the Games in general focused on popular ownership and community participation and campaigns presented these elements as the heart of the Olympic experience. In contrast, the promotion of OAF events was targeted at a specialist audience, with the programme being either not associated with the Olympics, or presented as high end cultural activities dedicated to traditional arts audiences and special guests utilising niche techniques common to established arts festivals. As a result, average Olympic audiences and the general public during Games time would perceive the free entertainment programme *LiveSites,* as the defining and most popular cultural event taking place in the city during the Olympic period, rather than the OAF.

In sum, from the perspective of management and communication, the Olympic cultural programme in Sydney, in common with most previous editions of the Games, did not play a central role in defining the cultural dimensions of the Olympic Games. Instead, this role is played by the Olympic Ceremonies, Torch Relay activities and, particularly since Sydney, by the wide range of community-oriented and free activity programmes organised by the OCOG or the local host authorities, such as the *LiveSites*. The tendency to use the Olympic cultural programme as a vehicle to support a traditional and/or elite-oriented understanding of culture as 'high arts' has contributed to this situation.

THE PERCEIVED RELEVANCE OF THE CULTURAL PROGRAMME

The fourth area of enquiry considered whether the Olympic cultural programme is perceived as a relevant component of the Olympic Games by key Olympic stakeholders and whether it has sufficient media appeal. As noted earlier, in Sydney, as in all Games editions for which evidence is available, the programme was not viewed as central in the portrayal of the Games cultural narrative. Instead, other Olympic programmes such as the Ceremonies, Torch Relay and the host city's open-air activities or *LiveSites!* were seen to take the lead. This can be partly explained on the grounds that the IOC places greater emphasis on these programmes and they are better linked with the Games marketing communication strategy. Additional answers to this question can be found by contrasting the way in which key Games stakeholders approach arts events as opposed to other Olympic programmes.

Government Bodies and the Arts Community

A fundamental limitation of the approach by government bodies that has prevented them from maximising the potential of the Olympic cultural programme has been the lack of a shared vision to enable and subsequently highlight the Games cultural impact and medium to long term legacy. The competing interests of different agencies in their claims of ownership over the Games tends to accentuate this situation. As a result, a majority of government bodies have failed to provide the kind of long-term policy support that the cultural programme requires.

In Sydney, public bodies such as the Australian Tourism Commission at a federal level and the City of Sydney at a local level, were keen to explore the potential to advance their agendas through the Olympics. However, they did not use a cultural or artistic discourse as a core element of their promotions. This suggests that, in the context of the Olympic Games, the public sector did not identify the Australian arts world as a priority area for promotion. Instead, the most effective sources to promote Sydney and Australia continued to be associated with the country's outdoors life, its sporting traditions and its growing business sector.[5] Government support towards the OAF was partially addressed with the creation of the Sydney Media Centre and the establishment of *ausarts2000*. This can be taken as a proof of the opportunities for greater visibility and centrality that joint government initiatives can bring to the Olympic cultural programme. However, these initiatives were only of use for the promotion of the final festival after it had been designed and produced, so it did not help raise the profile of the Cultural Olympiad as a four year initiative nor enhance the funding and planning for the final festival.

Beyond governmental limitations, another ongoing challenge is the failure of the cultural sector, arts communities in particular, to play a defining role shaping the Games cultural policy. In Sydney, the absence of pressure groups that could lobby on behalf of the arts institutions to bring about greater support towards the OAF suggests that the arts community did not have high expectations about the Games as a platform to advance a local or national arts agenda or indeed the OAF as the most appropriate vehicle for it. It also suggests that arts institutions were not strongly coordinated and that, as in the case of state agencies, they represented competing interests and failed to overcome their differences in time to influence the Games explicit or implicit cultural policy framework.

In the period leading up to the Games, the arts world in Australia was strongly dependant on government allowances despite them being increasingly rationalised. Consequently, although the government aimed to move towards a more entrepreneurial arts environment, institutions and artists were still lacking a corporate approach to events funding and production and thus struggled to understand how the Games (and, by implication, the OAF) were run. This was accentuated by the lack of common structures and networks within the arts sector which, contrasting with the sports sector, remains highly individualistic, with few channels of communication and interaction between venues, arts companies and artists within any given art-form and, notably, practically no common ground between different artforms. This situation, far from being unique to Australia and the Sydney Games timeline, is a widespread challenge for the cultural sector in most countries and one of the key reasons why it is difficult for the arts community to devise the kind of joint-thinking that is essential to capitalise on the opportunities brought by a large-scale event such as the Olympic Games.

Corporate Sponsors

From a commercial point of view, current Olympic marketing regulations make corporate support towards the Olympic cultural programme either unappealing or virtually impossible. Olympic sponsors are not encouraged to support the programme and tend to see it as far less attractive than other Games components, while non-Olympic sponsors are either denied the chance to contribute or have to face strong branding restrictions. Such restrictions are implemented in cases where corporate companies provide direct funding to new Olympic cultural events, but also if they are long-term supporters of companies or previously existing events included within the Olympic programme. The latter is relevant to explain the difficulties attracting corporate support for the Olympic cultural programme in contrast to the sporting competitions. Contrary to the majority of sports venues and sports teams, Olympic arts participants and venues tend to be partly funded by a large number of corporations that are not necessarily involved in Olympic sponsorship deals. These corporations might not have had any interest in being associated with the Games. However, they are still affected by Olympic regulations if the arts group they sponsor is included within the official cultural programme. In Sydney, as in many other host cities, most Olympic arts productions had not been exclusively funded and curated by SOCOG through the OAF, as a result, the conflict over acknowledgements—for instance, in terms of displaying of logos at venues—became a major issue that made marketing OAF events very difficult. For instance, a theatre that would be showing an official cultural programme event was, in OCOG terms, classified as an Olympic venue and would be subject to the same parameters of presentation, from the design of brochures and programmes to the dressing of the venue foyer.

Taking this into consideration, it is clear that the existing Olympic sponsorship regulations have had multiple negative effects on the ability to generate corporate funding for and cooperation with the Olympic cultural programme. First, Olympic sponsors are not likely to see the value of providing extra funds for the cultural programme given that it is not a high profile area and its marketing structure is perceived as confusing and less-value-for-money than other iconic Games components. Instead of supporting the Cultural Olympiad, global partners often run their own Olympic cultural programmes while local corporate partners often can benefit from pre-existing arts support deals. Given that many Olympic sponsors are involved in supporting the arts, they can attempt a connection with the Olympic cultural programme without extra costs through 'passive' ambush marketing. Even though this did not always occur, in Sydney, the general public was likely to associate with the OAF any established arts sponsor that happened to support Olympic sport. This was the case for *Telstra*, Team Millennium Partner, supporter of the swimming Olympic team and official sponsor of the high profile *Adelaide Festival*.

Secondly, non Olympic sponsors faced strong restrictions over how they could provide funds to the OAF. This was due to the prohibition on non-Olympic sponsors to be OAF sponsors, when the product category of the non-Olympic sponsor conflicted with the category of any of the TOP or Team Millennium Olympic partners. Although it had already been a major OAF achievement to secure the approval by the SOCOG Board to seek the support of non Olympic sponsors, the inflexible ban of conflicting product categories excluded most major Australian corporations that were not already involved in the Olympic project.

Finally, non-Olympic sponsors that were supporting the arts were likely to lobby against participation within the Olympic programme of the institutions they were involved with in order to avoid branding bans or limitations by SOCOG. For example, *Philips* was supporter of the Sydney Symphony Orchestra and its product category conflicted with Olympic sponsors such as *Panasonic* and *Samsung*. As such, it has been suggested that the company was inclined to discourage the inclusion of the orchestra within the OAF programme, so as to prevent the long process of negotiations that finally took place for the design of the concert promotional material in terms of sponsor acknowledgements.

The Media

From the media's perspective, in the lead up to and during the Olympic period, there are also multiple reasons to prioritise sports stories over coverage of the arts, over and above what is to be expected during an Olympic Games. In Sydney, an initial reason was linked to the strong sporting traditions of Australia and the pervasive sporting enthusiasm that winning the right to host the Games arose throughout the country. This led most publication companies and broadcasters to put a growing emphasis on Olympic sports news from a very early stage. In contrast, the coverage of arts related features was not perceived as an integral part of the Olympic project and, in some cases—for example, local and regional papers—it would be cut-down altogether in the lead and during the Games, to expand instead the amount of space dedicated to Olympic sport related stories.

During the 1997–1999 period, however, the coverage of sports in Australia was not the main media competitor against the arts festival appeal. Rather, it was the long chain of controversies resulting from the Games preparations in areas such as transport, budgeting or personal disputes among Olympic representatives. Academic researchers have argued that publication groups such as Fairfax and News Ltd. were looking forward to the chance of publishing stories about the difficult side of the Olympics because, during the bid period, there had been a shared agreement to avoid any sort of criticism in order to support the candidature (Cunningham 2000, pers. comm., 25 Aug). Others have added that SOCOG offered 'more than enough opportunities for negative and sensationalist coverage' (Sydney Arts Organisation 2000, pers. comm., 24 Feb) in contrast to the cultural programme that, after 1998, 'lacked the necessary insight to make for a good new-story' (*The Australian*, arts editor 1999, pers. comm., 13 Sep).

In any case, the most widely accepted reason for the lack of media appeal of the arts festivals in the lead up to the Games was not so much their intrinsic nature as their failure to establish a clear link with the Olympic experience. In that sense, the decision to design the final festival as a show-case of high-end artistic performances accentuated the perceived division between the arts and the sports programmes. This explains the decision of most papers to keep information about the *OAF'2000* in the arts editorial pages instead of integrating them within the Olympic coverage section.

SOCOG Communications and Community Relations general manager indicated that it is necessary to accentuate the popular or accessible side of the cultural programme to make it more relevant to the Olympic experi-ence, attract the interest of wider audiences and ultimately gather consistent media coverage. Chapter 7 notes how, at the end of an informal interview, the manager mentioned, as a missed opportunity, the names of broadly popular Australians from the world of cinema, fashion and music that could have been used to promote the OAF in parallel to the athletes pro-moting the sports. However, this links back to Berkaak's (1999) comments on the danger of an over-commercialisation of values and commodification of culture for the benefit of the media and corporate groups. Berkaak's arguments bring into question the merit of capitalising on culture, thus transforming it into a particular kind of entertainment with specific promo-tional objectives. The need to ensure a balance between the media appeal of a cultural programme that aspires to reach out to a global audience, the commitment towards offering a representative and sustainable cultural perspective of the local community, and the aspiration to stage a challeng-ing, ground breaking cultural programme that, in some sense, coheres with the excellence of the athletic achievements is discussed further in the next, concluding section.

CULTURAL POLICY TENSIONS

This book starts with the premise that over the last three decades, cul-tural policy frameworks have merged with communication policies and are being used as a promotional tool for cities and regions. Major events have been identified as a suitable platform for the implementation of urban cul-tural policies, as they can have a high level of impact through local and international media by acting as a focal point for attention. However, the analysis of the communication and cultural provisions for a paradigmatic mega event such as the Olympic Games suggests that there are ongoing challenges preventing the effective implementation of such policies and put-ting into question their actual purpose. These challenges could be defined as ongoing tensions within the cultural policy of major events and could be summarised as four main dichotomies: cultural imperatives versus eco-nomic imperatives; local representation versus global projection, and lived festival versus media event frameworks.

Cultural Imperatives versus Economic Imperatives

In the context of globalisation and with a view to informing a major event, cultural policy needs to address a range of economic imperatives. However, a balance should be maintained between the influence of economic and *cultural* objectives. In this sense, cultural policy must avoid becoming a means towards economic ends alone and should, instead, ensure that the right balance is struck between economic, social and purely cultural aspirations. In the case of the Sydney 2000 Olympic cultural programme, the tension between economic and cultural imperatives was particularly evident at the bid stage, with a cultural discourse gaining centre stage internationally while economic imperatives dominated the local discourse. However, once the organising committee for the Games was made operational, the economic imperative became the dominant guide for key decision-making, from managerial structures to promotions and interaction with stakeholders. In this context, the notions of cultural policy that had informed the original vision for the cultural programme tended to be used more as an instrument to assist the OCOG's economic (and often explicitly corporate) agenda than as a basis for developing the Games cultural narrative.

The dominance of economic imperatives in the structure of an OCOG can be explained by looking at the historical trajectory of the Olympic Games: from being a historical event led by humanistic values, into a highly lucrative enterprise dependant on the corporate values of the global market and the global media. The emphasis on corporate investment and media exposure has been critical to the development of the Games as the mega-event it is today. However, this has also implied a radical transformation of priorities and policies which has resulted in some imbalances. Sporting competitions, infrastructure management and symbolic components with a strong communication value such as the Opening and Closing Ceremonies have been adapted to this new corporate reality and have become major investment areas within an OCOG, SOCOG being a good example. In contrast, the role and purpose of the Olympic cultural programme is still presented in the idealistic manner that characterised the first period of the modern Games and thus has become out of touch with current Olympic priorities.

The lack of adaptation of the Olympic cultural programme to the current corporate trends has diminished its chances to be commercially viable. However, this situation also offers a potential for the programme to ensure an emphasis on cultural rather than economic priorities. For instance, one advantage of the lessened pressure to be commercially lucrative is the possibility for socially worthy aspirations to be more prominent and thus, for having greater chances of being representative of the local host's cultural context, regardless of its corporate appeal. Nevertheless, striving to be culturally responsible and ensuring local representation reveals another of the enduring tensions for cultural policy within major events, as discussed below.

Local Representation versus Global Projection

A further challenge for cultural policy-makers to inform the cultural programme of a major event is the potential conflict between the global, generic aims of the event international stakeholders and the specific aims of the local host. The Olympic Games can act as a powerful catalyst to renegotiate and showcase a nation's renewed cultural identity discourse and, as such, concerns about the presence of local communities within the Olympic programme are a significant priority. However, the discourse needs to be easily transmitted and understood by audiences around the globe, and this often curtails the required levels of sensitive negotiation and inclusion.

In Sydney, the selection of Australia's culturally aspirational 'brand images', despite their significance, did not receive widespread acceptance. Despite the fact that multiculturalism and reconciliation were internationally acclaimed concepts, their selection and articulation was not the result of an open and nationally owned negotiation with interested communities. Further, the implementation of the OAF, bound as it was by financial and managerial constraints, failed to ensure sufficient levels of collaboration and direct representation of those who were theoretically included in the concept, particularly during the Games, at the time of maximal global media exposure. In this context, one might draw attention to the varying politics of arts and sports as expressions of culture. It is my contention that the arts are ideologically more complex than what might be the dubiously-termed universalism of sports. At least, the programming of arts activities via its depiction of ideas and forms of excellence, are more difficult to adapt to a regimented process of Olympic programming, with its top-down hierarchy. While sports are also cultural activities, they do not present novel ideas that require the negotiation of Olympic interests in the same way as the Olympic cultural programme does.

In sum, the situation re-affirms the fragility of the cultural programme and cultural images in general as they need to be accommodated to a global marketing and mass media discourse. To use and maximise the benefits of media distribution can be positive for the programme, but only if the concepts, themes or brand images have emerged from a common or sufficiently negotiated vision by the host community, rather than just media imperatives. This points at the final identified cultural policy tension.

Lived Festival versus Media(ted) Event

The Olympic Games is essentially a cultural manifestation of which the official cultural programme is only one component. For its particular conditions—time length, flexibility in locations and freedom of design—the cultural programme offers considerable potential to act as a catalyst to project the image of the host-city and nation in more locally sensitive ways than other Games components. However, this possibility has been constrained by the lack of guidance and definition about the role of this programme in the context of the Games and, in particular, by the poor managerial and promotional structures set up to implement it. This indicates a great limitation in the cultural policy of the Olympic Games and reveals one of the great challenges for defining the cultural policy of other major events. The challenge is to ensure that an event's cultural dimension is supported by a defined policy that remains strategically relevant within the organisation and its key stakeholders throughout the event's life, instead of relying on the outcome of other successful event components in economic and/or political terms.

The cultural dimensions of the Olympic Games range from the traditional Olympic Ceremonies and related historical symbols to the design of banners, logos and the provision of street entertainment. All of these elements, characterised by their spectacular visibility, have the possibility of engaging the local community in memorable ways and offer a platform to simplify local host narratives so that they can be projected on to and easily understood by a global media audience. However, they could also be viewed as artificial and globally standardised impositions that stifle local creativity. For these elements to make a significant difference at a local level, it is necessary that they respond to a coordinated strategy and that, while remaining attractive to a global audience, they represent cultural values that are consistent with the values of the host community. This is where the official Olympic cultural programme has a critical part to play.

The official cultural programme should act as a bridge between the visibility and media appeal of the most iconic Olympic components, and the complexities involved in offering opportunities for genuine representation and direct participation of any given local culture. Further, the programme should provide the space where iconic (or apparently fixed) elements can be questioned, revitalised or challenged. For this, it is essential that the programme overcomes the tendency to focus on either elite-oriented or populist art manifestations building on out-of-date art festival models. The culture teams in Sydney as well as Torino, Vancouver and now London have tried to challenge this narrow conception of culture, particularly in the early years of the Olympiad. However, organisers tend to revert to elite-oriented high arts (or, most commonly claimed, 'world class') programming during Games time. This approach plays well with established arts audiences and critics but fails to advance the case for Olympic cultural programming as a distinct offering that is fully in line and appropriate within the Games hosting process. Ultimately, this implies that the cultural programme fails to play the kind of distinct and defining role that is necessary in order to better contextualise, revisit or advance what the Games are supposed to mean for particular communities at particular points in time. Indeed, as I have discussed elsewhere, the more oversimplified and standardised the underlying Games cultural discourse is, the lesser the chances for the event to lead on to meaningful and sustainable legacies (see García 2002, 2004b).

As an additional note, which would require further analysis elsewhere, it is worth commenting on the escalating loss of a festival atmosphere within the Olympic city since Sydney 2000. This has been due to the impact of global security concerns emerging in the wake of the 9/11 terrorist attacks in New York, which have had a marked effect on the way mega-events such as the Olympic Games are hosted. Establishing security measures throughout the Olympic city is now one of the most demanding tasks for any Games organiser. The expectation that crowds should be regularly screened so as to prevent potential attacks or disturbances, has diminished opportunities for open air and spontaneous activities during the Olympic fortnight, particularly in the perimeter of sporting venues or iconic city centre areas such as central squares around government buildings. This has, in turn, diminished opportunities for festive activities to take place and be easily accessible in the public realm, with organisers preferring to focus on enclosed (and easier to control) venue environments. The question of how to protect the Games 'festival' atmosphere is thus an increasingly important question to consider and one where the cultural programme could play an essential role.

MOVING FORWARD

In order for the Olympic cultural programme to fulfil its potential, the IOC must acknowledge and revisit its cultural policy framework. This should not lead to overly prescriptive and fixed policies. Instead, it should result in guidelines that provide clear pointers into the Movement's rich cultural and symbolic heritage but also open the door for respective local hosts to challenge and re-interpret the Games cultural priorities. Such position assumes that the Games local host will commit to engaging in a cultural policy discourse as well, and use the Games as a platform to advance a cultural dialogue with its local stakeholders.

Ultimately, the Olympic Games cultural policy must recognise the need to operate at the interface of the event's three main and interconnected cultural dimensions: the Olympic Games as the enactment of an international set of symbols of historical significance, the Games as a media dependent global brand and the Games as a locally-based lived festival.

The *symbolic* or *constructed ritual* dimension of the Games relates to the historical value of a centenary 'Movement', as defined by its founder, Pierre de Coubertin, and embodied in concepts such as Olympism (see MacAloon 1984). The notion of a Movement and Olympism as a 'philosophy of life' (IOC 2007) that frame and give meaning to the quadrennial celebration of the Games are presented in documents such as the Olympic Charter, which claim that the purpose of the Games is to advance a series of 'Olympic values', such as fair play, and that this is to be done by following strict rules for 'Olympic protocol' and protecting as well as promoting a series of 'Olympic symbols'. The *global brand* dimension of the Games refers to its embodiment as a media event. The Olympics as a 'brand' is owned by a global network, the Olympic Family, led by the IOC in over 205 nation states, and its commercial value is achieved via the sale of sponsorship as well as media rights worldwide. The strenght of the brand is directly proportional to the strengh of its symbolic and lived festival dimension, but it is mainly experienced through the media. Finally, the *lived festival* dimension of the Games refers to its location within a specific place and time: an Olympic host city, 16 days of competition, and over seven years of preparations that must be managed by a locally appointed 'organising committee' and require considerable investment not only in terms of finances, but also public support. This means that the Games, beyond their historical international roots, and global media impact, must achieve a high degree of local ownership and engagement to ensure a successful hosting process as well as result in sustainable and tangible local legacies. The latter is crucial in ensuring that the Games remain attractive to future hosts.

Without an acknowledgment of these three dimensions and the need to establish a more explicit cultural policy discourse capturing them all, the Olympic Games are bound to become progressively emptier of their cultural significance, to operate instead as a standardised global media event, efficiently run and financially viable but devoid of broader symbolic value. Ultimately, a revised and strengthened Olympic cultural policy is of critical relevance if the Games is to remain credible as the main vehicle for an international movement dedicated to advance universally relevant and locally sensitive social and cultural causes.

Appendix 1
Olympic Arts Festivals
Programme Description

This is a summary of the information displayed in the festivals promotional literature available at SOCOG web-site from 1999 to 2000, and the festivals promotional brochures and reports distributed in the same period (SOCOG 1997–2000, 1998a, 1998d, 1999a, 1999b, 1999c, 2000b)

1997: THE INDIGENOUS FESTIVAL— FESTIVAL OF THE DREAMING

Artistic Director: Rhoda Roberts
Time line: 14 September–6 October 1997
Location: Sydney
Slogan: Intimate Contemporary True

The Festival of the Dreaming was said to be the first of its kind in Australia. It celebrated the world's indigenous cultures, in particular, those of the Australian Aborigines and Torres Strait Islanders. SOCOG promoted it as one of the largest and most representative indigenous arts festivals yet to be held in the world, a description that, by the end of 1997,was widely supported by the Australian press.

> I believe that Rhoda Roberts has created an expectation that no festival planned here henceforth can exist without its indigenous contribution. And that's a defining moment (Eccles 1997: 14)

The festival aimed to increase the awareness and appreciation of Australia's indigenous heritage. It comprised 30 visual arts exhibitions, 14 dance and theatre productions, eight performance troupes, 50 films, a literature programme, three concerts and a number of specially commissioned open events.

Under the guidance of Rhoda Roberts, the content of the festival was determined by an all-aboriginal managing team to respond to the claim that the event was entirely indigenous, both in terms of authorship and

control. Roberts stated that this did not exclude non-indigenous artists from being involved in the festival. However, the final presentation
of indigenous works remained the responsibility of indigenous artists.
Most of the content was Australian, with additional representation from
indigenous cultures from other countries, including the United States of
America, Canada, Greenland, Korea, New Zealand, Western Samoa and
Papua New Guinea. According to the promotional material, the festival
explored the experience of indigenous people from their early origins to
current times, when they are in close contact with many and diverse foreign cultures.

Primarily, the festival took place around Sydney's regions, in the city
central business district, and in suburbs such as Western Sydney, Sydney Harbour, Parramata and Campbelltown. The majority of Sydney's
performing arts venues and galleries were utilised for the festival. Maintaining the commitment made by SOCOG to include the whole country
in all Olympic manifestation, every state and territory of Australia was
represented in the festival, with individual artists and writers, dance and
theatre companies, music groups and exhibitions coming from all around
the continent. Many of the projects from *The Festival of the Dreaming*
toured nationally in 1998 and internationally in 1999, as part of subsequent Olympic Arts Festivals.

1998: THE MULTICULTURAL FESTIVAL OF DIVERSITY AND TRANSFORMATIONS—A SEA CHANGE

Artistic Director: Andrea Stretton
Time-Line: April–November 1998
Location: All around Australia
Slogan: Transformations

According to artistic director Andrea Stretton, the title and theme for *A
Sea Change* was coined from Shakespeare's theatre play 'The Tempest'. The
festival intended an exploration of the idea of transformations in Australia
in the context of the influences of geography and landscape, immigration
and indigenous cultures. The festival included 98 separate dance, theatre,
visual arts, literary, music and educational events that were staged in all
Australian states and territories.

> Australia tells its own story in this nation-wide celebration. The events
> selected for this national festival were from all states and territories, from
> communities large and small. Together they show a 'sea change' in our
> life today. A life enriched by the geographic and cultural diversity that is
> Australia. A Sea Change explores the transformations that have occurred

in Australian culture with over one hundred events around the country—
from Darwin to Hobart, from Broome to Brisbane—to give a snapshot of
Australia in 1998. (Welcome by Andrea Stretton, SOCOG 1999a)

Among the highlights were a series of free lighthouse and harbour concerts
played at highly appreciated Australian locations in each Australian State
and Territories. These locations included Tweed Heads in northern New
South Wales (NSW); Darwin, Port Fairy and Cape Otway on the State of
Victoria's south coast; Fremantle and Broome in Western Australia; Port
Adelaide in South Australia; Towsville in Queensland and Low Head in
Tasmania. The other highlight was *Sculpture by the Sea*, a popular Sydney-
based event put on tour for the first time. One hundred works by Australian
sculptors were installed at outdoor sites on the Tasman Peninsula, on the
beach at Noosa (Queensland) and on the esplanade at Darwin. The location for the Sydney event continued the tradition of previous years, taking
place in the cliff-walk from the popular Bondi beach to Tamarama beach.

Events from traditional civic festivals across the country were also
included in the Olympic programme. Some examples include the Festival of
Darwin, Shinju Matsuri at Broome, the Festival Fremantle, The Port Fairy
Spring Music Festival, the Waterborne 1998 Innisfail Harvest Festival,
Tweed Heads Harbour Festival, Hobart's Wooden Boat Festival, the Pacific
Wave Festival and Carnivale, the multicultural festival in Sydney. Festivals
were complemented with a wide range of community-based events, most
of which involved the participation of schools and youth organisations,
which were included in the festival in co-ordination with SOCOG National
Olympic Education Programme. Educational initiatives within the festival
included 'A Sea Change Information Kit', a document listing most cultural
activities happening throughout the country. Support was given to promote existing school prizes and other popular education events, such as the
'Legacy Junior Public Speaking Award', the 'National Schools Cartooning
Competition' and the 'Australasian Intervarsity Debating Championship'.

For more traditional art forms, in theatre, there were nine emerging
and established companies and a selection of popular Australian actors
and playwrights including some of the most successful ones from *The Festival of the Dreaming*. Dance included Aboriginal shows from *The Festival of the Dreaming*, premiere collaborations between Australian and
foreign companies and new works by the young and popular Australian
group Chunky Move. In music, the Sydney, Melbourne and Tasmanian
Symphony Orchestras presented classical recitals. In Sydney for instance,
The Five Rings Concert was a multicultural concert in collaboration with
the city ethnic festival Carnivale. The visual arts section was composed by
contemporary paintings by Aboriginal artist Emily Kame Kngwarreye, a
photography exhibition by David Moore, a joint exhibition by indigenous
artists, traditional crafts from women of the Torres Strait Islands, works

by Australian traditional painters such as Russell Drysdale, Donald Fried, Ian Fairweather and Sidney Nolan, and a special exhibition mounted by the Australian National Maritime Museum.

Finally, literature took a role through the publication of an anthology of Australian short stories and photographs titled 'A Sea Change: Australia writing and photography'. The book was distributed to most schools, libraries and cultural institutions throughout the country.

1999: THE OVERSEAS FESTIVAL—REACHING THE WORLD

Artistic Director: Andrea Stretton
Time-line: November 1998–January 2000
Location: Around the world

> Reaching the World is a unique opportunity to highlight to the world the extraordinary breadth of Australia's cultural and artistic life. Our perceived geographical isolation has always inspired us to look outside of our own country, and as a result we have long been a nation of travellers. In that sense, our isolation has had a silver lining, and in 1999 the Olympic Arts Festivals gives us a once-in-a-lifetime opportunity to celebrate our cultural and artistic place on the world stage. (Andrea Stretton, artistic director of the 1998 and 1999 Olympic Arts Festivals, SOCOG 1999c)

Reaching the World aimed to showcase 'the best of Australia' to each of the continents that are represented by the five rings of the Olympic emblem: Europe, Africa, Asia, the Americas and Oceania. This showcase was to take place throughout the entire year. The festival was composed of 70 events by Australian companies and artists touring to more than 150 cities in 50 countries worldwide. It was promoted as being in partnership with The Australia Council, State funding bodies and the Department of Foreign Affairs and Trade. Find below a brief description of the various events that were presented in each continent.

The Americas: The Sydney Symphony Orchestra's 10th anniversary tour to the USA signalled the opening of the third Olympic Arts Festival programme in November 1998. The orchestra opened its season of concerts in 11 cities across the country at New York's Carnegie Hall, under Chief Conductor Edo de Waart. The Americas were also the destination for a number of exhibitions and performances featuring the work of 'some of Australia's most talented artists' (*Reaching the World* promotional documents). Events included a touring retrospective to the USA of the Australian photographer David Moore; Meryl Tankard Australian Dance Theatre and WOMAD in Seattle. In Latin and South America, the Stalker Theatre Company performed a new show: *Blood Vessel*; a retrospective of Australian film toured Brazil; *Seasons of the Kunwinjku,* an exhibition of Aboriginal art from West Arnhem Land was seen in Argentina, Venezuela and Chile, and the electro-acoustic ensemble, Elektra, toured Argentina, Brazil and Uruguay.

Europe: The Australian Chamber Orchestra, Melbourne Symphony Orchestra, Company B Belvoir, Legs on the Wall, Meryl Tankard and Sydney Dance Company toured to locations as diverse as the Canary Islands, Greece, Austria and the United Kingdom. Australian writers travelled to the Czech Republic to take part in the Prague Writers' Festival. Within the programme for Europe, a key focus was a major exhibition opening in September 1999 at the Royal Institute of British Architects (RIBA) in London, which marked the one-year countdown to the opening ceremony of the Sydney 2000 Olympic Games. It was called *Olympic Design of the New Millennium* and documented in detail "the most ambitious urban design and architecture project ever undertaken in Australia" (SOCOG 1999c). The exhibition showcased the process of design and construction of the stadiums, public parks, meeting places, arenas, exhibition halls and transport facilities for the Sydney 2000 Olympic Games. In Paris, Gallery Gabrielle Pizzi was designed to mark the one-year countdown with a major exhibition of Aboriginal painting and photography called *Myth and Reality*.

In Asia the programme included a dozen companies and exhibitions touring to Singapore, Japan, Hong Kong, China, Malaysia and Indonesia, among which Circus Oz, Barking Gecko, The Powerhouse Museum and Music Theatre Australia. A highlight was said to be *The Rose Crossing*, an exhibition travelling to Singapore and Hong Kong, of the work of nine Australian artists, most of them of Asian origin.

In Africa, Expressions Dance Company artistic director and choreographer, Maggie Sietsma (Brisbane) was guest-choreograph of a new work by the South African Dance Company. Other highlights included a season by the Australia Ensemble in collaboration with the community based programme Musica Viva and a residency and exhibition in Ghana by the Western Australian artist Walter Gomes.

In Oceania there were shows in Sydney, New Zealand, Fiji, New Caledonia and Vanuatu. The programme included performances, exhibitions and discussions by Australian artists and writers. Notably, Stalker Theatre Company: the Sydney-based physical theatre company. These, in collaboration with the Marrugeku company of Aboriginal dancers and musicians from Australia's north, presented the outdoor celebration of the Mimi spirits of Arnhem Land during The Festival of the Dreaming.

The OAF also enlisted the co-operation of the Australian Broadcasting Corporation (ABC), the Special Broadcasting Television and Radio Service (SBS), Film Australia, the Australian Film and Television, Radio School and independent producers in the initiative 'Australia On Show: The Guide to Australian Arts Broadcasting'. This work documented for the first time in a single publication the range of arts programmes available for international broadcast at a time when the eyes of the world were increasingly turning to Australia with the approach of the Sydney2000 Olympic Games (1999b).

2000: THE OLYMPIC ARTS FESTIVAL—THE HARBOUR OF LIFE

Artistic Director: Leo Schofield
Time-Line: August–November 2000
Location: Sydney city—the harbour

> At the dawn of a new millennium, *Harbour of Life* presents works
> of national and international significance when the eyes of the world
> are on Sydney. The festival runs throughout the Sydney 2000 Olym-
> pic Games and Paralympic Games and focuses on events of scale that
> embody excellence and exhibit a distinctive Australian quality. Har-
> bour of Life -like the Games themselves—provides an opportunity to
> experience events that we are unlikely to see again in our lifetime in
> Australia. (SOCOG 1999b)

The final festival started on the 18th August 2000, a month before the Opening Ceremony of the Olympic Games. Australia's cultural icon, the Sydney
Opera House, became a key venue for the festival and a major focal point
for entertainment during the Olympic period. Major events were staged on
the Opera House forecourt and in the House Concert Hall, Drama Theatre, Opera Theatre, Studio and Playhouse.

In words of its artistic director, the festival was designed to showcase
the work of both prime Australian artists and international stars of outstanding relevance. In the festival promotional literature, the programme
components were categorised as follows.

Open air events: Open air events were mostly performed by national artists and included the Festival opening ceremony, a dawn-to-dusk event called
Tubowgule: The meeting of the Waters, by Aboriginal troupe Bangarra
Dance Theatre; the nightly coloured lighting of the Sydney Opera House
sails; an outdoors music concert by national groups called *Australians All*; a
weekend of world music called *Hemispheres* and the festival *Jazz 2000.*

Visual Art programme: The visual arts programme embraced all public
museums and galleries and most renamed commercial galleries in Sydney
city. Exhibitions of national work included the Art Gallery of NSW Australian painting collection- *Australian Icons* and its collection of Indigenous art- *Papunya Tula;* also the presentation of the *National Aboriginal
and Torres Strait Islanders Awards* at the Customs House, the specially
commissioned *Shrines for the Next Millennium* featuring installations by
contemporary Australian Aboriginal and Pacific Island artists at Sydney's
College of Arts, and a retrospective of Lin Onus, one of Australia's most
appreciated Indigenous artists *Urban Dingo* at the Museum of Contemporary Art. Exhibitions of international work included *The Dead Sea Scrolls*
at the Art Gallery of NSW; an important Collection of *Greek antiquities*
that had never toured out of Greece and Leonardo da Vinci's *Codex Leicester* at Sydney's Powerhouse Museum.

Music and Opera programme: The music programme counted on many national groups including the Sydney Symphony Orchestra, the Australian Chamber Orchestra and Melbourne Symphony Orchestra. A major highlight in the music programme was Sydney Symphony Orchestra performance of Mahler's Symphony No. 8, *The Symphony for a Thousand* with a chorus of 1000 voices at Sydney Superdome in Olympic Park. Overseas groups included, initially, the L.A. Philharmonic Orchestra (which was cancelled by the middle of year 2000), the Asian Youth Orchestra, New Zealand Philharmonic Orchestra and *Orchestra Filarmonica della Scala de Milan*, among others. The Opera programme featured the Australian national opera group by excellence, Opera Australia, which presented a range of classical operas such as *La Traviatta, Tosca* or *Don Giovanni* among others. An overseas artist that was presented as one of the stars in the festival programme was Italian singer Andrea Boccelli, who performed at a special Torch Gala on the night prior to the Games Opening ceremony.

Dance: The dance programme included both classical ballet and contemporary dance performances. The classical ballet component of the dance programme featured works by national groups such as the Australian Ballet, which presented two ballet seasons, one of which starred French prima ballerina Sylvie Guillem. The contemporary dance component was composed by overseas groups such as the Cloud Gate Dance Theatre from Taiwan, US' Bill T. Jones/ Arnie Zane Dance Company, England's DV8 Physical Theatre which presented a new work commissioned by the OAF in collaboration with British authorities, and Germany's Tanztheatre Wuppertal Pina Bausch. An important national dance component situated between traditional and contemporary movements in dance was brought by indigenous troupe Bangarra Dance Theatre with their new work, *Skin*. Finally, the Sydney Dance Company presented a world premiere that was promoted as having been inspired in Olympic legends, under the name of *Mythologia*.

Theatre: The theatre programme was exclusively composed of national groups and, primarily consisted of new versions of theatre classics. Performances included new work by the Bell Shakespeare Company which presented the Trojan tragedy *Troius and Cressida*. Company B Belvoir revisited *The Marriage of Figaro*, while the Sydney Theatre Company presented the Jacobean 'thriller' *The White Devil*. Additionally, the Australian Theatre for Young People presented a version of Aristophanes' classic comedy *Birds* and the National Institute of Dramatic Art gave a world premiere. An event that was initially categorised as 'theatre' and later in time categorised as an 'event' was the performance by Australian acrobatic troupe the Flying Fruit Circus, which performed a new production, *Fusion*, in conjunction with the Shanghai Acrobatic Troupe of China.

The final festival official programme was launched on the 13th October 1999 and made available to the public the 15th October of the same month.

Appendix 2
Olympic Arts Festival Budget

Data provided by the OAF team under freedom of information act. (Actual figures from JDE: 23/09/1999)

	The Festival of the Dreaming	A Sea Change	Reaching the World	The Harbour of Life
A. Income				
Box Office	A$430,083	A$0	A$0	Not available
Grants	A$421,183	A$197,500	A$0	A$2,500,000[1]
Other	A$4,762	A$0	A$0	Not available
Total Income	A$ 856,028	A$197,500	A$0	A$15,300,000
B. Expenditure				
Artists Program Travel	A$395,877	A$166,594	A$ 8,269	
Hire & Lease of equipment	A$848,702	A$ 49,471	A$ 3,000	
Program costs	A$1,308,840	A$ 1,006,233	A$ 1,057,649	
Performance fees	A$1,218,967	A$ 388,211	A$ 75,938	Not available
Hospitality	A$ 44,650	A$ 17,970	A$ 16,648	
Personnel costs	A$627,369	A$ 65,178		
Technology & Stationery	A$64,306	A$ 7,675	A$ 190	
General Mng, Mkt & Prom	A1,093,000	A$ 1,093,000	A$ 1,093,000	
Total Expenditure	A$ 5,601,711	A$ 2,794,602	A$ 2,254,694	A$ 28,300,000
C. Net Cost	-A$ 4,746,000	- A$ 2,597,000	- A$ 2,255,000	- A$ 13,600,000

1. Projected figure in 1999. Data partially verified via personal interview with OAF senior staff in 2002.
Source: SOCOG (1999e) Summary budget. Olympic Arts Festivals (23/09/1999)

Interesting points to note are:

1. Promotion expenditure was exactly the same since 1997. Programming costs also remained stable.
2. The only financial support for *A Sea Change* was a grant by the Arts Office in Queensland. *Reaching the World* did not receive any external financial support.
3. *Reaching the World*, despite being the 'international' festival, was only allocated A$ 8,269 for travelling expenses.

Appendix 3
SOCOG Cultural Commission and Committees

In 1996 Cultural Commission members and heads of Artforms Committes, members were as follows:

- Edmund Capon, (Director, Art Gallery of NSW)
- Mary Vallentine (General Manager, Sydney Symphony Orchestra)
- Lydia Miller (Executive Officer, Dritt Council Aboriginal and Torres strait Islander Arts Board)
- Annette Shuh Wah (Media Producer and Presenter)
- Mary Kostakidis (Chief Newsreader, SBS)
- Lesley Bangama Fogarty (Performing Arts)
- Lynden Esdaile (Assistant General Manager, Culture and Community Services, Sydney City Council)
- Evan Williams (Secretary, NSW Ministry for the Arts)

Other members between 1997 and 1999 were:

- John Moore (Group General Manager, SOCOG Marketing & Image Division 1997–1999)
- Anna Booth (board member of the Torch Relay Committee & SOCOG board member)
- Rod McGeoch AM (CEO of Sydney Bid Ltd. and SOCOG board member until 1998)

In 1999 the Commission members were:

- Donald McDonald AO
- Frank Sartor (Lord Major of Sydney & SOCOG board member)
- John Valder AO CBE (Former President of the Liberal Party & SOCOG board member)
- Craig McLatchey (Australian Olympic Commission member & SOCOG board member)
- Brian Sherman (chairman of EQUITI Equiti)

Notes

NOTES TO CHAPTER 1

1. For a recent reflection on the role and future of Culture Observatories see the 'Monitors for Culture' project blog, funded by the European Commission : http://www.monitorsofculture.deusto.es/ (last accessed January 2012)
2. See Bianchini 1999, Bianchini, Fisher, Montgomery and Worpole 1988, Borja and Subirós 1989, Council of Europe 1997, Garcia 2004a, García Canclini 1999, Lacarrieu 2000, Landry 1999, Murray 2001, Roche 2000.
3. Notably, in the lead to the Beijing 2008 Olympic Games, and in response to severe criticisms by the international media on China's human rights record and calls for a boycott against the Games, Jacques Rogue, current IOC president was quoted in the UK press indicating that 'The role of the IOC is to organise the Olympic Games. We are not a sports association nor a political organisation and neither an association with humanitarian goals' (Macintyre 2008: 16). The depiction of the IOC as an organisation that is not mainly aimed at addressing humanitarian goals in part contradicts the ambitions expressed in the Olympic Charter, the main document outlining the Fundamental Principles, Rules and Bylaws adopted by the International Olympic Committee in representation of the wider Olympic Movement. These issues and apparent contradictions are explored in more detail in Chapters 2 and 3.

NOTES TO CHAPTER 2

1. In the Candidature Questionnaire published for the 2000 Olympic Games candidates, the cultural programme requirements were presented as 'Theme 14: Cultural Programme and Youth Camp' (IOC 1992). Following editions of the Questionnaire have presented it as 'Theme 11: Olympism and Culture' (IOC 1995) which has been maintained up to the 2012 Games edition for which the Candidature Questionnaire read as 'Theme 17: Olympism and Culture' (IOC 2004b).
2. The IOC Cultural Commission is the body that preceded the current IOC 'Culture and Education Commission'. Chapter 3 provides a detailed assessment of the Commission.
3. For instance see Arguel 1994, Burnosky 1994, Guevara 1992, IOC 1969–2000, 1993, 1995, 1997a, 1997d, 2000c, 2000d, 2000f, Levitt 1990, Messing 1997, Masterton 1973, Stanton 2000, Pfirschke 1998, Priebe 1990.
4. While I hold to the idea that this interpretation prevails, it is important to note an added dimension of ritual and classic ideals around the aesthetic

experience that I do not consider further in this analysis. Further details are explained by Gold and Revill (2007).

5. Yet, Coubertin was not the first to attempt a revival of the Olympics in the 19ᵗʰ century. For further details and suggestions for why other attempts did not flourish see Georgiadis (1998).

6. In the original conception of the Olympic Games, a key criteria for inclusion as an Olympic competitor was the need to be an amateur athlete, that is, not to be a full time professional and compete in sport for financial or commercial gain. This rule was also applied to the arts competition, and caused controversy as it became a challenge to attract artworks of the right quality if contributors could not be professional artists. Avery Brundage, was elected as IOC president in 1952 and was strongly opposed to any form of professionalism in the Olympic Games. His views prevailed during the lengthy revision of Olympic Arts Competitions formats and priorities that took place between 1949 and 1952 and led to their replacement by Arts Exhibitions.

7. The 'Olympic Truce' is the principle of stopping all wars for the duration of the Olympic Games, a notion that was originally implemented during the Ancient Olympic Games to ensure the safe passage of all athletes. See: http://www.olympictruce.org/.

8. See: http://www.cultural-olympiad.org.gr/.

9. See: http://en.beijing2008.cn/culture/festivals/ and Garcia 2008.

10. At a national level, London 2012 has established the *Unlimited* programme, dedicated to celebrating disability arts throughout the Olympiad (see: http://tinyurl.com/3pcg5xo).

11. In Beijing 2008 and Vancouver 2010, certain aspects of the sports programme were co-programmed as well between the Olympic and Paralympic organising committees, perhaps indicating some additional advancement towards merging activities and modus operandi.

12. In particular, see Brownell (2008: 94) who, in response to the many inquiries into whether Beijing 2008 would change or reinforce China's politics, highlights that 'the more important symbolism will concern the place of Chinese culture and the Chinese nation in the modern world'.

13. See: http://www.london2012.com/plans/culture/now-to-2012/getting-involved.php.

NOTES TO CHAPTER 3

1. Note that there are more updated versions of the Olympic Charter. However, this book has relied on the 1999 version as this reflected the rules that were in place at the time of delivering the Sydney Olympic Games and Olympic Arts Festivals.

2. This table compares the number of EB members and IOC members in each commission with total membership as at the beginning of 2000. The commissions have been ordered starting from the commission having a relatively higher percentage of EB and IOC members combined.

3. For a more extensive description of the negotiations involved in the management of television and related issues, see Chapter 7. Also see Moragas, Rivenburgh and Larson (1995) and Pound (2004), who describes the development of TV rights negotiations from the 1980s.

4. By 2009 there were 31 members and by 2012, 35 members.

5. John MacAloon has indicated that one of the key recommendations for culture to emerge out of the major reform process heralded by the IOC 2000 Commission was to create a separate professional IOC administrative department

concerned with cultural affairs, education and heritage. This recommendation was, however, not implemented. The only culture-related recommendation to be implemented was the merger of the IOC Culture Commission and the Commission for Olympic education, as noted elsewhere in the chapter. (MacAloon 2002: 272; full recommendations available via IOC 1999b).

6. During the period 1986–1994, an analysis of the key subjects treated by 'Olympic Review' has revealed that issues about the relationship between art, culture and sport ranged up to a 4% of all publications. This number stands well in comparison to other key issues such as: general discourses and speeches (6%), international federations (6%), chronicles of meetings (5%), sports aids (5%), members and personalities (5%) and National Olympic Committees (4.5%). The only subject that stands far over the rest is the articles about the Olympic Games in general (15% of all articles). These issues reflect the categories of the Olympic Review Thesaurus (IOC, 1994a); percentages have been calculated by the author out of the Summary of Olympic Review Articles, (IOC, 1994b).

7. In 2012, the Olympic Museum is undergoing major restructuring and the current Museum Director has indicated a commitment to highlighting the role of the Olympic cultural programme and related Games time cultural activity as part of his plans for the Museum's new permanent exhibition layout (2011, pers. comm., 5 Dec).

8. The IOC website includes updated information about the Cultural Commission and, on occasion, has displayed information about specific activities such as the Art and Sport contest in 2000. However, this does not incorporate an explanation about the wider cultural aims of the movement, including the existence of Cultural Olympiads and Arts Festivals. In this sense, remarkably, within the historical archives section of the Museum website, there is not a single reference or image about past cultural programmes to accompany the extensive information about past Olympic Games, athletes and special events such as the ceremonies.

9. Prior to the existence of a Cultural Commission in 1968, the IOC had a Fine Arts Sub-committee which had initially been dedicated to supervise the arrangement of Olympic Arts Competitions. After its dissolution in 1952, it would continue counselling the IOC about the need for an interaction between arts and sport activities. Avery Brundage was a strong supporter of the activities of the sub-committee. (University of Illinois, 1998).

10. The current state and functions of National Olympic Academies (NOAs) is difficult to summarise. Nevertheless, it must be noted that, as suggested by Prof Norbert Müller, who is a member of the Commission (2000, pers. comm., 9 Sep) the relationship of NOAs with NOCs and other Olympic Family members is not always an easy one. Arguably, this lack of interaction has affected the ability to establish cultural departments in either NOAs or NOCs and, ultimately, has diminished the existence of Olympic projects and networks with cultural interests other than sport.

11. The most notable example is the IOC's formal endorsement of the 'Sport Movies and TV International FICTS Fest', organised by the International Federation of Cinema and Television Sports and presided by a member of the IOC Commission of Culture and Education. (http://www.olympic.org/news?articleid=143478, last accessed Jan 2012).

12. The IOC archives and collections store most published records on Games programmes, including Arts Festivals and Cultural Olympiads. However, there is practically no stored material on the strategic and policy frameworks for cultural programmes, such as their aims and objectives, budgeting issues, approach to promotions, levels of participation attained etc. This is in

stark contrast with other Games programmes which, following IOC requirements, are documented in detail and thus provide a better basis for respective OCOGs to learn from previous experience. The IOC Transfer of Knowledge programme was supposed to establish a more consistent framework for programme monitoring and documentation.

13. The Cultural Commission chairmen have made many proposals but few have resulted in real implementations. For instance, during the 89th Session in Lausanne in 1986, the proposal by Ramirez Vázquez to create an Olympic gold medal in art (IOC 1969–2000: 1986, annex 16) was gradually reduced to a special prize, arguably unknown by most Olympic fans, that is currently called *Olympiart*. At another level, the applauded proposal by Ramírez Vázquez to invite Nobel Prize Winners to the Olympic Congress (IOC 1969–2000: 1987, annex 10; 1989, annex 6) did not have any following in the records of subsequent sessions.

14. This is the case of the 97th Session in Birmingham, 1991 and the 98th Session in Courchevel, 1992. The verbal proceedings of these Sessions do not include minutes nor annexes about the Culture Commission.

NOTES TO CHAPTER 4

1. According to the Aboriginal and Torres Strait Islanders Commission, the number of Aboriginal languages range close to 300.

2. See Sydney Bid Ltd. 1992b, 1992c, 1992d; SOCOG 1999i, 2000a.

3. The Youth Camp is an optional requirement described under Rule 58 of the Olympic Charter. It aims to bring together young people in the host-city from each participating country. Two youths are normally chosen by every National Olympic Committee, aged between 18 to 22 years old. The Charter recommends them to be hosted together during the duration of the Games in order for them to learn about the Olympic Movement and the host-city culture. The Youth Camp must include an education programme and implement cultural and arts activities (IOC 2001).

4. See Chapter 6 for more details on the role and involvement of the Sydney 2000 Games Olympic Cultural Commission. Do not confuse with the IOC Cultural Commission.

NOTES TO CHAPTER 5

1. The discontinued lines mark the difference in nature of the marketing and publicity services within the OAF programme. Both services were contracted as 'consultancies', while other positions such as operations or production were contracted as 'managerial positions' (SOCOG 2000d, internal sources).

2. *A Sea Change* in 1998 incorporated some activities that were coordinated by the National Education Programme but this did not imply any managerial interaction between the education and arts teams. The collaboration was limited to some promotional support, that is, the incorporation of mutual references in some of the printed materials.

3. See more information in Chapter 7.

4. Direct observation exercises were undertaken during the author's internship at SOCOG within the Public Relations programme and the Publications programme in the periods of March to September 1999 and August to September 2000.

5. By the end of 1998, suspicion of corruption and bribery within the bid for the Salt Lake 2002 Winter Games led to a major public scandal that put into question the IOC basic structure and working procedures. The scandal received expanded coverage throughout the beginning of year 1999 and had some repercussion on SOCOG image strategies.

6. Currency conversions into A$ and U$ have been calculated on the basis of the exchange rates existing at the time of respective budget confirmations in 1992, 1996, 2000 and 2004.

7. Ambush marketing is defined by the IOC as all intentional or unintentional attempts to create a false or unauthorised commercial association with the Olympic Movement or the Olympic Games (IOC 2000a).

8. The distribution channel of the festival 48-page guide varied depending on the state. Average newsagents were used to reach the population of the state of Queensland; Fairfax newspapers capitalised on the distribution for New South Wales and Victoria respectively; and *The West Australian*, Perth's metropolitan daily, was used to reach the state of West Australia.

9. The website designed for *A Sea Change* in 1998 was, arguably, the most detailed and informative of all the OAF festivals' webs up to 1999. However, after the launch of a new SOCOG Olympic site in September 1999, all references to past festivals were transformed into a single page information without links to the prior interactive webs, where details on programmes and venues had been stored. The extensive information on the 1998 experience was, thus, inaccessible to the increasing number of visitors to SOCOG's web in the final approach to the Games.

10. The communication and marketing strategy for the 2000 festival is analysed in detail in Chapter 7.

11. Due to the high demand for top sporting competitions (particularly the finals), tickets to Olympic events are sold within a 'ballot' system that does not guarantee first choice. The OAF was introduced within this system and presented to the public as a possible alternative or 'second choice' to the top profile sporting events.

NOTES TO CHAPTER 6

1. The information presented in this section has been compiled from internal sources and informal meetings at SOCOG. SOCOG has published official information on these issues as part of the Sydney 2000 Post Games Report (a version of this report is available at http://www.gamesinfo.com.au).

2. This was a proposal designed by the Bid Cultural Commission, many members of which became also members of the Olympic Cultural Commission.

3. Jonah Jones, OAF executive producer since 1995, announced his departure from the OAF in 1996. Numerous projects and arrangements for the inclusion of community artworks were cancelled soon afterwards, such as Jeremy Taylor's National Youth Music Theatre, London.

4. Personal communications in 1999 with representatives from Carnivale, Casula Powerhouse Regional Arts, SOCOG Multicultural Advisory Committtee, NSW Community Arts Association.

5. Among others, aboriginal performers Leah Purcell, Deborah Cheetham and the Bangarra Dance Theatre were commonly acknowledged as successful stars of the OAF who had the opportunity to get an international exposure. This was accentuated due to the early start of the 1997 festival, four years ahead of the Olympic Games.

6. The 'executive producer' model has also been the chosen approach for the delivery of other one-off cultural events such as the Manchester 2002 Commonwealth Games cultural programme (García 2003) and the Liverpool 2008 European Capital of Culture (see García et al. 2010). Such approach contrasts with the autonomous 'artistic director' model that tends to dominate within ongoing large arts festivals such as the Edinburgh International Festival, the Adelaide Arts Festival or the Festival d'Avignon.
7. See Chapter 8 for more detailed information on the involvement of the city of Sydney to support the OAF.
8. Some events in this table could not be included in the final festival programme. Please note that this table is based on projections rather than final, confirmed costs. Most of these costs were met, but the final confirmed table has not been disclosed.
9. Interesting cases to consider are non-Olympic sponsor Qantas promotional slogan 'The spirit of Australia' (SOCOG's promotional slogan for the Games was 'Share the spirit') and the successful 'Australia 2000' merchandising brand, which could be easily associated to the Olympic merchandising products although it had no legal rights for it.
10. The marketing kit for the 1998 festival, *A Sea Change*, indicates that a total of 1000 individual media representatives were contacted soon after the official media launch of the festival (SOCOG 1998d: 17).
11. To learn more about the IOC crisis of 1999 and subsequent reform see an official chronology, available at: http://www.olympic.org/Documents/Reports/EN/en_report_590.pdf (last accessed July 2011).
12. The Olympic Info intranet also included details of the biographies of all participant athletes and information about each NOC; information about all activities happening in the Olympic and Media villages and general information about the Games organisation and the Olympic Movement basic structure. The information was more detailed than the one available on SOCOG website.
13. See the official website: http://www.londonandpartners.com/ (last accessed May 2011).
14. See the initiative's official website: http://www.media2012.org.uk/ (last accessed May 2011).
15. The Cultural Olympiad section within London 2012 official website includes a note that states: 'BP and BT are Premier Partners of the Cultural Olympiad and the London 2012 Festival'. Another official sponsor is Panasonic, introduced as the 'presenting partner' of one of the Cultural Olympiad major commissions (Film Nation: Shorts). Other funding comes from the Arts Council England, Legacy Trust UK and the Olympic Lottery Distributor. Information available online at: http://www.london2012.com/cultural-olympiad (last accessed: April 2011).

NOTES TO CHAPTER 7

1. After the first IOC global advertising campaign in 2000, a second campaign has started with a focus on the notion of 'The Best of Us'. See: http://www.olympic.org./uk/bestofus/index_uk.asp (last accessed: Sep 2011)
2. See Figure 5.3. in Chapter 5.
3. Value in kind is a marketing term meaning that the support or investment provided by a particular partner or sponsor is not cash, but services. For instance, a flying company may offer flights and a media company may offer space for promotions. The market value of these services is accounted for as sponsorship investment.

4. The Look of the Games is a programme within the OCOG that is dedicated to guaranteeing the consistency of the Games corporate design. This includes the design of the Games/sports pictograms, staff uniforms, stationery design, publications design, city banners and so on.
5. At the beginning of 1999, the IOC had to face a series of public hearings about practices of bribery and corruption within the Olympic Movement. This was an effect of the publicity given, by the end of 1998, to suspicion of bad practices within the bidding process for the Salt Lake City winter Games.
6. For a brief definition of 'ambush marketing' see Chapter 5 notes.
7. In brackets in the original.
8. An overview of the marketing and communications strategy for the OAF as a whole and the festivals in 1997, 1998 and 1999 is presented in Chapter 5.
9. In following pages, the festival taking place in year 2000 will be referred to as *OAF'2000*. The title *The Harbour of Life* will be used only in reference to the early stages of the planning for the OAF.
10. Directional displays consist of the placement of temporary and very visible panels in popular areas of the city where a special event is going to occur. Their purpose is to offer an indication of where the activities associated with the event are taking place. Within the Olympic Games, there is a very strong tradition of way-finding displays, which have become a key component of the organising committee design strategy or Look of the Games.
11. See additional details about the *LiveSites!* programme in Chapter 8. This programme became the most popular aspect of Sydney's city celebrations and was often perceived as the main Olympic cultural programme.
12. The delivery system changed from the company Ticketek to SOCOG's centralised ticketing system and back to Ticketek.
13. Delays in the tickets mail delivery system led to requesting that customers picked up tickets at Ticketek offices and, secondly, to request that they picked them up at the venue on the day of the event. This caused great confusion and discontent among OAF audiences.
14. In Sydney, SOCOG agreed to appoint a number of internationally established academic professors dedicated to the study of the Olympic Games (Olympic scholars) as Games observers. This arrangement was supported by the IOC which provided them with special accreditation to access Games venues.
15. Find a detailed explanation of the media promotional schedule in the following section: 'Media distribution schedule'.
16. See Chapters 6 and 8 for more details on the *ausarts2000* programme.
17. As briefly discussed in Chapter 2, this has been the case in other Olympic editions, in particular, Athens 2004, where the Hellenic Ministry of Culture decided to establish a separate organisation to programme and promote the Cultural Olympiad. A similar approach had been taken in the context of Barcelona 1992, where the local city authorities were also aspiring to place culture and the arts at the heart of the Olympic experience.

NOTES TO CHAPTER 8

1. Arts Queensland offered a grant of A$200,000 to *A Sea Change*, leading to the inclusion of top Queensland arts organisations. Tourism Queensland kept updated information on the OAF at its web-site: www.qttc.com.au/media/olympic/arts (last accessed, September 2000).
2. The 'Major Festivals Initiative' was created to commission new work to an international standard with the capacity to reach audiences throughout the country and overseas (Australia Council, 1999: 10–11). It is indicative of the

low consideration given to the OAF that the Olympics were not seen to have such a capacity in the area of the Arts.

3. The Department of Communications, Information Technology and the Arts is an Australian government agency with a similar function to that of the Ministry of Culture in countries like Spain, or the Department for Media, Culture and Sport in the United Kingdom.

4. The IOC retains the right to accredit all media that want to gain access to Olympic venues and cover Olympic competitions. Accredited media are hosted at the Main Press Centre and the International Broadcasting Centre and are also provided with accommodation at the Olympic Media Village. The main focus of all information provided within accredited environments are the official competitions and related high profile Olympic events such as the Torch Relay and the Opening and Closing Ceremonies. The OAF has traditionally been underrepresented within accredited media environments.

5. As previously stated, the creation of SOCOG's Cultural Committee in 1995, led to suspicion within artistic circles about the power that Committee board members would have to determine who was to be part of the OAF and who was not to be.

6. A remarkable case was that of Rosehill, an area neighbouring Olympic Park and host of sporting competitions, that was to be host of *Australians all*, the only OAF event 'taking place out of the city centre' (SOCOG 1999b). After a year of strong promotions about the dedication of the final festival to expand out of the city centre and reach suburban Sydney communities, the initiative was finally cancelled by mid year 2000 and the concert was transferred to a popular park in the heart of the city or 'city business district', where all other events were taking place.

7. Carnivale is a festival dedicated to Australian artists from non-English-speaking backgrounds and organises shows throughout Sydney suburbs. The festival team was dissolved at the beginning of November 1999 due to changes in the board constitution (in hands of the NSW state government). By January 2000 a new team was put into place leading to new policies reinforcing the marketing potential of the event and stressing the need for the festival to be considered a display of professional artists and not just a community celebration. The festival was established in 1976 and underwent a major revision and 're-branding' in the aftermath of the Sydney Olympic Games (see Australia Council [online] http://tinyurl.com/3km27h6 (last accessed: July 2011).

8. The price for events taking place within Opera House OAF programme in year 2000 duplicated and, sometimes, triplicated the average prices of similar quality events in Australia (Morgan 1999: 15).

9. Two prestigious historic ships were brought to the venue and an exhibition about Australia sporting life was commissioned.

10. The only visual arts exhibition especially commissioned by the OAF was *Shrines for the New Millennium* which was an Oceanic indigenous art exhibition presented at Sydney College of the Arts in collaboration with Australian Aboriginal and Torres Strait Islanders, and institutions from France, New Zealand, Korea and New Caledonia.

11. The festival is currently called *Telstra Adelaide Festival* and it is nationally recognised as the leading festival in the country, the only one with an international profile at the level of the Edinburgh Festival.

12. Some of the most common criticisms were about the lack of new Australian work in theatre, opera or concerts. There was also much criticism related to some problems attached to ticket deliveries and some protest for the cancellation of the very few events happening out of the city central business district.

Notably, numerous artists and community leaders denounced the transfer of the concert *Australians all*, the only *OAF'2000* event that was supposed to happen outside the city centre, from its original placement in the western suburb Rosehill, into yet another venue in the city centre, Moore Park.

13. See UNESCO's memorandum of understanding with Greece's Cultural Olympiad, signed off by its Executive Board in 1998, available online at: http://unesdoc.unesco.org/images/0011/001134/113420e.pdf (last accessed: May 2011).

14. For Vancouver, see Legacies Now (online: http://www.2010legaciesnow.com/arts/). London has established a Legacy Trust Fund, which is one of the main sources of funding for community projects linked to the Cultural Olympiad (online: http://www.legacytrustuk.org/).

15. As discussed in previous chapters, reflections on national identity tend to be a favourite subject for Olympic cultural programmes, perceived as both timely in the Games context, and likely to attract wide involvement from large sections of the population. As such, this is seen as a safe cultural investment for corporate sponsors. Beyond the examples provided for London 2012, Vancouver 2010 did also embark in a nation-building exercise via its Canada CODE programme. For London 2012, see: http://roadto2012.npg.org.uk/ and http://tinyurl.com/45yzqdz. For Vancouver 2010, see: http://www.facebook.com/CODECanadaCODE (last accessed May 2011).

16. The case of Beijing is particularly telling. While Chinese authorities were adamant to avoid the dominance of commercial messages within iconic spaces in the city, such as Tiananmen square, and negotiated a Look of the Games with low sponsor branding presence in these select (and highly touristy) environments, they were open to the Cultural Squares being used in whichever way corporate sponsors may see fit. This resulted in some of the most extravagant branding displays of any Games, in sites such as the Coca-Cola branded Cultural Square within the large shopping mall, The Place (see Garcia 2008).

17. In the context of Vancouver 2010 see, for example: http://artthreat.net/tag/vancouver-2010/. In the context of London 2012, some examples include the work of Hilary Powell, ranging from film to community gatherings and university courses (http://hilarypowell.com/gatherings/salon-de-refuse-olympique/) or the piece of performance art and resulting visual exhibit produced by Jim Woodall, who in turn is a regular contributor to community activist-led debates on the subject (http://www.seestudio.com/#olympic-state-jim-woodall-14th-april-14th-may-2011-2 (last accessed January 2012).

18. During Beijing 2008, a Games edition which incorporated an extensive cultural programme taking place throughout all the major cultural institutions, some of the most dynamic and innovative gatherings between emerging artists and young intellectuals happened at the fringes, within small art venues located in traditional neighbourhoods or 'hutongs'. An interesting example was a gathering organised by the group Yah Interactive attracting social media designers, artists, media writers and university lecturers. See: http://www.yahplus.cn/leolympic/ (last accessed April 2011).

19. See http://www.bbc.co.uk/olympicsnewsletter/summer2007/cultural_olympiad.shtml (last accessed May 2011).

NOTES TO CHAPTER 9

1. As discussed in Chapter 4, *The Harbour of Life* was the original title for the 2000 Olympic Arts Festival as given within the bid documents, and coverage

about the plans for this programme used this heading from 1995 to 1999. The final festival title was changed in late 1999, appropriating the generic *Olympic Arts Festival* denomination and eliminating references to previous festivals or the notion of a four year Olympiad.

NOTES TO CHAPTER 10

1. The establishment of an OCOG liaison post with a specific remit for culture and educational matters should help raise the profile of the cultural programme and locate it in more operational rather than just aspirational debates within the IOC. However, this post has only been created in mid 2006 as a part-time function and it is unclear whether its cultural portfolio will be treated as central or, yet again, just marginal within day-to-day strategic priorities.
2. Such integration seems to be part of the vision behind the new '360 degree' Olympic experience narrative (see IOC 2009b) but so far, this has not been operationalised with culture and the arts in mind.
3. As mentioned earlier in the book, the major IOC 'shake-up' was the result of the international scandals or 'IOC crisis' emerging in the wake of the Salt Lake City Bid process, where there were allegations of corruption within the IOC structure. This crisis led to a major revision to the IOC modus operandi post year 2000 and resulted in a greater commitment to ensuring transparency and accountability, particularly within the Games staging process.
4. For example, other cultural and community programmes managed through the Communications and Community Relations programme were the *Olympic Journey* and *Share the Spirit Olympic Art Student Prize*, but these programmes were not linked to the OAF. Furthermore, in 1999, the official presentations of the mascots, the National Education programme and, especially, the Torch Relay preparations, received stronger media attention than the 1998 and 1999 arts festivals together.
5. At the time of writing, Australia has launched a worldwide tourism campaign under the slogan 'There's nothing like Australia'; in this campaign, the emphasis continues to be on traditional icons (from traditional Aboriginal culture to the Sydney Opera House sails, the outback and the people's relaxed character) and contemporary arts and cultural activity is not represented as part of the key tourist offer. On an added note, the people featured in this adverts is either of Anglosaxon descent of in traditional Aboriginal attire, thus not incorporating any of the more recent waves of immigration 'multicultural Australia' discourse that had been attempted at the time of the Olympic bid.

References

ACOG, Atlanta Committee for the Olympic Games (1997) Official Report on the Atlanta 1996 Olympic Games.

Adorno, T.W. (1991) *The Culture Industry*, London: Routledge.

Adorno, T.W. & Horkheimer, M., (1979) *Dialectic of Enlightenment*. London: Verso.

Ander-Egg, E. (1991) *Desarrollo y Política Cultural* [Development and Cultural Policy], Buenos Aires: Ediciones CICCUS.

Anderson, M. (2000) *States and Nationalism in Europe Since 1945*, London: Routledge.

Arguel, M. (1994) 'Sport, Olympism and Art' inCNOSF (Ed) *For a Humanism of Sport*, Paris: CNOSF and Editions Revue EP, pp. 179–186.

Arts Today (December 1994) Interview with Donald McDonald, Chairman of SOCOG Cultural Commission.

Ashworth, G.J. & Voogd, H. (1995) *Selling the City: Marketing Approaches in Public Sector Urban Planning*, London: Wiley.

Australia Council (1994) *Arts for a Multicultural Australia. Arts for Australians by Australians*, Sydney: AC.

Australia Council (1999) *Support for the Arts Handbook*, Sydney: AC.

Australian Bureau of Statistics (1999) *Statistics on the Australian Population* [online] http://www.abs.gov.au

Australian Tourism Commission (ATC). (2000) *Media Information Kit*, Sydney: ATC.

Berg, L, Borg, J. & Meer, J. (1995) *Urban Tourism. Performance and Strategies in Eight European Cities*, Avebury: Aldershot.

Berkaak, O.A. (1999) 'In the Heart of the Volcano: The Olympic Games as Mega Drama' in Klausen, A.M. (Ed) *Olympic Games as Performance and Public Event. The Case of the XVII Winter Olympic Games in Norway*, New York: Bergham Books, pp. 49–75.

Berlin Organising Committee for the Olympic Games (1937) *The XIth Olympic Games Berlin 1936 Official Report*, Vol.2 [online] http://www.la84foundation. org/6oic/OfficialReports/1936/1936v2sum.pdf

Bianchini, F. (1993) 'Remaking European Cities: The Role of Cultural Policies' in F. Bianchini & M. Parkinson (Eds) *Cultural Policy and Urban Regeneration*, Manchester: Manchester University Press, pp. 1—19.

Bianchini, F. (1999) 'Cultural Planning for Urban Sustainability' in: Nyström, L. (Ed) *Culture and Cities. Cultural Processes and Urban Sustainability*, Stockholm: The Swedish Urban Development Council, pp. 34–51

Bianchini, F., Fisher, M., Montgomery, J., & Worpole, K. (1988) *City Centres, City Cultures. The role of the arts in the revitalisation of towns and cities*, Manchester: Centre for Local Economic Strategies.

Bianchini, F. & Parkinson, M. (1993) *Cultural Policy and Urban Regeneration: The West European Experience*, Manchester: Manchester University Press.

Blake, A. (1996) *The Body Language: The Meaning of Modern Sport*, London: Lawrence and Wishart.

BOCOG (2008) *Beijing Olympic Cultural Festival*, (Official Programme), Beijing: Beijing Organising Committee for the Olympic Games.

Booth, D. & Tatz, C. (1994) 'Swimming with the Big Boys? The Politics of Sydney's 2000 Olympic Bid', *Sporting Traditions*, 11 (1), pp. 3—23.

Borja, J. & Subirós, P. (1989) 'The Rebirth of the City', *Documents and Subjects of the Eurocities Conference* (21–22 Apr), Barcelona, pp. 13–24.

Brittain, I. (2010) *The Paralympic Games Explained*, Oxon: Routledge.

Brownell, S. (2008) *Beijing's Games: What the Olympics Mean to China*. New York: Rowman & Littlefield.

Bureau of Tourism Research (2000) *International Visitors Survey*, Canberra: Australia Bureau of Statistics.

Burnosky, R.L. (1994) *The History of the Arts in the Olympic Games*, (MA Thesis) Washington DC: The American University.

Cahill, J. (1999) *Running Towards Sydney 2000: The Olympic Flame and Torch*, Sydney: Walla Walla Press.

Carl Diem Institute (Eds) (1966) *Pierre de Coubertin, The Olympic Idea: Discourses and Essays*, Lausanne: Editions Internationales Olympia.

Collins, J. & Castillo, A. (1998) *Cosmopolitan Sydney: Explore the World in One City*, Sydney: Pluto Press.

COOB, Comité Organizador Olímpico de Barcelona (1993) *Official Report on the Barcelona 1992 Olympic Games. The Means* (vol. IV).

Council of Europe (Ed) (1997) *In from the Margins*, Strasbourg: Council of Europe.

Craik, J.(2007) *Revisioning Arts and Cultural Policy. Current Impasses and Future Directions*. Canberra: ANU Press.

Crane, D., Kawashima, N. & Kawasaki, K. (2002) *Global Culture: Media, Arts, Policy, and Globalization*, New York: Routledge.

Cuilenburg, J. & McQuail, D. (2003) 'Media Policy Paradigm Shifts: Towards a New Communications Policy Paradigm', *European Journal of Communication* 18 (2), pp. 181–207.

Cunningham, S. & Sinclair, J. (2000) *Floating Lives: The Media and Asian Diasporas*, Santa Lucia: Queensland University Press.

Cutlip, S.M, Center, A.H & Broom, G.M. (1994) *Effective Public Relations*, Englewood Cliffs, NJy: Prentice-Hall.

Dayan, D. & Katz, E. (1994) *Media Events: The Live Broadcasting of History*, London: Harvard University Press.

DCMS (1998) *A New Cultural Framework*. London: Department of Media, Culture and Sport.

DCMS (2001) *Creative Industries. Mapping Document*. London: Department of Media, Culture and Sport.

DCMS (2004) *Culture at the Heart of Regeneration*. London: Department of Media, Culture and Sport.

Department of Communication and the Arts (Eds) (1994) *Creative Nation. Commonwealth Cultural Policy*, Canberra: Australian Government Publishing Service.

Department of Immigration and Multicultural Affairs (2000) *Australian Statistics 1998–1999*, Sydney.

DiMaggio, P. (1983) 'Can Culture Survive the Marketplace?', *Journal of Arts Management and Law* 13 (1), pp. 61–87.

Dodd, D. & Hemel, A. (1999) *Planning Cultural Tourism in Europe: A Presentation of Theories and Cases*, Amsterdam: Boekmanstichting.

Farrell, F. (1999) 'Australian Identity' in Cashman, R. & Hughes, A. (Eds), *Staging the Olympics. The Event and its Impact*, Sydney: University of New South Wales Press, pp. 59–70.

Fernández Prado, E. (1991) *La Política Cultural: Qué es y para qué sirve* [Cultural Policy: What Is It and What It is For], Gijón: Trea.

Florida, R. (2002) *The Rise of the Creative Class*, New York: Basic Books/ Perseus.

Foote, J. A. (1998) *Canada's Cultural Policy: A Model of Diversity*, Waterloo: University of Waterloo–Centre for Cultural Research Network.

Frankland, R. (2000) *Media Briefing, Indigenous Unit–Australian Film Commission*, (26 Nov), Sydney: Sydney Media Centre.

Fréchete, S., Roy, I. & de la Durantaye, M. (1998) 'Municipal Cultural Policies in Québec: Evolution in Light of Québec's 1992 Cultural Policy and Links to Cultural Practices' in Murray, C.A. (Ed) *Conference on Cultural Policies and Cultural Practices: Exploring the Links between Culture and Social Change*, Ottawa: Canadian Cultural Research Network, pp. 53–-54.

Galloway, S. (2007) 'A Critique of the Definitions of the Cultural and Creative Industries in Public Policy', in *International Journal of Cultural Policy* 13 (1), pp. 17–31.

Gans, H.J. (1974) *Popular Culture and High Culture: An Analysis and Evaluation of Taste*, New York: HarperCollins.

García, B. (2000) 'Comparative Analysis of the Barcelona'92 and Sydney 2000 Cultural Olympiad', 5th *International Symposium for Olympic Research. Bridging Three Centuries: Intellectual Crossroads and the Modern Olympic Movement*, London: University of Western Ontario, pp. 153–158.

García, B. (2001) 'Enhancing Sports Marketing through Cultural and Arts Programmes. Lessons from the Sydney 2000 Olympic Arts Festivals', *Sports Management Review*, 4(2), pp. 193–220.

Garcia, B. (2002) 'Securing Sustainable Legacies through Cultural Programming in Major Events', in Moragas, M., de Kennet, C. & Puig, N. (Eds), *The Legacy of the Olympic Games: 1984–2000*, Lausanne: Centre for Olympic Studies (UAB) and Olympic Museum , pp. 314–320.

Garcia, B. (2003) *Evaluation of Cultureshock, Cultural Programme of the Manchester 2002 Commonwealth Games*, Manchester: Arts Council England North West.

García, B. (2004a) 'Cultural Policy and Urban Regeneration in Western European Cities: Lessons from Experience, Prospects for the Future', *Local Economy* 19 (4), pp. 312–326.

García, B. (2004b) 'Urban Regeneration, Arts Programming and Major Events: Glasgow 1990, Sydney 2000 and Barcelona 2004,' *International Journal of Cultural Policy* 10 (1), pp. 103–118.

García, B. (2005) 'De-constructing the City of Culture: The Long-term Cultural Legacies of Glasgow 1990', *Urban Studies*, 42 (5/6), pp. 1–28.

García, B. (2008) 'Beijing Cultural Festivals . . . Bigger but Not Always Better', in Cerezuela, B. (Ed) *Beijing 2008—Academic Views of the Event*, Barcelona: Centre for Olympic Studies.

García, B. (2012 in press) 'The Cultural Olympiad', in: Girginov, V. (Ed) *Bidding, Delivering and Engaging with the Olympics*, London: Routledge.

García, B., Melville, R. and Cox, T. (2010) *Creating an Impact: Liverpool's Experience as European Capital of Culture*, Liverpool: Impacts 08 at University of Liverpool.

García, B. and Miah, A. (2006) 'Ever Decreasing Circles: The Profile of Culture at the Olympics', *Locum Destination Review*, 18, pp. 60–63.

García Canclini, N. (1999) 'Opciones de políticas culturales en el marco de la globalización', in UNESCO (Ed) *Informe Mundial sobre la Cultura. Cultura, creatividad y mercados*, París: UNESCO.

Garnham, N. (2007) 'From Cultural to Creative Industries', *International Journal of Cultural Policy*, 11 (1), pp. 15–29.

Georgiadis, C. (1998) 'The Significance of the Olympic Games for Greece in the 19th Century', in Barney, R,K,, Wamsley, K.B., Martyn S.G. & MacDonald G.H. (Eds) *Global and Cultural Critique: Problematizing the Olympic Games*, (Fourth International Symposium for Olympic Research), London: Centre for Olympic Studies, University of Western Ontario, pp. 191–196.

Getz, D. (1989) 'Special Events–Defining the Product', *Tourism Management*, 10 (2), pp. 125—137.

Getz, D. (1991) *Festivals, Special Events and Tourism*, New York: Van Nostrand Reinhold.

Gibson, C. & Klocker, N. (2005) 'The 'Cultural Turn' in Australian Regional Economic Development Discourse: Neoliberalising Creativity?', *Geographical Research*, 43, pp. 93—102.

Gibson, L. (2001) *The Uses of Art: Constructing Australian Identities*, Brisbane: University of Queensland Press.

Gold, J.R. & Gold, M. (2005) *Cities of Culture: Staging International Festivals and the Urban Agenda, 1851–2000*. Aldershot: Ashgate.

Gold, J.R & Ward, S.V. (eds) (1994) *Place Promotion: The Use of Publicity and Marketing to Sell Towns and Regions*, Chichester: John Wiley & Sons.

Gold, M. and Revill, G. (2007) 'The Cultural Olympiads: Reviving the Panegyris' in Gold, J.R. & Gold, M.M. (Eds) *Olympic Cities: Urban Planning, City Agendas and the World's Games, 1896 to the Present*, London: Routledge, pp. 59–83.

Goldstein, A. (1998) 'Conference Summary' in *New Directions in Cultural Policy Conference. Privatization of Culture Project*, New York: New York University.

Good, D. (1998) *The Olympic Games' Cultural Olympiad: Identity and Management*, (MA Thesis, unpublished), Washington DC: The American University.

Good, D. (1999) 'The Cultural Olympiad' inCashman, R. & Hughes, A. (Eds) *Staging the Olympics: The Event and Its Impact*, Sydney: University of New South Wales Press.

Guevara, T. (1992) *Análisis comparativo del programa cultural olímpico desde México'68 hasta Barcelna'92, como base para su realización en Puerto Rico'2004*, (unpublished) available at: Centre for Olympic Studies–Autonomous University of Barcelona.

Hall, C.M. (1992a) *Hallmark Tourist Events: Impacts, Management and Planning*, London: Bellhaven.

Hall, S. (1992b) 'The question of cultural identity' in: Hall, S; Held, D. & McGrew, T. (Eds) *Modernity and Its Futures*, Cambridge: Polity Press, pp. 273—327.

Hanna, M. (1999) *Reconciliation in Olympism, The Sydney 200 Olympic Games and Australia's Indigenous People*, Sydney: University of New South Wales.

Hassall, C. (2008) 'Sydney 2000 Olympic Games Cultural Programme' in Muller, N. & Messing, M. (Eds) *Olympism. Heritage and Responsibility*, Kassel: Agon Sportverlag, pp. 307—313.

Haxton, P. (1999) *Community Participation in the Mega-Event Hosting Process: The Case of the Olympic Games*, (PhD thesis), Sydney: University of Technology.

Hearn, G, Roodhouse, S., and Blakey, J. (2007) 'From Value Chain to Value Creating Ecology: Implications for Creative Industries Development Policy' in *International Journal of Cultural Policy*, 13 (4), pp. 419–436.

Heller, A. (1999) *World's Fairs and the End of Progress: An Insider's View*, Corte Madera: World's Fair Inc.

Hesmondhalgh, D. (2007) *The Cultural Industries,* London: Sage.

Hesmondhalgh, D. & Pratt, A. (2005) 'Cultural Industries and Cultural Policy', *International Journal of Cultural Policy*, 11, pp. 1—13.

Horne, J., Tomlinson, A. & Whannel, G. (1999) *Understanding Sport: An Introduction to the Sociological and Cultural Analysis of Sport*, London: E & FN Spon.

House of Representatives Standing Committee on Industry, Science and Technology (1995) *Olympics 2000 . . . And the Winner Is?* Canberra: Australian Government Publishing Service.

IFACCA (2008) *Cultural Observatories*, International Federation of Arts Councils and Cultural Agencies [online] http://www.ifacca.org/links/cultural-observatories/

International Network on Cultural Policy (2002) *Cultural Observatories*, [online] http://incp-ripc.org/observatories/index_e.shtml

IOC (1969–2000) *Verbal Proceedings of Cultural Commission Meetings* (unpublished) available at: Olympic Studies Centre-Archives, Lausanne.

IOC (1978) *Rapport about the IOC Commissions*, (unpublished) available at: Olympic Study Centre–Documentation Services, Lausanne.

IOC (1992) *Olympic Host City Candidature Guidelines,* Lausanne: IOC.

IOC (1993) *Proceedings of the 100ᵗʰ IOC Session,* Lausanne: IOC.

IOC (1994a) *Olympic Review Thesaurus (1968–1994)* (unpublished) available at: Olympic Studies Centre–Documentation Services, Lausanne.

IOC (1994b) *Summary of Olympic Review Articles (1986–1994)* (unpublished) available at: Olympic Studies Centre–Documentation Services, Lausanne.

IOC (1995) 'Theme 11: Olympism and Culture', *Report of the IOC Evaluation Commission for the Games of the XXVIII Olympiad in 2004*, pp. 290–295.

IOC (1997a) *Memorias Olímpicas por Pierre de Coubertin,* Lausanne: IOC.

IOC (1997b) *Olympic Decorations*, IOC Communication and New Media Department

IOC (1997c) *Olympic Charter,* Lausanne: IOC.

IOC (1997d) *Report on the Sport-Culture Forum* (6–7 June) Lausanne: IOC.

IOC (1998a) *1998 Marketing fact file,* Lausanne: IOC.

IOC (1998b) *Olympic Marketing Communications Manual,* Lausanne: IOC.

IOC (1999a) *Olympic Charter,* Lausanne: IOC.

IOC (1999b) 'IOC 2000 Reforms'. Supplement to: *The Olympic Review*, XXVI (30).

IOC (2000a) *2000 Marketing Fact File,* Lausanne: IOC.

IOC (2000b) *Olympic Marketing, Striking a Balance between Business and Sport,* Special Advertising Section (25 Sep) Lausanne: IOC.

IOC (2000c) *Olympic Art & Sport Contest 2000,* Lausanne: IOC.

IOC (2000d) *Cultural Commission Meetings. Verbal Proceedings.* (unpublished) available at: Olympic Studies Centre–Documentation Services, Lausanne

IOC (2000e) *Olympic Movement Directory,* Lausanne: IOC.

IOC (2000f) *Forum on the IOC and its Cultural Policy,* Lausanne: IOC.

IOC (2004a) *Olympic Charter,* Lausanne: IOC.

IOC (2004b) *2012 Candidature Procedure and Questionnaire,* Lausanne: IOC.

IOC (2007) *Olympic Charter,* Lausanne: IOC.

IOC (2008a) *Candidature Acceptance Procedure. Games of the XXXI Olympiad in 2016,* Lausanne: IOC.

IOC (2008b) *World Forum on Sport, Education and Culture—Action Plan* [online] http://www.olympic.org/Assets/ImportedNews/Documentss/en_report_1374.pdf

IOC (2008c) *Olympic Marketing Fact File,* Lausanne: IOC.

IOC (2009a) *The Olympic Movement. Mission Statement* [online] http://www. olympic.org/uk/organisation/index_uk.asp

IOC (2009b) *2018 Candidature Acceptance Procedure,* Lausanne: IOC.

IOC (2011a) *Olympic Marketing Fact File,* Lausanne: IOC.

IOC (2011b) *The Commission for Culture and Olympic Education.* Advocacy   [online]   *http://www.olympic.org/culture-and-olympic-education-commission?tab=2*

Jakubowicz, A. (1981) 'State and Ethnicity: Multiculturalism as Ideology', *Australian and New Zealand Journal of Sociology,* 17 (3), pp. 4–13.

Jakubowicz, A. (1994) 'Australian (Dis)contents: Film, Mass Media and Multiculturalism', in: Rizvi, F. & Gunew, S. (Eds) *Arts for a Multicultural Australia: Issues and Strategies,* Sydney: Allan & Unwin.

Jeffreys, T. (2011) 'Art and the Olympics 2012 in London: "They never had us in mind"', *Hart International,* 84 (14 July), [online] http://tinyurl.com/3go8sxu

Job, C. (2010) 'Vancouver's Olympic CODE', *Culture @ the Olympics,* 12 (2), pp. 3–11.

Kelly, O. (1984) *Community, Art and the State: Storming the Citadels,* London: Comedia.

Klausen, A.M. (1999a) 'Introduction' in Klausen, A.M. (Ed) *Olympic Games as Performance and Public Event: The Case of the XVII Winter Olympic Games in Norway,* New York: Bergham Books, pp. 1–9.

Klausen, A.M. (1999b) 'Norwegian Culture and Olympism: Confrontations and Adaptations', Klausen, A.M. (Ed) *Olympic Games as Performance and Public Event: The Case of the XVII Winter Olympic Games in Norway,* New York: Bergham Books, pp. 27–48.

Kong, L. (2000) 'Culture, Economy, Policy: Trends And Developments', *Geoforum,* 31 (4), pp. 385–390.

Lacarrieu, M. (2000) 'Construcción de Imaginarios Locales e Identidades Culturales en la Mundialización' in: *Nuevos Retos y Estrategias de Política Cultural frente a la Globalización* (Conference, 22 Nov) Universitat de Barcelona.

Landry, C. (1999) 'Towards a European Urban Culture: Cultural Policy at the Cutting Edge', *Summary of the 2nd Conference of European Cultural Metropolises* (Conference, 17–20 June), Hamburg.

Landry, C. (2000) *The Creative City. A Toolkit for Urban Innovators,* London: Earthscan.

Leishman, K. (1999) 'And the Winner is Fiction: Inventing Australia, Again, for the Sydney Y2K Olympics', *M/CA Journal of Media and Culture,* 2 (1). [online] http://www.uq.edu.au/mc/9902/sydney.php

Levitt, S.H. (1990) *The 1984 Olympic Arts Festival: Theatre,* (PhD Thesis), Davis: University of California–Davis.

Lewis, J. & Miller, T. (2003) *Critical Cultural Policy Studies: A Reader,* Oxford: Blackwell.

Luo, J. (2010) 'Betwixt and Between': Reflections on the Ritual Aspects of the Opening and Closing Ceremonies of the Beijing Olympics', *Sport in Society: Cultures, Commerce, Media, Politics,* 13 (5), pp. 771–783.

Lyberg, W. (1989) *The IOC Sessions II: 1956–1988,* Lausanne: IOC.

Lyberg, W. (1994) *The History of the IOC Sessions III: 1973—1994: Lord Killanin to Juan Antonio Samaranch,* Lausanne: IOC.

MacAloon, J. (1984) *Rite, Drama, Festival, Spectacle: Rehearsals toward a theory of cultural performance,* Philadelphia: Institute for the Study of Human Issues.

MacAloon, J. (1996) 'Olympic Ceremonies as a setting for intercultural exchange' in: Moragas, M.; MacAloon, J; Llinés, M. (Eds) *Olympic Ceremonies. Histori-*

cal Continuity and Cultural Exchange, Barcelona: Olympic Studies Centre, pp. 29—44.

MacAloon, J. (2002) 'Cultural Legacy: The Olympic Games as a "World Cultural Property"' in Moragas, M., Kennet, C. & Puig, N. (Eds) *The Legacy of the Olympic Games 1984–2000,* Lausanne: Olympic Studies Centre (UAB) and Olympic Museum, pp. 271–279.

Machet, E. & Robillard, S. (1998) *Television and Culture: Policies and Regulations in Europe,* Brussels: The European Institute for the Media.

Macintyre, J. (2008) 'Olympics Chief: I respect Spielberg's boycott decision' in *The Independent,* (16 February), p. 16.

Martín-Barbero, J. (1989) 'Por unas Políticas de Comunicación de la Cultura' in: *Procesos Socioculturales y Participación,* Madrid: Editorial Popular, pp. 173–181.

Masterton, D.W. (1973) 'The Contribution of the Fine Arts to the Olympic Games' in *Proceedings of the International Olympic Academy,* Athens: International Olympic Academy, pp. 200—213.

McArthur Chronicle (1995) 'Interview with Donald McDonald' (10 March) [online] http://www.macarthurchronicle.com.au/

McDonnell, I; Allen, J; O'Toole, W. (1999) *Festival and Special Event Management,* Queensland: Jacaranday Wiley.

McGeoch, R. & Korporaal, G. (1994) *The Bid. How Australia Won the 2000 Games,* Melbourne: William Heinemann Australia.

McMill, E. (1999) 'NSW Ethnic Communities, Advocacy & Lobbying–Past, Present and Future' in Multicultural Arts Alliance (Eds) *The Future of Multicultural Arts* (Conference, 7 Nov), Sydney: Australian Museum.

Messing, M. (1997) 'The Cultural Olympiads of Barcelona and Atlanta from German Tourists' Point of View' in *Coubertin et l'Olympisme. Questions pour l'avenir,* (Conference, 17–20 Sep), Le Havre: Comité International Pierre de Coubertin.

Miah, A. & Garcia, B. (2000) 'Olympic Ideals and Disney Dreams: Cultural Representation at the Opening Ceremony of the Sydney 2000 Games' in *Culture @ the Olympics,* 2 (4), pp. 15–20.

Miah, A. and García, B. (2008) 'We Are The Media: Non-Accredited Media & Citizen Journalists at the Olympic Games' in Price, M. & Dayan, D (Eds). *Owning the Olympics: Narratives of the New China.* University of Michigan Press, pp. 320–345.

Miller, T. & Yudice, G. (2002) *Cultural Policy,* Thousand Oaks: Sage.

Mommaas, H. (2004) 'Cultural Clusters and the Post-industrial City: Towards the Remapping of Urban Cultural Policy', *Urban Studies,* 41 (3), pp. 507–532.

Monreal, L. (1997) 'Sport, Olympisme et Culture' in: *Coubertin et l'Olympisme. Questions pour l'avenir,* (Conference, 17–20 Sept.), Le Havre: Comité International Pierre de Coubertin.

Moragas, M. (1988) 'Local Culture and International Audience Facing Barcelona'92' in S.P.Kang, J. MacAloon, & R. DaMatta (Eds) *The Olympics and East/West and South/North Cultural Exchange,* Seoul: The Institute for Ethnological Studies, Hanyang University, pp. 753–771.

Moragas, M. (1992) *Cultura, símbols i Jocs Olímpics,* Barcelona: Generalitat de Catalunya- Centre d'Investigació en Comunicació.

Moragas, M. (2001) 'Juegos Olímpicos: Cultura, identidad y comunicación', in: *¿Cómo una ciudad puede ganar o perder la Olimpiada?* (Conference, 21 May), Turin.

Moragas, M., Kennett, C. and Puig, N. (eds) (2002) *The Legacy of the Olympic Games 1984–2000,* Lausanne: IOC.

Moragas, M., Rivenburgh, N.K., & Larson, F. (1995) *Television in the Olympics,* London: John Libbey.

Morgan, J. (1999) 'Opera to Ask Its Audiences for Top Notes at Games' in *Sydney Morning Herald* (30 July), p. 15.

Muller, N., Messing, M. and Preuss, H. (Eds) (2006) *From Chamonix to Turin: The Winter Games in the Scope of Olympic Research.* Kassel: Agon Sportverlag.

Munro, J. (1999) 'Treaty between the Sydney Land Councils' in *Red, Black and Gold: Sydney Aboriginal People and the Olympics* (Conference, 22 October) Sydney: Centre for Olympic Studies—University of New South Wales.

Murray, C. (1998) *Cultural Policies and Cultural Practices: Exploring the Links between Culture and Social Change,* Ottawa: The Canadian Cultural Research Network—Simon Fraser University.

Murray, C. (2001) *Making Sense of Place,* Leicester: Comedia & International Cultural Planning and Policy Unit–De Montfort University.

Myerscough, (1988) *Economic Importance of the Arts in Great Britain,* London: Policy Studies Institute.

Napoli, P.M. (2006) 'Bridging Cultural Policy and Media Policy in the US: Challenges and Opportunities' in *McGannon Center Working Paper Series,* Bronx, NY: Fordham University.

NSW Ministry for the Arts (1999) *Cultural Grants. 2000 Guidelines,* Sydney: NSW.

Nugent, H. et al. (1999) *Securing the Future: Major Performing Arts Discussion Paper,* [Nugent Report], Canberra: Department of Culture, Information Technology and the Arts.

Olympic Museum (2000) *Annual Report,* Lausanne: Olympic Museum.

Paddison, R., (1993) 'City Marketing, Image Reconstruction, and Urban Regeneration', *Urban Studies,* 30 (2), pp. 339—350.

Panagiotopoulou, R. (2008) 'The Cultural Olympiad of the Athens 2004 Olympic Games: A Tribute to Culture, Tradition and Heritage', in Müller, N., Messing, M. (Eds) *Olympism—Heritage and Responsibility,* Kassel: Agon Sportverlag, pp. 315–337.

Petersen, A. (1989) 'The Olympic Art Competitions 1912–1948', in *Sport Science Review,* pp. 44–51.

Pfirschke, A. (1998) *Struktur, Inhalt, Resonanz und gesellschaftspolitische Funktion der Kulturolympiade von Atlanta 1996 im Unterschied zu Barcelona 1992 und zur Konzeption von Sydney 2000,* (MA dissertation, unpublished) available at: Sport Schule, Universität Johannes Gutenberg, Mainz.

Pound, R.W. (2004) *Inside the Olympics: A Behind-the-Scenes Look at the Politics, the Scandals, and the Glory of the Games,* John Wiley and Sons.

Priebe, A. (1990) *Die Kulturprogramme der Olympischen Spiele von 1952 bis 1988—Konzeption zur Integration von Kunst und Sport innerhalb der Olympischen Spiele.* (Diplomarbeit zur Theme, unpublished) available at: Sport Schule, Universitat Johannes Gutenberg, Mainz.

Purchase, S. (2000) *Overview of Activities in Free transportation Zone* (Fieldwork Report, unpublished). Griffith : University, Queensland Gold Coast.

Radbourne, J.& Fraser, M. (1996) *Arts Management, A Practical Guide,* Sydney: Allen & Unwin.

Reason, M. and García, B. (2007) 'Approaches to the Newspaper Archive: Content Analysis of Glasgow's Year of Culture', *Media, Culture & Society,* 29 (2), pp. 304–331.

Reczeck, W. (1970) *Circulaire 541* (19 Feb) (unpublished) available at: Olympic Study Centre Historical Archives, Lausanne.

Rentschler, R., Radbourne, J., Carr, R. and Rickard, J. (2002), 'Relationship Marketing, Audience Retention and Performing Arts Organisation Viability', in *International Journal of Nonprofit and Voluntary Sector Marketing*, 7, pp. 118–130.

Richards, G. (1996) *Cultural Tourism in Europe*, Wallingford: CABI Publishing.

Richards, G. (2001) *Cultural Attractions and European Tourism*, Wallingford: CABI Publishing.

Roche, M. (2000) *Mega-events Modernity. Olympics and Expos in the Growth of Global Culture*, London: Routledge.

Roughton, B. (1996) 'Return to Barcelona Prompts New Doubts' in Bruce, D.C. (Ed) *Impact of the Olympic Movement*, (Conference, 28 March–30 May), Georgia Public Television and the University System of Georgia, pp. 2–4.

Schofield, L. (1998) 'Supporting the Sydney Festival', *The Sydney Weekly* (21 Dec), p. 5.

Scott, C.A. (2005) 'The Olympics in Australia: Museums Meet Mega and Hallmark Events', *The International Journal of Arts Management*, 7 (1), pp.34–44.

Shubik, M. (1999) 'Culture and Commerce', *Journal of Cultural Economics*, 23 (1–2), pp. 13–30.

Smyth, H. (1994) *Marketing the City: The Role of Flagship Developments in Urban Regeneration*, London: E & FN Spon.

Stanton, R. (2000) *The Forgotten Olympic Art Competitions: The Story of the Olympic Art Competitions of the 20th Century*, Victoria: Trafford.

SOCOG (1995) *Cultural Olympiad. Sponsor Information Kit*, Sydney: SOCOG.

SOCOG (1997–2000) *Olympic Arts Festivals—Fact Sheets*, Sydney: SOCOG.

SOCOG (1997a) *Festival of the Dreaming. Complete Guide to the Festival*, Sydney: SOCOG.

SOCOG (1997b) *Olympic Cultural Ambassadors—Discussion Paper* (unpublished), accessed at: SOCOG Record Services, Sydney.

SOCOG (1997c) *The Harbour of Life 2000, Government Funding Strategy* (unpublished), accessed at: SOCOG- OAF Marketing Department, Sydney.

SOCOG (1998a) *Festival of the Dreaming.* Final report, Sydney: SOCOG.

SOCOG (1998b) *A Sea Change. Complete Guide to the Festival*, Sydney: SOCOG.

SOCOG (1998c) *Olympic Marketing. Marketing Communications Manual*, (unpublished), accessed at: SOCOG Record Services, Sydney.

SOCOG (1998d) *The Official Marketing Kit for A Sea Change*, Sydney: SOCOG.

SOCOG (1999a) *A Sea Change. Final Report*, Sydney: SOCOG.

SOCOG (1999b) *The Harbour of Life. Complete Guide to the Festival*, Sydney: SOCOG.

SOCOG (1999c) *Reaching the World. Complete Guide to the Festival*, Sydney: SOCOG.

SOCOG (1999d) *Summary Budget: Olympic Arts Festivals. Figures from JDE*, (unpublished), accessed at: SOCOG- OAF Marketing Department, Sydney.

SOCOG (1999e) *SOCOG Revised Games Budget.* (News Release, 22 July).

SOCOG (1999f) *Olympic Arts Festivals a Unique Four-year Celebration*, (Media release).

SOCOG (1999g) *OAF—Job Descriptions Documents* (unpublished), accessed at: SOCOG Record Services, Sydney.

SOCOG (1999h) *SOCOG Annual Report 1998*, Sydney: SOCOG.

SOCOG (1999i) *Media Guide*, May 1999, Sydney: SOCOG.

SOCOG (1999j) *Information Guide*, January 2000, Sydney: SOCOG.

SOCOG (1999k) *SOCOG Games Time Structure* (unpublished), accessed at: SOCOG Record Services, Sydney.

SOCOG (1999l) *SOCOG Expenditure Savings*, (Media release, 21 May).

SOCOG (2000a) *Media Guide*, September 2000, Sydney: SOCOG.

SOCOG (2000b) *Olympic Arts Festival—Media Information Guide*, Sydney: SOCOG.

SOCOG (2000c) *SOCOG Annual Report 1999*, Sydney: SOCOG.

SOCOG (2000d) *Post Games Report Background Documents* (unpublished), accessed at: SOCOG Publication Services, Sydney. (The final, official report is available online: 'Official Report of the Sydney 2000 Olympic Games' [online] available at: http://www.gamesinfo.com.au

SOCOG (2000e) *OAF'2000 Marketing and promotions plan* (unpublished) accessed at: SOCOG—OAF Marketing Department, Sydney.

SOCOG (2000f) *OAF'2000 Media distribution plan*, (unpublished), accessed at: SOCOG—OAF Marketing Department, Sydney.

SOCOG (2000g) *Olympic Art*, (Visual arts programme), Sydney: SOCOG.

Stanton, R. (2000) *The forgotten Olympic Art Competitions. The story of the Olympic Art Competitions of the 20th century*, Victoria: Trafford.

Sydney Bid Ltd. (1992a) 'Cultural Program and Youth Camp', in *Sydney Bid Books*, Sydney: Sydney Bid Ltd.

Sydney Bid Ltd. (1992b) *Sydney Bid Books*, Sydney: Sydney Bid Ltd.

Sydney Bid Ltd. (1992c) *Fifteen Good Reasons to Bring the Olympics to Sydney 2000*, Sydney: Sydney Bid Ltd.

Sydney Bid Ltd. (1992d) *Sydney is the Best Choice for the 2000 Games*, Sydney: Sydney Bid Ltd.

Tatz, C. (1999) 'Aboriginal Representation in the Olympics', in *Olympic Lecture Series*, (Seminar, 4 Nov), University of Technology of Sydney.

The Advertiser (1999) 'We are Exporting Our Arts' (24 Jun), p. 30.

The Australian Financial Review (1999) (28 May), p. 14.

The Sydney Morning Herald (1997) [Interview with Margaret Seares, Chairman of the Australia Council] (14 March), p. 29.

The Weekend Australian (1998) [Commentary about Leo Schofield] (20 Jun), p. 23.

Thompson, J. (2000) 'Aboriginal Tent Embassy Set to Stay' in *Green Left Weekly*, 418.

Tomlinson, A. (1996) 'Olympic Spectacle: Opening Ceremonies and Some Paradoxes of Globalization' in *Media, Culture & Society*, 18, pp. 583—602.

Towner, J. (1997) 'Tourism and Culture' in: *Annals of Tourism Research*, 24(4), pp. 1017–1019.

Tucker, K. & Phillips, R. (1999) 'Inquiry Foreshadows Major Rationalisation of Australian Performing Arts', *World Socialist Website* [online] http://www.wsws.org/articles/1999/sep1999/nug-s27.shtml

Turner, M. (1995) 'Impact of Hosts—World's Attention Raises Atlanta's Anxiety' (session XVIII) in Bruce, D.C. (Ed) (1996) *Impact of the Olympic Movement*, (Conference, 28 March–30 May) Georgia: Georgia Public Television and the University System of Georgia, pp. 2–4.

UNESCO, Swiss National Commission (1990) *Culture in the Neighbourhood: Cultural Animation in Urban Districts. Final Report* (International Expert Meeting, 30 Nov–2 Dec 1989) Bern: BOLDERN- Evangelical Meeting and Study Centre.

UNESCO (1996) *Our Creative Diversity*, Paris: UNESCO.

UNESCO (1998a) *Informe Mundial sobre la cultura [World Culture Report]*, Paris: UNESCO.

UNESCO (1998b) *Conferencia Intergubernamental sobre Políticas Culturales para el Desarrollo* (Conference, 30 March–2 April), Stockholm: UNESCO.

UNESCO (1999) 'Culture: A Form of Merchandise Like No Other?', in *Symposium of Experts on Culture, the Market and Globalisation* (Conference, 14–15 June) [online] http://unesdoc.unesco.org/images/0012/001228/122892eo.pdf

UNESCO (2000a) *The Strengthening of UNESCO's Role in Promoting Cultural Diversity in the Context of Globalisation*, (CLT/CIC/BCI/DC.DOC 5E), Paris: UNESCO.

UNESCO (2000b) *Cultural Diversity in the Light of Globalisation*: *The Future of the Cultural Industries in East and Central Europe,* Symposium of Experts organized in collaboration with the Polish National Committee for UNESCO, (30 June–1 July), Warsaw.

UNESCO (2000c) '2001–2010: Diversité Culturelle: Les Enjeux du Marché' in: *Table ronde des Ministres de la Culture,* (Round Table, March), Paris : UNESCO.

University of Illinois (1998) 'Correspondence 1950–52. Box 158. Cultural Programme 1950–52', in *Avery Brundage Collection (1908–1975)* University Archives at University of Illinois, Urbana Champaign.

Urry, J. (1994) 'Cultural Change and Contemporary Tourism', in *Leisure Studies* 13 (4), pp. 233–238.

Usher, R. (1999) *The Age* (9 Mar), p. 21.

Williams, R. (1981) *Culture,* London: Fontana.

Wong, D. (2011) '*No Manual Available'. Creating a Youth Olympic Legacy*: *A Case Study of Singapore 2010 Youth Olympic Games.* (Final Report to the IOC Postgraduate Research Programme), Lausanne: IOC.

PRIMARY SOURCES: INTERVIEWS

This monograph builds on over 90 personal interviews conducted in Sydney between 1999 and 2000. Interviewees represent key Olympic cultural programme stakeholders including the organising committee for the Games, government organisations, arts organisations, corporate sponsors and the media. Particularly insightful were the interviews conducted with all senior representatives of the Olympic Arts Festivals team in SOCOG, including five interviews with the OAF General Manager and Programme Manager (anonymised as 'Senior staff'). Interviews have also been conducted between 2001 and 2009 with representatives from the IOC and organising committees, arts organisations and government representatives from subsequent Games host cities.

Find below a list of the interviewees that have been quoted directly within the monograph.

Arts Queensland, Marketing Team (25 August 1999)
Athens Art Gallery Director (2004)
Australian Tourism Commission, Olympic Liaison Team (3 March 2000)
Ausarts2000, General Manager (4 October 2000)
BBC Sports team senior representative (2008)
Carnivale & NSW Multicultural musical coordinator (15 November 1999)
Casula Powerhouse Regional Arts Director (14 Sep 1999)
City of Sydney, Cultural Affairs and Protocol Unit (16 August 1999)
City of Sydney, Executive Director of Major Projects (8 October 2000)
Citta di Torino, Culture Commissioner (February 2006)
Cunningham, Stuart (2000) Head of School, Media & Journalism, Queensland University of Technology (25 Aug)
Department of Communications, Information Technology and the Arts—Australian Government, General Manager- Arts Branch (August 1999)
IOC Head of Bid City Relations and OCOG Liaison for Culture and Education (15 December 2009)

IOC Head of Publications (24 April 2001)

IOC OCOG Relations Team (20 March 2001)

IOC Olympic Museum Manager of Collections and Exhibitions (19 April 2001)

IOC Olympic Museum Director (5 December 2011)

IOC Secretary General (5 April 2001)

Kidd, Bruce (30 September 2000) *Olympic Scholar,* Appointed Sydney 2000 Observer by SOCOG with IOC accreditation; Dean, Faculty of Physical Education and Health, University of Toronto

London 2012 Culture team (16 January 2012)

London 2012 Culture team (8 December 2006)

London 2012 Regional creative programmers (15 December 2008, 10 July 2009)

Louw, Eric (25 August 2000) Senior Lecturer in Communications, The University of Queensland

MacAloon, John (23 June 2008) *Olympic Scholar,* Appointed Sydney 2000 Observer by SOCOG with IOC accreditation; Associate Dean, Graduate Division of Social Sciences, University of Chicago

Müller, Norbert (9 September 2000) *Olympic Scholar,* Appointed Sydney 2000 Observer by SOCOG with IOC accreditation; President of the German Olympic Academy, Professor at Johannes Gutenberg University

NSW Community Arts Association (13 September 1999)

OAF Marketing Manager (14 September 1999 and 22 August 2000)

OAF Publicity Manager (1 September 1999)

OAF Senior staff (23 August 1999, 14 August 2000, 11 November 1999)

OAF Senior staff (15 September 1999, 6 October 2000)

Powerhouse Museum, Evaluation & Visitor Research Manager (4 October 2000)

Schofield, Leo (9 March 2000) Artistic Director of *The Harbour of Life* or *OAF'2000*, SOCOG

Seven Network, Olympic Sponsorship Officer (2 October 2000)

SMH- Sydney Morning Herald, Olympic Editor (13 October 1999)

SMH- Sydney Morning Herald, Olympic Sponsorship Manager (23 August 1999)

SOCOG Communications and Community Relations General Manager (17 September 1999)

SOCOG Multicultural Advisory Committee member (13 Sep 1999)

SOCOG Sponsors Relations staff (1 September 1999)

Swatch, Public Relations Manager (2 October 2000)

Sydney Arts Organisation, Principal (2000, pers. comm., 24 Feb)

Sydney Opera House, Olympic Media Relations—Arts & Events (5 October 2000)

Tatz, Colin (4 October 1999) Director of the Australian Institute for Holocaust and Genocide Studies, University of New South Wales, Sydney

Telstra, General Manager- Special Events & Olympics 2000 (2 September 1999)

The Australian, Arts Editor (13 September & 5 October 2000)

The Australian, Olympic Editor (28 September 1999)

Turner, Graeme (25 August 2000) Professor Department of English, The University of Queensland

Veal, Anthony (15 April 1999) Associate Professor, Dept of Sport, Tourism and Leisure Studies, University of Technology of Sydney.

Index